o Mexico.
hinks I like it when six Catholics get cut up.
I would rather die standing than live on my knees!
Estado

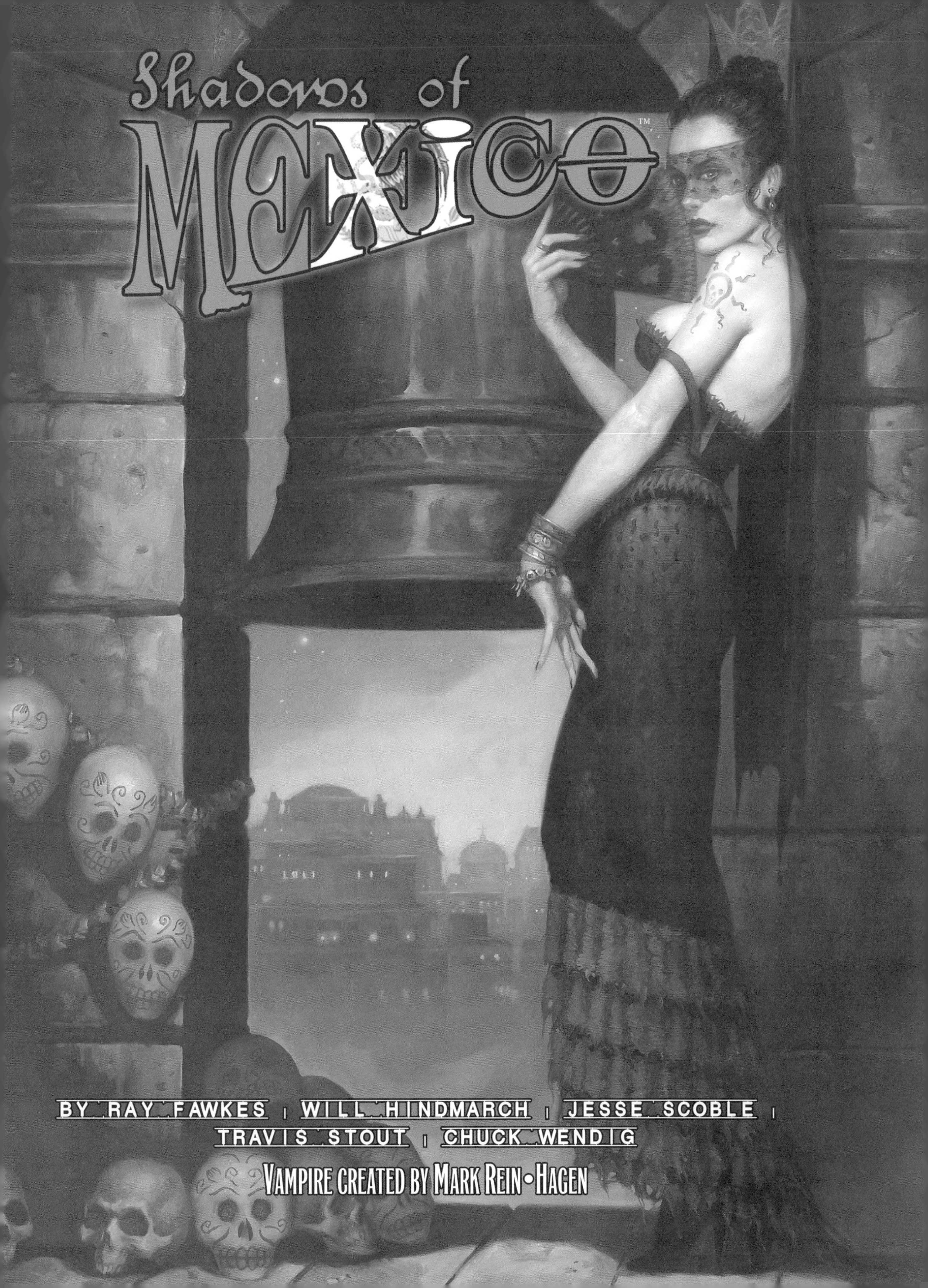

Shadows of MEXICO™

BY RAY FAWKES | WILL HINDMARCH | JESSE SCOBLE | TRAVIS STOUT | CHUCK WENDIG

VAMPIRE CREATED BY MARK REIN•HAGEN

Prologue: La Justicia

The multicolored tarps of the Tepito market snap and flutter in the mild midnight breeze. It is quiet now, all the bustling business of the day long packed and hidden away. In the deep shadows between two stalls, Emilio Montejano turns to glance into the street, just to see if anyone is there. He runs a hand through his dark hair, letting a few strands fall over his forehead. Cristobal el Indio is standing nearby, toying with a cigarette, turning it around and around in his fingers. There is a scent in the air tonight, the barest hint of something foul, and the boys are on edge. Emilio spits, clearing his mouth. He briefly wonders if he could not have given this job to someone else, someone younger or more eager. He nods once, quickly, to Cristobal, and the huge, burly teen pushes on an unmarked door, throwing it open. They enter.

Inside, a frail old man rises from his torn chair before a flickering black-and-white television, his eyes wide with fear and surprise. "No," he shouts, "no, we are paid! We are paid! La Justicia has no— "

Cristobal shoves the old man back by the chest, making him sit down again. Emilio walks past him, pressing on the makeshift wall at the far end of the room with his fingertips. He puts an ear to the thin plaster for a moment, closing his eyes. The wrinkled old man stares at the tattoo on the boy's shoulder: two hands clasped in prayer. A bead of sweat rolls over his brow, and he blinks rapidly.

Emilio nods, moving away from the wall. "This one," he says, and Cristobal steps up to it, feeling along the ceiling for an edge. Finding it, he hooks his fingers underneath.

"Don't you know I can smell a thief a mile away?" Emilio asks, turning to the old man as el Indio rips the flimsy sheeting away, exposing a passage into an unlit room beyond. "You steal from La Justicia, old fool, and we find out. You try to hide something from us? That is like stealing, no? We always find out. Tepito is ours now, and so is whatever you've been hiding."

Cristobal peers into the dark room, inching forward carefully. The old man is babbling now, on his knees and gripping at Emilio's pants leg, begging. "*Por favor*, you don't understand, you don't know…" Emilio scowls, shaking him loose.

"It's a passage," el Indio says, moving further into the shadow. "Maybe through two or three apartments, behind them." A sickly sweet smell floods the room, and Emilio coughs, once, covering his mouth. The loose edges of the opening in the wall tremble faintly, and there is a muffled sound — a crack, as of lightning striking in the distance.

"Indio," Emilio says, listening. "Indio." There is no response. The old man falls to his knees, clasping his hands over his head and babbling a hurried, desperate prayer in some Nahuatl dialect. Emilio pulls a pistol from the waistband of his pants, putting it to the man's head and dragging him to his feet by the collar with his free hand. "Is there a trap? Did you trap your stash, you crazy old *chingado*?" The old man can only shake his head and weep, his mouth open in a distorted, silent howl. "Anything happened to him, it's going to happen to you ten times," the boy says, shaking the old man. "Do you understand me?"

"Indio!" Emilio calls again.

And then there is a voice in the black passage. Quiet and low, like the thunder that follows the light. The voice flows like black tar, like blood-thickened bile. "Intolerable," it says. "In my home, this insult." There is something behind it, moving forward in a wave of ancient, unutterable, depraved hate.

And Emilio is running. There is no resistance, no hesitation. The sound of that terrible voice cuts his mind at the root, and he flees, left only with the animal, the desperate, terrified beast. He is knocked into the wall by something strong and hard, something cold as ice, and an agonizing pain shoots through his arm as he bounces off the stone. His gun is forgotten, falling to the matted carpet. He does not stop running — the doorway looms before him, and he throws himself out, skidding across cobblestones slick with garbage.

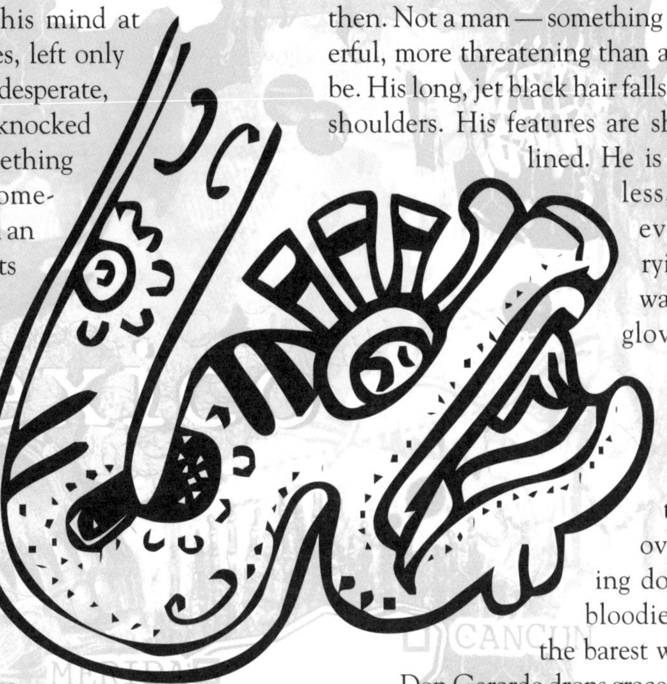

Something moves with him. He cannot see it, but he feels it close by, brushing him with the stink of rotten meat. Something old and dry, like a great serpent. His heart pounds wildly, painfully, and for a moment he imagines he can hear hoarse laughter, and wonders deliriously if it is his own. Into the night he runs, as fast and long as he can. The peeling billboards and rusted shells of cars flash past as he races wildly, blindly, to the very limits of exhaustion. When he can no longer run, he drops to his hands and knees, crawling through the ruined shacks and filth of the *barrio,* but still it is with him. When he can no longer crawl, he collapses, struggling to pull himself forward on shredded fingers, and still it is with him. And when he can no longer move even thus, he lies on the cold stone, twitching, his lips moving just slightly as he mouths some final phrase or prayer in reflex, in preparation for death. All he has left now is the final call of his gang. Thus is the strongest living member of La Justicia brought low, without a touch.

A man steps out from under the awnings then. Not a man — something older, more powerful, more threatening than a man could ever be. His long, jet black hair falls loose over broad shoulders. His features are sharp and deeply lined. He is dressed in spotless, old-fashioned eveningwear, carrying a gentleman's walking stick in his gloved hands. Don Gerardo de Alvarado, vampire of Tepito, momentarily distracted, stands over Emilio, looking down at the boy's bloodied fingers. With the barest whisper of sound, Don Gerardo drops gracefully to one knee, bringing his face close to the boy's own. The vampire listens carefully.

"P-por que no, come mi mierda? Viva La Justicia."

Don Gerardo purses his lips. He lifts Emilio up with one hand, propping him against the corrugated steel wall of a half-collapsed shack. The boy's head lolls on his neck, and the vampire pushes it back with two fingers, letting it rest on the wall. After a moment, he slaps him once across the cheek, one palm flattened against his chest to keep him from sprawling to the ground. "Intolerable," Don Gerardo says, and slaps him again, back the other way.

Through bloodied lips, Emilio speaks once more.

"Viva La Justicia. I will be avenged."

Don Gerardo lets the boy drop and stands, putting two knuckles to his chin. He considers his options. Death would be too quick for this disrespect.

A storm rolls over Tepito this night. The criminals and wanderers huddle beneath ragged awnings, shielding themselves from the driving rain. Nopal cacti are battered by the water, bending and shedding their needles. Clouds crash overhead as Emilio stands at the border of the *vecindad*, staring off into the darkness. His eyes are sunken in dark, bruised circles. His body is thinner, whip-hard and covered in scars. He fingers a long, sharp blade, letting the cool rain wash it clean. The locals assume he is a *tecato*, addicted to heroin and willing to subject himself to any degradation for his next hit, serving the whims of his dealer. They are half-right.

He can go no further. The vampire has seen to that. The edges of the *barrio* are now the ends of Emilio's world. He cannot will himself to step across the border. If he is taken against his will, he collapses in agony.

La Justicia is finished. This night, Emilio has murdered the last of his living brothers, slitting his throat and letting him drain into the gutter. For more than a year, Emilio has flickered through the alleys and the junk piles, a half-man shadow dwelling in filth, destroying everything he has ever cared or lived for. Dozens lie dead now in payment for his brief trespass. The empire they were building is gone, lost to scavengers and rivals all over the neighborhood. Their homes are torn down, their cars ripped apart for scrap. Emilio's apartment has been gutted and turned into a new haven for his master, decorated with the bones of his victims.

And through all the misery and shame of his crimes, he thirsts for Don Gerardo's blood. There is no pleasure beyond the gift of the vampire's blessing now. Emilio is a ghoul, a soul lost utterly to shameless, perpetual slavery. He has endured every insult, every injury and indignity. His body is beaten and broken, a mass of ugliness and pain. Here among the wracked souls of the decrepit market, he is the lowest living creature, mocked and spit on by passersby, cursed by all.

Tonight, he will report his success to his master. The murderous task complete, he expects that Don Gerardo will finally finish him off, tearing the still-beating heart from his body as promised. He welcomes it now and hopes it will be quick, knowing that even if he cannot be redeemed, he will at least find peace in death.

Two figures appear in the downpour. He folds the blade away into the torn sleeve of his jacket, taking a couple of steps backward. They tread confidently toward him, and he notices immediately that they are not human. There is something in the way Don Gerardo moves, something fluid and predatory. They move this way. They are Kindred. Neither seems to care about the rain, acting as if it does not exist. The male grins as they advance on Emilio, glancing off to the side, placing a toothpick between his lips. He looks *mestizo*, and his skin is a smooth, dark, ashen gray, showing through his open white shirt. The female pulls a black cowboy hat low over her straight blonde hair, letting her eyes fall into shadow underneath. Her crimson lips part at the edges, revealing just the barest tips of her fangs. "Shit, look at this. The Don's dog at the very edge of his land." She hooks her thumbs into the belt loops of her jeans. "Here, doggie. Why don't you let me give you a kiss?"

Emilio knows better than to run or speak uninvited. He watches them carefully, fighting the instinctive bubble of fear growing within him. Rain patters on the brim of the female's hat, and the male chews the end of his toothpick. "*Chilito*," he says, still grinning, "where is your master? Hmm?"

"He is nearby."

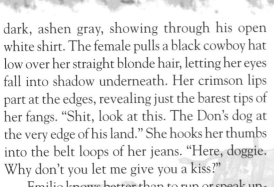

The male nods, and for a moment, Emilio sees something familiar in him. Emilio half-turns, trying to get a better look. "Yes, you know me," the gray one says, "but not for a long time. You were thin and small and only just looking to make a place for yourself. I brought you into La Justicia."

"Ramon," Emilio whispers.

"Yes." His smile fades. "Emilio. Yes. I have been away from *la vecindad* for too long, too long. La Justicia has come apart, no? My boys… my legacy… because of that ancient *maleton* and his fucking insanity. I should have come to you earlier."

"Ramon, I — " Emilio begins to shake uncontrollably, staring at the ground. Water soaks his back, his legs, weighing him down. The blood of his brother drips from his fingertips.

"I know, my brother, I know. You had no choice. He forced you to do it, all of it, and for what? Did one of you piss on the wrong wall? Did you spit on his favorite sidewalk?" Ramon rolls the toothpick with his tongue. "His problem is that he thinks you all must still respect him. He thinks this whole filthy place is a temple to his name, and he doesn't understand that you have no fucking idea who he is. Why should you? His people are long gone."

Ramon extends a hand, and Emilio glances at it, confused. The female crosses her arms, muttering under her breath. "Quickly, Ramon." The rain hisses in the early morning hours, blurring their bodies at the edges. She turns her head this way and that, beginning to show some nerves.

"You die tonight, Emilio. One way or another. Come with me, and we see if we can't give you something better than his rotten reward. Then you pay him a visit."

Emilio flinches as Ramon steps forward, putting a hand on his shoulder.

"You are nobody's dog, my brother. And La Justicia never dies. Not while we stand."

The moon sits full and heavy in the sky, a glowing halo surrounding it in the residue of the day's smog. A large altar of flowers stands at the end of the street, where the old man's apartment stood, years past. A statue of the Virgin of Guadalupe rises from the center, lit by hundreds of candles. The good citizens of Tepito dance, drink and sing, rejoicing on the eve of *La Día de la Virgen de Guadalupe*. What little they have is offered up as adoring tribute, a celebration of the holiness in life and love.

Emilio sits on the roof of a tiny, ramshackle apartment, gazing down at the crowd below. He notices his niece there, fully grown now, holding a small child in her arms. Further along, his uncle hobbles on a cane, helped to the *fiesta* by his wife.

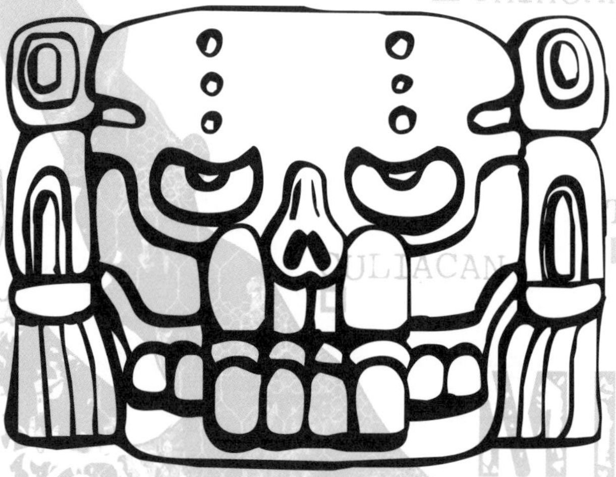

The young gangster runs a pale hand through his hair, and the loose strands fall over his forehead, as always. The clothes he wears are not fine, nothing better than those of the crowd. He runs a tongue quickly over his fangs, a habit that has stayed with him ever since he was changed.

A wasting sickness has taken the citizens of the *barrio* in recent months, as Emilio and Don Gerardo circle one another, testing themselves and each other, placing greater and greater demands on their power. Their need for blood is growing. The people have a vague idea of what is happening to them — rumors of a monster in their midst are gaining momentum. *El hombre pálido*, they call him, and they do not yet realize that they are speaking of two men, not one. Emilio tries to feed on outsiders as often as possible, tourists and police, but they are beginning to stay away from Tepito, and he has never completely shaken the conditioning of his old master. He still cannot bring himself to leave this place. He knows that Don Gerardo will never leave, either. One must kill the other, and it must come soon, before the people can no longer bear the weight of their battle.

Ramon has told Emilio that he is responsible for eliminating the wretched old creature alone. If he can do it, he will inherit Tepito. No others will interfere with him if they know he has the strength to destroy Don Gerardo. If Emilio cannot, Ramon will be forced to handle the problem for him — but then there will be no end of trouble.

Down below, music is playing. Emilio's niece is showing her daughter the lights, the flowers. She wears a scarf around her neck, hiding the bruises that Emilio left there by accident this week. He looks away, whispering a curse. Don Gerardo leaves these ones alive because he knows that Emilio will kill them himself, sooner or later, and that he will torture himself for it. The old one is an awful opponent, well practiced in his wickedness.

He fingers a medallion of San Gabriel, whispering a quick prayer. *Lord*, he thinks, *I am proud and I am stupid. I have done terrible things because I did not have the strength to deny the devil. I promise, I will change my ways. I was a man once. I will protect these people. I will watch over them and I will not take from them. There is hope, even for a wretch like me. And if there is hope for me, there must be hope for us all.*

In the distance, out of the corner of his eye, he notices a momentary flicker in the dark. His lip curls in a wry grin. "I see you," he whispers, scuttling to the edge of the roof, gripping it with his fingers. He empties his mind, letting his prayers die away. At the end of the street, Don Gerardo moves unseen among the mortals, fading in and out of view. He scans the crowd, searching tirelessly, furiously for his foe. The flush of a recent feeding is visible in his face. He has come prepared.

Slowly, inexorably, his eyes wander up to the rooftops. There Emilio waits, rocking forward in a mix of eagerness and trepidation. He clenches his fist. The clasped hands tattoo stands out in stark contrast to the dead flesh of his arm, muscles knotting underneath as he calls on the strength of stolen blood.

Don Gerardo's mouth twists in a monstrous scowl. His rage is palpable, even at this distance, projecting from him as it did that night long ago, when Emilio first met him. The boy is not so easily frightened away, this time. Don Gerardo strides toward his enemy, across the white petals scattered on the road. He picks up speed, breaking rapidly into a flat run. His black suit and hair shiver into a blur, and his eyes shine in the moonlight as he opens his mouth, exposing his terrible fangs. Emilio leaps from the roof, drawing his fist back, the cables of muscle tensing under his skin.

Fireworks light up the sky with dazzling color, and a cheer rises from the unsuspecting mass of people below. In the passing flash, the two vampires seem frozen in mid-leap, nearly touching, their snarling calls lost in the din of the crowd.

Credits

Authors: Ray Fawkes, Will Hindmarch, Jesse Scoble, Travis Stout, Chuck Wendig
Vampire and the **World of Darkness** created by Mark Rein•Hagen
Developer: Will Hindmarch
Editor: Scribendi.com
Art Director: Pauline Benney
Book Design: Aileen E. Miles
Interior Art: Samuel Araya, Avery Butterworth, Andrew Hepthworth, Travis Ingram, Tomasz Jedruszek, Jim Pavelec, Conan Venus
Front Cover Art: Brom

For use with the
World of Darkness Rulebook

Coming Next for Vampire:

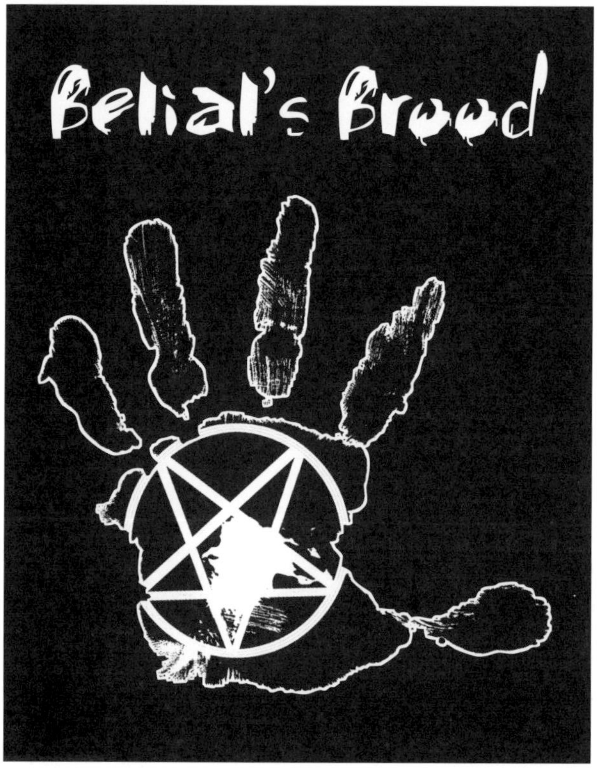

1554 Litton Dr.
Stone Mountain, GA
30083
USA

White Wolf
Game Studio

Check out White Wolf online at
http://www.white-wolf.com
PRINTED IN CHINA

Shadows of Mexico™

Table of Contents

Introduction

> **"Wisdom lies neither in fixity nor in change, but in the dialectic between the two."**
> **– Octavio Paz**

Facts and Fictions

This book lies.

This isn't a history book. This isn't a travel guide. This isn't a book that'll give you the basics about Mexico, its culture or its people.

Today, it just feels like a ridiculous notion to take up a bunch of space in a book like this with facts and data and reports that you can get at the library or off of the Internet. If you want a complete list of Mexican presidents or the specific century that the Olmec civilization is thought to have begun its decline, that stuff is easy (and often free) to find out. You came here because you want to know what happened when the vampires of the New World first encountered the Kindred of the Old World, or why werewolves patrol the U.S.-Mexico border or just what the hell is up with that goat-sucking monster. That we can do for you.

This is a book about telling stories in a frightening modern fantasy world created in the image of Mexico. You may find historical minutiae, precise travel times and hotel reviews to be vital in your stories, but you won't find many such things in here. This is a book about fiction, not fact.

Fair Warning

This book does not exactly paint a flattering picture of Mexico. Before you get angry about anything, remember this: it's foolish to base your opinion of any place solely on the horror stories you read about it.

Shadows of Mexico is about what's dark, what's mysterious and what's scary in the southern stretches of North America. This is Mexico in a World of Darkness. The following pages are preoccupied with criminals, liars, miscreants and monsters not because they are necessarily representative of the land but because they are good sources for conflict, fear and adrenaline. Remember that the daytime streets of Mexico City are thick with a silent majority — a population that doesn't get so much stage time in tales of damnation, murder, fury and the occult.

Likewise, this book isn't your complete guide to Mexican history or culture. This book hardly scratches the surface of that. This book wasn't written to tell you about the real Oaxaca or the genuine Cancún. This book was written to help you tell stories in a frighteningly fantastic version of a real country. That is, this book is about evocative fiction, about telling lies worth hearing — lies that *feel* true, whether they're realistic or not.

When you're reading this book, think of the Mexico we're writing about as an imaginary place based on a real one. Remind yourself that this is a grim and wondrous fantasy. Let your imagination loose. Let it bolt across the border from reality, let it careen through Mexico City like a getaway car, let it kick up dust like a Mustang sprinting away from the sun. Once you've given yourself that freedom, then you can walk your imagination back closer to the bricks and bars of what's authentic to get the sense of realism you want.

Remember, the World of Darkness isn't about what you know. It's about what you fear.

Sources and Inspiration

Whether you want to read everything you can about Hernán Cortés and the conquest of New Spain or you just want to spend 120 minutes seeing and hearing snippets of Mexico in preparation for your next game session, the best we can do is give you a few places to start.

Books and Magazines

The Myths of Mexico and Peru, by Lewis Spence, is one of those charmingly weird snapshots of another era's outlook on a foreign land. Published first in 1913, Spence's survey of Mesoamerican history and myth reveals as much (or more) about how scholarly approaches to Mexican culture have changed as it does about the material it means to examine. Spence was writing at a time when the truth of the Toltecs in Mexico (AD 11th to 14th centuries) and in Mesoamerican culture was hotly debated (at least within his pages), but information about the earlier Olmecs was practically unavailable. The facts of a book such as this are highly suspect today, but its bold conclusions (often since disproved) and enthusiasm with barely understood ancient peoples excellently evokes the mysticism and marvel that surround histories pieced together with broken artifacts and conjecture. This is what the truth about the ancient past looked like 90 years ago. What are we getting wrong now?

Pre-Columbian America: Myths and Legends, by Donald A. Mackenzie, originally published in 1923, is freer with its theories than Spence's book and great fodder for any World of Darkness game. For example, Mackenzie relates the theory that the migration of the Aztecs into Mexico corresponds with the 12th-century arrival of Welshmen into the region of the Carolinas — so perhaps the two are linked? Even if they are, the arrival of the Phoenicians in the Americas predates them by many centuries, if the artifacts Mackenzie describes are real. Even if the "Lost Atlantis" he writes about isn't the same as the one mages debate about, this book is an imagination-inspiring relic and a great source for secret histories and fanciful occulted myths that give off an eerie fog of mysticism.

The Course of Mexican History, by Michael C. Meyer, William L. Sherman and Susan M. Deeds, is a textbook (and reads like one). It's great for bare data and background information on the past Mexicos from which your elder vampires emerge. Contrast this book with one of the above books (and how certain they seem to be of their facts), and you'll get the hang of tweaking and altering real information into the kind of subtly warped alternate history that suits the World of Darkness.

The Art of Mesoamerica: From Olmec to Aztec, by Mary Ellen Miller, is a terrific guide for Storytellers looking to evoke pre-Columbian visuals in their chronicles. Whether you're looking for ancient artifacts to lure characters into stories, ruins to haunt with terrifying ghosts or pages from ancient codices to decorate the walls of some sorcerer's den, you'll find inspiration in here. Miller packs in more background, illustrations and analyses of architecture, glyphs and history than such a small book should reasonably be able to hold. (This is part of the Thames and Hudson "World of Art" series.)

Colonial Latin America, by Mark A. Burkholder and Lyman L. Johnson, is a detailed examination of the "Iberian colonies in the New World." For most Storytellers, this is probably more information than they'll need, but if you want to know about things such as "registered silver production in Peru and Mexico, 1581–1810," this book's got that. One thing that's very easy to take away from this book is that life in colonial Latin America was difficult, bloody and often complex.

Eyewitness Travel Guide to Mexico, part of the handsome DK series of travel guides, is full of maps, diagrams, photos, illustrations and key phrases you can use to add quick color and clarity to your game. In many ways, a copy of this book (or one similar) is the ideal Storyteller's companion to any story or chronicle set abroad. Highly recommended.

Archaeology Magazine isn't just about what was happening in Mexico 1,000 years go. More and more unbroken threads are uncovered each year that con-

nect modern Mexican culture to those of the "ancient" civilizations broken apart by the conquistadors. The Maya may no longer be a separate civilization, *per se*, but they're still a living culture in southeast Mexico. Mexico's archaeological record is as much about who modern Mexicans *are* as what they *were*.

Other Titles

By the Lake of Sleeping Children, *The Devil's Highway* and *Across The Wire: Life and Hard Times on the Mexican Border*, by Luis Alberto Urrea; *Lines and Shadows* by Joseph Wambaugh; *Always Running, La Vida Loca: Gang Days in LA*, by Luis J. Rodriguez; *Drug Lord: A True Story, The Life & Death of a Mexican Kingpin*, by Terrence E. Poppa; *Hard Line: Life & Death on the US-Mexico Border*, by Ken Ellingwood; *Coyotes*, by Ted Conover; *Chicano Folklore*, by Rafaela G. Castro; *Latin American Folktales*, edited by John Bierhorst; *Magical Urbanism: Latinos Reinvent the US City*, by Mike Davis.

Movies and Television

For the sake of simplicity, we've stuck with movies you're likely to be able to find wherever you are. Many mass-market movies seem to focus on the same few parts of Mexico, though, just as so many American movies seem to be about New York and Los Angeles. Also, we've ignored the famous Westerns here, revisionist and classic, though plenty of them can be inspirational for modern-day Storytelling. *Treasure of the Sierra Madre* and *The Wild Bunch* are both thematically apt places to start if you're looking for an excuse.

Outside of National Geographic specials and documentaries, not many studio moving-picture cameras get lugged into the Yucatán, for example. So get yourself a documentary if you want facts or travelogues.

If you're going to stick with dramatic films, though, you can glean some historical or cultural lessons along the way. *Frida* (a visually excellent film) and *The Motorcycle Diaries* are both about real people and at least somewhat-biographical events. They do better than tell you about historical periods in Mexico — these films dramatize them for you. *Amores Perros* and *Y Tu Mama Tambien* offer well-textured, character-driven stories that, despite not being somehow "uniquely Mexican," ooze Mexicana.

Movies such as *Traffic* and *Man on Fire* are more about thrills truly than about evoking Mexican culture, but at least both were shot on location. *Traffic* at least has something to say about modern Mexican life, and *Man on Fire* shows you several different sides of Mexico City.

Robert Rodriguez's popular and bloody fairy-tale trilogy (*El Mariachi*, *Desperado* and *Once Upon A Time*

In Mexico) shows you lots of colorful Mexico locations without dipping into resort towns or jungle ruins. Plus, these films play with notions of modern legendry, so you'll have something to think about while you watch these violent cartoons with great guns. While we're on the subject, the amusing *The Mexican*, by Gore Verbinski (you saw his pirate movie) also toys with modern mythology and a lovely gun (plus J.K. Simmons and Bob Balaban are in it).

The Shield and *The Crow: City of Angels* demonstrate two different ways Mexican culture can be incorporated into stories outside of Mexico. *The Shield* is populated with countless Latino characters who have much more to do, dramatically, than fill a token minority role; besides being a stellar show, *The Shield* shows how cultures can tangle, embrace and clash every day. That *Crow* sequel is pretty, at least.

From Dusk 'Til Dawn, *John Carpenter's Vampires* and *Cronos* are just three movies that show how filmmakers have mated Mexico with supernatural bloodlust. Numerous other vampire movies are set within a night's ride of the U.S.-Mexico border (or at least feel like it), and many of them are unremarkable sequels to two of the previous titles. *Near Dark* has something of a Southwestern bent, too, though there's not much particularly Mexican about it.

You can also find varying degrees of darkness, violence, bloodshed and Mexican culture in movies such as *Way of the Gun*, *Bring Me the Head of Alfredo Garcia*, *The Mask of Zorro* and *The Three Burials of Melquiades Estrada*. *Way of the Gun* is an underappreciated specimen of Peckinpah idolatry full to the brim with terrible, scheming bastards hurting each other for an ignoble chance to change their stations — a terrific Vampire film despite the lack of vampires.

At the time of this writing, we have no idea if Mel Gibson's *Apocalypto* is any good.

Music

Trying to describe the music of Mexico is like the trying to describe the music of the US: 100 magazines do it every month and still never get closer to covering it all. Even if we restricted ourselves to something like Latin music, we'd be skimming one corner of a huge pond. If all you're looking for is a shallow end to wade into, you can try popular artists as diverse as Del Castillo and Shakira, as different as Los Lobos and Nelly Furtado, who represent a wide-enough array of musical styles to give anyone a foothold into the "Latin music" category. The US band Calexico (try out *The Black Light*) has a dusty, sometimes spooky Southwestern sound that's the musical equivalent of Tex-Mex, while the Mexican group Kinky ranges so far from traditional Latin music that they signed on with a Canadian record label. (Still, Kinky recorded that version of "Oye Como Va" you hear in *Man on Fire*.) Beck's *Guero* is a recent example of American music injected with a variety of Latino styles.

Outside of American pop music, you've got plenty of other styles to experiment with. Durangunese music (from Durango) went through a big boom in Chicago not so long ago, brought north by the Windy City's large number of immigrants from Durango. *Norteño* is a style of music with accordions and guitars, which you've probably heard, while *banda* is essentially big-band music from Mexico. Everybody knows a mariachi is. Put some of these terms into a search engine and see what other styles you get led to.

Ultimately, you're looking for music that fits your stories, whether they're set south of the border in the 1920s or in tonight's Los Angeles. Whether you're looking for timeless folk ballads or the newest indie hip-hop sound, someone in Mexico in singing it.

Lexicon

a toda madre: Anachronistic use of "mother," means something is the best. Literally translates into "at/to total mother." Can be seen as rude in professional company.

así es, así sera: This is how it is; this is how it's going to be.

a todo dar: Literally "at total give." A slang phrase that means "to the extreme end." It is considered a polite way to say *a toda madre*. Similar to saying "to the max."

barrio: Neighborhood, or gang territory.

blancas: Amphetamines. White pills.

bruja: Witch.

cabrón(es): Technically means "male goat," but used as slang for "bastard." Can be used both in a positive and negative way.

caló: The slang of Chicano gangs, originally from the pachuco culture. Not simply "Spanglish," but a bastard dialect of its own. *Caló* uses archaic words, code-switching and some rhyming slang, and ties to the argot of the Spanish Roma.

cantón: House or "crib."

carga: Heroin. (See *chiva*.)

carnal(es)/carnala(s): Brothers or sisters. Literally means "of the flesh," but used to indicate one's gang is one's family.

chale: Slang for "no."

chicanos: People of Mexican descent in the US.

chinga tu madre: Slang for "Fuck your mother," a tremendously powerful insult due to the sacred esteem Mexicans have for their mothers.

chingao: Slang for "What the fuck?"

chiva: Heroin. Literally "goat." (See *carga.*)

cholo(s)/chola(s): Originally means "low-life," but now slang for members of Chicano gangs. From archaic Castilian word meaning "Indian."

chota: Police.

clica(s): A clique, used to mean a particular gang or set (such as a coterie of vampires).

coloradas: Barbiturates. Red pills. In the 1980s and 1990s, this term was also often used by vampires as slang for human blood.

con safos: Slang for "nobody can mess with this." In graffiti tags, represented as just "c/s." More recently used as slang in the *barrios* to describe something as cool.

corridos: Mexican "running" ballads. Normally used to relate an epic story of heroism and heartbreak.

cuete: A gun. Literally means "firecracker."

curandera(o): Mexican healer, usually tied to a mix of spiritual magic, a blend of native and Catholic beliefs.

dedos: Snitches. Literally means "fingers."

El Mero Chignon: Top dog. Literally "biggest/meanest fucker." In some North and Central American cities, this is considered a respectful but informal way to refer to a vampire Prince, though this phrase implies loyalty or subservience on the part of the speaker; i.e., "the biggest/meanest fucker in my organization."

East Los: East LA.

Eme: A term for the Mexican Mafia, normally "La Eme," or "EME."

Ése: Greeting among young men. Literally means "hey you." Non-Mexican gangs sometimes use the term to mean any member of a Mexican gang.

feria: Money. A Spanglish word derived from "fare."

grifa: Marijuana. A joint. Sometimes also used by vampires to describe a human vessel high on marijuana.

huevos: Literally means "eggs," but slang for "testicles" or "balls."

homes (holmes): A man, possibly derived from the French *home* for "man." Used to describe a friend, similar to "homie" or "homeboy."

Jaspia, La: The Hunger; the peril of Wassail.

Jefe: Boss. This is typically considered a rude, even contemptuous way to refer to a vampire Prince.

llanta: Derogatory term for African American. (See *mayate*).

marqueta: Market, a Spanglish term.

mayate: Derogatory slang for African American (*see* Llanta).

Mezcal: A colorless spirit, distilled from desert plants such as the agave or maguey cactus.

mestizo: In Mexico, a person of mixed European and Amerindian blood.

Migra, La: Slang for the Border Patrol.

orale: A word with many uses, including "OK," "Hey," "Hello," "Yes," "Yeah," "Right on," etc. Also used as an exclamation of surprise, similar to "Hell yeah!" or "Hell no!"

pachuco: Mexican-American *barrio* culture of the 1930s and 1940s. They developed their own showy style (such as zoot suits) and favored jazz, swing and jump blues. Originally derived from Mexican Spanish to mean "flashily dressed," and originated in California or Texas before spreading throughout the Southwest. The style effectively died out in the 1960s and 1970s as gang life became more violent and associated with prison culture, but cliques of the style still persist (especially among vampires Embraced during the pachuco era).

padre: Literally "father," but slang from Mexico City meaning "it's really good." Similar to saying *a todo dar*. For vampires, to call one's sire *padre* is considered amateurish or embarrassingly "white bread."

padrísimo: Slang from Mexico City meaning something is excellent. Similar to saying "better than padre," or "more father."

pandilleros: Slang for members of a gang; tough guys.

pinche: Slang for "fucking," as in the adjective, not the verb.

pinta: Prison. In northern Mexico and parts of the US, sometimes also to mean the torpor of the Kindred.

pinto: Ex-con. In northern Mexico and parts of the US, sometimes also to describe a young (neonate or ancilla) vampire recently awakened from torpor.

por el amor de Dios: "For the love of God."

puta: Whore or prostitute. For vampires, also a derogatory term for a disposable mortal vessel.

puta madre: Whore mother, often used as a term of praise or exclamation of shock. (Also a derogatory label for Hierophants of the Circle of the Crone, regardless of gender, and Mother Moon of the Uratha.)

rateros: Spanish for thieves, literally "ratmen."

rocanrol: Spanglish for "rock and roll." Among some young vampires, this is also used to refer to mystical physical alterations through the Blood (i.e., any use of a Discipline or Vitae to alter Physical Traits or form).

Santísima Madre de Dios, La: Holy Mother of God.

simón: Caló slang for "yes."

soldados: soldiers of the Mexican Mafia, often called *soldados azules*. Sometimes also applied to the Kindred role of Hound in some domains.

tecato: Traditionally, a heroin addict. May also refer to a Vitae addict.

Tijuanense: Tijuana slang for a native or local.

torcida: Time served in jail, or jail itself. Literally means "twisted." Sometimes also used in reference to vampiric torpor.

vato: Man, or dude. Unlike some mortal slang, vampires use this term in reference to their own kind as well. (That is, *vato* is free of the linguistic baggage that comes with "the Man" and "the Beast.")

Vida Loca, La: The Mexican gang experience, from life in the *barrio* to prison. Literally "the Crazy Life." In recent years, this term has been diluted almost out of use, but is returning to usage in a kind of ironic parody of itself.

veteranos: Veterans of the *barrio* gangs, similar to the O.G.s of black gangs. In most Kindred domains, it is dangerously improper to use this term in reference to elder vampires.

yonke: Spanglish word for "junkyard."

That Word: Indians

Yes, it's an archaic, politically incorrect, bullshit label. Mexico is not India. The native inhabitants of the Americas are (not were), in reality, a great many distinct and diverse cultures, nations and peoples. We're not saying otherwise.

The fact is, though, that the word "Indian" has stuck as a vernacular term for "indigenous Americans." It became clear, while researching this book, that the native Americans of what is now Mexico are still quite often referred to as Indians in lots of perfectly respectable publications, from newspapers to travel guides to history books. The word has a pedigree of ignorance, but it is not a dishonest term. We use it in this book because the word is authentic — not in its relationship to the history or lineage of the Mexican people, but in its modern usage. The word Indian is genuinely used in reference to Mexico's indigenous people, even though it originated in error.

Be offended if you want, but that's not the reason we use the word in this book.

Mexicans and Their Mothers

Mexicans revere their mothers. They hold a sacred place and are seen as virginal. Thus insulting someone's mother can be seen as a dangerous insult. *Madre* is the technical word for mother, but using this term among a rough crowd almost always has the connotation of *chinga tu madre*. Similarly, *tu madre* tends to mean "fuck your mother."

Variants include *mamacita*, which is often seen as rude or crass, similar to "hot little mama." *Mamosota* transalates into "great big mama," but is stronger than *mamacita* (perhaps "sexy momma, or even MILF). *Vieja* is "old lady," as in girlfriend or wife (but specifically not mother). In contrast to all of these, *mama* ("mommy") is a far more acceptable form of address.

Ni madre translates as "not mother." In this instance, the phrase has no object — it's an abstract mother being discussed, not anyone's specific mother. This term also implies "fuck." It is a very strong way of saying "No!" — something like "no motherfucking way."

An even more extreme (and strange) phrase is *no tiene madre*. It translates into "he or she (or it) has no mother," and roughly means that something is as good as it can possible be. Something without a mother — be it a woman, a car, a drug, whatever — is sublime perfection.

As mothers are so highly charged, there are various obscene forms to say one is the "son of…" or "daughter of…" Even the seemingly benign *hijo(a) de tu madre* (son/daughter of your mother) is seen as an insult, let alone *hijo de tu chingada madre* ("son of your fucked mother") or *hijo de puta* ("son of a whore").

Perhaps the ultimate Mexican curse is to cry out *hijo de la chingada.* "Son of the fucked" encompasses a sense of abject despair. Culturally, it expresses a terrible bleak and cold state, attempting to contain an entire history of blood, torture, conquest, submission, failure and rape. From an academic standpoint, this term even describes the state of the *mestizo* population — the offspring of Amerindian women raped by European conquistadors.

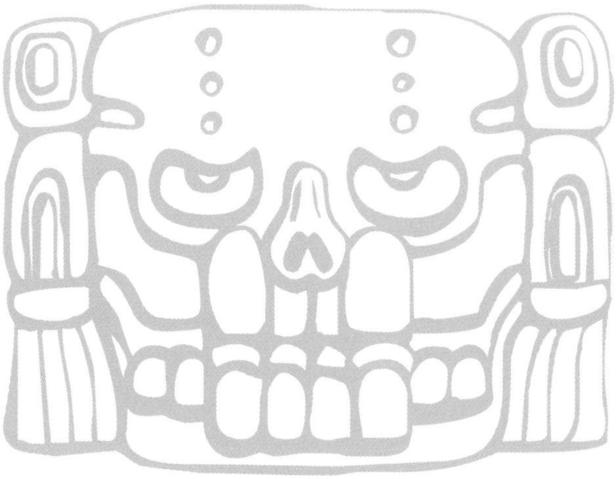

TIJUANA
CIUDAD JUAREZ
HERMOSILLO
CHIHUAHUA
MATAMOROS
TORREON
CULIACAN
MONTERREY
Gulf of Mexico
MEXICO
TAMPICO
CANCUN
MERIDA
LEON
CHICHEN ITZA
GUADALAJARA
Pacific Ocean
VERACRUZ
MEXICO CITY
ACAPULCO
SALINA CRUZ

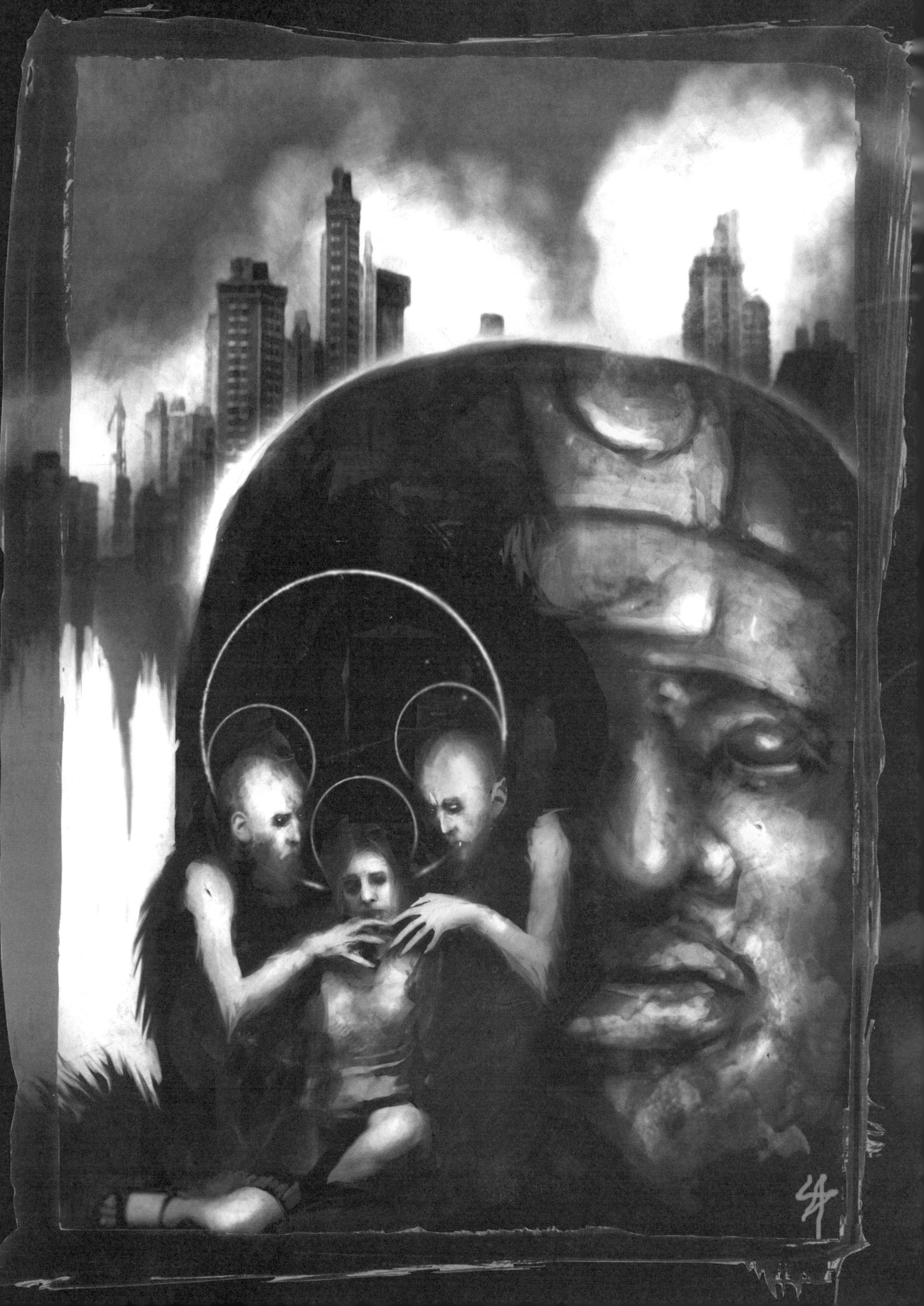

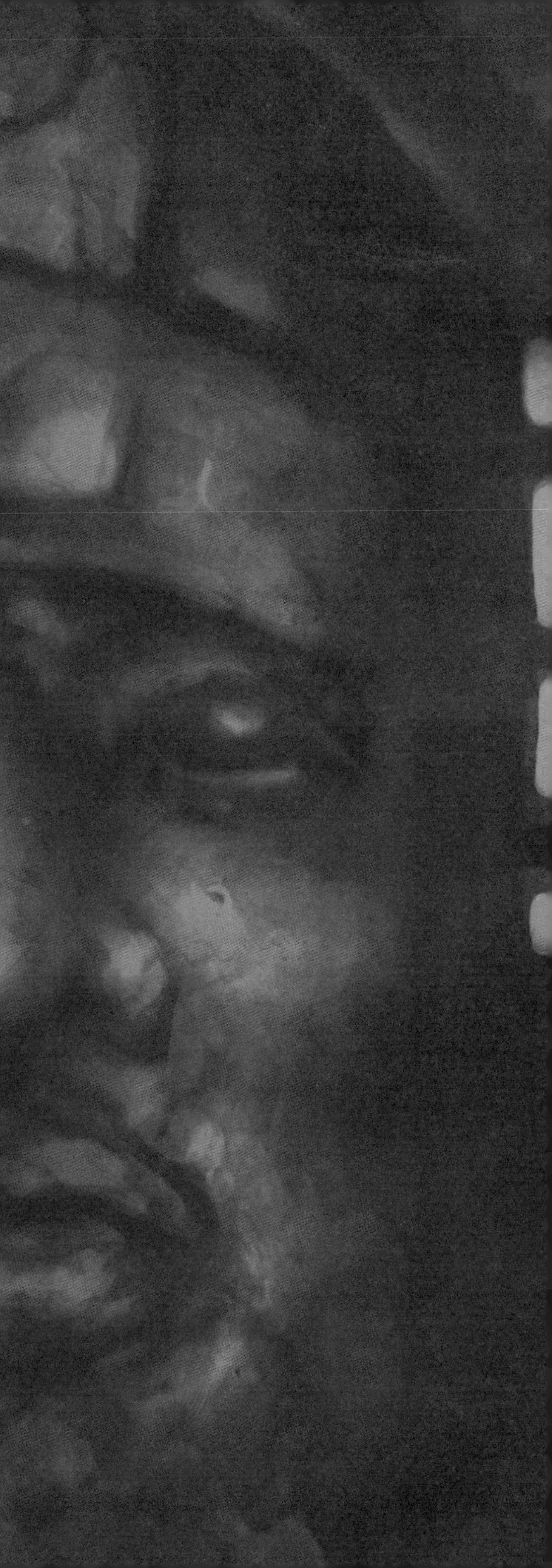

It's easier than you think.

You're easier to rob than a
bank or a liquor store or a bar.
We can't fit one of those in our car.
We can't take them back to our
territory and empty them slowly.
We can't ransom a bank back to its family,
then leave it dead in the desert.

You hail the wrong cab and we're the drivers. We
go where we want and you're in the back. There's
no rush, because you're the only
real witness to your own kidnapping.
We spend Wednesday night driving around,
going to one ATM after another,
until your account is empty.
The cash slips out of the slot in little spurts.
You give us the PIN
because otherwise we cut off your fingers.

We cut your wrists
and blood drips out of the slit in fat drops.
You hold the wadded-up t-shirt we give you
around the wound or else you bleed to death in
the oil stain on the floor of our garage.
Then we cut off some of your hair
or maybe one of your fingers anyway.

The hair goes to your family,
who pays us cash through an insurance broker
we work with five or six times a year.
They think it's a ransom,
but they'll never see you again.

The blood goes to an auction
where hundred-year-old monsters bid on it.
The winner gets you for one night,
which is your last.
He holds you down and bites your throat
or your wrist or your thigh
and when your blood spurts out into his mouth
it smells like the cash that comes out of the ATM.
At least to us.

Your blood goes around for a few nights in his
veins, but we get a cut of it.
We lick your blood off his fingers
as it drips down from his wrist.

We send your family a letter,
so that they can come and find you.
You're lying dead in a blue plastic tarp in the desert,
limp and empty like a snake's shed skin.
Then your family goes on with their lives.

It's easier than you think.

Chapter One: Overview

> **"I forgive everybody. I pray that everybody may also forgive me, and my blood which is about to be shed will bring peace to Mexico."**
>
> **– Maximilian, Emperor of Mexico**

A Gross Look at Mexico

The raw facts of Mexico are the naked flesh that defines the shape of the land as a setting for your stories. Those facts are readily available at the library, on the internet and in your local bookstore. They're easy to find. What this book focuses on are the details that you're likely to look at when you bring Mexico on stage. This book is about what Mexico wears in the World of Darkness, what it hides under its jacket, what scars it's got on its back and what its sweat smells like.

Nahua, Mexica, Aztec, Mayan

Throughout this book, you'll find reference to the Nahua, the Mexica, the Aztecs and other peoples. Just who these people are and what exactly we mean when we use these words is, honestly, uncertain. From the position of a modern reader, the cultural boundaries of the Aztecs and the Mexica are somewhat fuzzy — certainly they're not the same as they might have been thought of fifty, a hundred or five hundred years ago. For the sake of easy readability, we're using these words a little more broadly than some historians or anthropologists would probably like.

The Nahua are (not "were") the indigenous peoples of much of what's now Mexico and Central America. "Nahua" is an ethnic and cultural descriptor, though, not a political one. Nahua peoples covered much more ground than either the Aztecs or the Mayans, for example, and their core language (Nahuatl) was spoken throughout Mesoamerica in various dialects and sometimes heavily modified offshoots. One form of Nahuatl was an administrative language for the Aztecs, for example, while other derivations of the language became the tongues of the Comanche and the Yaqui further north.

The Aztecs, as you probably already know, were the people residing in central Mexico when the Spanish arrived in the 16th century. Although we know them as Aztecs, and refer to them as such, they were actually a Nahua-descended people who called themselves Mexica (me-SHEE-ka). Though we sometimes use the words Aztec and Mexica interchangeably in this book, in general the difference between the Aztecs and the Mexica, for our purposes, is the difference between cultural and national identity. That is, though the so-called Aztec Empire is gone, the Mexica are still many. Through the peculiarities of undeath, however, some currently active vampires may consider themselves to be Aztecs, even though they mortal nation they identify with no longer exists. A great many of Mexico's vampires probably consider themselves to be Mexica, however, at the same time that they consider themselves to be Mexicans, in sort of the same way that a person can consider himself Irish and American at the same time. The Mayans, although often thought of as an ancient civilization, are still around today. By some counts, there are still a million people in the Yucatán who speak Mayan as a part of their daily lives. Though the Mayan civilization, in the sense of its governments and uniquely Mayan cities, is no longer a political power in the modern world, Mayan culture continues to flourish and flower. (For Vampire players, it's worth considering how it is that a civilization can be both dead and alive, active but so often unregarded.)

In general, in this book, we divide the mythological and cultural trends in Mexico between the Mexica and the Maya. This is a gross simplification of the truth, but a necessary one for a book of this scope. Ultimately, we're more concerned with characters and drama than the truth in here, and though we've chosen to focus on the more populous cultures in Mexico, you don't have to. If your stories and your characters lead you to focus more on the culture of the Yaqui or the Olmecs, follow those leads as far you like. Genuine history and anthropology books are a better source for facts than this game book (which is a source of inspiration), anyway. The broad sense of the Mexica and the Maya in here can provide a valuable context for whatever other details you choose to dig up and use in your stories, though — whatever your stories are about, in Mexico it's hard to ignore the impact of the Mexica and the Maya on the modern day.

10,000 Years of History

The human history of Mexico goes back more than 10,000 years. Even if this book had the room to explore all that time, it wouldn't be possible. Mexico's history is a mysterious collection of contradictory legends and speculation. The Aztecs, whose cultural descendants are still alive today and whose written records still survive, had little information on the people who built Teotihuacán or the people who razed it.

Even the history of the Aztecs only goes back to about the 12th century. Before that, Aztec history and mythology tangle into an enticing mix. We know that the Aztecs considered themselves to be travelers from the land of Aztlán, to the north, but it's unclear whether Aztlán was even considered a real place by the Aztecs.

Before the Aztecs were the Otomi, who seem to have given the Mexica the custom of the Flower Wars, but whose origins are also lost in legend. When the Maya were building their spectacular cities in the jungles of the Yucatán, the Toltec civilization had already come and gone. The colossal stone heads of the Olmecs were already mysterious ruins.

The point is that Mexican history, like all history, is fleeting and fantastic. Even though we have the words of people who were alive to see ancient days, we know little about them (or what's real). Even in a world of immortal vampires, facts are slippery. The recollections of one millennial vampire may offer little information on facts of the night outside of his stone city. The fog of eternity that distorts all vampire memories through the long sleep of torpor leaves many of the Damned with clear, reliable images of a dead wife's face, the smell of Aztec chocolate or the taste of a lover's blood, but it does little to reveal the sweeping facts that give history its shape.

The story of one undead Mexica warrior can provide the moving and awesome climax to a chronicle's mysteries even if it reveals nothing of who built Teotihuacán or why it was abandoned. Mexico's mysteries are precious and frightening because they are mysteries. Though we reveal some possible truths (and imply many more if you read carefully), we're not about to spoil the power of the land's fantastic forgotten history by filling in all the blanks for you.

Whatever truths lay in Mexico's past should be the ones that are right for your stories.

A Mexico of Monsters

Mexico, like every other country on Earth, is at its heart a nation of people. And people, ultimately, are the source and subject of all monsters. Some people become monsters, some become the target of monsters, but nowhere is free of the impact that monsters have on life. Throughout this book you'll find details of life for humans and monsters throughout Mexico, but first get your bearings with a zoomed-out look at the cultures of vampires, werewolves and mages in general.

Vampires

Mortal humans provide the structure to every major supernatural society in the world. Werewolves battle spirits, but spirits feed on the resonance created by the actions of living men and women in the material world and werewolves themselves are born and raised as mortals. Mages begin their lives as ordinary folks, and many continue to live their Awakened lives with the same families they new before their magical change. Vampires are as dependent on mortal civilization for food and companionship as any living person is, just in different ways.

In Mexico, for a thousand years, vampires have also defined the essential social framework for other supernatural societies that interact with the mortal world. Vampire priests, spies and warriors, though dwelling secretly away from most mortal eyes, represented an essential link between the physical world and the divine. They were masters and cultivators of blood, the mystic currency of the gods. They transcended death. They were conduits of heavenly power on earth.

But they were also closely tied to mortal society, especially compared to the Kindred of Europe. Mexican vampires did not organize themselves into states or churches outside those of the mortal world. Rather, the Damned bridged the gap between the mortal and the supernatural, between the past and the present. Thus vampires became supernatural overseers for mortal realms, advisors and landlords with an ancient knowledge of the land and an integral connection to the blood of the people.

The vampires of ancient Mexico organized into feudal city-states just like their living Mayan and Aztec counterparts did, just as modern vampires do tonight from Oaxaca to New York. The vampires of a particular domain organized within the city based on their age, with the eldest vampire commanding the fate and duty of all those below him. In general, the eldest vampire of each clan in residence formed something of a ruling council. This council had significantly less temporal power than a modern vampire might expect. The vampires of the Mexica and the Maya saw themselves as hidden extensions of mortal society, like essential keystones rooting the mundane world to the mystic cycle of blood that powered the cosmos, and continued to obey many of the same laws and customs as they did in life. Mortal kings and priests were considered to have authority over vampires, even if they did not know it themselves.

The Masquerade, or some version of it, was known to vampires of the Mexica, who held it in high esteem. It wasn't seen quite as a vampiric convention, however, but more a mortal one. It was the responsibility of vampires and werewolves to maintain a fog of secrecy around mortals, to prevent them from turning on their supernatural cousins out of fear. The Damned and the Forsaken conspired to maintain the secrecy of their cultures.

Mostly. Trustworthy individuals were much more likely to be brought into the fold of vampire or werewolf society in those ancient nights. Many Aztec priests were ghouls. Many warriors were rallied by a werewolf they thought was known only to them. Although the common Nahua person may have believed in vampires and werewolves in some form, they probably didn't realize that their most exalted priests were housing the undead within the city's pyramid and feeding them the blood of the enemy warriors sacrificed on their altars.

Damned and Forsaken Society

Vampires, in the ancient nights, had a degree of authority over the land and the way other supernatural creatures were allowed to interact with mortals. Werewolves consulted with vampires over matters of local politics and religion. Vampires consulted with werewolves over matters of mortal territory and warfare. The Damned were priests, the Forsaken were generals and they were both splashed with blood, gleaming in the moonlight.

Werewolves weren't subject to the vampires in power, exactly (not usually). Rather, vampires acted as the religious and intelligence-gathering branches of the secret supernatural world while werewolves were the spiritual soldiers and proto-federales of the land. Vampires and werewolves conspired to protect desirable mortals and to destroy enemies, whether living or dead, fleshy or ephemeral. Vampires kept tabs on the kine, and werewolves kept track of the spirits. Vampires dwelt underneath the temples and in the stone tombs of the land, sucking blood as it fell through the cracks between stones, pouring down the pyramid steps and pooling in cisterns within. Werewolves prowled at the edge of the mortal firelight, where the smooth stone plazas of the civilized world turned into the mud and roots and ruins of the jungle.

The Masquerade is infused into the blood of the Damned. Even in ancient Mexico, when the protective curse of the Masquerade manifested only through twisted reflections in water and glass, it was seen as the responsibility of vampires to oversee the maintenance of human ignorance of certain mystical truths — like the existence of monstrous, vulnerable beasts supping off their blood and hiding from fire. Vampires had the task of keeping vampires and werewolves hidden from mortal reckoning.

It was their responsibility to identify potential threats to their secrecy, to avoid a war with mortal civilization. In the event that the secrecy of the Damned and the Forsaken was threatened, vampires or werewolves would take action to prevent it, whether that meant slipping into a mortal's hut in the dark and biting his throat or charging like wolves into the midst of a military formation.

Which isn't to say that vampires and werewolves didn't do battle with each other. Within a particular domain, they strived not to, but even that was impossible given the Beast and Uratha rage. Still, the majority of conflicts between the Forsaken and vampires occurred across the same lines of tension that they occurred for mortals: physical resources (including mortals), territory and religion. These conflicts didn't escalate into bloody midnight wars because vampires and werewolves all began as mortals. They shared a common view of war: War had rules. Kindred and werewolves engaged in Flower Wars just like their mortal brethren (see below).

Underneath this umbrella of customary conduct, with vampires prowling around inside temples and werewolves sprinting through the jungle after reckless spirits, werewolf society was very much like it is today. Isolated, intimate packs took responsibility for their own patches of ground and kept their infighting inside the boundaries of their own kind.

Mages

Despite their powers, mages were regarded much like mortals by the vampires of the Mexica. Mages received grants of land, food and sacrifice from the local vampire overseer. In exchange, the mage provided the vampire with a degree of protection and a promise to stay out of trouble. Vampires distrusted mages for their power, and led mortal Mexica to fear them as well.

In Pre-Columbian Mexico, wizards didn't have the same degree of complex but occulted society that a modern Consilium does. Real willworkers were as attached to their mortal allies as any poseur-wizard. Mages were largely independent from one another, however, drawing on traditional divisions of duty not unlike the modern Orders, but organizing into loose cabals out of function rather than ideology. One city might be home to a handful of mages, each with a different responsibility roughly in line with the Atlantean Orders, but they might only meet to discuss crises or to conspire against another mage in the domain.

Without the rich society that modern mages use to share knowledge and experience, Aztec and Mayan mages progressed more slowly through their understanding of the Arcana. Rotes were less common. Mages were, generally, just as powerful but less diverse in their applications of magic. Thus they were capable of astounding mystic feats that dazzle even modern mages, but they left behind precious little information on Atlantean ruins or how to repeat such impressive magical feats because they were seldom writing for an audience. Magic was passed down from mage to mage.

With the line of Mexica and Mayan mages broken during the conquest, and so many mages killed in magical battles against European willworkers, an unknowable volume of precious arcane secrets have been lost. When the Mexica wizards died, they took their arcane knowledge with them. Today, modern mages must puzzle out the few ancient allusions and symbols that can be found at sites like Chichen Itza, the same as any modern archaeologist.

Flower Wars

Nothing shows off the culture clash of the Aztecs and the Spanish better than their notions of warfare. The Flower Wars of the Mexica were carefully considered military and religious engagements whose cultural and political significance defined the way people lived and died. To modern people, the systematic capture of enemy soldiers for later sacrifice to the gods can seem like an alien way fighting, but it's not so difficult to grasp when you understand its purpose. The importance of understanding the idea of the Flower Wars isn't just in the insight it offers into Mexica culture, though — it's also vital to understanding how things work behind the scenes in Mexico tonight.

The Flower Wars never stopped.

Then

As the Aztecs described it in the 16th century to the Spanish monk and proto-anthropologist, Brother Sahagún, the Spanish killed their enemies in battle, while the Aztecs killed their enemies after the battle.

Flower Wars were elaborate affairs that combined bloody tribute with ritual warfare. Aztec cities were obligated to participate in the Flower Wars with Tenochtitlán, though exactly what form the battles took was different from city to city and century to century. Some cities fought screaming with sweaty abandon to defend their people and reduce the number of combatants given over to a victorious enemy. Other cities ceremoniously delivered up chosen souls without any real fight, paying a tithe in blood as if the battle had already been fought and lost.

The souls who were collected during a Flower War were brought to the victor's city for ritual sacrifice. Blood was essential for oiling the cosmic machinery of the gods,

regular gifts of the sacred stuff had to be paid to the gods for the maintenance of the universe. This was how that blood was gotten. The more impressive, important or fearsome a city, the more bodies it could produce during a sacred war and the more blood it could pay forward to the heavens.

But not all of that blood went to the gods. Some of it went to the vampires who lurked behind the princes of the Aztec cities, who consumed sacrificed blood in a secret part of the holy ritual. The Damned were, they said, the couriers of blood to the gods. Some must be spilt on the stones of the pyramids in the daylight, in full sight of the heavens, but some must also be allowed to dribble through the stone into the sleeping mouths of waiting vampires.

The Damned had insinuated themselves into the mortal religious ceremony and fanned its flames into a wildfire. Thousands of people might be sacrificed each day at the height of a sacred war, and much their blood went into the bellies of hungry monsters who licked it from the temple steps or drank it straight in nighttime ceremonies.

The scale of the Flower Wars was reduced by the Spanish, but the practice was too essential to the culture of the Aztecs to be killed outright. The undead kept it alive.

One aspect of the Flower Wars that often goes unappreciated by sensationalist historians blinded by the shocking practice of human sacrifice is the honorable civility of ritualized warfare. The Flower Wars delivered all the proud, bloody spectacle and financial benefits of warfare without the same level of socially destructive hate and vengeance that comes with European warfare. Though you may carry off my brother for ritual sacrifice, I know that his noble death guarantees the perpetuation of our world. Rather than avenge his death with an unending cycle of escalating violence, I vow to fight more fiercely in his name during the next Flower War. Our rivalries are channeled and honored.

These customs of death were adopted by werewolves in vampires in the early nights of Aztec culture, if not earlier. The Forsaken had a spiritual obligation to keep the actions of the wicked Damned in check, but a practical appreciation for vampires' abilities to police themselves (unlike the spirits Uratha regularly battled). Likewise, vampires had a need to see werewolf activity limited, to prevent average mortals from engaging in monster-hunting crusades that would expose and destroy the vampires in their midst (as supposedly happened at Teotihuacán).

The solution was a supernatural counterpart for the Flower Wars. Every year, in most Aztec cities, the Damned and the Forsaken paid each other a tithe of blood. In some cities, a champion of the Damned simply faced a Forsaken champion in ritual combat for an honorary prize of respect. In other domains, the Forsaken were given leave for seven nights to reduce the number of Kindred by a fixed number (one, three or seven, usually, depending on the territory). In exchange, the Forsaken had to pit one werewolf against the Damned for one night — if the vampires could catch and contain him, they could have him.

For centuries the Damned and the Forsaken kept their differences in check through these ritualized wars. Eventually, in many cities, these customs eventually dissolved into outright allegiance. In others, the Flower Wars still go on.

Now

Mexico City is the kidnapping capital of the world. Some of the victims are returned for a simple ransom. Many are never seen again. The Flower Wars continue in secret.

Terrified that the world will end if the humanity fails to deliver its blood tribute to the gods, cults of Aztec-inspired men and women throughout Mexico abduct people off the streets and deliver them to the heavens through ritual slaughter. Many of these cults — many more than they know — are secretly directed by cunning vampires, just like the Aztecs of old.

Some of these cults work against each other in imitation of the old Flower Wars, competing to collect the most sacrificial bodies from the other's extended ranks. The cult who offers the most blood to the heavens wins.

In this case, "extended ranks" means the unknowing families, coworkers and neighbors who make up the public communities surrounding each secret cult. Beneath the surface, even these cult kidnappings are often a front for the Danse Macabre. Many kidnapping victims are the property of rival vampires, abducted and murdered by cultists with no idea that their religious fervor has been hijacked and manipulated for political power plays by ancient corpses.

Cenotes

Cenotes are peculiar natural wells located throughout the Yucatán. Like gaping mouths in the earth, they often lead to complex networks of caverns and tunnels were rainwater and groundwater collect. Some cenotes touch the surface of the Mexican landscape as shallow stone bowls filled with mossy green water. Others are long, narrow shafts, like throats, ending in deep blue pools. Some say the Yucatán's cenotes are fractures in the earth created when the Gulf of Mexico's extinction crater was pounded into the globe by a colossal meteor.

The Yucatán has no surface rivers, so all of its rainfall eventually falls through these pores into a vast, dark underground stretching beneath vast tracts of the land. The Mayans believed these caverns bordered on Xibalba, their Underworld. This gave cenotes a sacred significance beyond their essential purpose of providing local people with fresh water. Ancient cities and religious sites like Chichen Itza were founded around clusters of cenotes, but countless hundreds of other isolated cenotes lay scattered throughout the jungles of the peninsula, forgotten by modern folk or never discovered in the first place.

SACRED CENOTE

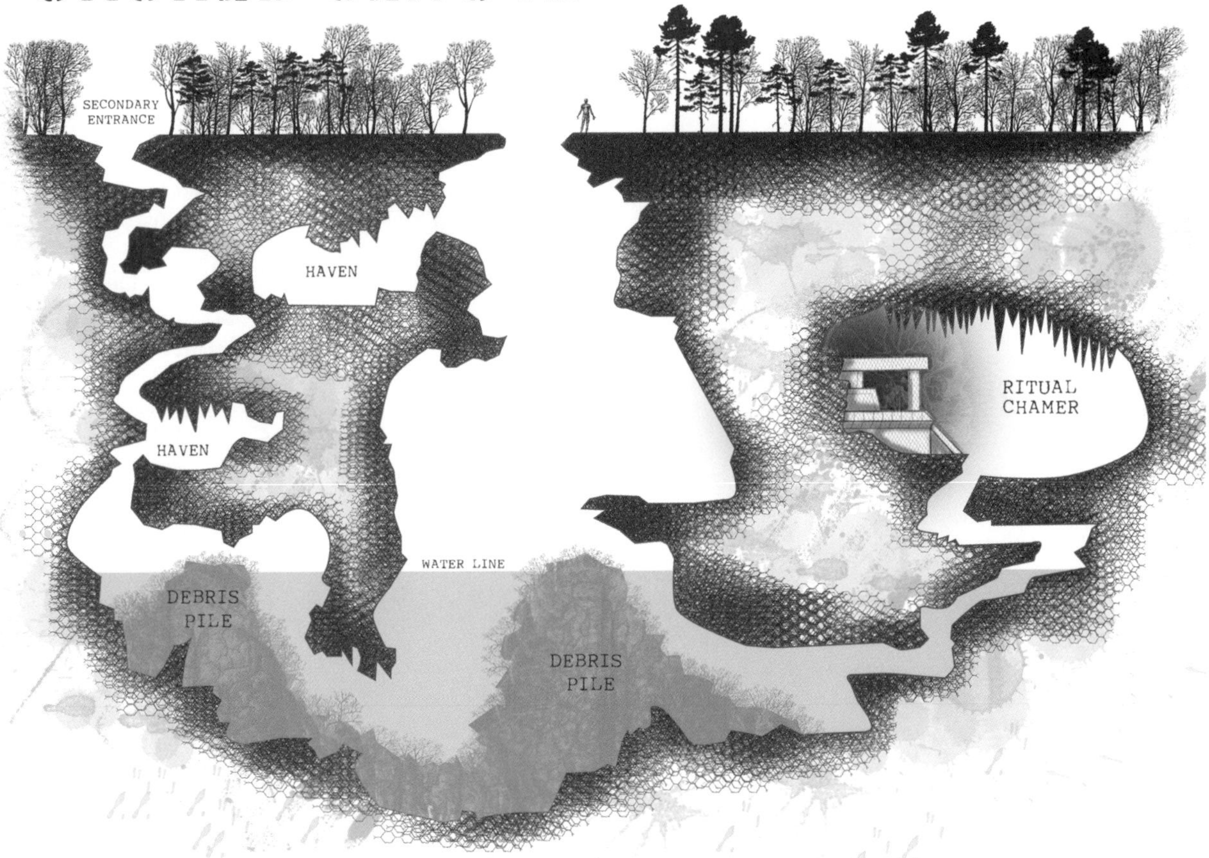

Ancient artifacts and human relics pass through these pores in the earth like they were holes in time. Mayan shamans made regular gifts to the gods and the Lord of the Underworld by throwing slaughtered animals, stone sculptures, woven baskets and human sacrifices into these portals. After centuries at the bottom of these black pools, many of these artifacts still survive today. The bottom of many cenote shafts are littered with antlered skulls, scrubbed bones and stone glyphs.

Over time, as the water levels in cenotes rise and fall, caverns are revealed. Many cenotes just represent one point where labyrinthine cavern networks make contact with the sunlit world. Hidden chambers sometimes sprawl up above the water level between a cenote well and the salty murk of the Gulf. Some of these chambers were reachable by the Maya centuries ago but have since been blocked by eerily quiet, lifeless waters. With scuba gear and nerve, though, modern divers can reach these secret sites and find out what buildings and treasures were valuable enough to the Maya to warrant the trek through the Underworld.

Thousands of people come to the Yucatán to swim on the surface of cenotes. Hundreds go so far as to strap on tanks and dive into the dark. Dozens disappear along the way.

The number of cenotes is much larger than the number of cavern complexes under the ground — that is, many of them are connected. A vast, sunless world lurks under the Yucatán, accessible only through these breaches in the ground.

Some of these caverns are inhabited by bestial vampires who come forth only to carry away local villagers. Some of these caverns are host to caches of sleeping elder blood-suckers, waiting to be awakened by their long-dead attendant shamans. Some caverns are stalked by monsters that have never known the light of day. One tunnel network is home to an immense, legendary beast whose limbs stretch for miles and end in grotesque, fanged human faces.

And beneath them all are the tiny fissures in the land through which these hellish monsters seep through from the Underworld.

Across the Line

The paradox of US-Mexico integration is that a barricaded border and a borderless economy are being constructed simultaneously.

— Peter Andreas, *Sovereigns and Smugglers*

The U.S.-Mexico border stretches for 2,000 miles, from San Diego/Tijuana on the West Coast, then travels east through Calexico/Mexicali, El Paso/Ciudad Juárez, Laredo/Nuevo Laredo, and finally ends at Brownsville/Matamoros on the East Coast. The border is a solid mark on a map, and a hard line bisecting many urban regions: a wall of fences and spotlights and guards. Yet the barrier is ephemeral when it comes to culture, money, drugs and horror.

There is an important difference in Spanish between *La Línea* — the physical line on the map, the barrier that 300 million people cross every year — and *La Frontera*, the nebulous border zone, culturally distinct from both the northern United States and the interior of Mexico. The border has always been a greater political tool than a corporeal barricade.

A Recent History of the Border

The border between Mexico and the United States has a long, complicated and bloody history, stemming from the desire of Empire and Hegemony of an even older conflict migrated over to the New World from Europe. The two founding cultures, the English and Spanish, set the early tone of the fledgling nations as one of conflict. The historical animosity and political and socio-economic desires of both countries fuel the complex mix of issues present today. From an American perspective, cheap labor and profitable industry are highly desired, but not so much the actual people. From San Diego, Americans flock across the border daily to manage the gleaming, ultramodern, bi-national assembly plants, called *maquiladoras*. Others zip down to buy prescription drugs at cut-rate prices, or may enjoy a leisurely fresh lobster dinner down the Baja coast. The Mexicans, meanwhile, look across the border and see a luxurious world they have only heard about from stories of family members who have gone across, from friends who have returned with American luxuries and from the Hollywood images that no border can stop.

Night Fell Like a Curse

In recent history, up until about the mid-1990s, night ushered in bedlam along the border flashpoints such as Imperial Beach, California. As the sun set, the beaches and canyons would suddenly come alive, crawling with thousands of bodies. Illegals looking for work, smugglers moving drugs and bandits looking to cause terror all boiled over the border, terribly outnumbering the US border agents stationed there to keep the peace.

Similarly, in San Ysidro, another neighborhood of San Diego, the worst elements of the border could be found every night somewhere along the wild outskirts. While the river of cars that flowed between Tijuana and San Diego was a slow current, the foul waters of the Tijuana River teemed with illegals, all moving to make a mad dash across the six lanes of Interstate 5. Once they reached the freeway, they would weave through speeding traffic and use oncoming cars as shields against the Border Patrol, knowing the agents would not risk the deadly gauntlet. These "banzai runs" would carry the illegals hundreds of yards into US territory, and from there they would make their way to truck pick-up points.

In response, the Border Patrol dealt with the symptoms. They closed four of the six lanes of I-5, and put up yellow highway caution signs depicting a family holding hands, moving at full sprint — Caution: Illegal Alien Crossing. The border fence would be marked up in bright orange paint, labeling the names of nearby landmarks — a water tower, a clinic, a yoghurt shop — on the Tijuana side. U.S. Border Patrol agents could radio their Mexican counterparts and indicate where the trouble parts were south of the fence.

Small teams of special police units — Border Crime Prevention Units — were assembled to patrol these treacherous zones. Few in number, they did their best to not only deter migrants from crossing but also protect them. These desperate workers were easy prey for predatory criminals who roamed the canyons and mesas. Poor travelers, if caught by these animals, were robbed, raped and often killed. But the Border Units, so few in number, could only stop a small trickle of the flood.

Angry U.S. citizens mobilized themselves to help defend their nation's boundaries. By 1990, a couple of hundred regulars would show up to participate in "Light Up the Border," a veritable nightly spectacle. Residents parked their cars along the line after nightfall and aimed their headlights south. These "light-ups" were led by the widow of a decorated border agent. As the drivers helped the agents watch the border, the community was abuzz over the talk-show networks. Furthermore, it didn't take long before counter-protestors showed up, increasing the tension.

Hold the Line

Clearly a new strategy was needed, and the senior Border Patrol agent in El Paso was willing to take bold risks. The Rio Grande was a flimsy barrier at best — anyone who couldn't actually cross the river by himself or herself only needed to hire a *lanchero* to be floated over. The line-up of Mexicans began in the morning, long queues standing along the levee to cross from Ciudad Juárez, Mexico, into El Paso, Texas. The migrants would lie face down, purses and bags clutched beneath them, two or three to a "raft" — little more than inner tubes covered by wooden boards. The *lanchero*, for roughly two dollars per two-minute trip, pulled the raft across the river by wading through the thigh-deep, filthy water.

The El Paso Border Patrol agent's new initiative was called Operation Blockade, and it involved stationing hundreds of agents, nearly shoulder to shoulder, all along the concrete river bank. The strategy hit like a landslide, changing the landscape of the border. Three days into the new plan, the migrants, finding their path blocked once again rioted angrily. The chief held the men in place, however, and within a week tempers calmed, and the flood of illegal immigrants had slowed to a trickle.

Gatekeeper

El Paso's Operation Blockade was so successful that it became the model for a much larger government program

instituted by the presidential administration and launched in 1994: Operation Gatekeeper. Gatekeeper was unveiled in San Diego, and targeted Imperial Beach, likely the worst spot on the border.

Several hundred new agents were added along the line, like a long string, a truck stationed every quarter-mile apart, all the way to the sea. Each able to watch a section of the border, and keep one or two other agents in sight.

A layered series of fences was erected along the border. National Guard troops were deployed in the region to help with the massive construction project. The front line of defense was the "landing-mat barrier," a dark, rust-colored wall built up from the corrugated steel panels the military uses to make battlefield airstrips. The welded plates ran from the waterline nearly 14 miles inland, ending at the foot of the Otay Mesa mountains. Behind the landing-mat wall was a second barrier, the "bollard fence," a forest of foot-thick concrete poles planted so densely that a person could not squeeze by them, and tough enough that a truck could not smash through them. In other spots was the "Sandia fence," a shiny steel barrier dimpled like a grater, and curved south at the top — toward Mexico — making it hard to scale.

Certain sections of the border look like permanent construction sites, where the National Guard stays deployed and slowly builds out the fence. The walls stretch out of the urban corridors and into the desert. By the end of the 1990s, 60 miles of barricade snaked along California's border with Mexico. And to the west, the border-wall ran from Imperial Beach into and under the water; it ended in an enormous blade, 100 yards long, that lurked just beneath the waves to discourage swimmers.

Wiring the Border

Fifty years ago, watching the border meant a single observer stationed atop spindly steel towers, 75 feet into the air, peering into the desert. Operation Gatekeeper brought an influx of new technology to the Border Patrol to help them patrol the night. In addition to the new fences and additional personnel, floodlights mounted on high poles were installed to bathe the barriers in harsh light (in some spots stretching for as long as a mile), portable klieg spotlights could be relocated to new trouble spots, motion and heat sensors were buried beneath the desert sand or hidden along known smuggling routes, set off by vibrations of someone passing by and nearby, remote cameras (sometimes located in tall towers) scanned the area when an alarm was tripped. Alarm signals were transmitted instantly to Border Patrol control centers, such as the one at Imperial Beach Station.

The men and women of the Border Patrol also benefited from new equipment, including night-vision goggles and military-style infrared scopes. New funds allowed the purchase of new ATVs and SUVs and even Blackhawk helicopters.

At the border stations, a new high-tech lookout database, called IDENT (Automatic Biometric Identification System) was installed. IDENT takes a set of digital fingerprints and couples them with a digital mugshot, to better track undesirables processed through the border no matter where they cross.

San Diego's Border Research and Technology Center is developing various future-tech prototypes, including a device that broadcasts an electric current that can shut down a speeding car, a camera that can see through the body of a car or truck to look for concealed people and computers that can scan and identify voiceprints of subjects.

The Human Scarecrows

Today, the Border Patrol guards are sometimes mockingly referred to as "human scarecrows" by the coyotes and the smugglers, for all the agents seem to do is stand along the border and wait. The rough-and-tumble, cowboy image is faded, like a photograph of the old frontier.

Still, to those who know the Border Patrol, their trackers, or Signcutters, are men to be respected. Armed with military topographical maps, GPS units, powerful radios, handcuffs, pepper spray, batons and .40 caliber sidearms loaded with hollow-points, Border Patrol agents are self-sufficient. They patrol in custom-retrofitted, four-wheel drive Explorers, built out with heavy mesh cages, a shotgun rack behind the seat and the mother-of-all air conditioners. And the Signcutters are some of the best trackers in the field.

Signcutters read tracks by how sharp or faded they are: as a track ages and dries, its details soften. Similarly, while most walkers travel the desert during the heart of night, bugs begin their frenetic chores just before the day's first light. "Bug-sign," the telltale scurrying of lizards, rodents and insects, leaves a distinct pattern. If the bug-sign lies atop the walker's trail, the tracks are older; if the walker's steps crush the bug-sign, the tracks are fresh.

The average men and women of La Migra do the bulk of the grind work, sitting on the line, patrolling endless stretches of desert, helping illegals in dire straits as much as arresting them; yet these agents are the unsung heroes of the Border Patrol. Most of the glory goes to the superstar units, BORSTAR (the Border Patrol Search, Trauma and Rescue) and BORTAC (Border Tactics). The BORSTAR units are the air cavalry of the border; they ride in on hot desert winds like giant dragonflies, hovering over the dunes. BORTAC, however, is their dark shadow. A fully armored and heavily armed SWAT team, some of the local sheriffs wryly refer to them as "hunter-killer" or "terminator" units. They are trained to bust heavily armed drug dealers, survivalist militias and roaming banditos. BORTAC commandos dress in military-style blacks, are outfitted with infrared goggles and night-vision scopes and equipped with jet-colored, monster SUVs and cutting-edge Blackhawk helicopters.

Myths of La Migra

The rugged Western myth of the Border Patrol is not uncommon in the United States, but south of the border, the stories told of La Migra have the echo of bogeymen:

La Migra Malo

Rural women who have never gone north, but have lost men across the border (a brother who never came back, a husband who disappeared) whisper horror stories to their children: La Migra are monsters, who catch young men and women and stake them out in the desert for *el chupacabra*. Old men sit on decaying porches drinking *cerveca* and telling tales of how they almost made it… until La Migra swarmed over the hills like a nest of scorpions, faces masked by demonic goggles, screaming like coyotes and firing their guns wildly! In some stories, La Migra storm in on ATVs, motorcycles and gleaming 4x4s; in older tales, they wear cowboy hats and carry assault rifles and ride in on a cloud of dust kicked up by monstrous horses! La Migra chased them down and beat them with batons. La Migra stripped them of their clothes and sent them back along the highway naked and without water. La Migra took their money and promised to shoot them between the eyes next time. And if there are ever women or girls in the group… everyone knows that La Migra takes them into their buildings and molests them.

Shadow Wolves

While the BORTAC units are the most widely known terror-units of the Border Patrol, there is one agency with an even more fearsome reputation. Customs is rumored to field a legendary unit called the "Shadow Wolves." Stories claim that every member of the Shadow Wolves is a Native American tracker — full blood to the last — the best of the best Signcutters, able to follow a coyote, or drug smuggler or vampire across the badlands no matter where they run and hide.

The Border Czars

Both the United States and Mexican governments are interested in controlling the gateways across their shared border. Of course, they are not the only powers interested in the flow of traffic. A new initiative of the U.S. government created the position of the "Special Representative for Southwest Border Issues," or the Border Czar. The Border Czar is a politically appointed position, who reports directly to the Attorney General. The Czar's responsibilities include mobilizing taskforces to combat drug smuggling (in cooperation with the Drug Czar), coordinating multi-agency projects (such as overlapping cases of the FBI, U.S. Customs Service and INS) and investigating official corruption among U.S. border agencies.

The Border Czar acts as the Attorney General's representative when dealing with the Mexican government on issues of drugs, immigration and other bilateral border issues. Border politics are sometimes difficult to negotiate, as both sides recognize the other as a valuable trading partner. Yet social and cultural issues must also be negotiated, as American citizens are often paranoid about unchecked migration, while Mexican citizens often complain about ill-treatment at the hands of border officials. The Border Czar must argue the government's agenda but also help placate the Mexicans (though skeptics might describe it as simple lip-service).

Mexico also has a Border Czar, or "Foreign Ministry Institutional Liaison for Northern Border Affairs." The Mexican Border Czar is a presidential appointee, and in the modern era is a position geared to fight for a more open border, such as the invisible lines that cross the European Union. Additionally, the Border Czar deals with the Mexican side of border security measures.

The Future of the Border

The border is never far from the headlines. As Mexican President Vincente Fox comes to the end of his term, the border is once again in the media's focus. On one side are those pushing for a comprehensive immigration bill that provides for guest-worker programs and allows for the legalization of undocumented workers already established in the United States. On the opposition side are those who fear such a bill would open the floodgates to tens of thousands of desperate aliens, all seeking to claim a piece of the United States for themselves.

Opponents have reawakened the notion of a 700-mile-long fence between the United States and Mexico, but many experts believe that such drastic measures only drive people into more dangerous terrain, increasing the risks while doing nothing to actually stem the tide. It is said that more people than ever before traverse the border, but a rough average of one Mexican dies per day crossing la frontera.

Crossing the Border

There is one constant concerning the border — and that is that it is ever changing. Paradoxically, at the same time, it never changes. Whether one is going north or south, rules, regulations, corruption, racism, politics — all of these may color the details.

It is a common assumption that it is much easier to cross into Mexico than to come north into the United States. Stereotypes of rampant corruption, boredom and laziness cling like cheap cigarette smoke to Mexican customs agents. As with everything on the border, the truth shifts depending on where one is standing.

Jim Ozark worked with a Christian charity organization that helped build orphanages. Driving down with a convoy of fresh-faced, UT Christian co-eds, they crossed into Mexico at McAllen into Reynosa. When they stopped at Customs, the Mexican agent told them to pull over for inspection. When Jim and his girlfriend, Peri, talked to the agent, he rattled off in rapid-fire Spanish how they were not allowed to transport goods along this road, and that they should have crossed over at Brownsville/Matamoros. He told them to turn back. Jim knew he needed to pay off the agent, but also realized he couldn't just blurt out an offer of a bribe. So he said, "I understand that we don't have the right permit. But maybe we could pay you, and you could take care of the paperwork for us?" The agent pondered this, and replied, "Yes, I can do that." Jim asked, "How much is the permit?" "Sixty American dollars." Jim was a bit shocked by such an outlandish amount, but before he could say anything, Peri exclaimed, "Sixty dollars for each truck?" Jim groaned as the agent's face lit up with a wide grin.

A few years later, Jim was driving through the interior of Mexico with his pal, Ed. The two were driving gear to the Mayan archaeological site at Uxmal, but traffic was terribly slow on these small roads. Night was coming quickly, and Ed did not want to be stuck on the roads in the dark. Ed encouraged Jim to pass the slowpokes. Jim gunned the engine, and shot ahead, zipped along the curve, crossed a bridge — and suddenly a car was coming right at them! Jim cut hard back into his lane, but the other car — a police car — drove off the road. Ed said, "Let me handle this," as the policia stalked up, furious. Ed blamed it on the hot day, the cold beer, and offered the officers smokes, and a bribe. The officers mellowed, thanked Ed for the cigarettes and told them to be more careful. As they started off again, Jim asked Ed, "How much did you slip them?" "Five whole dollars," Ed laughed.

- It is illegal for foreigners to possess guns, ammunition or other weapons while in Mexico. Gun laws are very strict in Mexico, and foreigners will, at a minimum, be detained, and are normally formally arrested. Penalties for possession normally consist of prison time, and while the American consulate may be able to help out, foreigners often sit in jail for weeks if not months during the labyrinthine, and expensive, legal maneuvering.
- Border stations at large urban centers, such as San Diego/Tijuana, are open 24 hours. Smaller stations, however, are often closed from midnight until 6 A.M.
- The border stations allow both automobile and foot traffic. Travelers are randomly stopped (a green or red traffic light) for questioning.
- Americans do not need visas to travel within the "border zone," which encompasses the border towns and many resort areas, and extends roughly 12 miles into the interior of Mexico.

Crossing into the United States from Mexico often involve long lines at the border, where travelers may sit for several hours. While customs agents are on the lookout for obvious contraband, many Americans travel across the border for cheap prescription drugs. Individual drugs may have a particular limit (such as a three-month supply), and others may not be allowed at all across the border.

The U.S. Border Patrol occasionally sets up secondary "surprise" checkpoints a few miles inside the United States' border, well beyond U.S. Immigration and Customs. These agents are on the lookout for illegal immigrants and drug smugglers who may have slipped through the first line.

Illegals who make it past La Migra often hole up in drop houses. Some of these are private houses owned by friends of the coyotes, who make a few bucks per head that passes through. Other drop houses are abandoned properties that provide shelter to anyone passing through, though the migrants may have to defend themselves from the local homeless population now squatting there. The coyotes jam their chickens into the house like an overstuffed coop: 10, 20, 30, 40, 100 people crammed into a tiny, ramshackle building whose only "luxury" is that it is located near the highway, thus providing an excellent pick-up point.

Mexico Side

The Mexican side of the border is colored by poverty, drug smugglers and the masses of hopeful, albeit hopeless, illegals. The towns have names that are familiar, yet still possess a touch of the exotic, of the lawless West. Tijuana. Mexicali. Agua Prieta. Ciudad Juárez. Nuevo Laredo. Matamoros. The newly erected walls of Operation Gatekeeper had a secondary effect of creating a baffle that directed the flow of illegals into the badlands. While the Border Patrol agents had predicted this would happen, they were unprepared for the sheer volume of people who risk such hostile terrain.

The border towns have migrant shelters — essentially way stations for the stream of illegals, either planning the journey to *el norte*, or already failed and deported back to their homeland. Illegals dumped back across the border in the middle of the night often have no other place to go, for their homes might be hundreds of miles in the interior of Mexico. The migrant shelters are a lodging of last resort, a little bit of protection in the cold world.

Desolation and the Devil's Highway

You need a new kind of prayers to negotiate with this land.

— Ofelia Zepeda, Tohono O'Odham poet

The stretch of Sonoran country that straddles Pima and Yuma in Arizona, and Sonora in Mexico, is known to a few as Desolation. It is also more commonly known as the nightmarish *Camino del Diablo* — the Devil's Highway.

There are some religious texts that describe a vast desert, called Desolation, where God has buried rebel angels. Some mystical theologians suspect an angel, bound in chains, lies here, beneath the broken plains, and the shifting sands. What is for certain is some terrible spirit makes its presence here, overseeing the Devil's Highway.

The region was named for the many travelers who died during the gold rush of the mid-1800s. Even previous to this, however, Mexican settlers were besieged by native bands, such as the Sand Papagos. Skeletons — both human and animal — were found along the road. Horses and cattle were transformed into withered mummies and blanched bones, settled among the ironwood trees. Graves marked only by heaped-up cairn stones lay scattered throughout the area. Even today, the Border Patrol's unofficial policy is to leave bodies where they are found. It's simpler this way.

The Devil's Highway is found within what is today a large wilderness reserve. The Spanish conquistadors named the region *Cabeza Prieta* — or Dark Head — in reference to a large, lava-topped granite peak on the western edge of the refuge. Superstitious folk think the name refers to the fallen angel, devil or other evil spirit that lives in the land. The Amerindian peoples of the region (such as the Tohono O'Odham and the Hopi) blame the evil on the wicked pranks of a coyote-spirit, called Ban, who runs through the wide-open places. When the Spanish first arrived, they believed that the natives of the area were barbaric and evil, savages who feasted on human children. Throughout history, this place has been a place of legend and myth. In years past, the Yaqui Indians believed that their ancestors, the tiny Surem, lived underground here. After the Spanish arrived, Catholic apparitions began to haunt the region, such as a white woman bearing a cross, and La Mujer Azul. Today, stories of La Llorana and the *chupacabras* both are told by ragtag travelers.

The Blue Lady

The myth of the Blue Lady, or *La Mujer Azul*, seems to have originated in the Southwest in the mid-1600s, throughout the regions of New Mexico and Texas. She was described as either wearing a blue veil, or dressed in a blue nun's habit. She was a blessed spirit, who helped the sick in their time of suffering, in particular women in need and poor children. In Texas, she was called "the Mysterious Woman in Blue," and was said to be concerned with bringing God to the native tribes.

In San Antonio, the folktales say that she appears once in a generation, always emerging from a hidden underground passage beneath the Alamo, to visit a chosen woman. The woman, whether old or young, is always a native Texan — a woman pure of heart, blessed with faith, smart and wise, mannered and patriotic. The Blue Lady bestows a gift upon the chosen woman, an ability to see "the true heart of all things," and charges her to use her abilities for the good of her people.

Hostile Country

The entire land is hostile. The historic route linking frontier Mexico to the Spanish settlements of California is desolate, dry and barren. The main trail is easily navigable, but the surrounding terrain is primarily desert flats, shifting sand dunes and lava rock. There are old abandoned mineshafts waiting to collapse upon the unwary, or potentially hiding things that do not want to be disturbed. There are few signs or navigational aids. There are no sources of safe drinking water, and many of the waterholes dry up. And there is danger from unexploded munitions, for sections of the desert were used as military firing ranges.

Even the plants are unforgiving, angry and sharp. Cacti such as saguaros and nopales are common, as are many varieties of the shrubby cholla pants. The silver and gold cholla have white or yellow sheathes on their spines, respectively. They are bushy, and often grow woven together. The buckthorn cholla is extremely widespread, a straggly green cactus with bright yellow, orange, pink or red flowers and inconspicuous spines. Then there is the devil cholla, which has no sheathes and seems to be all spines. The devil cholla grow together, forming walls of spines, which may be in all colors, but are always sharp as knives.

Most of the wildlife only makes its presence known at night. The day is just too much of a killer. And everything seems to be a predator. Ringtail cats, coyote and foxes all hunt through the night. Bats feast on insects for the most part, although the long-nosed bats drink from the saguaro flowers. The desert seems to welcome dangerous creatures, from rattlesnakes (sidewinders, diamondbacks and the almost silent Mojave) to coral snakes, from black widows and tarantulas to brown recluse spiders (whose bite can cause permanent tissue damage), from giant centipedes and killer bees to scorpions and beaded Gila monsters. Everything is ready to bite and spread its venom. Those that aren't deadly may be strange and alien, such as the regal horned lizard, which defends itself by squirting blood from its eye sockets with precision aim! Even the bite of the seemingly harmless kissing bug may cause an explosion of red welts… or may cause the victim to go into anaphylactic shock.

Death comes in many forms in the Devil's Highway. It gets so cold at night that travelers can freeze. But the Border Patrol also finds illegals who drowned, were hit by trains and trucks who did not see them in the dark or were bitten by deadly animals. Of course, the most common killer is hyperthermia — death by sunlight.

Tucson

Tucson, Arizona, is a small chunk of civilization in the vastness of the desert of Desolation — an urban center riddled with secrets and holes, which hide the night's terrors.

Coyotes

The smugglers who deal in human cargo are called *coyotes*. These paid guides control the ebb and flow of human traffic, and are often viewed as parasites by both the border guards who try to catch them and the very migrants who pay them for their services.

Roughly within the last decade, the cost of a coyote's service shot up. As the border became harder to penetrate, the journey became more dangerous, and the coyote became richer. Before Operation Gatekeeper, it could cost between $300 and $500 for a guided trip across the line. More recently, the price has more than doubled, running between $800 and $1000 per head.

If the smugglers are coyotes, the migrants who desperately need them are *pollos*, or chickens. Coyotes are therefore also known as *polleros*, or "chicken-wranglers," although in some communities they are instead called *iguanas*.

Patron Saint of Illegals

A priest from Jalisco, Toribio Romo, was killed in the early 20th century (in the Cristero War, when the government closed churches and banned worship). Romo was shot and murdered as a martyr in the town of Tequila; Pope John Paul II canonized him and two dozen other fallen from Cristero, but Romo had long been a saint to the locals. Even today, illegals carry Saint Toribio prayer books; they pray for miracles when they are lost and alone in the desert. Some claim he has appeared and led them to water, hidden them from La Migra, rescued them from valleys of desolation and brought them to the highway and civilization. A few even recount stories in which Saint Toribio has picked them up in his truck, driven them across the border and given them a package with money, food, water. Toribio is also known as *Santo Pollero* (Holy Chicken Wrangler).

His appearance is normally chronicled as a white-skinned youth with blue eyes, who speaks perfect Mexican Spanish (sometimes dated, sometimes very current). He asks for little, except for prayers once those he helped have established themselves in safety and security.

Watchdogs

E Pluribus Unum — Out of Many, One

The Watchdogs call themselves a citizen's watch group, but in the harsh desert nights, it's clear that they are a paramilitary, vigilante organization. They espouse a racist and paranoid philosophy; in their rhetoric, illegals are effectively less than human, all criminals, terrorists and junkies. They carry diseases, and they threaten our neighborhoods, our families, our women and children.

A Houston congressman who backs them has spent a lot of energy on anti-immigrant campaigns. He issued statements linking Muslim fundamentalist terrorists and Chinese spies to the myriad workers crossing the border in search of jobs, and called for investigations into rumored paramilitary training camps being operated near Matamoros. These spurious accusations breed ignorance and sow the seeds of fear.

The Watchdogs believe they are doing good, red-blooded patriot work. Work that their government has failed to do. Although in their formal writings they claim to be unbigoted, in reality they recruit from white supremacist websites and private clubs. They take it upon themselves to spy on suspicious members of their communities, threaten and assault migrant workers and, in extreme cases, commit acts of sabotage or murder.

From a Watchdog website: *Be aware that terrorist, drug-smuggling, job-stealing, gang-raping, criminal alien barbarians are roving through YOUR STREETS every night while you are ASLEEP. These ANTI-AMERICAN Che Guevara pussies will attack you if they find you alone. They will STEAL your truck and MOLEST any defenseless women, whether young or old. Do not travel alone and stay LEGALLY armed.*

Border Towns

Every year we get poorer and poorer, even though we create more and more wealth.

— Mayor Gustavo Elizondo (of Ciudad Juárez), *New York Times*, Feb. 2001

All border towns have their peculiar traits and distinctive landmarks. Yet many of their problems, and quirks, are shared with every urban center strung along *la frontera* like a string of burnished pearls. No matter how gritty and run-down the reality, from a distance, at night, each is a gleaming paradise.

What follows are broad-stroke descriptions of Tijuana, yet many of the core elements — the crime, the bloodshed, the poverty, the shantytowns, the dumps — exists in Ciudad Juárez and Nuevo Laredo and Matamoros and all the others.

Tijuana

Tijuana is the archetypical border town. It came into its own during the early part of the 20th century, one part dusty Spanish ranching town, and one part Hollywood resort. During the 1920s, Prohibition in the United States caused Tijuana's first big tourism boom, and it featured the "longest bar in the world" at the Tijuana racetracks. In 1927, the glittering gambling den and gilded spa, Agua Caliente, opened to much fanfare. (When the casino closed in 1938, its action-seeking patrons found a new refuge, in Las Vegas, Nevada).

Now, as then, money pours in from the gringo tourists who treat Tijuana as their own personal playground. Bars and resorts spill over with white Americans looking for *cerveza*, tequila, mescal, cheap sex and soft (or hard) drugs. Poor kids sell bubble gum, cigarettes, bottles with dried scorpions and spiders and whatever else they can get their hands on. There's always someone selling, and always someone buying, at any hour of the night.

Money also circulates freely through the underworld, as some of the top drug smugglers operate from here, spreading their cash flow among the *judiciales*, the judges, the politicians. It's not that there aren't honest cops in Tijuana, it's that they get paid far less than US minimum wage, and have to buy their own car, gun and handcuffs. How can that compare to a *narcotraficante*'s fat stack of greenback dollar bills, fast cars and big guns? It's no surprise that most cops supplement their paychecks with the *mordida* — "the bite" — a traditional system of bribes that runs throughout the country.

Tijuana is San Diego's sister. The connection is easy to see, for they sit side-by-side and have coexisted for decades. According to some census reports, Tijuana is the bigger sibling, now larger than San Diego, yet Tijuana's economy is barely equal to a U.S. city one-third its size. Tijuana's infrastructure is at least a decade, and more likely a generation, behind the times. Among certain *Tijuanense* intellectuals, the city's modern nickname shouldn't be TJ, but Palestijuas: Tijuana-Palestine.

La Mujer Blanca

In the *barrio* of Colonia Aeropuerto, a woman reaches up to the sky. She is concrete, five stories tall and stripped bare before the world. A naked statue to liberty, La Mujer Blanca ("the White Woman") was made by a local artisan as a symbol. Painted white, and towering about the garbage-filled alleys, she represents purity, and perhaps contains a number of contradictory meanings about the condition of Mexican women, if one studies her closely.

La Mujer Blanca, or La Mona ("the Doll") as she is more colloquially called, is both hollow and yet filled with secrets. Her creator eats in her belly and sleeps beneath her massive bosom.

Outside of the resorts, plazas and *mercados*, the city seems to devolve rapidly. The poverty and dilapidation spread out in waves. Of course, there are some fine neighborhoods where the rich and dwindling members of the middle class live, but the majority of *Tijuanense* live the night-to-night grind in poor *barrios*. And at the extreme fringes of the *barrios* are the garbage dumps — *dompes* — where the poorest of the poor hunker down.

In the mid-1990s, a hot war seemed to erupt on Tijuana's streets. Prolonged gun battles between warring cartels, complete with their personally bought and owned police departments, screamed across the headlines. State police were allied with one cartel, and reportedly murdered a federal *comandante* (in the pocket of a rival drug baron). In retaliation, the federal police arrested the deputy state attorney general on charges of corruption… and then apparently took it upon themselves to also kill the city's police chief. A presidential candidate was slaughtered in cold blood, and the most likely assassins were his own bodyguards.

Hundreds of murders per year were attributed to the drug business, and the aftershocks of the central conflict brought death to innocents, tourists and outsiders. Beyond the borders of the city, bandits battled each other within sight of San Diego. Farther into Mexico, communal Native Indian lands that had been turned into marijuana operations for certain cartels, complete with hidden airstrips, also became war zones. On one such reservation, in Baja, California, one of the cartel's roused an entire colony in the heart of the night. Members of the Pai-Pai tribe (a pre-Columbian people) worked for the cartel because they had no other options; the group included young children, infants and a pregnant woman. They were all massacred.

Cat and Mouse

In response to some of the most dramatic killings, the Mexican Attorney General put together an elite, three-man team to target the heads of the cartels. The team, graduates of various special forces services, kidnapped a few key captains of the cartel, and broke up several lucrative smuggling rings. To keep the team off the grid, the Attorney General arranged a U.S. DEA safe house in San Diego as the base of operations.

Despite these precautions, someone at the top talked — someone always does. The team members' vehicle was found cracked up at the bottom of a canyon between San Diego and Tijuana. They bodies had been flayed — skin torn with pliers, all limbs broken, faces torn off, skulls reduced to a wet pulp.

The Plaza

The face of Tijuana's drug trade seems to be ever changing, but there are certain constants. The head of the underworld holds *la plaza*, and everyone beneath him — who pays appropriate tribute — is also protected by the authorities. Yet rivals may seek to do him in, or the authorities may become displeased with him or more powerful forces (such as the U.S. government) may demand his head; it's good to be at the top, but one is never secure.

The Archetypal Druglord

Miguel Tomas de Castillo is one of Tijuana's paragon drug lords. He directs his organization from a fortified estate outside of the city, and his name commands fear and subservience. He travels with a pack of armed thugs. In previous years, when he decided to dine, his soldiers would secure the chosen restaurant. They would not let any of the other diners leave, or use the phone, but in exchange for the inconvenience, de Castillo would pay for all their meals. The nights have become more dangerous in recent years, and now de Castillo has his men completely clear any establishment he decides upon, ushering out any other patrons and outsiders with a speed rivaling the American Secret Service.

De Castillo expects his men to be loyal and follow his orders without question. He has no tolerance for dissidents, and no mercy for traitors. He is quick to order the deaths of any who threaten his operation, and he is just as likely to order the execution of a client who fails to pay him — his strict enforcement policy ensures all his clients know he means serious business.

De Castillo is flamboyant, and too quick to take an active hand in meting out punishment. He likes to be there when they die. His favorite death sentence is *carne asada*, in which the victim has a gasoline-soaked tire forced on him, and is then burned to death. Although not a big man, De Castillo is not afraid of violence or getting his hands wet with blood. He carries a signature .357 Desert Eagle ("Silver Eagle Series") with him at all times, and has been in several shoot-outs with his enemies. De Castillo is known to wear a bulletproof vest or flak jacket when expecting danger, and his bodyguards are outfitted with fully automatic weapons, bulletproof vests and modern cell phones.

Most of the smuggling is done over land, although some is done by small, private airplanes. The organization also deals in stolen vehicles, and is responsible for 70% of the stolen jeeps, SUVs and pickup trucks in southern California and western Arizona. Stolen trucks are often driven straight into Mexico, with a small bribe to the Customs agents, and traded directly for heroin. De Castillo has more than 500 people in his organization, scattered from Tijuana to Ojinaga and Chihuahua to Acuña and Coahuila and throughout many U.S. cities, including Calexico, Yuma, Tucson, Amarillo, Dallas, Fort Worth, Odessa, the Presidio, and even has agents and distribution channels as in states as far away as Kansas, Missouri, Nevada, Georgia, Michigan and Minnesota.

Unconfirmed intelligence reports conclude that de Castillo and his cartel have protection that reaches all the way to Mexico City. Local ties include the governor of Baja, California, and the Mexican general in command of the region. In fact, a number of his men are believed to hold positions in the local Mexican Federal Judicial Police

(MFJP). These men carry MFJP credentials and travel heavily armed with impunity.

De Castillo pays and pays well for this tremendous freedom and extensive web of contacts. He is not only ignored but actively protected by the local and federal levels of the Mexican government, and can expect to be treated as a guest of the government, given immunity and can even order military raids upon enemies. For all of this, he pays at least US$100,000 per month.

Finally, de Castillo protects himself through his own family. His closest advisors and lieutenants are all blood relatives. He only deals with them, and they in turn deal only with close family friends or long-time business associates. These people, then, deal with the next levels on down. The core of the cartel is thus well insulated, as most members only know a few contacts within the hierarchy. This keeps outsiders from penetrating to the upper echelons, and learning de Castillo's deepest secrets.

Due to the constant state of warfare and volatile nature of the *narcotraficante's* lifestyle, drug lords are arrested, killed or driven into exile with some regularity. The Storyteller should feel free to populate her Mexico with whatever cartel bosses she feels best suit the chronicle. For example, instead of de Castillo she might use Los Hermanos Aztlan from "Mexican Snow" in the **Requiem Chronicler's Guide** (p. 107).

Colonia Libertad

Colonia Libertad is the most infamous *barrio* in Tijuana, a collection of ramshackle houses and apartments that line the hills and box in the narrow streets. Although Colonia Libertad is one of the oldest neighborhoods of Tijuana, those who live there can almost reach out and touch the lights of the San Diego nights. Many of the older residents never leave the *barrio*, even to go into Tijuana proper. There are meager butchers and modest bakers in Colonia Libertad, and even skeletal hospitals and dilapidated hotels. There is also an expanding shantytown of scrap wood and tar paper, despite being on the doorstep of San Diego.

The local population of Colonia Libertad is constantly swollen by those pushing for the border. Not only do many of the younger men and women cross regularly for their jobs in the United States, but many impoverished travelers end up here on their long journey north. Mexicans from the interior, from Oaxaca, Chiapas, the Yucatán, all cram into cheap rooms, looking for coyotes or trying to ford their own way across the *frontera*. Beneath them are the indigenous — Mixtecas, Zapotecas, Mayas — who cannot pass as Mexican and face further discrimination and abuse. Then there are the travelers who are illegal aliens even in Mexico — Guatemalans and Salvadorans and Hondurans and Nicaraguans. They are wary and nervous, often country peasants as much as anything else, led on by the lure of a better life in the United States, of course, but also directly fleeing the abject poverty, natural disasters, political terror, violent crime, even death squads of their homelands. So many end up in Tijuana, in Colonia Libertad, struggling for a new life. Not all of them make it.

Colonia Libertad suffers from lack of adequate water for its residents. Drinking water must either be hauled in or collected in improperly dug wells. Sometimes it is stored in barrels, which were often used in industrial plants (some labeled, "not to be used for water.") The water quickly becomes contaminated by human waste, chemical cleaners and pesticides, or heavy metals in the ground. Factories on the edge of the *barrio* dispose of hazardous waste by dumping it straight into the sewers. One of the side effects is children born with leukemia, lupus or anencephaly: a birth defect resulting in undersized, malformed or missing parts of the brain.

The Barrio Priest

Tío Coatl Coatl (from the Nahuatl Tezcacoatl, or "reflecting snake") is nobody's blood relative, yet he is everyone's uncle. He is old, and scraggly, yet seems to know the old Indian traditions and the ancient Mexican healing arts. "This will hurt you," he says simply. "Be brave."

He slices open sores and lets the blood and pus drain out. He bathes the wounds in steaming water, and covers them with herbs purchased for a few pesos from a botánica, or scrounged from Heaven knows where. He covers each injury with a different concoction, and he prays over each individually.

The border priest is the master of the snake, the herb, of the Holy Virgin. His magic is old, and subtle, and it requires faith — or at least a wild desperation. And for many, his magic works.

No Man's Land

There are a few square miles between the lights of San Diego and the shadows of Colonia Libertad that are regarded as no man's land. The distinction is clearly defined on the map, but it is harder to see, despite the fences and signs and walls, out in the canyons.

One of the gashes in the earth is called Deadman's Canyon. It is pitch black, even on moonlit nights, and has swallowed the blood and cries of countless desperate *pollos*. For years, bandit gangs have ambushed poor and frightened illegals. Coyotes — real coyotes — no longer take their charges this way, because too many of them have ended up caught in a bandit's trap. Bandits like to hamstring the coyotes, slicing through their tendons, leaving them writhing on the ground, begging for survival. Coyotes don't

carry much money and hate the robbers for preying on their marks. There are still many men in Tijuana who claim to be coyotes, but if they lead a party into Deadman's Canyon it's likely they plan to drop the illegals into the jaws of hell.

There are many canyons and trenches in these few miles of blood-watered mesquite and cactus. Spring Canyon is also known as the upper soccer field, where ragtag, pick-up teams will play before they try to sneak across the border when the sun sinks down. Airport Mesa is even higher up the hillside, providing a spectacular view of planes gliding into San Diego International Airport.

Dompe

Somewhere on the edge of Tijuana, outside of even Colonia Libertad but not quite in the no man's land and certainly daring to cross San Diego's shadow is the *dompe*, the garbage dump that is home to the most miserable creatures in Tijuana.

Dompes are common in most border towns. The abject and insane and broken who drift north, yet who would perish on the journey into the United States or perhaps can no longer even figure out which was is north, end up here, clawing out a pitiful existence. The lowest classes of Mexico end up here — peoples illegal in Mexico, running away from death squads and civil war, native peoples who could not pass as Mexican in the United States, the handicapped and the sick.

The police almost never come here, and when they do, they come in full force and in riot gear. Water is filthy when available, and fires eventually tire and fade, leaving gutted ruins in their wake. In some *dompes*, organized crime controls the territory, and taxes the homeless who pick through the trash. There is always a pecking order, sometimes a "mayor," sometimes a shady syndicate, no matter where one goes.

There is a feral pack in the garbage — the *cementeros*, glue addicts who have an almost religious zeal when it comes to getting their high. If they sense an outsider, especially someone who seems weak (and white), they swarm in a fluid mass of arms and legs, tearing and clawing and often stabbing with sharp metal fragments pulled from the garbage. In the light, they primarily young boys, cast-off bastards of hookers and crippled homes. But in the dark, they are wild.

At the very bottom are the zombies. Most often junkies, their souls are shattered and their minds are gone. Their odor is horrendous, but luckily they are barely capable of functioning. Still, they hunt in large shambling packs, and the Mother of God is probably no help to those they corner or catch sleeping.

Burning Hill

The most spectacular view of San Diego — one of the richest cities, in one of the richest states, in one of the richest countries — is from the

Tijuana garbage dump. In particular, it is the spot not where people collect bottles or cans, but a unique graveyard; it is the hill of dead animals that the city unloads in heaps. And then torch.

In the greasy haze, in a sculpture garden of twisted dreams, cat skulls and dog faces, smoking ribs and burnt fur and fat, one can watch San Diego's lights sparkle and gleam under the coal-blue sky. A city of gold and silver sitting along the coast, San Diego looks like Paradise.

Nuevo Laredo

Nuevo Laredo, in Tamaulipas, Mexico, is one of the "*dos* Laredos." Its dusky sister, Laredo, Texas, sits on the north bank of the Rio Grande. Three bridges across the river marry the sisters by economics, history and common culture — unfortunately, for many years that culture has been one of savage violence. Nuevo Laredo is the largest inland port in Mexico, and a tremendous amount of goods pass through here. Despite the trade boom, or more likely because of it, the *narcotraficantes* have long eyed Nuevo Laredo with a greedy eye — and recently, a group with enormous *huevos* has seized control.

Although Nuevo Laredo is supposedly the scarier of the two cities, they are so closely married that one must reflect the other. In today's Laredo, many businesses have closed down, tourism has dried up and the general population scurries along, terrified of the night.

Equis

As a town along *la frontera*, Nuevo Laredo has always had its own rules. For years, two modest cartels waged a thinly concealed war over control of the bridges and regional drug trade. As the cycle of violence threatened to spiral out of control, the Mexican and U.S. governments put together an ambitious plan to re-establish order. A unit of 31 elite Mexican army paratroopers from the Special Air Mobile Force Group was clandestinely sent to the United States to go through an extensive training regimen led by U.S. Army special forces. The program was held at the School of the Americas, the U.S. Army's Latin America-focused training facility, in Fort Benning, Georgia.

The United States spent millions of dollars on the program, teaching these airborne troops how to disrupt smuggling operations, intercept and decode smugglers' communications, interface with authorities on both sides of the border and deal with coyotes and human smuggling.

When the paratroopers were finally deployed, a young entrepreneurial drug baron nicknamed La Vibora ("the Snake") sought out their leaders in a Gulf Coast bar, and explained the economics of how much they were making ($700 a month) compared to what they could be making ($15,000 a month).

They took the better deal. They fell into La Vibora's employ, calling themselves "Equis" (X's) after a secure radio code used by Mexican federal police in Tamaulipas to identify high-ranking battalion commanders. The Equis, heavily armed and expertly trained as special forces operatives, took the offer. They became mercenary soldiers whose services included acting as bodyguards, smuggling aliens, providing intelligence reconnaissance and conducting assassinations.

Once they had learned enough of the drug trade from the *narcotraficantes*, the Equis went into business for themselves. Driving military-style vehicles and armed with fully automatic weapons and heavy weapons, they murdered many of their former bosses, including La Vibora, and offered the lowest runners and mules a choice — join them or disappear. The ultra-violent commandos were responsible for hundreds of deaths that year, as they laid siege to the entire countryside around Nuevo Laredo. They shattered both cartels, what limited local law enforcement remained, and declared themselves in charge.

The leaders — many of the original 31 — still remain, though a number have been arrested in spectacular skirmishes with the Mexican army, or killed in the constant power struggle. They have become that which they were trained to destroy. They outfit themselves in ostrich-skin boots, sport huge gold watches, drive enormous armor-plated Hummers and raise exotic animals on their fortified ranches.

Yet the group has maintained its hardcore military mystique — the notions of honor, courage and loyalty run deep. These principles, coupled with their ability to spy out their enemies plans, and bring devastating firepower to the field, have made them a force to be reckoned with. The Equis have grown in size by bringing in sons and nephews of the original group, as well as accepting deserters from the Mexican army and rotten *judiciales*. Recruits (Equitas, or Little Equis) are put through harsh six-week training courses in weapons, tactics, recon and intel; these paramilitary camps are in Tamaulipas and Michoacán. When a new police chief in Nuevo Laredo, during his first press conference, declared that the Equis' rapid deployment across the Rio Grande would not be tolerated, he was gunned down in the streets nine hours later.

Their increased numbers have allowed them to expand their trafficking routes through six American states. They charge a 10% tax on all smuggling operations — whether drugs, weapons, vehicles or humans — that pass through their territory. Anyone caught not paying is summarily executed, hands tied behind their backs and blindfolded. The Equis' cold-blooded killing extends to enemies, witnesses, law-enforcement authorities and the occasional innocent bystander.

Soldados de Cuera

A side business that the Equis still dabble in is paid assassinations. A core group of their deadliest assassins, known as the Soldados de Cuera, are still hired out to the highest bidder for jobs in Mexico and in the United States. Reportedly, there are 10 Soldados, all capable of easily navigating the border and able to freely cut across it. Their custom is to sport fine black leather jackets, and while they are expert marksmen, the brotherhood carries a traditional puñal dagger. Hiring them costs anywhere from $30,000 to $50,000 and up.

Initiation into the Soldados is said to require a recruit to hunt down and execute a member of the Border Patrol, preferably one of the daredevil commandos. Regardless, any member of Equi who manages to slay an American law-enforcement officer gains tremendous status within the organization and may one night be invited into the Soldados brotherhood.

Common Myths

The following are a collection of myths, tropes and stories that seem to circulate around the seedy underbelly of border and drug culture.

The Reign of the Don

Roberto "El Guapo" Rodriguez y Rodriguez was a small-time hood from Ciudad Juárez who impressed Miguel Tomas de Castillo with unflinching nerve and a canny ability to drive loads of marijuana across the border. De Castillo was impressed by El Guapo and gave him more and more responsibilities. Roberto had a long career ahead of him, if he had stayed to that path.

When American and Mexican authorities cooperated to bring the heat down on de Castillo, Miguel was forced into hiding. With Miguel cut off from his people, no one knew who was in charge of *la plaza*. Roberto wasn't sure if Miguel had been killed, or was ever coming back, so he declared himself the new don of Tijuana.

However, when the government agents pulled out, as they always do due to boredom or lack of funding, de Castillo crept out from hiding to find El Guapo parading around Tijuana. De Castillo and a few loyal men found El Guapo at a bar he frequented and butchered him in the parking lot. They cut him apart with machetes and fed his body to a pack of mongrels in Colonia Libertad — everything except for his head. De Castillo took El Guapo's skull, had it scoured clean and then smashed into bone chips, each about the size of a quarter. He had a favorite jeweler drill them and lace them with fine gold chains; de Castillo gave one to each of his lieutenants, so that everyone would know de Castillo was always around, even when out of sight.

The Survivor

Certain *padrinos* make their reputation by surviving certain death. The close brush with the next world, and the subsequent death of their enemies, fuels their *machismo*. One particular drug lord survived an assassination attempt although his red Ford Bronco did not. He had the truck towed to a square next to the main highway, where the truck sat on a pedestal of cinder blocks, the bullet holes and shattered glass a symbol of his immortality.

The Ubiquitous Drug Boss

Sometimes, when one drug lord rises to extreme prominence, other, smaller drug barons in the surrounding region will counsel their runners to lie if caught, and claim their association is with the boss who runs *la plaza*. This practice conceals the smaller rivals in a veil of anonymity, which offers them some protection, while simultaneously builds up the reputation of the drug boss who seems to control every last junkie or drug runner in the territory.

Payment

Drug lords demand that payment must be made, as efficiently and brutally as any mafioso or triad boss. One common method, to prove the drug lord's seriousness, is to take a customer who owes money, tie his hands behind his back and then throw him into the Rio Grande. The debtor is fished out of the filthy water before he drowns, but has learned not to be late.

Silencing Enemies

Many of the most powerful drug traffickers prefer anonymity to making headlines. It certainly helps their life expectancies. As such, they often retaliate fiercely when the media attempt to expose their identities or the details of their organizations.

There are numerous reports of journalists who have been shot dead in the street, or whose homes have been blown up, after a particular in-depth article that names names. Freedom and security of the press is but another American myth in many border cities in the grips of the *narcotraficantes*. Many newspapers self-censor, although even this isn't enough to guarantee their safety, for while uncommon, it is not unheard of for a cartel's hit men to burst into the offices of a random paper or television studio and shoot the place up to sow seeds of terror and paranoia.

Human rights activists, undaunted journalists and idealistic politicians are all seen as dire threats to the kings of the underworld. Such enemies, if not scared off with the threat of force, may find a friend or loved one slain, or they themselves may be disappeared — vanishing into a black Suburban with tinted windows in the middle of the night — a long-standing Latin American tradition.

The Capital of Murdered Women

"12 Women Slain in Juárez" is one headline, six apparently horribly raped and killed by three men from the Los Toltecas gang, and the other six dead at the hands of Los Rebeldes.

"400 Women Killed Since 1993" screams an Amnesty International report focusing on sexual violence in Ciudad Juárez, known as "the capital of murdered women."

A construction worker finds a body of a girl in a ditch near a major intersection. When police search the ditch, two more skeletons are found. Bulldozers are brought in, and unearth five more bodies. An arrest is made, a likely scapegoat: a bus driver who shuttles women between the *maquiladora* and a run-down apartment complex. Yet a week later another body is found — another girl, dead less than a day.

All along Avenida Juárez, the discount and dollar stores have photos taped to the windows. Many are now faded, and many sound so similar it breaks one's heart: "Missing… tan skin… long brown hair." "Missing… long dark hair… young… slim." "Missing… thin… long-haired." A score or more of young women who vanished without a trace, yet fit the profile of dozens more who had been raped, savagely mutilated and dumped with the trash.

Yet young women come from small towns for the jobs despite the danger. The factories demand they start before dawn, and often work until after dusk. The factory doors slam shut on the hour, so if a girl is late, she is trapped outside, alone and vulnerable. Billboards warn, "*Cuidado* — Watch for your life!"

The ditch where the bodies were found holds eight crosses and the remains of thousands of candles from past vigils. Eight wooden stakes are still jammed into the ground where the girls were discovered. Each stake bears a sign with a number: "*Cuerpo Uno,*" "*Cuerpo Dos,*" "*Cuerpo Tres*"…

Nearby, on a major street, a lamp post bears a painted sign — a black cross, and the word "Justice," in English. Perhaps that voice will be heard.

Underground Doorways

Authorities uncovered a fantastic feat of engineering, a massive 2,500-foot tunnel running from San Diego's Otay Mesa neighborhood for nearly half a mile, emerging in Tijuana, Mexico. One end of the tunnel was hidden in a cavernous warehouse in Otay Mesa, while the other poked out near the Tijuana airport.

The 48,000-square-foot Otay Mesa warehouse housed 12 loading docks. For weeks on end, the warehouse would be silent as if the place were vacant, with only a single container sitting at Dock No. 9, obscuring the entire door. Some days, the container would simply be gone.

And then without warning, the warehouse would become a hub of hyperactivity. Trucks would pull in and depart at all hours of the day or night. This could last for 10 days, and then everything would return to quiet.

No one heard the tunnel being dug, or saw evidence of the hundreds of loads of dirt hauled away. Authorities could not even hazard a guess as to how long it took to build, or for how long it was in use before they discovered it. While it seems more likely that the tunnel was dug with jackhammers and clay spades, one expert mining engineer suggested that, with enough time, the tunnel could have been dug by hand.

A shaft descends 90 feet into the ground, then the five-foot-high tunnel travels north from Tijuana, through sandstone and compacted sand, for several hundred feet. The floor is concrete, and electric lanterns are bolted to the wall at fairly regular intervals. Ventilation shafts pipe air down through the length of the corridor, which becomes very muggy in the depths. Drainage systems were built in to avoid total flooding, as water can rise three to four feet during periods of significant rainfall. The tunnel even contains a water-pump system and a pulley and winch for hauling goods.

The tunnel branches, and the minor branch dead-ends a few hundred feet later, but the main branch runs under the busy streets of Otay Mesa, and leads up into warehouse via a nine-story shaft. The dead end is an enigma: Did the engineers get lost and make a mistake in their digging? Was this a continuation that was never completed? Or is there something important, buried or released, that mortal authorities simply overlooked?

In the past decade, more than two dozen tunnels have been found crossing from Mexico into the United States. Most, if not all, of these tunnels are carved out by drug smugglers, going to any length to avoid detection. This find, complete with more than two tons of marijuana, was a big bust for authorities. Whether the owners will let this battle go or retaliate remains to be seen.

The Policia

The local authorities often claim they will investigate the murders and kidnappings and robberies, especially in high-profile cases with media attention. Quite often, while the officials publicly promise an investigation, in fact the arrests are blocked by a senior federal police *comandante* or military officer who directly benefits from the drug payments. In most cases, no results of the investigation are ever made known, and no one is ever arrested.

Rarely, one does find an honest cop who is willing to pursue a wanted criminal despite the signals that he should let it go. Such an officer quickly makes a name for himself among the underworld, and unless he secures his own protection from a power-player, the cop's days are then numbered.

Torture

The Mexican military (and some branches of corrupt police) relies on certain tried and true methods of torture. Victims are taken away, often disappeared under the cover of night with no witnesses and no official word of their imprisonment. A victim, cut off from the world he knows, may have no idea if or when he will be released, which begins breaking down his resistance.

The torturers may break prisoners who are reluctant to talk with a drink of water — from a hose, at full blast. The torturers don't stop until the prisoner resembles a drowned rat, sodden and quivering on the floor, bloated by water straight from the tap — in other words, certain to be suffering gastric distress.

Another common, and more severe, method is to strap a victim to a chair, and place a hood over his head. Low-ranking guards pummel the victim, pausing occasionally to demand answers to particular questions. The lack of sight and the inability to sense when the next blow will fall tends to heighten the terror.

From that point, the punishments only grow worse. A victim may have his head thrust into a bucket of water and held down so he cannot breathe. Alternatively, a victim might be strapped naked to a bench and then suffer a cattle prod to the thighs and testicles.

Beatings may last on and off for days, broken up by fitful sleep in a bare, concrete room. Inevitably, after a length of time, the senior commander appears during one of these periods of relative calm to find the victim naked, hungry, exhausted and terrified. The commander takes the role of sympathetic friend and protector, demanding clothes and food and that the brutal treatment be stopped. When the commander then questions the victim in a fatherly tone, it is as if the victim has found the ultimate confessional.

A Mexican specialty is to use Coke — Coca-Cola — to break down a prisoner's resistance. The victim has his arms hooked behind a chair, wrists handcuffed behind his back and is tilted so far back he feels as if he's going to spill out of the chair. One officer vigorously shakes up a can of soda, then pops the top and aims the violent stream of fizzy bubbles up the victim's nostril. As he gasps for air, another officer jams a small rag down the victim's throat, forcing him to breathe through his nose. The sensation has been described as an explosion in the brain. But because the pain goes away quickly enough as the bottle empties, officers are never content to use only one. Normally, an entire six-pack (or more) is used; by the end, the victim cannot control the tears streaming down his face. The soda feels as if acid is eating through his sinuses, and he will confess to *anything*. Or so they say.

Variants of this technique use ginger ale (which some says stings to an even higher degree), but the nastiest derivative is to mix soda with orange habanero peppers. Victims have described it as a white-hot iron jammed into their skull. If a victim's hands are free, he might dig gouges into his cheeks and nose, leaving bloody furrows as he tries to scratch out the peppers.

Shadows on the Border

It stretches nearly 2,000 miles across the desert, winding like a serpent along the Rio Grande and Colorado rivers, driving across hundreds of miles overland from the Gulf of Mexico to the Pacific Ocean. It crosses major metropolitan centers and vast, inhospitable deserts. It is the border, and it is locally thought to be one of the most spiritually active locations in the Western Hemisphere. From the Bruja vampire gang's drug-smuggling and illegal-crossing operations to the Uratha's attempts to block off the border's spiritual reflection to a brisk trade in mystical artifacts among mages, the border draws all manner of supernatural interest — and that doesn't even include the ghosts of border-runners who ran out of luck, spirits of division that prowl the Shadow and even stranger things.

The Bruja

The scourge of every border domain from Tijuana to Matamoros, Bruja gang members are easily among the most influential power-players on the border, at least in vampiric terms. While individual Princes of the border cities might have more control of the border in their territory, the nomadic Bruja have interests along the entire border. They run drugs out of Juárez, prostitutes out of Tijuana and traffic in human beings (and inhuman beings) across the border from anywhere to anywhere. The Bruja's influence is broadly felt and about as subtle as a sledgehammer to the brain; the Bruja don't buy off *federales* or bargain over turf with drug lords, the vampires drag the poor bastards behind their choppers until they see reason. Despite the Bruja's crude nature, Kindred across the southwestern United States and Mexico know that if they need something moved across the border without all those awkward questions the immigration agents like to ask, the Bruja are the bloodsuckers for the job.

The Many Faces of the Bruja

Throughout this section, numerous references are made to "the Bruja" as a whole. In this case, the term is used not to refer to the entirety of the bloodline, but to the core of the Bruja gang, which is made up of the bulk of the Bruja bloodline, assorted Gangrel wannabes and hangers-on who haven't joined the bloodline yet and a smattering of ghoul bitches and blood dolls kept around for convenience's sake. While certainly a significant percentage of the bloodline belongs to this gang, by no means is every Bruja on the planet embroiled in drug trafficking, white slavery and prostitution along the United States-Mexico border. Bruja have left the gang for many reasons, ranging from a desire to start a new branch of the gang in another city, to trying to find greener pastures for personal advancement, to even (admittedly rarely) as a result of simply becoming sick of the gang's philosophy of mindless violence and personal gratification.

Of course, references to "Bruja," sans the definite article, refer to the founder of the bloodline, Carlos Saavedra, the original *"hijo de bruja."*

Drugs

The bulk of the Bruja's drug trade comes out of Ciudad Juárez, Chihuahua, and comes into the United States through El Paso, Texas. While the gang has a few members who possess the first level of Obfuscate (quite possibly the most useful Discipline a drug runner could ask for), the bulk of the gang's mules are ghouls or mortal blood dolls the gang views as expendable. Kindred members of the gang avoid immigration for the same principal reason they avoid air travel: unexpected delays. Traffic at the border checkpoints can back up for several hours, and the last thing any vampire wants is to be boxed in by other vehicles on the freeway, sitting on a Harley as the eastern skies begins to redden. A few enterprising Bruja have experimented with teaching their ghouls Obfuscate, but this is a slow, difficult and frustrating process. (Bruja ghouls *can* learn Obfuscate, but as Obfusate is out-of-clan for Bruja, their ghouls must pay double the normal cost, new dots x 14, to learn Obfuscate.) The gang occasionally demands that a prospective member make a border run as an initiation; if the vampire gets from Juárez to El Paso with a few keys of Mexican black tar heroin in his saddlebags, he is allowed to join the gang. If he's busted, the local cops end up with one hell of a story when the morning sun hits the holding cell's window and fries their mule like an egg. Needless to say, such callow disregard for the Masquerade does not endear the Rabble to the Princes of Juárez or El Paso.

Story Hook: Behold a Black Horse

Most Bruja have been running (and using) heroin since long before they were Bruja, and they're no strangers to the bad shit the cartels try to move sometimes. Usually, when one of the Bruja's suppliers tries to sell them some badly-cut smack, the Bruja just roll in en masse and beat the shit out of him, but this latest batch isn't just your garden variety, watered-down-with-quinine junk. Sure, it kills

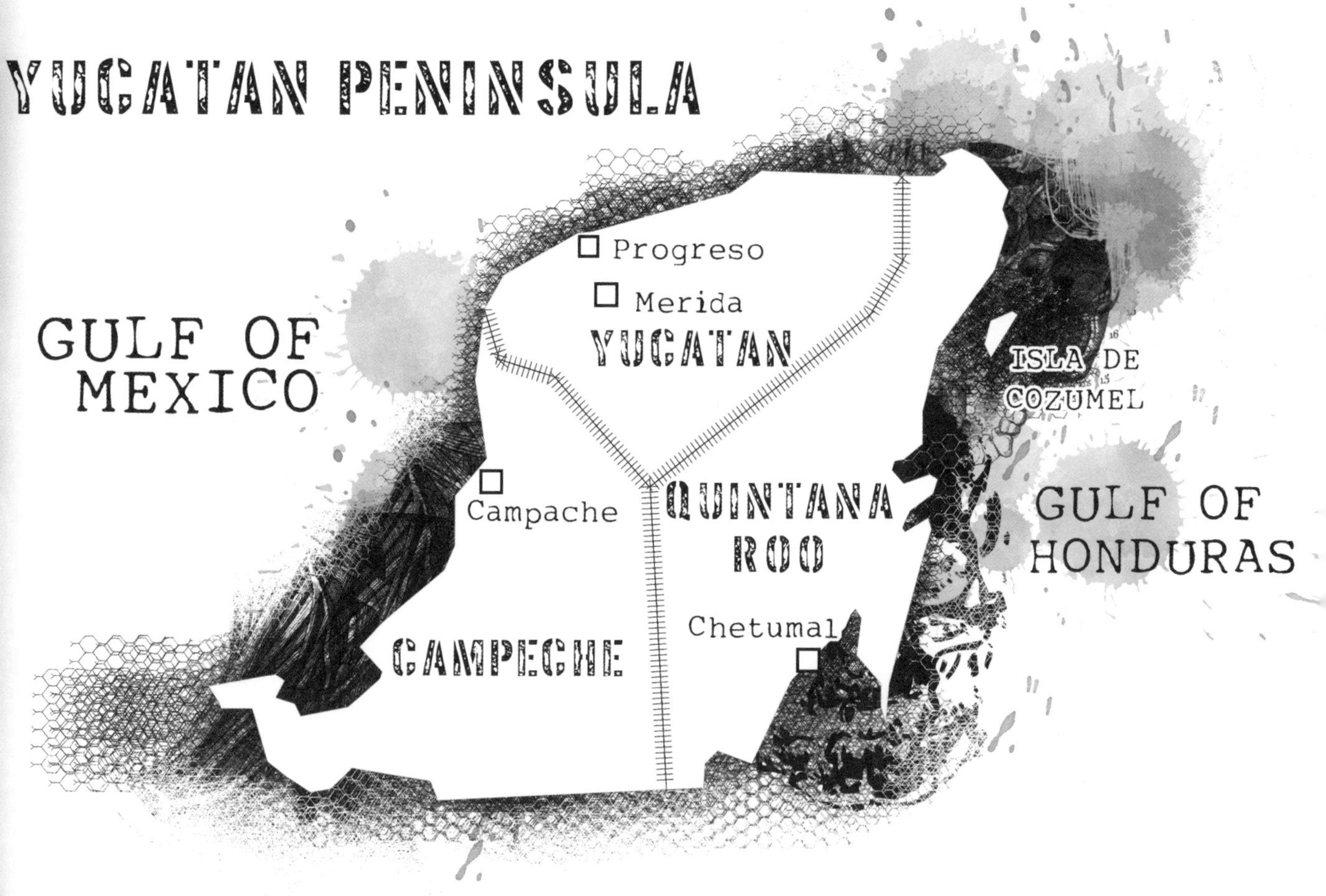

any poor bastard unlucky enough to shoot up with it, but after that, the junkie sort of... sticks around. Most Bruja are familiar with the concept of ghosts, of course, but few have any direct experience in dealing with them. As much as it galls the gang to admit weakness, they might have to call in some outside help to deal with the large number of poltergeists who are none to happy with the Bruja for selling the dope that killed them.

Prostitution

The Bruja started their prostitution operations running streetwalkers in Tijuana, pimping girls (usually blood dolls) out to mortals looking for a cheap fuck or Kindred looking for an easy meal. The Bruja began importing girls into the United States in the early '70s, and now have several smaller stables in southern California and Nevada, whose earnings the gang collects whenever the Bruja (or even just one of the senior members) roll through town. The gang isn't stupid, and knows that dead bodies — even the bodies of dead hookers — tend to draw more unwelcome attention in American cities, and as a result, the Bruja are considerably more cautious about selling their "stock" to other Kindred without strong assurances that the feeding won't be fatal.

Recently, the gang has begun using one of the brothels in Nuevo Laredo's *zona de tolerancia* ("tolerance zone," a six-block walled area in which prostitution is legal) as a money-laundering operation. The Club Sangre has rapidly garnered a reputation as a violent place where fights are nightly and disappearances weekly, and wise tourists avoid the brothel in favor of "safer" brothels in the zone, but the money keeps rolling in from the locals and the long-haul truckers. In addition to the services provided by the girls, the Bruja control the sale of any and all illegal drugs in the club and make a tidy profit renting out light-proof back rooms to traveling Kindred (meal service, of course, is not complementary).

Girls on the Side

The Bruja are a mostly male-dominated gang, but there are a few tough-as-nails biker broads among their number. While not exactly scions of the feminist movement, some of these female Kindred (and a few ghouls as well) have begun to try to set up an underground railroad of sorts to get girls out of the worst of the brothels the Bruja operate. The gang at large will tear these Kindred to shreds if they find out, of course, and it's unlikely that the "conductors" (being as they are mostly young Kindred with a decent amount of Humanity still intact) would survive such a confrontation intact. The biker chicks might turn to outsiders for help — but is holding onto your Humanity worth the risk of having a bunch of big, brutal, shitkicking Kindred pissed at you?

Human Trafficking and Smuggling

The phrase "human trafficking" is a bit of a misnomer in the Bruja's case. Certainly they play coyote to any number of mortals, whether Vinculum-bound blood dolls or ordinary kine with no idea of the true nature of their escorts across the border, but the Rabble do a brisker trade in Kindred looking to cross the border. There are multiple reasons for this, but among the most prominent are that, for one thing, not having to plausibly explain the myriad difficulties of Kindred travel to a mortal border-runner makes a would-be immigrant Kindred's Requiem a great deal easier, and secondly, because a vampire can be smuggled across the border in situations or environments that would kill a human. A vampire can be sealed in an airtight box barely big enough to fit her body, or brought across the most barren, inhospitable stretches of desert that would lead any mortal border-runner to a slow death by exposure. Bruja sometimes demand monetary services for their operations, but in the case of Kindred border-crossers, a more common form of payment is instruction of one or more members of the bloodline in a Discipline (usually a rare Discipline such as Nightmare or Majesty) or a Devotion. Because of this practice, it's not uncommon for coteries of Bruja coyotes to exhibit extremely diverse sets of powers, beyond the bloodline's usual Disciplines.

While the Bruja do smuggle humans across the border for a tidy profit, the gang's more common fare is in providing blood dolls to wealthy, powerful Kindred primarily in the southwestern United States. The Bruja's tactics in acquiring their chattel range from good old-fashioned press-ganging to the same techniques used by mortal coyotes: offering promises of a life of freedom in America, then, when their impoverished charges are unable to pay the "immigration fee," selling them into blood slavery. Few of these blood dolls last more than a few weeks, but that suits the Bruja just fine: there are always more people desperate to get across the border, after all.

Rumor in some border cities, including Mexifornia and Calimex, is that the Bruja have a standing pact with the Lupines called the Lodge of Coyote (see below). The Lupines let the Bruja traffic through the werewolves' territory, as long as the Kindred aren't moving anything especially spiritually malignant, and in return the Bruja do their *Easy Rider* routine on isolated border towns the werewolves point out from time to time. Exactly what *los lobos* get out of the arrangement is something of a mystery to the Bruja — some sort of mumbo-jumbo about *espiritos* and creating a wall across the border, but for the most part, any explanation goes right over the Bruja's heads.

Story Hook: Out in the Desert

There's a rumor circulating among the Kindred dwelling near the border. According to this rumor, the Bruja were paid a very generous sum — in blood, money or supernatural knowledge, depending on the source — to ferry an elder Kindred down el Camino del Diablo, the Devil's Highway, from Caborca, Sonora to Yuma, Arizona. Exactly why this elder wanted to follow an ancient trail used by conquistadors and gold prospectors, but the fact remains that this Kindred and his Bruja escort never reached Yuma. The rumor further speculates that this elder, sometimes of the Ordo Dracul, sometimes the Circle of the Crone, had found information regarding a potent mystic artifact lost somewhere on the Devil's Highway, perhaps by a mage traveling with the conquistadors or a Lupine pack killed fighting God-knows-what in the high desert.

The Lupines

To the Uratha, the border is more than just a stretch of geography dividing two countries. The border is a powerful symbol of division, of hope and despair, of wealth and poverty, of the First World and the Third. The border teems with spirits, and many more try to cross it every day: perhaps ironically, spirits generally want to get from the United States, a highly-developed, rationalized society, into the more wild and rural Mexico, where superstition and folk religion still have a strong hold on the people. In much of Mexico, the Gauntlet is far thinner than it would be in a similarly developed region of America. Whether this is a natural phenomenon of the region's Shadow or an effect of human belief and religion is a topic hotly debated by Uratha sages.

The superstition and folk religion common throughout the rural areas of Mexico mean that clever spirits have ready access to an abundant supply of Essence. Spirits have been known to masquerade as patron saints or divine manifestations, drawing Essence from the beliefs of the locals while simultaneously using Influences to bring the mortals completely under their sway. In small, isolated towns and villages, this arrangement can continue, Innsmouth-like, for generations, allowing the original spirit to grow stronger and draw its own brood of servants and "offspring." Such villages may have a Claimed population larger than its human population, and God help the lost traveler who stumbles across one of the "lost towns" in search of shelter.

Story Hook: Rosalita, La Santita de Cocozca

Cocozca, Oaxaca, is a tiny, isolated farming village in the southern region of Mexico. The village had been foundering for many years, with poor harvests and many of the younger generations leaving the village for the big city and the hopes of a better life. Ten years ago, a local farmer, Benicio Espinosa, was plowing his fields in the middle of the day when he saw a vision of an emaciated young girl in a white dress, surrounded by ears of corn. The little girl called herself Rosalita, and said that she would give of the food that sustained her to feed the village if they would honor her.

The village elders were skeptical at first, and wrote off Espinosa's tale as a hallucination brought on by too much time in the sun, but when Benicio's crops began to grow when the rest of the village's fields remained barren, the people were convinced. They began offering prayers to Rosalita, dubbed "the little saint of Cocozca" every Sunday, and the village's crops improved — not enough to be called truly bountiful, but enough to keep the village from starving, barely.

"Rosalita" is actually a famine-spirit, Pangs-of-Emptiness, that was drawn to Cocozca by its poor crop. Since the spirit's arrival 10 years ago, the spirit has slowly gained more and more control over the village, to the point that the people of Cocozca will do anything to appease their little saint. Every spring, on the first day of planting, one person (an outsider if one can be found, but often one of their own) is chosen to "feed Rosalita." The unfortunate victim is bound and thrown into a 10-foot-deep hole dug in the church's basement, where the victim is left to starve to death as an offering to Rosalita. Dissenters and anyone trying to leave the village are dealt with by *los Hambres,* the hungry ones — Spirit-Claimed ridden by lesser famine-spirits of Pangs' brood.

The Border in the Cities

Since the early 1970s, a loose alliance of Uratha packs in border cities along the Arizona and Texas stretches of the border has been working to stem the flow of spirits into the Shadow of Mexico. Through a radical process of spiritual landscaping and a careful cultivation of superstition and fear,

the Closed Borders, as the packs have come to be known, seek to create a spiritual barrier that echoes the physical border, a kind of Gauntlet-beyond-the-Gauntlet to keep spirits from escaping into the wild, untamed spaces of Mexico.

To accomplish this goal, the werewolves have made overtures of alliance to spirits of division and separation, creating a kind of spiritual border guard that monitors spiritual movement and interdicts any spirit attempting to head south. Border-spirits are popularly bonded to this task, but Elunim have been known to serve the same purpose, at least for a short period before their fickle natures take over. The packs themselves patrol the border as well, of course, but if such an ambitious reshaping of the Shadow is to succeed, the Uratha are more useful in the physical world. They put their effort into catching mortal border-runners and smugglers, creating an impression in the minds of the mortal residents of their cities that the border is an impenetrable wall, and that any attempt at crossing is doomed to failure. Sometimes this involves alerting the Border Patrol (and in fact, many Uratha, Irraka in particular, take jobs with the Border Patrol) to make an arrest, but more often this involves simply making the unfortunate runner disappear into thin air. Fear of arrest and incarceration is very real and potent, of course, but fear of some invisible, divine force doing God-knows-what to any poor unfortunate who tries to jump the fence is far more ephemeral and uncertain, and thus, more terrifying by far.

Although many of the packs involved in the Closed Borders alliance have had a fair amount of success within their own territories, the overall goal of the alliance — to extend this spirit-border across the entire length of the United States-Mexico border — can only be categorized as a dismal failure. The packs are too spread out, too territorial and too focused on their own immediate needs and goals to extend the wall beyond their own territorial borders. Even in cities like El Paso, where the Closed Borders alliance began, the spirit-border may stretch from territory to territory across the city, but out in the wild places where Uratha are either absent or pass through on patrol only infrequently, the border ceases to become a meaningful boundary in the Shadow. The best-case scenario most packs can hope for is to slow the tide of migrating spirits through Uratha territory — which, given the mindset of most Uratha, suits the werewolves just fine.

Story Hook: Totem Go Bye-Bye

A pack from up north is making a road trip to Mexico to deal with the source of a spiritual infestation in their territory (this might be the players' pack, or the players might be the ones living on the border). While passing through one of the border cities, the packmembers send their totem to scout the Shadow and run afoul of the guardian-spirits manning the border, who seem to think the totem is a migrant heading south. Now the nomad pack's totem is missing, and the packmembers are looking for answers. If they don't get them soon, the situation could turn ugly fast.

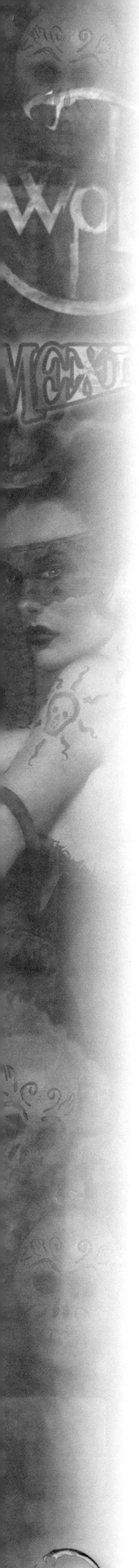

Story Hook: The Silken Curtain

The territory of a neighboring pack, part of the Closed Borders alliance, has begun to stagnate and decay spiritually. All signs point to the machinations of the Spider Hosts, but the pack seems unable or unwilling to look into the problem. In truth, one (or possible all) of the pack's members has made a deal with an Azlu Gauntlet-weaver, agreeing to let it work unhindered within a small region of their territory in exchange for fortifying the border as well. Naturally, this pack will go to extreme lengths to keep this information from reaching the larger werewolf community, lest the pack be dubbed traitors or worse.

Why the Border?

Werewolves care very little about mortal political boundaries, and spirits care even less. So why are the Closed Borders packs trying to create their border along the actual, political divide between the United States and Mexico? It's not as though the Rio Grande is a magical line, on one side of which lies a land of cold logic and ordered reason, with the far bank being a land of rampant superstition and magic. There are communities in the United States that are isolated and superstitious that would make ideal feeding grounds for spirits, and there are towns in Mexico that scoff at divine visitations, the dead returning and all of those archaic folk beliefs. Why not draw the line somewhere else?

The answer to that question lies in the extant spiritual energy that surrounds the border. Humans already have a great deal of emotion and thought centered on the border between the United States and Mexico, and drawing upon and manipulating that emotion is far easier than creating it from scratch.

The Wild Border

Outside the cities and the major border checkpoints, the border region becomes less distinct from the surrounding desert. Spiritual echoes of barbed-wire fences and guard towers appear occasionally, especially at locations where major border-running operations have been shut down or where they went disastrously wrong, but for the most part, the terrain is indistinguishable from the rest of the desert that stretches for hundreds of miles in every direction.

Werewolf packs that patrol the wild border are usually nomadic, simply by virtue of the vast and relatively inhospitable territory they control — even a small pack might control hundreds of square miles of high desert, where temperatures can range from over 100 degrees to 20 below zero — often within 24 hours. Even werewolves are advised to have transportation and a ready supply of water in that kind of environment. Biker gangs, truckers and RV campers are among the most common werewolves to hold territory along the untamed regions of the border.

Story Hook: Court Is Adjourned

Most of the time, when a spirit tries to make the run down into Mexico, the spirit is of minor status, no higher than Greater Gaffling. Word coming down the spiritual grapevine, though, says that an extremely powerful spirit — a Greater Jaggling or maybe even an Incarna — has pulled up roots along with its entire court and is moving on to greener pastures in Mexico. The spirit's nature and motives are unknown; perhaps it lost out in a bid to become the spirit of a city, or perhaps the spirit is an urban-spirit whose growth was checked by environmental legislation that kept the spirit's city from expanding into a protected forest. Whatever the case, the spirit will reach the pack's territory soon, and it's a pretty safe bet that the spirit's very presence will throw the pack's territory into chaos.

The Lodge of Coyote

"So, you think you got what it takes to fool the federales, huh? You think you can just wade across the Rio Grande and start living large in the U.S.? Wake up, ese, it ain't that easy. They got dogs and spotlights and guns — I hear they even got landmines in some places. You want to get across that fence, you gotta be clever. I know these guys, they're fucking unreal — swear to God I saw one of them walk right through a border checkpoint with five keys of smack taped under his shirt. The damn drug-sniffing dogs didn't even look twice at him. Of course, it's true — hand to God, amigo. Would I lie to you about something like this?"

The Lodge of Coyote is a fairly small, loosely organized lodge scattered across the American Southwest, although recently the lodge's members have begun to spread out to Southeast Asia and other locales where the smuggling of human beings is a lucrative business. Unlike most lodges, which are organized around a spiritual or philosophical ideal, the Lodge of Coyote is almost totally focused on the material. The lodge's members supply a useful service to other werewolves who need to cross the border quietly or move certain objects or substances out of the country with no questions asked, but the lodge's primary motivation is profit.

The Lodge of Coyote was founded in 1946, by several members of the Lobos del Rio pack. The Lobos had been using their unique talents to smuggle humans, werewolves and drugs from Mexico into the United States for years, as a way of funding themselves, but shortly after World War II, the pack, led by the Bone Shadow Irraka Andrew Carlton, began to talk about expanding the pack's operation. The packmembers approached several neighboring packs, especially those whose territory abutted or contained the border, with overtures of alliance and promises of major profits. Reactions ranged from cautious acceptance to violent rebuffs, but after a shaky start, the packs began to work in tandem. Mortal coyotes' operations were absorbed or outright eliminated, and for a time the Lodge of Coyote (which became a formal lodge in early '48 with the binding of Coyote as totem) was the most influential border-running operation in the supernatural underworld. In addition to humans and drugs, the lodge's members moved vampires, other werewolves and even mages. Fetishes and other artifacts "liberated" from museums were smuggled across the border to Ithaeur and mages alike.

That changed in 1949, when the Bruja vampire gang started moving into human trafficking. The two groups have clashed repeatedly ever since, sometimes even spilling over into open warfare on the streets of the border cities. The lodge was further weakened when the idigam returned in the early '70s; many members of the Lodge of Coyote were killed or captured while attempting to ferry critical supplies and information across the border in both directions, keeping the front-line warriors in the fight. Many werewolves across the American Southwest and northern Mexico still remember the lodge's sacrifice, and accord members of the Lodge of Coyote more respect than their normally mercenary nature might indicate otherwise.

Today, the Lodge of Coyote still operates, albeit on a smaller scale than the members did in their heyday. Their operations remain as versatile as ever, and even though their range is restricted in North America, they have been making inroads in Asia and the Middle East. Lodge members are technically forbidden to traffick in slavery or exploitation, but as that mandate comes from the Lodge's original founders and not Coyote himself, that rule is often ignored.

Prerequisites: Cunning ••, Wits ••, Stealth or Subterfuge •

Membership: The Lodge of Coyote is open to Uratha of all tribes, though Iron Masters and Hunters in Darkness are the most common. Iron Masters excel at bullshitting their way past Border Patrol checkpoints, while the Hunters in Darkness are unparalleled trailblazers when it comes to finding paths across the border in the high desert. Likewise, membership is unrestricted by auspice, though many members are Irraka, for obvious reasons. Perhaps surprisingly, the lodge makes an active effort to recruit Rahu, mostly to deal with the Bruja and other rival human-smuggling gangs.

Initiation into the lodge is at once simple and extremely rigorous: the prospective member is simply told to smuggle someone or something across the border, usually from Mexico into the United States, but occasionally the other way around. Depending on how well-liked the applicant is, the cargo to be smuggled might range from a small artifact or a single individual who speaks fluent English to a quantity of drugs or multiple individuals who only speak Spanish. One particularly disliked hopeful was notably instructed to smuggle a truck carrying 37 passengers, mostly elderly people and small children, all of whom spoke nothing but Zapotec (the original language spoken by the indigenous peoples of Mexico), and approximately 100 kilograms of Mexican black tar heroin. In some versions of the story, the truck dated from the early '30s and had a bent front axle.

In most cases, though, the task is nowhere near that impossible, and membership is granted simply based on whether or not the applicant succeeds. The prospective member must run the whole operation alone, without help from his packmates — he may use them as contacts to acquire information or gear, but cannot call on them for direct assistance. Failed applicants are usually in jail or dead, but in the event that a failure is not immediately apprehended by the law, he may try again (though he may have to wait some time until the lodge has an appropriately expendable cargo for him).

Benefits: Members of the Lodge of Coyote are still respected for their lodge's efforts in the war against the moon-banished. Members purchase Allies, Contacts and Status at an experience point cost equal to their new dots in the Merit, rather than new dots x 2. The Allies, Contacts and/or Status purchased at this reduced cost must relate to Uratha society.

In addition, Coyote allows members of his lodge to buy Stealth Gifts as if they had affinity with that Gift list.

Artifact Smugglers

Mexico has a long and rich history in the Awakened world. The indigenous peoples of Central and South America had a remarkably advanced culture, and the Atlantean Orders supposedly had a strong presence among them, sometimes even operating openly alongside Sleeper priesthoods, according to legend. Some Mysterium scholars say the mages of the Olmec peoples were among the earliest descendants of the original inhabitants of Atlantis, and those mages held arcane secrets that much of the rest of the Awakened world lost during the Fall of the Awakened City.

Whether that theory is true or not, the mages of pre-Christian Mexico were certainly impressive magical artisans, and they crafted many artifacts imbued with Supernal power. Perhaps even more precious, though, were their writings on the Mysteries. Volumes upon volumes of arcane lore were written by the wizard-priests of the Aztec nation, much of the lore carried down in an unbroken line from the time im-

mediately following the Fall. Few of these manuscripts have been recovered, but those that have show a remarkable degree of insight into the Supernal World and its relationship with the Fallen World after the creation of the Abyss.

For all that those early mages wrought and wrote, little enough of it has made it into the hands of the Awakened, and almost none has made it out of Mexico. The Spanish destroyed a huge amount of Aztec writing and art during their crusade to convert the heathen, and what was not destroyed outright is now locked away in museums, showcasing Mexico's rich cultural heritage and remaining tantalizingly out of the reach of Awakened historians.

As is the case anywhere a valuable commodity is difficult or illegal to acquire, a brisk smuggling trade has arisen among the mages of Mexico's Consilii. These black markets of the occult underground have contacts all throughout Mexico and South America, and buyers across the United States and even as far afield as Europe. Artifact smuggling is one of the most profitable illegal operations in Mexico, after narcotics, automobile theft and human-trafficking, and as such it is not at all uncommon for these mages to supplement their operation by trafficking in perfectly mundane, non-magical artifacts of Mesoamerican cultures for sale at relic shows and auction houses (or more rarely, directly to private collectors). All artifacts are, of course, treated to the most thorough magical examinations imaginable to ensure that no mystical artifacts are sold to Sleeper collectors. This generally has less to do with protecting the Veil, though the Guardians of the Veil come down hard on smugglers who let Sleepers get a hold of Awakened artifacts, and more to do with simple economics: a mage will pay far more for a genuine relic of pre-Columbian willworkers than a Sleeper collector will pay for all but the most precious of ancient cultural curiosities.

Story Hook: Angel's Bones

There's a popular legend that the bleak desert called Camino del Diablo, also known as Desolation, is the place where God threw down Lucifer and his rebel angels and bound them in chains. A cabal of artifact smugglers operating out of Yuma, Arizona, has recently begun to quietly advertise certain artifacts they call Angel's Bones for sale to the Awakened community. These artifacts are small slivers of a substance that resembles bone, but defies any attempt to identify its composition. The shards are roughly the size of a pencil, and seem to be able to mitigate Paradox to a certain extent. (In game terms, holding an Angel's Bone while spellcasting reduces the Paradox dice pool by one; a single Angel's Bone works 10 times before cracking and becoming useless.) Several wealthy mages have paid top dollar for these artifacts, but now,

three months later, the buyers have begun to die one by one in horrific, obviously magical ways.

Acquiring Artifacts

Despite what popular movies and video games imply, the days of daring tomb robbers dodging insidious traps to recover precious relics of long-forgotten kings are mostly gone. (Sleeper scholars will tell you that ancient curses and death-traps to ward off grave robbers are nothing more than an invention of pulp writers and film directors. They've obviously never set foot in the tomb complex of an ancient Aztec archmage of the Guardians of the Veil.) The easy-to-find archaeological sites have all been found in the 500 years since the Europeans arrived, and those that have been found have largely been stripped bare, either by opportunistic tomb raiders or by archaeologists and historians looking to preserve the cultural record. Only the most remote and inaccessible temples and tombs have remained undiscovered, and mounting an expedition to find such a site is usually more costly than any artifacts that might be recovered are worth. On the relatively rare occasion that mystical or mundane research unearths the location of a previously unknown site, Awakened artifact dealers aren't averse to investigating, but they generally prefer less-risky means of acquiring the relics they sell.

Most illegally acquired relics, magical or otherwise, are acquired through rather mundane means. The majority are simply purchased from bribed museum employees looking to pad their paychecks a little bit. Museums typically receive large shipments of pottery, flaked-stone artifacts and assorted other relics on a regular basis from archaeologists in the field, and it's the museum's job to identify those relics and their significance, if any. Unless the relic is obviously valuable or tremendously significant (such as a gold-inlaid burial mask set with gems, or a map depicting the coastlines of Europe and Africa dating from before the Spanish arrived), altering shipping manifests to list the scepter of the wizard-King Xaloctotl as "miscellaneous pottery shards" is a relatively easy matter.

Other artifacts are acquired directly from archaeologists working in the field or from private collectors (who usually acquired them in one of the manners already discussed). This has the benefit of cutting out the middle-man and reducing the chance that an honest museum employee will notice the discrepancy, but also requires more effort on the part of the purchaser. Private collectors are usually wealthy enough that a simple bribe isn't enough to convince them to part with a piece, and monitoring archaeological dig sites for potentially lucrative artifacts takes time and manpower. Thus, these approaches are usually employed only when artifact smugglers are looking to acquire a specific artifact, rather than just combing for lucrative prospects.

Of course, inevitably situations arise in which the current owner of an artifact isn't willing to sell. Maybe it's an ancient obsidian-edged club on display in a museum, or a statuette of Tezcatlipoca that is the prize centerpiece of a private collection, but whatever the case, a smuggler looking to acquire such an artifact must sometimes take more drastic measures. Acquiring the services of professional thieves is harder than to buy off a museum curator, but there *are* individuals, both Sleeper and Awakened, who specialize in acquiring various items that the owners of said items would prefer remained right where they are. Obviously, the risks of this method are extreme — the thieves could be caught and roll on their employer, one or more of the "thieves" might be undercover law enforcement or any other of a number of problems could come up — so most artifact smugglers prefer to avoid it unless there is no other choice, or unless the prospective buyer can pay enough to make it worthwhile.

Legal Issues

According to Mexican law, all pre-Columbian art, artifacts and other relics are property of the federal government, and any attempt to buy or sell them is treated as trafficking in stolen merchandise. Transporting such artifacts across the border is no respite, because the U.S. Stolen Property Act regards cultural artifacts as stolen property if a clear case of national ownership exists (and a federal law stating that the Mexican government owns all pre-Columbian artifacts is about as clear as it gets). That makes it a federal crime to traffic in illegally obtained artifacts. Furthermore, in 1971, the United States and Mexico signed the Treaty of Cooperation between the United States of America and the United Mexican States Providing for the Recovery and Return of Stolen Archaeological, Historical, and Cultural Properties, more commonly abbreviated as the 1971 Treaty of Cooperation, which allows either nation to request law-enforcement intervention to recover and return stolen cultural artifacts. In other words, even if a smuggler acquires an artifact, evades the Mexican police and gets it across the United States border to sell, all the Mexican government has to do is pick up the phone and make a call, and the smuggler will find the full weight of U.S. law enforcement bearing down on him.

In the United States, enforcement and investigation of stolen cultural artifacts falls under the dominion of U.S. Immigration and Customs Enforcement (ICE), the largest investigative arm of the Department of Homeland Security. In Mexico, La Administración General de Aduanas ("General Customs Administration") investigates the theft and smuggling of artifacts.

Awakened Society and Artifact Smuggling

In general, most Consilii turn a blind eye to mystical artifact smuggling, if they don't actively support it. The potential rewards, in terms of power and greater understanding of the Mysteries, are simply too great to ignore on vague, moral grounds. Most Hierarchs take a considerably less pragmatic view about the theft and smuggling of mundane cultural artifacts with no relation to the Awakened of pre-Columbian Mexico. Not only is it dangerous for all the reasons described above, it is blatant thievery for no motive other than profit, with no benefit to the mage community at large. Such a callous disregard for both the law and the history of a civilization reeks of hubris and is often met with censure or harsher punishments. Nevertheless, many gifted smugglers of Awakened artifacts line their pockets on the sly through the illicit sale of cultural artifacts to Sleeper collectors, and if the smuggler is talented enough to bring a steady flow of magical artifacts and manuscripts with mystical significance, the Consilium will usually overlook the indiscretion.

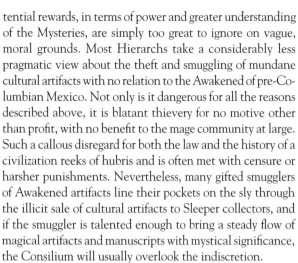

Among the Orders, the Adamantine Arrow is the least likely to produce dedicated artifact smugglers. Focused as Arrows are on protecting their fellow Awakened, these mages tend to be less interested in the acquisition of ancient relics or mystic texts. There are a few exceptions to this rule, such as in the case of relics that could see use as weapons, or that might serve as a key to defeating some current threat. Even in these cases, though, Arrows are more likely to hire a professional artifact smuggler rather than acquire the relic themselves.

The Guardians of the Veil, by contrast, have perhaps the greatest number of "artifact acquisition specialists," though they seldom engage in smuggling relics. More than a few ancient, mystical artifacts have ended up in museums and private collections, admired by ignorant Sleepers for the objects' craftsmanship or cultural significance. Many are relatively harmless, as they require an Awakened soul to operate, but some could be used by Sleepers, if those Sleepers were to discover the correct keys. The threat such artifacts pose to the Veil is tremendous, and the Guardians devote some of their best members to recovering them. A few Guardian "aquirers" have no qualms about selling recovered artifacts for a tidy profit of money, favors or arcane knowledge, but as long as the buyer is a member in good standing of one of the orders and not under censure from her Consilium, the order generally turns a blind eye to the process.

The Free Council, like the Adamantine Arrow, sees little interest in acquiring ancient magical artifacts. In keeping with the Libertines' "out with the old, in with the new" philosophy, the Free Council prefers to focus on developing innovative new magical praxes, not rediscovering old ones. On occasion, Libertines serve as contacts or middlemen between smugglers and buyers — after all, there's no reason not to profit off some fool who wants to cling to the Dark Ages, is there?

The Mysterium, unsurprisingly, is both the largest supplier and consumer of smuggled artifacts in Awakened society. The keen exploratory drive of this order's mages makes them the most likely to unearth long-forgotten tombs and the treasures therein, and their thirst for knowledge compels them to acquire artifacts in the possession of their fellow mages. Mysterium artifact smugglers can be as mercenary and profit-driven as those of other orders, but many engage in a free trade program in an effort to ensure that the greatest number of Mysterium mages can benefit from studying the artifact as possible.

The Silver Ladder only occasionally engages in artifact smuggling directly, but these mages are often purchasers of artifacts acquired by others. The Silver Ladder sees one of its mandates as being to prepare for the eventual renewal of the war against the Exarchs, and a properly stocked arsenal is key to that goal. The Silver Ladder is particularly keen to get its hands on artifacts that can be used by Sleepers, as the mages see the potential to use such artifacts to push Sleepers toward an Awakening.

Smuggling and the Others

This section has focused on mage artifact smugglers, but it should go without saying that nearly every major group out there has reason to smuggle artifacts across the border. Werewolves smuggle dangerous fetishes to places where they can be used or destroyed safely, vampires might covet relics of ancient, blood-soaked gods and cults might seek artifacts of whatever blasphemous thing they worship. Any of the information and story hooks presented in this section can easily be adapted to any other group; don't feel constrained to using mages as described.

Crime

Crime in Mexico runs the gamut from drug-smuggling to robbery to rape to murder. This section focuses on drug- and border-related crime: the drug lords of the interior, the specialized dangers of the border communities and the Chicano gangs that have spread throughout North America. Each has its own culture and focus, and can add a particular spice to a World of Darkness chronicle. Each is rife with its own distinct elements of criminality, thuggery, misery and horror.

Lords of the Underworld

As much power as the border militias and street gangs seem to command, awash in drugs, money and firepower, in truth their influence pales in comparison to that of the *narcotraficantes* who rule the Mexican underworld.

The drug cartels are essentially a third, invisible government whose policies directly impact *la frontera*. A sense of their true power begins to emerge when one realizes that the combined forces of the Mexican and U.S. governments, despite the grand forces they command, seem incapable of arresting the most notorious drug barons, who brazenly relax at high-end resorts throughout Mexico. Obviously, on multiple levels, the system fails and the politicians have ulterior agendas.

Most of these men (and most are men) live in opulent estates in the Mexican interior. Yet their shadows are long, indeed. *La plaza* literally translates into "a place of gathering" — the plaza, the town square, the market — but colloquially is used to mean authority. The person who holds *la plaza* is in charge. It often means police or military jurisdiction, but also has a more sinister meaning, referring to the lord of the underworld.

The few who hold *la plaza* are at the top of the hierarchy, in a much more entrenched position than most American or Western European drug lords. Although notions of corrupt police and bribable politicians are common worldwide, in Mexico the sickness runs deep. Those who command *la plaza* have the thinly veiled blessings of the government, from police to judiciary to military, all the way up the chain. He pays the authorities in sufficient coin to keep his operations safe from interference from state and federal police and from the military. He also pays in intel, providing information on independent rivals in the drug trade (often small-time operators who cannot or choose not to pay the necessary taxes). The authorities bust the small-timers, making headlines and visibly seizing product (which is often traded back to those who hold *la plaza*, or trafficked by the authorities themselves), and the system goes round and round.

The Role of Don

Traditionally, the drug lords of Mexico have assumed the role of "Don," or *padrino*, a sort of godfather role, to the poorer people in their region. Although an odd role for someone who deals daily in violence and profits form addiction, this role makes good business sense. By spending money on the locals — buying groceries for the hungry *campesinos* (peasants), building clinics and schools, even setting up families to raise pigs or goats or sheep — a drug lord earns their loyalty and respect. These poor people become the drug lord's eyes and ears, noting the presence of outsiders and known rivals, and spreading the word along a nearly invisible communication network. Spending money on the poor may also assuage the drug lord's conscience (assuming he still has the vestiges of one), by letting him believe he is doing more for his brethren than the government.

One *padrino* started every day by doling out 1,000-peso notes to the young beggar children, who sold water or gum or shined shoes to the tourists as they came out of their opulent hotels. Another had a bed placed next to the wrought iron gate that surrounded his home; whenever the poor women of town rang the bell, they were given an audience with the *padrino*. A good *padrino* never gives money to beggars, but instead "loans" it to them, so that these proud people, noble despite their poverty, save face.

In addition to the regular, and high, *plaza* payments, the *padrino* often makes gifts to local officials. Cars and trucks stolen from the United States and driven across the border and traded for drugs made excellent presents. Rarer treasures include fancy weapons and hip electronics.

The *narcotraficantes* also play the role of magnanimous hosts, inviting their colleagues and favored clients to share in their opulence. Private parties that run all night, fuelled by booze and high-grade product, are common after a particularly big deal has gone off successfully. Publicly, the drug lords may change the landscape of the town into a drug runner's paradise, by building large, opulent estates. For example, a man with a fondness for racing horses might build a large stable in an otherwise sleepy Mexican town, and arrange matches as big as any in the country. Invited guests — other drug lords, corrupt military officers, favorite clients — often show up in convoys that include expensive trailers to shuttle their horses about. On race days, the most infamous drug lords walk around town with automatic pistols jammed in their belts, accompanied by a handful of armed guards, fraternizing with the renowned jockeys or local *chicas*. Although the locals might not care much about the big betting going on, such events became fiestas where hundreds or thousands might come out, milling about stands serving corn tortillas, *cerveza*, tacos, *carne asada*, *churros*, while mariachis stroll about playing their rhythms.

Blood In, Blood Out

Most Mexican gangs follow the philosophy of "blood in, blood out." To be accepted into the gang, blood must be spilled. Similarly, the only way to leave the gang is by having one's blood spilled (often meaning that death is the only release). Arguably the most powerful Hispanic gangs are the two prison gangs, Los Tigres and La Nuestra Casa.

Los Tigres

Los Tigres is one of the most powerful Latino gangs in North America, although the gang's strength is primarily in the southwestern United States. State and federal law-enforcement agencies estimate Los Tigres's membership at roughly 30,000 members, heavily concentrated in state prisons, but also based in southern California, New Mexico, Arizona, Texas and Mexico. The gang's power resides in their use of intimidation, taxation (primarily of drug dealers throughout the region) and bloodshed to wrestle control of the region's lucrative underworld activity.

The origins of Los Tigres can be traced to the Duel Vocational Center, a youth offender facility in Los Angeles, where the gang was first conceived in the late 1950s, and then later Folsom Prison, where the gang truly took shape. Its original purpose was to help Latino inmates band together against the many rival factions within the pen, but they were forceful enough to take power on the inside. It wasn't long before they were running prostitution, gambling and the drug network inside the prison's walls. They controlled a stable of homosexual prostitutes, whose services would be sold to other inmates for money or trade. Los Tigres would break up any rival operations, often by killing any prostitutes not under the gang's thumb. Similarly, they had a lock on the drug traffic into the prison, and established a system for distribution, including importing product by visitors, bribing guards, hiding product in mundane shipments, regular taxes for non-members who trafficked, "advertising" the product, setting price lists and, of course, using the threat of violence for breaking the chain.

It is said that the original leaders were Luis "Tigre" Chavez and Sean Glenn, a one-legged Irishman who spoke fluent Caló Spanish. Flores seemed to fall off the face of the earth after his release. The members of Los Tigres presumed the police killed him; the police and feds, meanwhile, assumed he either fled to Mexico or was done in by an enemy. A few others temporarily rose to the leadership prison, but Morgan was eventually recognized as the number one "shot caller" in their informal hierarchy.

Los Tigres's influence spread until it effectively ruled the prison, dominating even the black, Italian and white gangs. As new inmates arrived at Folsom, they had to learn how to work in Los Tigres's world.

Characters from Latino street gangs are given a chance to "graduate" from their small-scope criminal activities and move into the big leagues. Before ending up in prison, gang members might hear about the fierce Mexican Mafia. They might even encounter a representative of the gang, for as members are released from prison they carry the gang's presence out into the streets of the L.A. *barrios*. Any of the hundreds of *cholo* kids throughout the Southwest hear about Los Tigres as badass lowriders and gangsters and envision an exciting life of money, drugs and women. The only way to be accepted into Los Tigres is to go through its classic ceremony — the first step is to be convicted and sent to prison. The next stage is for a convict to either have a significant reputation, or to work hard for the leaders of Los Tigres to notice him. The member will be contacted if he is believed to have potential to become a hard worker and big earner. The gang controls its members through loyalty or fear. The recruit is asked to perform a traditional initiation rite requiring the death of another inmate or prison officer.

Once the inmate is accepted into Los Tigres, he must follow several rules. First and foremost, a member has to obey any orders immediately and without hesitation. The shot caller might tell a member to commit a crime and then confess, in order to be sent to a particular prison, or to indoctrinate a younger brother into the gang or even ask a member to murder a friend or family member. Reluctance or non-compliance to carry out the orders could result in the member's own death.

Members are ordered not to engage in homosexual relations. This was partly due to the *cholo machismo*, but also to ensure members do not dally with the male prostitutes inside prison, or worse, become one.

Most importantly, members may not be Christians. This is problematic for some new recruits whose families may be very religious, and thus are ordered to renounce and turn against their Church. Los Tigres is now the members' family, their history, their future and their God — they must abandon all others.

As members ended up incarcerated in jails and penitentiaries around the country, the gang's influence stretched throughout the prison network. By the mid-1980s, Los Tigres was one of the four most powerful gangs operating on both sides of *la pinta*. Los Tigres was loosely organized around the structure of La Cosa Nostra, with a head shot caller in the role of the don. Beneath the shot-caller were various "generals," who took charge of the group's various enterprises. A general's territory could be the prostitution ring, the guards in the yard, Boyle Heights, LA, county jail or even a specific death row. Beneath the generals were the armies of *carnales*, the foot soldiers as it were.

A shot caller can raise a dealer's tax, or erase a debt, with a whispered word to a general. Members are notoriously clever in getting messages out, no matter where they are locked up. Even dropping them into solitary confinement does not cut off their lines of communication, as corrupt guards or inmates in the right location will pass written messages, called "kites," to the appropriate general. Orders are sent from prison to prison by various lawyers or family visitors.

Similarly, outside of the prisons' walls, generals may conduct their business from favorite cafes, at family gatherings or through legitimate-seeming front businesses. In one example, a senior member of Los Tigres started a roof-repair company. He purchased heavy equipment and hired contractors to do the real work. But when he needed to talk gang business, he'd meet his contacts on the roof of whatever project his company was undertaking. It provided a good cover, made it hard to spy on him and gave him a commanding view of the surrounding area.

Los Tigres is long-standing enemies with another major Mexican-prison gang, La Nuestra Casa. The Shield of Thule, despite their racist leaning, has allied with Los Tigres (in part because La Nuestra Casa works with the Black Marx Family). Most of the time this partnership solely revolves around a militaristic truce and an economic trade relationship — in other words, Latino bangers can stroll through the Brotherhood's part of the yard without being jumped, and a neo-Nazi can sell drugs in jail with only a light tax. But when the hammer needs to be brought down, and some plausible deniability needs to be created, each side can call upon the other for a violent strike against an enemy. Los Tigres also calls the Texas Syndicate (a group of Texans who bonded in California prisons before returning to the Lone Star State) friends, and both gangs trade information and contacts freely.

The Women of Los Tigres

Although Los Tigres does not accept women into the gang, the wives, girlfriends and sisters of the gang are held in much higher regard than in some gangs. This is because they are a secondary information and trade network, used to pass along messages, help conduct financial transactions, facilitate mail-forwarding activities (which may result in violence) and, at times, distribute drugs.

Folsom

Folsom Prison was built in the late 1800s, but has an older air, with its massive granite walls, square guard towers and arched entrances. Inside, the walls are gray, the light is muted and artificial and the walls close in like a medieval dungeon.

The main exercise yard is relatively spacious — open to the sky and sun — and is one of the most dangerous places in the prison, where inmates are thrown together to play. Although the guards watch over them with a heavy hand, there are just too many opportunities for drug deals, passing of messages or murderous retribution for the officers to maintain any real sense of control. Gangs stick to their territories and members stick to their own; blood and violence are only ever a heartbeat away.

Greystone Chapel lies deep within Folsom, a house of worship at the heart of sin. To reach it, one must pass through heavy metal doors that buzz open and slam shut at the hands of armed guards deadened to the horrors inside. They stand white like skeletons behind smoke-stained bullet-proof glass, and mutely watch worshippers pass into the bowels of the prison.

There are no windows in Greystone Chapel, and its doors are never locked, but few come here of their own volition. There is a secret here, which stains the chapel with an acrid miasma, and reaches throughout the entire prison like foul air. For Greystone Chapel is the haven of Luis "Tigre" Chavez, the Gangrel Prince of Los Tigres. Flores is content here, at the center of the world. From the darkness of Greystone he is able to learn about the outside world and issue commands through the lines of Los Tigres. He has everything he needs here, including a ready supply of blood and tremendous security. What was home for so many years in life naturally stayed his home in undeath.

The Real Mexican Mafia and Folsom

Historically, the Mexican Mafia (La EME) really does trace its routes to the Duel Vocational Center in Tracy, California, and to Luis "Huero" Flores, a member of the Hawaiian Gardens street gang (based along Hawaiian Gardens Street, in East LA). One unconfirmed story states that there were 13 original members (which ties nicely to "eme," or "M," their symbol, as the 13th letter of the alphabet). Furthermore, bringing Folsom into the World of Darkness is especially fitting as one article about the prison has the Latino inmates referring to it as the "House of Dracula."

Mara Cuscatlá

Mara Cuscatlá, or MC-9, is a gang whose origins can be traced back approximately 20 years to the El Salvadoran civil war. Young refugees, often no more than children, had seen firsthand the horrors of war and now had to struggle to survive in the *barrios* of Los Angeles. Some had fought with either the Salvadoran leftist guerillas or on the side of the government, and many more had been hardened by the death and torture they had seen.

Lost in a strange land, they found few jobs and a difficult social situation. Many of these immigrants were peasants and farmers, but they were not accepted by the local populations and faced new threats and persecution from Mexican gangs, especially the 18th Street Gang and Los Tigres, and from African American gangs, such as the Crips and Bloods. These kids, many of whom had firsthand experience with guns and combat, clustered in MacArthur Park, just west of downtown LA. They formed their own gang for protection and self-identity — Mara Cuscatlá was born. "Mara" is a Salvadoran term for gang, while "Cuscatlán" is a prehispanic name for El Salvador; they adopted the number "9" in a similar fashion to American gangs (and from 9th Street, where many originally lived).

MC-9 opened its arms to other Latinos, especially other Central American immigrants who were also at risk in the battlegrounds of the *barrios*. Guatemalans, Hondurans and even Mexicans joined MS. The gang has spread from California to 33 other states and DC. MC-9's many businesses include murder, extortion and drug running. Investigators say many of these moves have been calculated steps by its leaders, based in LA, to expand their power base. While the gang's leadership is somewhat centralized, the greater body of the gang is linked through a network of fairly independent *clicas*. The leadership is more organized than some suspect, with a flexible transnational network that can assist with recruiting, logistics, targeted attacks and intelligence operations. The disparate *clicas* allow redundancy in their operations, so if one operation is blocked they can often continue from a different direction. Although this occasionally breeds fierce rivalry among *clicas*, the leadership cadre actively works together at the highest levels.

As the gang gained in exposure and influence, the U.S. government battled MC-9 by deporting many of the illegals to their home countries. This had the unforeseen effect of spreading the MC-9 gang into these respective countries, where they established a strong foothold.

MC-9 members may be recognized by their unique tattoos, gang tags and hand signals. One of MC-9's most defining characteristics is the intense level of violence that permeates the gang's culture. Initiation rites often involve a recruit being beaten for 13 seconds by multiple gang members; the recruit cannot resist, and is only allowed to protect his face and groin. Girls who wish to join must prove themselves to be as tough physically, enduring the same brutal beating. If they refuse, they must be willing to have sex with all the male members of the *clica*.

The initiations continue until the recruit is forced to kill a victim, simply to show the newcomer's commitment to the gang, known as *Sangre Afuera, Sangre Adentro* ("Blood Outside, Blood Inside").

Today, it is believed that MC-9 has between 30,000 and 50,000 members in half a dozen countries, with perhaps as many as 10,000 throughout the United States. They deal in drug trafficking (primarily concerned with cocaine, marijuana, heroin and methamphetamines), weapons smuggling, human trafficking and extortion. Currently, their two primary sources of income are drugs and extortion. They do not hesitate to use violence, and since their earliest days have been known as one of the most violent gangs throughout the Americas.

Other Gangs

There are many other Mexican gangs operating throughout North and South American today. They share similar symbolism and mannerisms, though all have their particular set of mores and customs. For example, the teardrop tattoo beneath the eye — for some, each tear signifies one year lost to Hell, for another it may stand for a family member dead in the street wars and yet another may use it to represent each man the gang member has killed.

Appeasing Darkness

The religion of Mexico, from the old ways of Mesoamerica to the more modern Catholic and Pentecostal beliefs, has always been about appeasement on some level. Appeasement means, of course, satisfying or placating some divine power. Appeasement is not about rejection, or about conquering the divinity or somehow going "above" it. Appeasement involves giving the power what it wants so that the populace may either be safe from harm or given reward for the supplication granted.

Examples of appeasement in the ancient religions include, at the most obvious, human sacrifice. The Aztecs in particular maintained a fascinating array of sacrificial methods: hearts cut out, heads removed, whole bodies crushed beneath stone, chests pierced with dozens of arrows. The Aztecs performed these sacrifices because they believed in many cases that to *not* perform them would end the world. The sacrifice appeased the gods, and convinced them to let the sun rise upon the people. To neglect the sacrifice meant that the gods would be angry, and the world would grow cold and dead because the sun would stay hidden behind the horizon.

Catholicism in the country also offers various levels of appeasement. Pray and satisfy God. Make offerings (*milagros*) of gold and silver votives, and the saints will be pleased and grant favor (maybe even a miracle). The Church's idea of pacifism is also a form of appeasement: only in a "just war" should one commit to any path of violence.

Mired within — or married to — the Catholic religion are strains of the old ways, as well. The forcible conversion of various Mesoamericans left strong threads of ancient religions, each still bound to the tapestry today. Echoes of those religions place powerful prominence upon those gods and creatures outside the mortal realm.

Small Surrender

One could suggest that this old manner of appeasement applies to the levels of crime and corruption in Mexico. The government is crooked, the cops are dirty and every corner is a hook in a new road toward some transgression. Some say that if only 10 — or even five — percent of the country's nearly 100 million people would stand up and take notice, then maybe they'd make a dent in the human evils that persevere. Why don't they? Perhaps some urge to appease lies concealed within the psychology of the country's citizens: the criminals have the power, and maybe giving them what they want will make them go away.

Living Folklore

The old ways were not lies. Ancient folklore is given very real life in Mexico — some tales more honestly than others (is a god truly a god, or merely a powerful spirit or vampire masquerading as one?). But belief and appeasement continue to give these things life and power over the people. Humans aren't the only ones beholden to old ideas, either. The ingrained principle of placation exists across all levels of creature within Mexico's borders, be they Kindred, werewolf or mage.

Does it work? Can appeasement satisfy the darkness and keep it at bay? In some cases, absolutely. Some creatures are like wolves or bears: throw them meat and they will leave you alone. A sane spirit that demands service from a small cadre of farmhands may very well stop when the spirit receives whatever favor it desires. Having consumed what it was given, the spirit may leave the farmers alone, or even grant them small favor. A vampire who lords over a mountain village may be satisfied with the blood that the villagers tithe to him weekly. The Kindred's temperance gives him the wisdom to know when he has a good thing going, so why ruin it?

All beings are not so restrained, however. Selfish urges drive many of Mexico's parasites — they are not wolves or bears, and want satisfaction above and beyond what they originally demanded. Their bellies never grow full, and satisfied urges only give way to new cravings. A spirit may want power enough to cross over into the physical world, and so

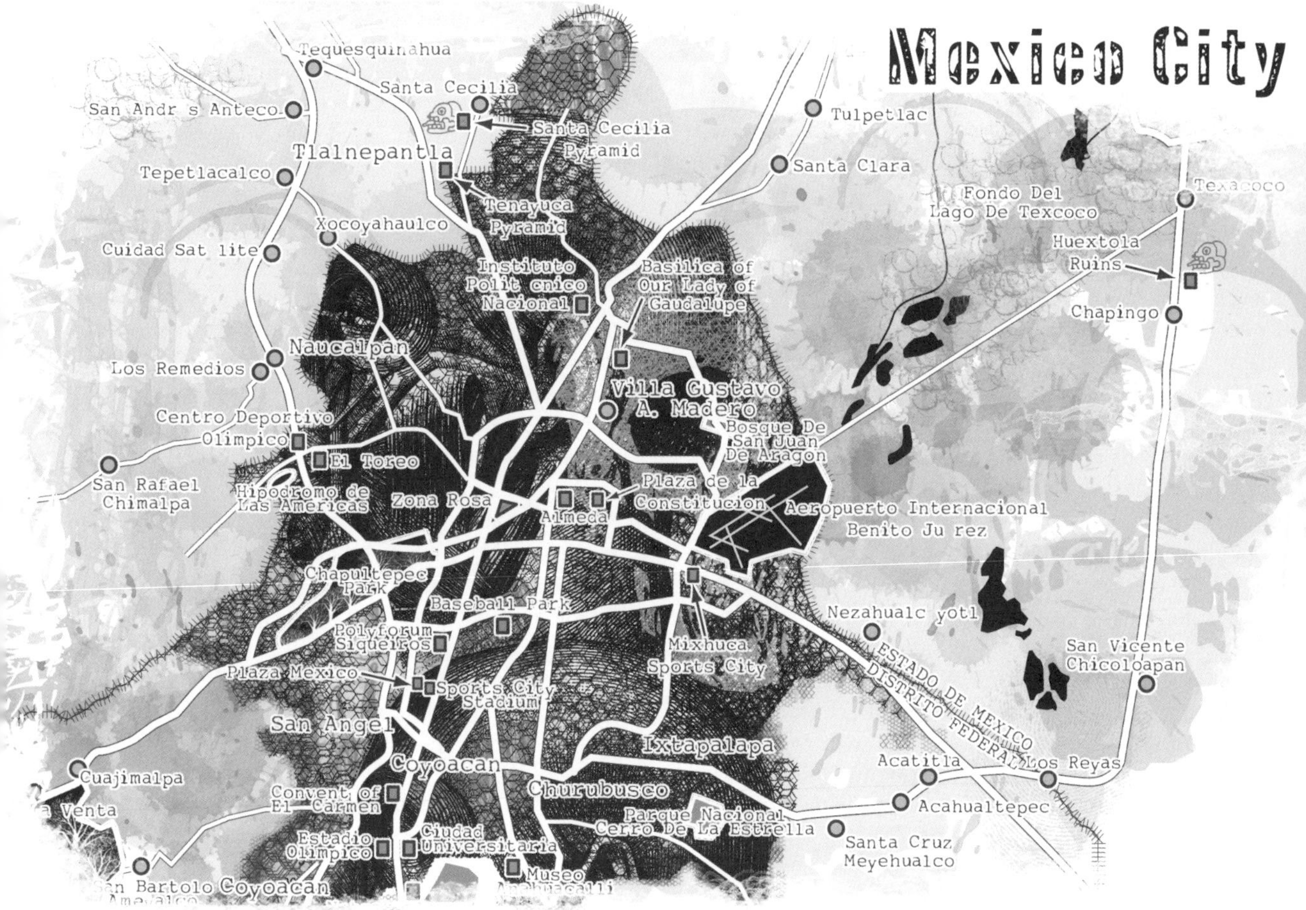

does not stop at what small kindness the farmhands give. The vampire may eventually grow more powerful and seek more blood — or his own lost Humanity may drive him to seek moral perversions above and beyond the Vitae his supplicants offer him. At what point does appeasement stop? When does the cultural principle give way to rage and action?

Examples

What follows are some examples of how appeasement exists in Mexico in regards to the supernatural realm.

Bloodstain at the Palenque

In some places, the old ways are like bloodstains on the floor: persistent, ugly, born of bad tidings. Some suggest that living with a bloodstain is easier than cleaning it up — covering it with a rug, perhaps, or simply ignoring the darkened mark.

This is literally the case in the Palenque Suite at the small-but-ritzy Villanueva Hotel in Mexico City. For the last 10 years, the suite's carpet has been marred by a bloodstain the size of a small child. Nobody knows how the stain got there, only that it won't go away. Cleaning it works, but only for a night — the next night, the stain reappears. Tearing up the carpet didn't work, either — the dark blot showed upon the wooden floor beneath, and upon the new rug laid atop it.

Octavio, the hotel's proprietor, has since closed the suite off to visitors. He visits the expansive room once a month, usually at night, carrying with him a chicken or iguana. There he kills the creature by breaking its neck — and he drizzles a little fresh blood over the old spot. Those who know of Octavio's odd ritual have asked him why he does this, and he gives the same reply every time: "I do this to stop it from spreading."

Within the last month, however, Octavio has gone missing. Nobody knows where he has gone or if someone has taken him (a ransom note would have appeared by now had he been taken by one of the local gangs). The time for his little ritual has come and gone. With the ritual left unperformed, the guests at the hotel have begun to experience odd, seemingly unconnected visions: a jaguar running through a busy street, a gobbet of dripping meat hanging from an extravagant chandelier, a circle of women in red face-paint stabbing knives into a squirming sack. Worse, the bloodstain in the Palenque Suite has nearly tripled in size.

The Man in the Lake

In the state of Querétaro, near El Bosque de Encino y Pino (Forest of Oak and Pine), sits a little village called La Oración. Only a few hundred people live in this village, mostly farmers and out-of-work laborers.

The townsfolk believe that a nearby lake, Moyolehuani ("The Enamored One" in Toltec) houses the spirit of a man with the same name as the lake. This man is said to be little more than a shadow standing at the water's edge, and yet, women claim to be drawn in by his handsomeness (despite being nothing more than a dark silhouette, even on the brightest day).

Those women who venture near to the lake's edge to get a closer look at Moyolehuani awaken hours later, often back at home, with little recollection of what happened in the interim. Pregnant women who go too close to the lake have a worse experience: their babies are universally born with some kind of defect or deformity. Many infants end up with club feet (or *Calcaneovalgus*, where the top of the foot bends sharply upward, pressing against the shin) or cleft palates or are missing fingers and toes. Doctors from other towns or Mexico City come from time to time, entreating the mothers of the village to give their children the treatment necessary to fix or at least mitigate such defects. The villagers uniformly refuse, claiming that the children are born that way because of the sins of the mother, and that such deformity is deserved.

The men of the village never see Moyolehuani, and never suffer any effects when going near the lake. The villagers whisper that a cadre of farmers offers wives and daughters to the lake spirit in the hopes of earning a good year for strong crops and healthy livestock. Nobody has ever seen this happen, of course; those with particularly robust harvests claim that such accusations are ridiculous.

Mud Cellar

About 10 miles from La Oración is the Sótano del Barro ("Mud Cellar"), a massive sinkhole nearly 2,000 feet wide and 1,500 feet deep. Just getting there is a two-hour hike through the forest, and getting down into the hole requires climbing knowledge (Athletics 3 with a Specialty in Rock Climbing). The massive hole (the second-largest vertical shaft in the world) is home to thousands of green macaws.

Local werewolves claim this place "touches the Shadow," and at its nadir, the space between worlds is inordinately thin. This thinness goes both ways: while it is easy for the werewolves to cross over to the Shadow, it is just as easy for things deep within the Shadow to find their way into this world. (Consider this a locus with a rating of ••••.)

St. Virgilio of the Broken Campanario

Mexico City is home to countless homeless children. Conservative estimates say there are potentially 20,000 street children in the city's slums, but some statistics suggest far greater numbers. One vampire — an outcast Priest of the city's Sanctified — dwells among these children, claiming a herd of them as his own. "Saint Virgilio," he calls himself, demanding little sacrifices from his puerile herd: blood, mostly, but he also asks them to bring him money and goods stolen from tourists, as well as icons stolen from various churches around the city.

He watches the children, sometimes moving among them like a lion amidst grazing gazelle. He plays them against one another, granting goodwill to some while unpredictably denying others. The children have, in the past, tried to fight him, but it never came out in their favor. Whenever they displease him, he takes one of them. Children who go missing in this way are never seen again — at least, not whole. Virgilio is fond of showing off little trophies (or little *milagros*, he calls them): an ear, a toe, a patch of skin from a child's back.

He claims that what he gives them — and what they give him in return — is love. Then he smiles beneath that pencil-slash mustache, his dark cratered cheeks full and round and almost cherubic. At the close of every day, he returns to the crumbling bell tower (*campanario*) in an old church. The children are afraid to go there, to see what he will do should they try to destroy him. But they grow increasingly fierce, some even feral. Some hunger to end their so-called patron saint. (Though, a few of them hunger for something else: to become like Virgilio, to have the power of a small god through the Embrace.)

The List

This five-person cabal of Mysterium mages receives a list once a year. The list is delivered differently every time: once, a lobotomized homeless man approached their sanctum with the list pinned to his chest. Another time a bird dropped out of the sky, dead, with the list bound up in a small copper tube around the creature's neck. The list always features 100 tasks to complete.

The tasks upon the list range from the foolishly simple ("Each mage must prick his index finger with a pin and drip a single drop of blood upon a flower") to the wildly complex ("The mages must track down the *Los Libros de la Serpiente de Sangre*, which remain hidden on a mummy in the catacomb roads beneath Guanajuato"). The cabal has one year to perform this tasks.

And the mages make every effort to do so. Because each list also comes with a number of consequences that will occur should the mages fail to accomplish the tasks set before them. The first year they received the list, three consequences were listed: 30 people will die as a hanging bridge in Tapjulapa collapses, one of the mages in the cabal will lose a hand, Banisher *exorcistas* will sweep through San Cristobál, destroying every mage who dwells there. When the cabal failed to complete the list as given, the consequences were made manifest. Since then, the mages endeavor mightily to finish the tasks.

Moreover, as mages of the Mysterium (*Las Alas del Dragón*), this cabal believes that the list is tied to some secret knowledge, perhaps from Atlantis itself. The mages

in the cabal have, since receiving the annual list, dreamt frequently of the Cenacle of Sighs, the old Atlantean library said to contain the writings of all the world's secret creatures. The cabal believes that the list is tied somehow to the Cenacle, a thought that is only further cemented by the fact that, upon completing a list, the cabal is rewarded with an old page written in some mystical (and so far unseen) tongue.

The cabal, formed of mages Awakened at el Colegio de Mexico university, calls itself the Learned Dancers because the mages dance to whatever song the list-makers sing. The mages appease whomever — or whatever — gives them the list year after year, but not blindly. They have other Mysterium cabals working on the back-end, trying to uncover exactly who or what creates and sends the list. Are these mages the puppets of the Seers of the Throne? Do Exarchs or Oracles somehow contribute to this list and the consequences of incompletion?

Kindred as Gods

In old Mexico, one dark practice of the native elders stirs more controversy than any other. Still discussed and debated in modern nights, this practice is alternately alluring and reprehensible, poetic and profane. It is the public declaration, to Kindred and mortal alike, of personal divinity, and the active manipulation of mortal religion in order to better serve the needs of vampire society. Despite efforts to destroy the practice and, in some places, all records of it, the temptation to follow in elder footsteps still claims vampires tonight. Wherever Kindred succumb, the fundamental traditions and laws of a domain are challenged, forcing conflict that is as desperate as it is fierce.

Some believe that the mistakes of the past will never truly be resolved until all evidence of their commission is erased. Others argue that without understanding the ancient ways, preventing their repetition is impossible.

Gods of the Old World

"Lord, let me not falter in this place of devilish sin. The Kindred here, far beyond encouraging the worship of ungodly demons, seek to embody those wretched beings themselves. They present themselves in vile material splendor, calling for the blood of the faithful in their guttural tongue. They whip the mortals to a frenzy of vice and degradation at every opportunity and laugh at their debasement in filth-spattered temples. There is no possibility of alliance — they must be erased."

— from the writings of Francesco de Maluenda, Nosferatu of the Lancea Sanctum, dated 1534

Presumption to Divinity

For centuries, the practice of masquerading as gods was so popular among the Kindred of the region that a great many myths bear the distinct mark of interference to anyone astute enough or informed enough to understand. With the passage of the centuries and the near-impossibility of accessing untainted eyewitness reports, the untangling of myth and truth is unlikely. It is known that some Kindred truly believed they embodied the earthly manifestation of great powers and behaved accordingly. There must have been a few who made consciously insincere claims to divinity, but

how common they were and how they managed to convince the people of their legitimacy is unknown.

First and most popular among the ancient gods, the Feathered Serpent deity (Quetzalcóatl to the Aztecs, Kukulkan to the Maya) was the god of wind and waves, creator of the human race and inventor of writing. He taught the mortals their intricate calendar and introduced them to the technology of agriculture. Death and resurrection were commonly tied to him, and he was honored with frequent animal sacrifice — two elements that modern Kindred scholars point to when arguing that his personage was tainted early on by the claims of early vampires in the region. There are a number of accounts of Kindred claims to embodiment of the great serpent throughout the history of the indigenous peoples of the region, leading to a series of confusing, contradictory myths and ritual practices. Among the few Mayan codices that remain intact and shielded from the eyes of mortals, there is one particular account of a clash between two warring forces led by beings that both claimed the identity of the creator and displayed great powers. Their refusal to abandon their claims eventually led to the mutual destruction of their armies — an eventuality that paved the way for a perplexing legend about a lesson from the great god to faithless warmongers.

It is possible that tales of a twin deity, both in collusion with and opposition to the Feathered Serpent, began to arise because of this battle. The deity was known as the Smoking Mirror (Tezcatlipoca), and was allocated dominion over beauty, fire and warfare. He is said to have co-operated with his sibling in the creation of the world, sacrificing his foot in the process, and is commonly depicted carrying a mirrored shield that gave off toxic vapors. Modern scholars among the Kindred believe that claims to manifestation of Tezcatlipoca were less popular among the vampires than claims of manifestation of his brother, since records of Tezcatlipoca's activities are both fewer and more consistent. This fact alone leads some to theorize that the majority of divine claims were false. Early in the 1920s, the skeptics were lent further support when a Gangrel in Tijuana arose from a long torpor, claiming that he was truly Tezcatlipoca and challenging the Prince of the domain for supremacy. The local Kindred, who observed that the Gangrel displayed no special abilities or knowledge as evidence of his divinity, quickly eliminated him. He was dismissed as an ordinary, if deluded, member of his clan.

Another popular divinity, whose original name has been lost, is known the Man of Crops: a selfless fertility figure who is said to have given his life so that starving people could grow food. Images of maize growing from his grave or ground soaked in his blood are common. Manifestations of the Man of Crops were extremely frequent among the Kindred of the time because the sightings encouraged ready sacrifice from the mortals who were all too happy to honor him.

The Rain Spirit (Tlaloc to the Aztecs, Chac to the Maya) was a great being who oversaw a legion of servants, presiding over the rains and waters. Worshipped for his association with agricultural plenty and feared for his ability to create both floods and droughts, Tlaloc was often appeased with the sacrifice of children. Several vampires are known to have addressed the mortals in the guise of Tlaloc, including one Daeva who, in modern terms, was particularly sloppy. Because of his frequent appearances among the people of Tenochtitlán, the god was depicted in several texts as blue-skinned (in an attempt to approximate the ashen tone of his flesh) and sporting great fangs. It is believed that the Daeva in question may have actually been the Prince of Tenochtitlán for some time, but the exact date and duration of his rule are unknown. Some believe that the old vampire entered torpor and remains thus, buried somewhere in the ruins beneath modern Mexico City, waiting to rise again. Despite fervent denials, certain Daeva in Mexico City have suffered persecution over the last few centuries because of rumored blood ties to this Tlaloc.

The frightening Death God (Mictlantecutli to the Aztecs, Ah Puch to the Maya) presided over the underworld of his people. Some of the first European Kindred in the Yucatán claim to have done battle with a skeletal vampire who was revered as the earthly embodiment of Ah Puch in the Maya city of Ti'ho (now the modern city of Mérida). He was described as a gaunt, physically powerful figure who dressed in the bones of his fallen worshippers and commanded an army of owls. He was eventually driven into the Mayan jungle, where he disappeared without a trace. Strangely, some of the same Kindred who drove him out later began to express fears that his claims may have been legitimate. The city was struck down by two great outbreaks of smallpox after his departure, and the local vampires became unwitting transmitters of the disease. Sacrificial attempts to appease the so-called Ah Puch and encourage his return became common enough that the Prince of Mérida was moved to forbid them in 1622, but the hidden practice continues into modern nights.

No doubt, there were other Kindred who made claim to godhood among the mortals, others whose names and stories are lost to the centuries. Nobody really knows what hidden monsters may yet dwell within the ruined temples and under the dusty plains of the region — or what sacrifices they might expect if they ever return.

The God-Noble Hybrid

Not every vampire posturing as a divine being laid claim to the uppermost positions in the local pantheon. Many were religious themselves and knew better than to pretend to speak for the fearsome powers above, and some were simply too canny to place themselves in the spotlight, knowing quite well that they would be called upon to take responsibility in times of crisis.

To retain a superior position without risking the wrath of the gods, the Kindred of ancient Mexico invented a third stratum of power: that of the god-noble. Those who were designated as such were dedicated to the service of a single god as his or her representatives on Earth, but not considered equal to that god. Many of the god-nobles practiced as high priests and priestesses, presiding over great sacrificial ceremonies and services. Some served as advisors, scholars and judges, mixing with mortals while maintaining an air of divine advantage.

Documentation has revealed the existence of six god-noble groups (each composed of multiple lineages), but it is believed that there may have been more.

The Cihuateteo, considered the envoys of the Aztec Underworld, were exclusively female and haunted the roads and byways of the empire. It is believed that there were two distinct lines of Cihuateteo, one Gangrel and one Daeva. Because of their status as representatives of the gods of death, the mortals of the region treated the Cihuateteo with fear and respect and always made sure to give them a wide berth. How, exactly, the Cihuateteo identified themselves to the mortal populace is unknown. They are described, in certain texts, as having "fleshless faces" and "eagle claws."

The Xipe were representatives of Xipe Totec, the Aztec god of agriculture and rebirth. They were wholly or partially flayed, and wore the skins of sacrificial victims while presiding over mystic ceremonies. Several Gangrel lines have been associated with the Xipe. European Kindred who encountered them briefly believed that they were a deformed bloodline until they discovered that the patches of missing skin on their bodies were self-administered.

The Chacs conducted ceremonies to honor Chac, the amphibious Mayan god of rain and agriculture. One of the few lines of god-nobles that had direct contact with European Kindred, the Chacs were composed almost exclusively of Mayan Mekhet, who would identify themselves to the mortals by showing their fangs and weeping blood tears. Each would take on an individual name, making the distinction from the god himself clear with descriptive terms.

The Balam, a fierce warrior faction of Mayan Kindred, were described as jaguar gods, devoted to the protection of their mortal communities. The Balam did not associate with any one heavenly presence in particular, but served as priests to all of the major deities. So many vampires referred to themselves as Balam that European invaders first mistook the word to mean "vampire," when, in fact, it means "jaguar." Some Princes still forbid their subjects to speak it, remembering the cruel holdouts who bore the title with pride.

The death-worshipping Xibalbans identified themselves as the ambassadors of a hidden underground city, claiming that they were tasked by the Mayan gods with bringing misery and pain to the living. The Xibalbans engaged in acts of spectacular cruelty for sport, humiliating and murdering humans who were unlucky enough to excite their malicious attentions. Two distinct lines of Xibalban Kindred are known to have existed — one Daeva, one Mekhet. Both warred constantly with their vampire neighbors and were utterly eradicated by the forces of conquest.

The terrifying Tzitzimime, believed to be demon stars manifest on earth, were ravagers and harbingers of evil. Servants of the skeletal Itzpapalotl (the "Obsidian Butterfly"), who ruled the dead world that served as the source material for the creation of humanity, the Tzitzimime presided over dark cults and violent sacrificial wars. Several Mekhet lines and one Daeva have been associated with the Tzitzimime. How they chose to make their divinity known to the mortals is not known.

Apotheosis in Blood

Although each domain was said to have its own unique rituals and requirements, investigations by modern Kindred and the testimony of some surviving ancients has revealed that the process of elevation to divine status always seemed to follow one of three paths: elevation by Embrace, omen or conquest.

The simplest (and, some would argue, most logical) approach was simply to declare that all Kindred descended from a powerful ancestor were heavenly creatures. This often occurred in domains where vampires made claims to high divinity. In the old domain of Yautepec, a vampire who identified himself as Mictlantecutli surrounded himself with female descendants who were all Cihuateteo by right of Embrace. There are rumors that some of these lines have survived into modern nights, but little has been made of the possibility. Some vampires have acknowledged their descent from self-declared gods on Earth, but most deny the attribution of truly divine influence in their line.

A number of Kindred are said to have achieved god-noble status by the fulfillment of prophecy: appearing in a certain place at a certain time, bearing specific deformities or eliciting an unusual reaction from the local priests. No doubt, several vampires took advantage of established beliefs, altering themselves or working to ensure that the predictions would be met. However, assuming that all of the vampires who qualified thus were engaged in practices of deceit would be incorrect. Modern Kindred are more comfortable attributing the stories of prophetic selection to mundane trickery, of course, but they cannot explain every case away. In the absence of evidence to the contrary (and, in general, the absence of any remaining eyewitnesses), the documents of strange coincidences are usually dismissed as blind myth and canny self-promotion.

Conquest, however, was the most common means to elevation among the ancient Kindred of Mexico. By destroying one who claimed to embody a god, some renewed the claim themselves, arguing that superior strength was their evidence of divine right. Unfortunately, making the claim this way would pave the way for hopeful future successors, leading, in general, to a Requiem of paranoia as the new vampire god fended off hopefuls. It is known that warring Kindred once plagued the Mayan city of Uxmal, each working to destroy the other in an endless procession of divine claims until their ultimate fall at the claws of Spanish invaders. In some domains, those who brought a heavenly vampire to Final Death would claim some fragment of her power, raising themselves to the god-noble position (if they did not already hold it) but avoiding the temptation of further ambition. In some cities, the destruction of an elder or the conquest of a domain would only qualify a vampire for divine elevation if the Kindred satisfied specific requirements: performance of the deed on or before a certain date, for instance, or the sacrifice of a limb in battle.

There was no discernible rhyme or reason to the character of the selection process from domain to domain. No two seemed to hold the same criteria, and some were so different from their nearest neighbors as to seem completely alien. European Kindred who later attempted to reconstruct the rules of apotheosis in ancient Mexico were baffled by the wide range of legends, many of which were in opposition to one another, and the testimony of those few surviving vampires who could remember the nights of their Aztec and Maya kin usually serves only to confuse matters further. Some scholars dismiss the practice as chaotic to the point of madness, but others labor on out of fascination, stubbornness or a dedicated belief that some powerful secret might be hidden in the maze of half-truths and myth. Recent rumors claim that members of the Ordo Dracul have made staggering discoveries on this subject in the Mexican south. True or not, this story alone has been enough to spark renewed interest in the ancient practice.

What about the real gods?

There's a question that most vampires are loathe to ask, but many consider. If the Kindred of old were merely masquerading as divine powers, what happened to the true gods of the people? Skeptics might dismiss the gods as convenient constructs, but believers must come to terms with the notion that the true gods either tolerated the claims of the vampires or they were unable (or unwilling) to prevent them.

Some make the case that the Kindred who claimed to embody the gods on Earth must have been serving the divinities, whether the vampires knew it or not. If they weren't, the argument goes, the true gods would never have allowed them to make the claim. Logicians point out that the argument is flawed, based as it is on a circular statement impossible to prove or disprove. Logicians, however, rarely enjoy widespread support on matters of religious faith.

A slightly more rational, faith-based argument points to the eventual collapse and failure of every vampire who made these claims as demonstration of the supremacy of the gods. Perhaps, say this argument's proponents, the gods accepted statements that furthered their goals and acceded to their wishes. When a vampire let her self-interest eclipse the true message of the gods, though, she would be brought down by their divine will.

Some claim that the vampires in question may well have been actual manifestations of the gods on Earth. They may have chosen to take possession of the undead bodies for convenience since they were stronger, tougher and generally more powerful than the mortal population. The blood-hungry gods of the old civilizations might well have decided that the bodies most capable of holding and demonstrating their strength were their best choice for temporary habitation in the material world.

Perhaps the gods chose not to involve themselves directly in the affairs of mortals and Kindred at all. It's conceivable that the gods simply didn't notice the pretenders. It is impossible, of course, to know the truth — in the end, one can only believe in one explanation or another.

Reward and Punishment

Many modern vampires wonder how the ancient ones could keep the mortals at bay while routinely threatening (or outright violating) the Masquerade. Those Kindred who pretended to divinity made no attempt to hide their supernatural power, and, if records are to be believed, the mortals accepted their presence for quite some time. It is clear to many supernatural scholars that the very structure of native Mexican society was tainted by the public presence of inhuman powers. The blood-drenched religion of the Aztec civilization seems tailor-made to support a vampire population, and the confusion of vampires with gods all across the region must have made it incredibly difficult for mortals to determine which interferences should or should not be tolerated. Kindred must have displayed their power during the early formation of native mortal societies, entwining themselves with the natural myth and legend of the region and inuring themselves against an unfavorable designation in the future.

Once the vampires were accepted and their claims to godhood and god-noble status were entrenched, they enjoyed a position unique in the known world. Whole societies were aware of their presence, but made little or no effort to eject them. Some even worshipped them, tying the communities' own fates to the monsters in their midst. The vampire gods began manipulating the whole cloth of ancient Mexican civilization, deluding themselves into believing that they had the right to steer the course of nations.

The testimony of some remaining native Kindred has revealed that the majority of their kin who were known to the humans maintained a position of relative safety by behaving as the gods would — dispensing reward for faithful practice among their adherents and punishing those who defied them. Disciplines and sorcery were applied to the benefit of mortals who fell in line, wherever possible — in magically furthering crop production, attracting animals for food, providing battlefield intelligence and intensifying pleasure. Those who opposed the self-proclaimed divinities were subject to horrifying tortures as interpreted through the same powers: the devastation of crops by invasion of mandragora, deadly visitations of jungle predators, exposure of embarrassing secrets and plagues of addiction. To modern Kindred, the mark of Discipline use is obvious, but to credulous mortals the power display must have been awe-inspiring.

A World Without Tradition

There are modern Kindred who would have us believe that their ancient Mexican counterparts held little regard for the vampire Traditions. The Masquerade was clearly interpreted differently, and testimony of surviving witnesses indicates no ban on either Embrace or diablerie. Was ancient Mexico a world of unconcealed vampires, prowling the streets and temples without regard for the necessities the Traditions embody?

In fact, it was nothing of the sort. The Masquerade was, to the old ones, just as important as it is now. They found it absolutely necessary to conceal their true nature from the mortals of the time. The Kindred's claims to divinity only worked because of carefully crafted lies, set one over the other in a centuries-long latticework of complicated deception and reinforcing self-delusion. If the mortals were to understand what they were really dealing with, the whole structure of Kindred power would have collapsed.

It is also known that some sort of ban on Embrace must have been in place, because the vampire population was relatively low in all but the most populous areas. Simple intelligence must have guided the decision to keep their numbers down, and superstition on the part of faithful vampires would have kept the creation of new "gods" to a minimum.

As far as diablerie goes, there is simply no evidence that it was common practice. In truth, diablerie is never mentioned in surviving Kindred codices of the region, and testimony relating the practice is rare to nonexistent. Some of the members of the Lancea Sanctum promote a view of the ancient Mexican vampires as soul-eaters, but there is no concrete evidence to back up this portrayal whatsoever.

The Vampire Nations

With divine influence came the imperative for divine guidance. Mortals were not satisfied with paying tribute to a god unless they were amply rewarded, and after a time, the communities that sprung up around the worship of Kindred could not be sustained by the spot tactics of magical incentive that had previously sufficed. Mortal tribes amalgamated into nations, crediting their prosperity to the vampire divinities who appeared at their temples. The population of god-noble Kindred increased proportionally, and the demand for blood grew with them. Most realized that the drain on the mortals could not be sustained without coring the nations that supported the Kindred, so they engineered a greater imperative for blood sacrifice, leading to the program of perpetual war that dominated the societies of the Mexican region.

As the great war machines of the vampire nations spread further and further outward, many Kindred began to understand the horror of their situation. The less humane vampires who tended to encourage the bloodshed were free to gorge themselves, growing wildly in power even as their capacity for virtue diminished. Those who attempted to steer their charges to more peaceful pursuits were constantly in danger of being overrun by their violent neighbors. Some were trapped into advising mortals who wanted justification for war and would threaten rebellion without it.

Those mortal tribes without vampire influence remained mentally healthy, but were often subjugated or destroyed by their bloody counterparts. Those who could not retreat to territories that were unknown or otherwise inaccessible to the aggressors were forced to do battle, often against overwhelming odds. Mortal armies, unwittingly bearing the standard of a vampire Prince, would occasionally carry off the entire population of an untainted village to feed their gods. Slowly, inexorably, the territories of Mexico fell to the hungry nations of Kindred followers.

Some vampires rose against the trend, fighting to protect the mortal societies that remained untouched before all could be consumed. These Kindred prophesized a future in which no mortals existed outside of the hungry taint of the increasingly ravenous creatures at the core of their civilization, and the eventual self-cannibalization that was sure to follow. These rebels cast off the mask of divinity, withdrawing from public view and turning their energies toward undoing the damage their entrenched influence had done. Still, the warmongers spread further and further out, running on a deep-set philosophy of accomplishment and oppression that seemed to roll forward with a constantly increased momentum.

The Fall of the Gods

By the beginning of the 16th century, the mortal population of the region was strained beyond capacity. Most of the territories had been scoured clean of those societies not already corrupted by Kindred divinities, and yet the vampires continued their gruesome demands. Inevitably, the cities under heavy Kindred influence began to turn inwards, depleting themselves in violent civil conflict. Oppressed peoples, no long able to stomach the constant need for fresh blood, turned on their priests and god-nobles, refusing to sacrifice any more of themselves.

A number of vampires who made claims to godhood were betrayed by their own servants and childer in an effort to appease the people. Some Kindred responded with terrifying force, subjugating those who had once served their masters willingly. Even those vampires who would not crush the rebels refused to step down from their temples, choosing to endure the attacks and insults rather than suffer the humiliation of a fall from grace.

In the midst of the great, self-destructive chaos that followed, the first Spanish forces arrived. The conquistadors swept across the region, scattering and demolishing the mortal armies that stood against them. Even the Kindred gods of Mexico were not prepared to do battle against sword and cannon. Beleaguered by the harassment of disillusioned, younger vampires and mortals, few even bothered to meet the Spanish in battle — and fewer still cared to face the European Kindred who followed shortly thereafter. The Mexican Kindred who did not retreat into slumber were caught and destroyed by fervent enemies on both sides. As each vampire god fell, the faith in all of the gods was cast into doubt, and the devotion of even their most stubborn followers dissolved.

By the late 1500s, the majority of Kindred with claims to ancient Mexican divinity were either destroyed or forced into hiding. The mortals of the region were released from the grip of traditional influence, for better or worse.

The Role of Kindred in the Spanish Conquest

Contrary to modern assumption, European Kindred had little to do with the progress of the conquistadors in ancient Mexico. Vampires rarely made a habit of traveling with sailors and explorers because of the many dangers of ocean transit, and there was no guarantee that the vampires would find an abundant food source when they arrived. Once the news of continental discovery filtered through to the Elysium gatherings of Spain, it took some time for those Kindred brave enough, desperate enough or foolish enough to undertake the voyage to arrange transport, and most of them missed the initial advances of Cortés' conquering army.

The Spanish vampires who first set foot on Mexican soil did grapple with the vampires who survived the first stages of the Spanish Conquest, and made war on their own terms. Their natural cautiousness, encouraged by the now-familiar established tradition of the Masquerade, kept the battles they fought hidden from mortal eyes.

Gods of the New World

"Shit, man, you gotta be kidding me. This guy actually thought he could run a confidence scam in our domain? He didn't ask Mariposa for permission, did he? I guess he didn't understand — crime isn't just organized in this town, it's religiously organized. Our Mariposa, she's the fucking god of thieves, and everybody pays her their respect. Well, kill him before she finds out — otherwise I'm getting out of here, fast."

— Ruiz, Nosferatu neonate of San Antonio

Old habits die hard in Mexico. Despite the lessons of the past, Kindred in the region seem drawn to the temptation of divine claim, whether they understand it or not. It may be that they sense the compulsion of torpid ancients, interpreting it through a filter of modern thought. It may simply be a manifestation of ambition, revealing itself in a manner unique to Mexico. Whatever the cause, the tendencies of Kindred both young and old are beginning to alarm European traditionalists who fear a return to ancient native practices.

Power and Influence

It is not unusual for some vampires to seek a modicum of control over their environment. Those with the means or the will tend to carve out a niche for themselves, building their fortunes or accessing the flow of information so as to enhance their position in a city. The advantages of awareness and influence are clear to most. What is unusual (and nearly unique to the vampires of the region) is the tendency to claim strict exclusivity in a field of endeavor. For some reason, it is not uncommon to find a vampire in a Mexican domain who decides to become the prime mover in a certain field and devote his attentions to eliminating the investments of fellow Kindred — even, in some cases, the mortal competition. Among the Kindred who stake these claims, there is an alarming tendency to refer to themselves as "gods," whether in humorous tones or not.

In the 20th century, a Ventrue by the name of Antonio Catalan de Guillen in Saltillo, Coahuila, was commonly referred to as the "god of guns" because of his established and extensive ties to the illegal weapons trade. Mortals and Kindred alike knew his title, even if they had no idea who or what he really was. His wealth and influence grew to staggering extremes in less than 20 years, and his violent exclusivity ruffled enough feathers that it was only a matter of time before he was called to heel before the Prince. Astonishingly, the Ventrue refused to attend Elysium for a meeting, sparking a conflict that lasted several months and resulted in his destruction. Those who knew him in his final nights claim that his Pride may have gotten away from him, but at no time did he seem delusional or overtly mystical in his assessment of the situation.

There is no discernible pattern to these claims. Lineage doesn't seem to be a consideration — there are just as many modern "gods" among Kindred of European ancestry as there are of native. These Mexican "gods" aren't just risen ancients looking to recapture the divinity of the past. Many are relatively young, and most seem more concerned with their endeavor than the title. Still, it can't be denied that almost every vampire who gains this divine (or pseudo-divine or mock-divine) status becomes inordinately proud of her position and defends it fiercely. There must be more to the phenomenon than simple ambition, because it seems to happen relatively often, and in similar terms each time.

It doesn't help that a portion of the mortal population seems all too eager to assist in the assumption of these roles. Superstition guides many of them, influencing the credulous and providing a manipulative tool to the unscrupulous. To refer to someone as a god is to ascribe unusual powers to that person, frightening the believers.

But What Happens to the Vampire?

A vampire who lays claim to divinity in Mexico, whether she believes it or not, is flirting with powers she may not understand. The influence of the ancients is so deeply ingrained in the land that the claim may actually resonate with the old ways, sparking a mystic reaction. In mechanical terms, the next time the vampire in question fails a degeneration check and gains a derangement, he will begin to suffer from a grandiose delusion, with the following effects:

Grandiose Delusion (mild): Your character fixates on her favorite territory, occupation or subject, feeling an inflated sense of knowledge and influence in relation to it. She will believe that she knows best in all cases related to the matter of choice, and will begin to guard the object of fixation jealously, working to ensure that nobody else can "interfere." Whenever your character encounters an individual who is attempting to exert influence in the matter (and isn't already in her service), roll Resolve + Composure to keep her from responding aggressively.

On a failed roll, your character must immediately answer the perceived threat with an attempt to exclude the interloper. The attempt can take any form that seems appropriate to her — bribery, intimidation, coercion — whatever she thinks will work. For the remainder of the scene, this attempt must be the character's first priority, even if there are more pressing matters at hand.

Example: *Beatriz, a Mekhet drug dealer, suffers a Grandiose Delusion with regards to her heroin business. One night, on her way to Elysium, she sees a pusher she doesn't know making a sale on the street. Beatriz' player fails the Resolve + Composure roll, so she can't help but respond immediately. She grits her teeth, deciding to beat the "competition" down, even if means ending up late for the gathering.*

Modern Gods and the Masquerade

The Kindred tendency to claim exclusive province in modern Mexico has raised some serious concerns in recent years. Certain European elders recall the behavior of the Mexican ancients and note the startling similarities in the

HEARTLAND

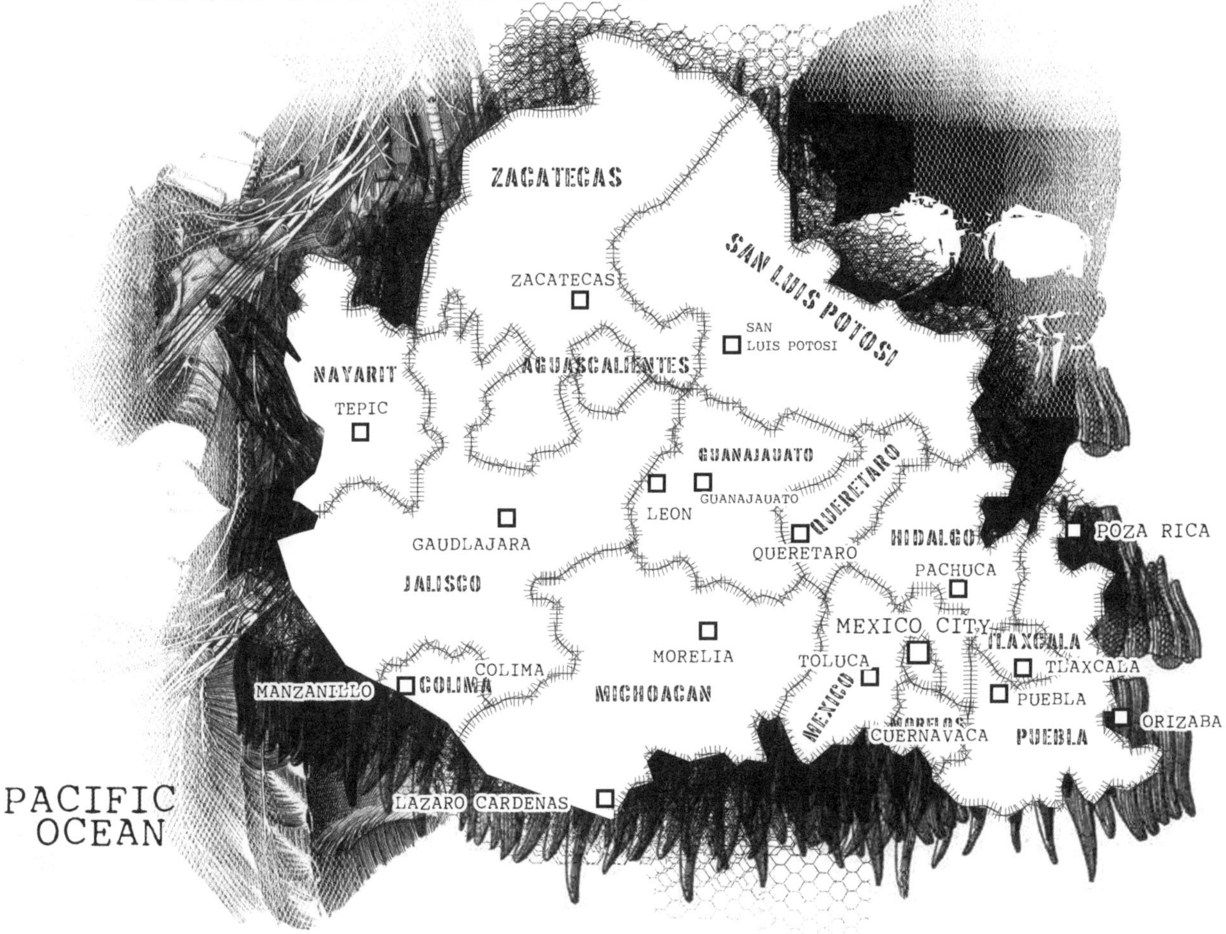

practice. Strict conservatives believe that playing on the superstitious nature of the mortals is, at best, a dangerous game, at worst, an outright violation of the Tradition of the Masquerade. In some domains, expressions of personal divinity, regardless of tone, are firmly banned. Even boasts of extraordinary skill or talent make some Kindred nervous.

To the vast majority who cannot recall the nights of the Spanish Conquest, the reaction seems overzealous. Most don't see the harm in cowing the mortals, so long as the actual existence of Kindred and their true weaknesses are never revealed. If a spook story about heavenly authority does the trick, they say, why not use it?

Interpretation of the Masquerade is a hot topic in contemporary Mexican Elysiums. Passionate calls for strict reform and enforcement are frequently met with populist arguments for lenience. Too often, the respective arguments undergo a swift metamorphosis, sliding into fearful violence or sarcastic derision. Both sides are easily tainted: the former by racist alarm, the latter by faithful agents of the old ways.

New Religion

Mortal believers often form accretions of reverence around these modern gods, feeding the power of the Kindred involved and establishing themselves in positions of favor. Many have no idea what they're actually associating themselves with — some think they are joining organized crime families, political societies or even celebrity fan clubs. Sooner or later, little by little, they are drawn into the vampire's orbit, isolating themselves from the outside world and dedicating themselves to his service.

These faithful followers are not likely to consider their efforts religious, and generally scoff at anyone who draws the parallel between their organizations and cults. They see nothing spiritual in their worship. In most cases, the rationale for obeying the Kindred in the center of the group seems perfectly mundane, even when Discipline use or the bond of blood reinforces it.

Strangely, there are some organizations that form without the participation or approval of the vampire at the core. Mortals like to identify themselves with a group, and Kindred with a powerful force of personality attract weak-willed humans with little effort. While most vampires wouldn't be eager to discard the potentially useful accumulation of mortal devotees, some Kindred consider it annoying at best. On the other hand, those who aren't careful get sucked in by their own followers, coming to believe that they are more than ordinary vampires. The constant praise and offers of servitude corrupt such Kindred, and some are inspired to pretensions not unlike those of the ancient god-nobles.

Flirting with Danger

Careful Kindred will notice that those who gather a dedicated group of mortals around them are actually engaging in seriously risky behavior. Besides the potential risk of revealing themselves to curious admirers, Kindred who tie themselves too closely to mortal affairs flirt with emotional vulnerability, temptation to abuse Disciplines and the ever-present threat of frenzy in the presence of allies. Many argue that keeping close company with a mortal group actually tends to diminish a vampire's Humanity over time. Keeping company with a group that takes pains to separate and elevate the vampire can only be worse.

The gathering of a modern, secular (or semi-secular) cult offers a Storyteller the chance to explore the inadvertent damage vampires are capable of. While players shouldn't be made to suffer for their Merits (Herd, Allies and Status, for example), the presence of admiring mortals can create story opportunities. A fan club might provide a vampire with a ready supply of blood and willing servants, but the Kindred involved should begin to understand that some of the admiring mortals are throwing away their lives for him, ignoring real prospects for love or missing out on genuine spiritual experiences. The choice between Man and Beast rears its ugly head with each revelation — should the vampire cut the mortal loose, improving the mortal's chances while making the vampire's own unlife more difficult, or will he continue to abuse his power?

As with any story about temptation, the conflict is largely interior. The real antagonist involved is the character's own Beast — so it works best as a subplot, running concurrent with a more external event.

Enduring Cults of Faith

Modern claims to divinity aren't the only ones the Kindred of Mexico have to worry about. It's commonly assumed that the Spanish Conquest was responsible for the destruction of most, but not all of the self-titled vampire gods of the pre-Columbian tradition. Some must have escaped the program of elimination enforced by European Kindred, retreating into hidden slumber or disguising themselves as unbelievers.

In recent decades, it's become increasingly apparent that old vampire deities didn't just survive the Spanish Conquest — these Kindred inspired both mortal and Kindred followers to keep the deities' traditions alive in an attempt to guarantee their eventual return to prominence. Whether these followers are encouraged by active influence or not, they work ceaselessly to pave the way for a vast and terrible reclamation at the hands of their hidden masters. Several organizations and factions have been uncovered over the passing years, and most have proven frustratingly resilient despite a concerted attempt to wipe them out.

The Black Sun Cult is said to boast more than 2,000 mortal members in the northern states of Mexico and the American Southwest. The cult's adherents believe that they serve the ancient Tzitzimime, hoping to hasten their apocalyptic return with precisely timed ritual sacrifices and a number of fierce, destructive mystic practices. The followers, to satisfy the demands of their faith, periodically conspire to stage disastrous mishaps via careful sabotage of mass transit and well-traveled structures. In addition, they are engaged in a number of widespread archeological investigations throughout the region, hoping to uncover clues that will lead them to their gods. A number of cells have actually located the bodies of torpid vampires who once identified themselves as the demon stars and were laid to rest by their followers in hidden, age-old tombs. Four elder Kindred have been discovered to date, and one was awoken and encouraged to feed freely in the aftermath of the deliberate derailment of a passenger train. Neither the cultists nor the vampires they seek know exactly what is supposed to happen when all of the Tzitzimime have been located and revived. The dogma of the cult predicts a vague, cataclysmic reckoning that is to be visited upon the denizens of the living world, possibly destroying all who fail to honor the demons (and, according to some readings, even those who don't).

An organization that refers to itself only as "La Sociedad" is an elite secret society of some two dozen wealthy mortals dedicated, ostensibly, to cooperation beyond the law and entrenchment of influence in Mexico City. In truth, the three members who founded the cult are dedicated worshippers of Tezcatlipoca and have cleverly woven mystic and pseudo-mystic references to him and his power throughout the complicated oaths and rituals of the group. While some members don't believe in the old god, all of them are blinded enough by greed to treat the traditions of the group with deadly seriousness. By the time a single member realizes that there might be more to La Sociedad than meets the eye, he is already committed — evidence of embarrassing and unlawful acts he partook in to prove his dedication are on record, and an attempt to desert the group would only attract the wrath of its potent established membership.

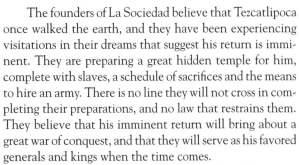

The founders of La Sociedad believe that Tezcatlipoca once walked the earth, and they have been experiencing visitations in their dreams that suggest his return is imminent. They are preparing a great hidden temple for him, complete with slaves, a schedule of sacrifices and the means to hire an army. There is no line they will not cross in completing their preparations, and no law that restrains them. They believe that his imminent return will bring about a great war of conquest, and that they will serve as his favored generals and kings when the time comes.

Xibalba Churches are scattered throughout the region, attracting both mortal and Kindred worshippers. The fanatic devotees of the Xibalba Churches believe that the gods of the Mayan underworld still exist and are rapidly regaining prominence in the living world (as evinced by the perceived steady increase in suffering in the modern world). The followers seek to understand the complex and demanding rites of the mythic city, hoping to appease the gods or, in some cases, to join them and become citizens of Xibalba. Members subject themselves to tests of staggering cruelty in order to prove their worth and prepare themselves for a living (or undead) journey to the underworld. Ingestion of poisons, willful contraction of painful diseases and ritual branding and bleeding are just a few of the common practices of the churches. Several mortal Xibalba Churches have been subverted by Kindred who are dancing on the edge of revealing themselves to their flocks in an ill-advised, potentially disastrous attempt to increase the pitch of worship.

Combating the Climate of Madness

If there is a consensus among the modern Kindred of Mexico on the subject of gods, it is that the people clearly need something to believe in. A policy of non-interference is promoted by the most clear-headed vampires, who suggest that the mortals ought to be allowed to find their own way. Any interference, especially interference on the part of the vampires, is bound to cause harm. The temptation to guide mortal belief leads inexorably to disaster, as indicated (or so it seems) by ancient Kindred accounts from around the world. It contributes, as they say, to the "Climate of Madness" in the Mexican region, a circumstance that seems clearly visible in all aspects of Mexican society in the World of Darkness.

Unfortunately, the call to withdraw contact from mortals and refrain from feeding their superstitions is intertwined with debates about the nature of divinity, which often lead to clashes between religious systems of belief. The passionate inability of Kindred on all sides to tolerate one another's creed interferes with measured discussion, and the issue is often buried in unrelated dispute. If the problem (if the Kindred can even be encouraged to agree there is a problem) of pretension to divinity can never be solved, the Mexican region may never be pulled out of the centuries-long spiritual tailspin it seems to be caught in.

Mexican Weirdness

Mexico has its fair share of lunatics and geniuses. Each has uncovered a variety of bizarre and frightening phenomena throughout the country. Some of these phenomena are utterly mundane things dressed up in drug-induced hallucinations or paranoid imaginations. Others mystify even the most jaded occultists and well traveled wizards. The trouble is in knowing which phenomena to fear.

For safety's sake, fear it all.

Turn of the Worm

Time to destroy a myth: one will not find a worm at the bottom of Mexican-produced tequila. Some American companies put a small worm at the bottom of bottles, but only as the embodiment of expected legend: naïve buyers assume that a pickled worm in the alcohol means it's somehow more potent, or even psychotropic. It's not.

The myth does have an origin in reality, however. In the 1940s, producers of mezcal (tequila's forebear) put butterfly worms (gusano) in the bottles to draw attention to the product. The worms (gusano rojo and gusano de oro, or "red worm" and "gold worm," respectively) were edible, sold in food markets all across Mexico. The worm wasn't magic. It didn't produce aphrodisiac or psychedelic effects. It was just pickled protein.

Lately, though, dingy nightclubs and crummy barrio bars have begun selling unlabeled bottles of mezcal that have fat, black worms (gusano negro) floating in the murky fluid. Bartenders offer a bottle, calling it *infusión especial*, claiming that it is a truly potent brew. Not magical, exactly, but deliciously sweet while packing twice the punch of normal tequila. Some sellers say it provides effects similar to those received from Ecstasy. Others say the drink causes hallucinations. Most, however, just claim that it gets the drinker deliriously drunk, very quickly, and without a soul-dragging hangover.

The drink does get the drinker inebriated faster. Having twice the normal alcohol content of regular tequila, this mezcal brings on a fast buzz. Drinkers of *infusión especial* subtract two dice from any Dexterity, Intelligence or Composure-based dice pools for every drink the character consumes in excess of his Stamina in an hour (Defense is reduced accordingly, as well). Nobody is a mean drunk on this drink, so assume that a drinker gains +1 Social bonus per drink (maximum of +3). These effects fade at the rate of one die per two hours until all the alcohol is purged from the character's system. Again, no hangover is suffered in the morning. (Note that these effects differ somewhat from the normal alcohol rules found on p. 177 of World of Darkness Rulebook.)

The beverage has an odd effect come morning, though. If the character eats the black worm at the bottom of the brew, eight hours later he will find two things of note. First, somewhere on his body he now has a smallish tattoo — no bigger than a dime — of a moth or butterfly. Second, he will vomit up a living moth (usually white), which then flies away.

That's it. He suffers no other effects, no hangover, no penalties or bonuses. He burps up a white moth, and has a tattoo.

What Then?

Nobody knows what happens next. The availability of this odd drink with its black worm is relatively recent. Some whisper about things they've seen, or heard, though, regarding the *infusión especial*.

- Rumors among the Kindred suggest that some vampires have little wire cages full of white moths. Some whisper that these moths carry pieces of the souls of those who have eaten the black worm. Others say that the worms do not carry souls, but information from the victims' minds: anything from phone numbers to their greatest fears.
- In Mexico City, a pair of serial killers — brothers, actually — were finally caught after a months-long spree of murders. The brothers always cut off the arms of the victims, letting them bleed to death in a closed room. The two brothers — Hervé and Raoul — had been policemen in Toluca, and by all accounts were good family men. When they were caught, they had small black moth tattoos on the skin between thumb and forefinger of their left hands.
- An old mage — a hermit living outside the Toltec Tula ruins in Hidalgo — returned to society after 50-some years. He claims to have had dreams of el cielo de polillas, or a "sky full of moths." This disturbed him enough to bring him out of hiding.
- Nobody has been able to find out just where the infusión especial is produced. A local vampire discovered a warehouse in Metepec's industrial corridor, finding crates full of the empty, dusty bottles — some spattered with bits of blood and what may have been milk — but that's the sum total of available information. Bartenders claim to not know where the stuff comes from, only that they find it in crates packed with dried grass outside their establishments. They sell bottles for about 500 pesos apiece.

Drunk in Public

It is illegal to be visibly drunk in public in Mexico. If police see a character exhibiting any signs of inebriation, they can arrest him. Of course, in most situations the police are willing to look the other way for a price. If the character can summon the wherewithal to offer a bribe, she can probably escape the arrest for about 200 pesos (less with a successful Presence or Manipulation roll). Some police, however, sensing opportunity, may try to get more out of the drunken individual than is perhaps warranted.

UFOs in Mexico

Within the last five years, Mexico has seen a sharp increase in the number of Unidentified Flying Objects sighted. More than half of these sightings take place in the skies above Mexico City. Some see lights flying in odd formations at night. Others see triangular-shaped metal crafts hovering over a dormant volcano or an odd polyhedron glinting in the sun over wide tracts of city slum. The military have spotted shapes in the sky visible only by infrared. Tourists have seen things in the sky as their flights land in Mexico City.

The strange sightings are oddly prevalent, and yet, none claim abduction. Few if any assert that they have seen any kind of actual alien being, only weird shapes and lights in the sky. What, exactly, is going on? Why here? Why now?

Transformación

Sometimes, witnessing one of these shapes or lights opens a door inside a person that cannot be closed. The experience seems to turn on some dormant part of the brain, or perhaps it merely draws closed the gap between the witness and other realities. Below are several possible consequences that a witness may suffer. Note that not every observer is subject to these transformations and events; probably about one in 10 actually suffer these effects. Also, while a rare few witnesses experience a number of the effects, most only suffer one (if any at all).

- The witness gains a Mental Merit she did not have before. This Merit is likely Unseen Sense, but can also be Danger Sense, Eidetic Memory, Encyclopedic Knowledge or even a new Language. (These can all be found on pp. 108–109, **World of Darkness Rulebook**.)
- Character gains a mild derangement from the following list: Fixation, Phobia or Vocalization (pp. 97–99, World of Darkness Rulebook). You can also choose the Hypnagogic Hallucination derangement, found below.
- Some observers become oddly religious. This may mean regularly attending Mass at the local catedral (cathedral) or capilla (chapel), going to the local ruins to "commune" with the old ways or finding some new kind of faith.
- The character may encounter members of UFO cults who seek to question her, torture her or recruit her. (See below.)

Hypnagogic Hallucination (mild)

The character suffers hallucinations while in the state between waking and sleeping. Just before going to sleep, the character might see one or several dark shapes standing around, a shadowy hag, dark insects on the walls or some other "presence." The hallucinations are often accompanied by sleep paralysis, discomfiting sounds (such as wind rushing in one's ears or a high-pitched mechanical whine) or the feeling that something is squatting on the character's chest and thus inhibiting his ability to breathe properly.

The hallucinations seem to occur following days (or nights, if a vampire) that were particularly stressful. The Storyteller may request a Resolve + Composure roll before going to sleep. Failing the roll results in the pre-sleep hallucinations.

Effect: Experiencing the hallucinations leaves any character, even one of the Kindred, feeling oddly fatigued the following day or night. The character can suffer a –1 penalty to all Mental rolls during that day, or can instead spend a Willpower point to ignore that penalty.

UFO Cults

Mexico is home to an alarming number of UFO cults, most of which have sprung up in the last few years. They seem to be able to find witnesses with unerring accuracy. What follows are just some of the cults a character might encounter in Mexico.

Tocado por los Dioses

Roughly translated: "Touched by the Gods." Members of this cult believe that they have literally witnessed — and thus have been graced by — the old gods. The cult seems to separate its members into groups of four or five, each of which offer belief and veneration to a particular god of the Mayan, Aztec or Toltec pantheons. One might worship Ekchuah, a scorpion-tailed god of war, while another "cell" might follow Itzpapalotl, the "Obsidian Butterfly" goddess of fire. Stranger still is how these cells venerate their patron powers — the followers do not seem to do so in traditional ways such as prayer, poem or even sacrifice. They perform odd, obsessive-compulsive habits to "honor" the gods: counting bricks in a wall and writing the number down in chalk, writing one word over and over again each day, gathering together and making small incisions upon one another in the same place. These cells don't necessarily bring harm to those they approach, but they are ceaseless and invasive.

The National Secret Army

This cult (also called the *Ejercito Secreto Nacional*, or the ESN) was founded about five years back by ex-military personnel who witnessed UFO activity while on active duty. Some were pilots for the Air Force, others officers in the Army. The founders believe — and still espouse — that a terrible conspiracy has infected the government. This conspiracy, they say, has not only crossed all levels of the government, from the president on down, but also is shared by several other countries (Brazil and the United States, chief among them). The group refuses to speculate on the precise nature of the conspiracy, but believe that it has to do with the "replacement" of military and governmental officials with *paracidos*, or "look-alikes." This group isn't gentle in its recruiting methods. Once the group is sure of a witness' identity, the group's members often kidnap him. They attack en masse, grabbing the victim and putting tape over his mouth and a bag over his head. From that point, the abducted has the choice of joining the "cause" or being part of the conspiracy. And the Secret Army does not abide the presence of conspirators.

Heaven's Light

The Heaven's Light cult (or *Luz de Cielo*) believes that the crafts in the sky are piloted by aliens, who are actually angels, who come to bring God's mercy upon the world. Lead by the extravagant (and wealthy) recluse, Jesus-Ernesto Flores, the group claims that the angel-aliens will one day come and free the souls of the living, causing a holy mass exodus into space (which apparently is the same as Heaven). The group is fairly public, giving tons of money to both charity and scientific causes. There is cause to worry, however. Flores, with the help of several of his chosen aides, has begun stockpiling all manner of weapons: from AK-47s to canisters of nerve gas. Flores has become increasingly paranoid, and believes that unnamed "enemies" will come and try to destroy the group's good works, thus circumventing the mass exodus that humanity so dearly requires. The weapons are his way of not only protecting the group, but of jumpstarting the mass exodus if necessary — which, of course, involves freeing a lot of souls by killing large numbers of people. The group recruits new members with honey, not vinegar, offering a warm community and handouts of money. Only later are recruits given weapons training.

The Truth

The reality is this: sometimes, there are lights and shapes in the sky, and people see them. These people are sometimes affected. Some join cults. Others become recluses. Most go about their day.

That's all that anybody knows, so far. Certainly, some speculate. The werewolves believe that the sightings amount to spirits that, for a short time, are able to cross the Gauntlet in an effort to mess with people's heads — thus drawing Essence through belief and action. Some mages agree with this, while other sorcerers believe that the UFOs are anything from Exarchs to Oracles, from Goetic demons to living mysteries. Few vampires have solid ideas (or even care about the phenomenon), though some within the more religious covenants believe that something is going on, but exactly what remains unclear.

Villa Luz

Cueva de Villa Luz — Cave of the House of Light — is unlike any other cave system found in the world. The main passage is safe: its opening length is vented by a couple dozen openings in which shafts of light illuminate the grotto (and allow poisonous gas to escape). Further into the cave, however, things get dangerous. And weird.

The waters that enter the cave and run through it are milk-colored, and stocked with thousands of blind, troglodytic fish. As a character goes deeper in the cave, he will find stranger creatures: hand-sized spiders, fat millipedes, vampire bats and the bizarre pseudo-scorpion called the amblypigid. Most of these bugs and beasts are blind, just like the fish.

The air is hazardous deep in the cave, with obscene concentrations of carbon monoxide and hydrogen sulfide. The mud is a bacterial brew; if it touches skin, it leaves a vicious, itchy rash (causing a –1 penalty to other rolls due to the distraction). The walls and ceilings, too, are covered in microbial snot — so much so that the slime drips down and forms living, mucousy stalactites (called "snottites"). The microbial waste that forms these is highly acidic: enough to burn through clothes and damage skin (two bashing damage per quarter-sized drop if it touches skin).

Many of the cave's deeper passages require cavers to crawl through tunnels on their bellies. Tyvek suits and rebreather masks are essential to avoid poisonous air, itchy mud and acid waste.

Cave of the Gods

The locals of nearby villages (such as Tapijulapa) are descended from the Zoque and Mixe Indians. They believe that the cave is sacred, that gods dwell within.

During the ritual of *La Pesca de la Sardina* (Fishing of the Sardine), the villagers gather at the milky waters at the entrance of the cave and smash barbasco roots to a pulp, then release the pulp into the stream. The pulp drives the blind fish to the edges, where the villagers catch them in the hundreds. After this is done, the villagers thank the gods in the cave by leaving flowers at the entrance while others drum and dance. Believing the gods placated, the villagers return to the village with their fish.

Gods of the Cave

The deepest lengths of the cave — where humans have not yet gone — are not entirely unpopulated. Three Gangrel vampires, all of native descent, dwell in the darkness of the cave. They have been there for nearly a century. Their normally bronze skin has gone ashen gray. Their eyes turned white and shriveled in their sockets, making them totally blind. Their other senses have become attuned to every sound and smell, their skin tough against the heady biological brew that should burn their skin.

Naked and mad, the vampires feed on the cave's strange offerings. They bait bats with bugs and stones, and eat them. Weirder is the "red goo" that forms on the walls in the deepest recesses: this blood-red paste provides sustenance to the three. It isn't blood, not exactly — and yet it acts as Vitae once in the system.

Rarely do they leave the cave. Sometimes they go to the nearby villages and drag victims back to the cave into the darkness and poison air — but doing so is a mad dash, for even the light of the moon above irritates them.

These three Gangrel believe themselves to be *dioses de la cueva*, or the gods of the cave. They no longer think of themselves as vampires, but as something else entirely.

Pilgrimage

The villagers are not the only ones who seek to placate the gods of the cave. Those Kindred who know of the cave come, from time to time, on a pilgrimage of sorts — though, it is a selfish journey, not a spiritual one.

Whether the cave itself possesses a supernatural property or whether it comes from the vampires remains unknown. What vampires do know is this: the three Gangrel "gods" know far more about the Damned of Mexico than they should. These "gods" know what secrets the Prince of San Cristobal holds. They know why one Tijuana Mekhet betrayed his childe, or what the childe did to get revenge. They know the names of ghouls, the locations of havens, the identities of loved ones and hated enemies. How do these Gangrel know this information? Nobody knows. They certainly aren't forthcoming about it, attacking any who get overly curious.

What these three *will* do, however, is answer one question. If a vampire makes the long trek to the cave and the uncomfortable journey deep inside, he may ask the "gods" a single question about himself or another vampire. The vampire must bring with him some kind of food: whether that means a dog, a bottle of blood or a whole human is up to the vampire. The three consume the offering, and then answer the question.

The vampire gets only one question during his whole existence. They remember him. He can never come back and get another answer (though, he could theoretically make another Kindred go in and ask a follow-up question). If the vampire dares to ask a second question, the three attack without mercy. Their strength and ferocity is terrible to behold.

Zona del Silencio

Located between Durango, Coahuila, and Chihuahua is Mexico's stretch of mythic desolation. Thought to be on par with the Bermuda Triangle, Mexico's "Zone of Silence" (also known as the "Sea of Thetys" or the "Dead Zone") is an unmarked swath of land in the middle of the desert that reportedly features a wealth of bizarre paranormal activity. That supposed activity includes, though is not limited to, the following:

- Strange lights in the sky and along the ground.
- An area littered with meteorites.
- Unique electromagnetic principles that can stop cars from working properly or radios from functioning.
- Mutations in flora and fauna.
- Visitations by odd, Nordic-looking men as well as "gray" aliens.

Theories about the area are limitless. Some suggest a conspiracy (with tales featuring experimental aircraft, uranium deposits, wayward missiles, all usually born of the U.S. government). Others believe that this place is frequented by aliens, perhaps even forcibly drawing extraterrestrial craft to the region by dint of its weird electromagnetic properties. Apocryphal tales speak of ghosts, demons, angels and even suggest that this is where Lucifer himself landed when he fell from Heaven.

Stranger than Fiction

This is the reality of the zone: the meteorites are just hematite and magnetite. The flora and fauna are just fine, and any so-called mutations are features normal for the plants and animals indigenous to the area. Strange lights are the province of heat lightning and other atmospheric conditions. The *area itself* also has no effect on radio signals or other electronic devices.

Conspiracy theorists point to the research station in the middle of the zone as proof of clandestine wrongdoing, but in reality the research station just a biosphere: a facility meant to help scientists study terrestrial biomes in a closed ecosystem. No conspiracy there. Similarly, no proof exists of extraterrestrial visitation.

That's not to say the area is without its enigmas — or more appropriately, its enigmatic figures. Both the researchers and the locals are fond of saying that they do not see strange things in the desert, only strange *people*.

The first strange group is the *zoneros*. Some come to the zone as curious tourists, and that's fine (though many leave behind litter and come knocking at the research station, believing it to be some kind of hotel or public sightseeing center). Other tourists exhibit curiosity that skirts dangerous obsession. They come to the zone bristling with theories. They collect meteorites. They camp in tents or stay in vans, remaining in the area for weeks, even months. Some claim to be psychic, others "scientists" (rarely with actual degrees) and nearly all of these *zoneros* seem unable to talk about anything but the Zone of Silence. They cause far greater concern for the researchers and locals than normal tourists. Some have attempted to break into the biosphere. Others leave gates open, resulting in the unwanted escape of whole herds of sheep or cattle. These individuals seem certain that they are taking part in something cosmic or spiritual, and can rarely be convinced otherwise.

The second group of strangers are the odd unearthly men and women seen frequenting the zone. They do not appear to be *zoneros*: they aren't unwashed, don't live in vans and don't possess so-called scientific equipment. These individuals are often seen with oddly pink skin, blond hair and perfect features. They seem to speak a multitude of languages, though all do so with a slightly musical lilt. Many smell strongly of flowers or sweet perfumes, and wear somewhat generic clothing. They never have any of the accoutrements expected of someone wandering in the middle of the desert: no vehicle, water bottles, backpacks or food rations. They seem to appear out of nowhere, and disappear in the same way.

Instituto de Ecologia

The biosphere is the property of the Instituto de Ecologia in Veracruz. The station has anywhere from five to a dozen researchers on staff at any given time; many come and go after a period of several months, replaced by other scientists and students. Most of the staff know of the realities and myths of the zone, including details about the strangers who frequent the region. Characters seeking to learn information from these researchers probably fall into the "stranger" category, however. Seeing as how the staff has had many problems with zoneros (breaking in, harassing the scientists, spying) and has seen the strange androgynous "unearthlies," the staff members aren't likely to trust characters without serious overtures (and Social rolls).

Zoneros

Some *zoneros* are stranger and more hostile than others. One *zonero* might be a so-called psychic, living under a tent and dowsing for water and praying over crystals. Another might be a conspiracy theorist who sticks to the shadows

with a rusty machete just in case he meets "the enemy." Some are content to live peacefully, eschewing their old lives to try to understand the area, while others are unclean psychotics who have lost all semblance of social propriety and civilization. One group might even attack another in the middle of the night. Rarely do such attacks result in death — but some certainly go home bleeding.

All *zoneros* believe that *something* is going on in the Zone of Silence, however. Whether this means something of religious importance, psychic significance or pseudo-scientific revelation is up to the individual — but they all believe themselves part of something larger. No evidence exists to support this, not really, but faith doesn't need proof to subsist.

Unearthlies

The blond androgynes of the area represent a greater enigma than the *zoneros*. These unearthly strangers seem overly polite and unrealistically knowledgeable about all manner of things. They're clearly ill-prepared to exist in the desolate region, and yet they show no signs of dirt, malnutrition or sunburn. In fact, they seem unusually pristine and well-kept.

Those who come in contact with the strangers are likely to notice the following:

- They appear and disappear with relative ease. They never do so in full sight, however, instead emerging or vanishing when characters have their heads turned for a split second.
- They are rarely alone, usually appearing in pairs or threes. However, lately some locals and researchers have noticed them in the distance gathering in far larger numbers — as many as a dozen in a "herd."
- Their presence is often preceded by electromagnetic dysfunction: radios cease to work, vehicles sputter and stop working, watches and compasses go crazy. This can happen up to an hour before meeting one, and up to an hour after.
- When directly in their presence, characters are unable to access certain interpersonal or supernatural resources: mortals cannot expend Willpower, vampires cannot spend Vitae and both mages and werewolves are unable to access Essence. (Any Abilities that require expenditure of these items fail to function.)

Unlike the *zoneros*, these strangers don't seem hostile, and in fact are often unusually helpful (offering advice or directions even before being asked to do so). And yet, some feel that the androgynes represent something sinister behind the courteous veneer, giving off a palpable aura of menace. (Those with the Unseen Sense or Danger Sense Merit may feel this tangible air of malevolence about them.)

Who, or what, are these "unearthlies?" Few signs indicate truth. That said, some *zoneros* claim to have an idea: they believe these androgynes are actually *zoneros*. They claim that some of the strangers encountered look similar to *zoneros* from months or years past, except now with fair skin, blond hair and blue eyes. The *zoneros* no proof of this, of course — and who trusts a *zonero*, anyway?

Story Seeds

The area is rife with potential for stories. What follows are just a few quick possibilities for things going on here:

- The biosphere in the middle of the zone is government-run, as it turns out, and its researchers experiment on "odd" fluctuations in flora and fauna. They also study psychic phenomenon. What happens when they kidnap some of the zoneros, or even some of the Nordic-looking unearthlies? Worse, what happens when the researchers bring a coterie of vampires back to the laboratory in an effort to study these "new" creatures? The Mexican government is willing to go any lengths to uncover the truth.
- The characters, regardless of how far they are from the Zona del Silencio, begin having dreams of the region. The androgynous strangers feature prominently — and some of them look like the characters themselves. Moreover, the strangers predict little occurrences of the future — nothing big, but small events that may occur during the next few nights. Do they go to the desert, hunting the strangers? If the characters don't, the dreams intensify, so much so that penalties during waking hours are incurred.
- Everything eats. Mortals need food. Vampires consume blood. What do the unearthlies eat? Could they be psychic vampires, eating thoughts and mental energies? Do they consume electromagnetic waves (both from electronic equipment and from human bodies)? Perhaps they've been literally eating the sanity of the local zoneros — sucking at them like leeches. Maybe the consequence of this is that small packs of roaming zoneros form, half-mad and feral, now cannibals as a result of having their minds eaten away by the unearthly strangers.

TIJUANA
CIUDAD JUAREZ
HERMOSILLO
CHIHUAHUA
MATAMOROS
TORREON
MONTERREY
CULIACAN
Gulf of Mexico
MEXICO
TAMPICO
CANCUN
MERIDA
LEON
CHICHEN ITZA
Pacific Ocean
GUADALAJARA
VERACRUZ
MEXICO CITY
ACAPULCO
SALINA CRUZ

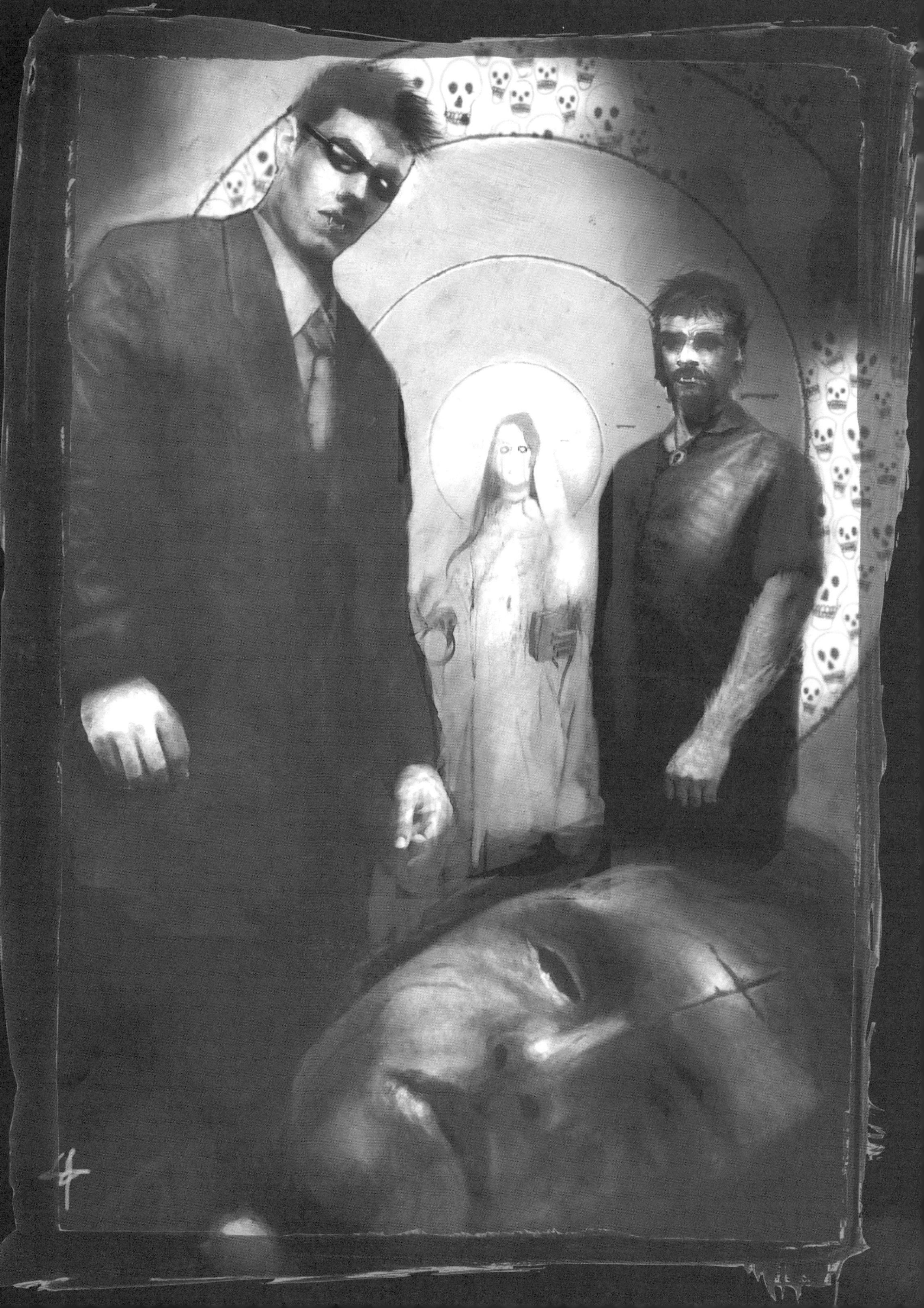

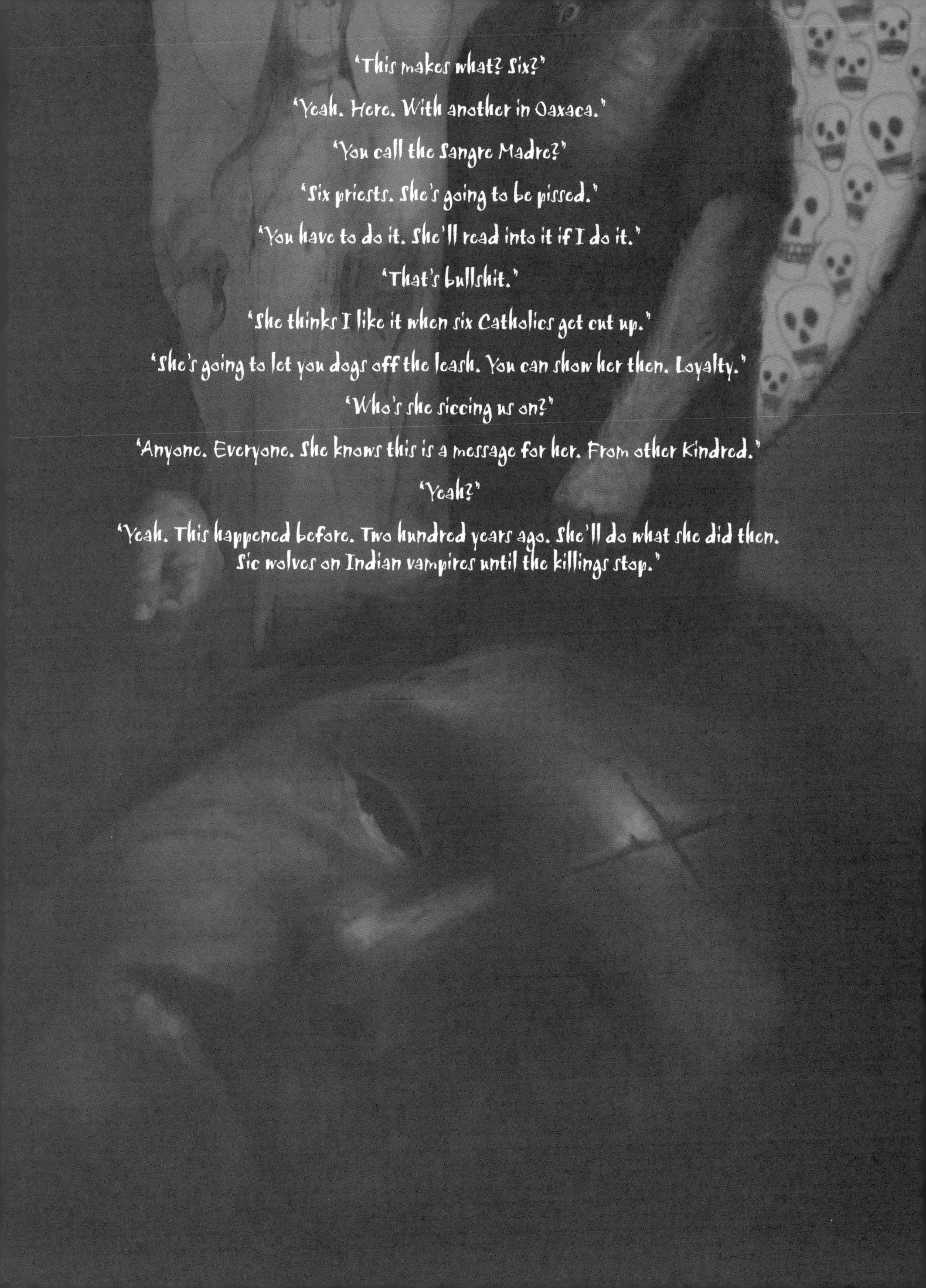

'This makes what? Six?'

'Yeah. Here. With another in Oaxaca.'

'You call the Sangre Madre?'

'Six priests. She's going to be pissed.'

'You have to do it. She'll read into it if I do it.'

'That's bullshit.'

'She thinks I like it when six Catholics get cut up.'

'She's going to let you dogs off the leash. You can show her then. Loyalty.'

'Who's she siccing us on?'

'Anyone. Everyone. She knows this is a message for her. From other Kindred.'

'Yeah?'

'Yeah. This happened before. Two hundred years ago. She'll do what she did then. Sic wolves on Indian vampires until the killings stop.'

Chapter Two: Player's Guide

> "I would rather die standing than live on my knees!"
>
> —Emiliano Zapata, Mexican revolutionary

Monsters in Mexico

This chapter is your guide to playing in a chronicle set in Mexico or themed with Mexican culture. For most of the creatures made by applying supernatural templates, the best way to infuse Mexican culture into the character is at the mortal level. The monomyth of the Uratha is not much different in Mexico than it's described in Werewolf: The Forsaken, for example. What makes a Mexican werewolf different from a werewolf from some other country is the same thing that makes a Mexican human being different: his upbringing. Look at Chapter One for some core information your character might know that could inform her goals, motives and opinions.

The Day of the Dead is a common touchstone for Mexican culture, and for good reason. Not only is it an exciting, distinctive holiday, but it's celebrated in cities throughout the Americas (and anywhere else with large Mexican populations). We've used it here as a sample of Mexican culture because its likely to be of use to Mexican characters living outside of Mexico, and because it's so thematically appropriate for the World of Darkness.

Uratha

Aside from the fact that Mexican werewolves have a historical interest in helping vampires maintain the Masquerade (see p. 22), they are not so unlike the Uratha described in Werewolf: The Forsaken. In general, Indian and mestizo werewolves grossly outnumber European werewolves, except perhaps in Mexico City.

The Mexican Wolf, the smallest wolf species in North America, is virtually extinct. Though its numbers might swell to as many as 100 or more in your World of Darkness, the situation is still grim for the breed. Thus wolves of any sort are rare sites anywhere in Mexico. No encounter with a wolf gets easily forgotten by a Mexican citizen. Mexican werewolves do tend to resemble the Mexican Wolf, which is redder and more slender (looking not terribly unlike a coyote to untrained eyes), but the body type and spiritual heritage of the individual werewolf probably has more influence on his wolf-form appearance than anything else.

A werewolf from Mexico can be made using the normal character-creation guidelines in Werewolf: The Forsaken.

The Awakened

Mexico's modern mages are almost exclusively foreigners. Even in the 500 years mages have had to entrench themselves in Mexican civilization, few have actually done so. More mages come to explore and dig up Mexico than to settle here.

Cities with enough resident mages to warrant the formation of a genuine Consilium are rare. Many of those that do attempt to organize end up with a single, loose clique of wizards than any kind of arcane government. More often, cabals operate like opposing gangs or business ventures, competing for the finite resources of ancient magical artifacts. Those cities with sizable mage populations are likely to be fiercely protective (or overprotective) of their arcane resources.

New mages certainly do Awaken in Mexico, but without a well developed magical society to absorb them, many fall victim to creatures of the Abyss or to agents of the Seers of the Throne before they truly understand the nature or extent of their powers. Life is terrifying for a Mexican mage, isolated in a hostile occult world. But it can also be exciting, because of the sheer volume of unexplored ruins and ancient sites hidden under the earth, off the Mexican coastlines and in the thick of the Yucatan that only spells can reach easily.

A mage from Mexico can be made using the normal character-creation guidelines in Mage: The Awakening.

Prometheans

The Created are a new addition to the shadow cultures of Mexico. Just how many there are and who has created them is still unknown. Vampires eager to know the nature of the monsters in their territory have attempted to investigate the created beings in several major cities, but even eye-witness accounts are often little help. Not only is it difficult to identify a Promethean, but it's difficult to understand what you're seeing when you do. Even if a vampire Prince could get his hands on a Promethean — or even manage to arrange a visit from one — rapidly spreading rumors would mutate and obscure the truth anyway.

A Promethean created in Mexico can be made using the normal character-creation guidelines in Promethean: The Created.

The Damned in Mexico

Modern Mexican vampires closely resemble the standard described in Vampire: The Requiem. With the colonization of Mexico by Spain, and the subsequent progressions of mortal culture over the past 500 years, the society of the Mexican Damned has come to look very much like that of American and European vampires. The neo-feudal structure of independent vampire Princes ruling over shadow societies in de facto city-states is the basis in Mexico as it is virtually every land where the Kindred dwell. This locally focused society was already in place when European vampires arrived in the 16th century. All the invading Invictus had to do was insinuate themselves into the local power structure, and the conquistadors and the Catholic Church were providing plenty of examples of how that might be done.

What sets the Kindred of Mexico apart from vampires of other lands is the unique culture clash occurring under the surface of the Danse Macabre. Sometimes this conflict cuts through the veneer of Kindred politics and turns bloody (some of the undead can still vividly recall the nights of the conquest), but it's always there to some extent, under the surface.

This culture clash manifests in clan and covenant relationships throughout Mexico. These issues color the way any Mexican vampire sees his neighbors, peers and enemies in the Danse Macabre. If you're going to create a vampire originating or operating in Mexico, you'll need to keep this in mind.

The Covenants

Despite what some loud-mouthed modern malcontents shout in their efforts to rally street-level vampires, the Kindred of Pre-Columbian Mexico had no real covenants of their own. At least, not as modern vampires would regard them. Mexica and Mayan vampires considered themselves to be a part of the mortal religions and states from which they were Embraced. The Kindred of Tenochtitlán would have considered themselves to be members of one covenant and the Kindred of Texcoco to be members of a different covenant, but neither city-state's vampires would've separated themselves from the mortal society they mirrored so closely by inventing a vampires-only church or political system.

In part, this is due to the small numbers of vampires thought to be awake at any one time in Aztec or Mayan lands. Smaller cities mean fewer vampires. It's been speculated by modern vampires who recall the ancient nights that less than a quarter of all known Aztec vampires were awake and active at any one time. A great many Damned must still lay buried beneath Mexico's pyramids and ancient cities, waiting to be set free by childer who were burnt to ash by the conquistadors a century after they went into torpor.

In modern Mexican domains, the Kindred covenants are as ubiquitous and varied as they are in any American city. Any generalization made for the whole of Mexico is sure to seem ridiculous to the vampires of some covenant. Even if these generalizations are proven wrong in the night-to-night existence of Kindred in many domains, they reveal something of how the Mexican Damned see themselves.

The Invictus and the Carthian Movement

Mexico's modern history has produced a large population of young, Carthian vampires still cruising on the momentum of revolutions that failed years, decades or centuries ago. The stereotype of the modern Mexican Carthian is practically a cartoon: the vehement, grandiose and disorganized Pancho Villa type with more passion than sense. The politics almost don't matter. Viva la revolucion! No matter what la revolucion is!

In practice, Mexican Carthians seek to break the line of Princes that stretch back to the conquistadors. As long as the land continues to be dominated by vampires who derive their power from Spanish conquest, Indian and mestizo Kindred will always be, on some level, a conquered people. It's time for a new era of independence.

The truth, of course, is more complicated. No city-by-city vampire census has ever been possible in Mexico (you can't just show up and poll a secret society of occulted monsters you've never met), but from the perspective of the modern, archetypal Invictus, very few cities still retain a line of rule from the conquest. Even those cities where the Invictus continue to maintain a controlling influence on Prince or Primogen (and there are many such cities), the vampires in power are often some "new" guard that has usurped rule within the last couple of centuries. But the stereotype of the Invictus lord as Spanish don continues to persist.

The Lancea Sanctum and the Circle of the Crone

On its face, the divide between the Circle of the Crone and the Lancea Sanctum is one of Indian versus European vampires. In truth, it is more of a conflict between Pre-Columbian and Post-conquest vampires. The Lancea Sanctum of Mexico has evolved alongside the mortal Catholic Church, from which most of its neonates are drawn. The Virgin Guadalupe is as much a part of the Sanctified faith as she is a part of Mexican Catholicism, for example. Though most of Mexico's devout European Kindred are members of the Lancea Sanctum, the bulk of the Lancea Sanctum's membership is actually made up of Indian and mestizo vampires Embraced within the past 450 years.

The Circle of the Crone is divided into two major factions in Mexico: the collection of miniature cults that is common of Acolytes in any city and the gradually expanding body of ancient vampires for whom the religion of the Mexica was their first, in life. The small cults of the Acolytes are largely imported neo-pagans from the United States or local attempts to re-imagine and redefine Aztec faiths. The acceptance of native traditions into the Sanctified church, however, means that many of the counter-culture quasi-Christian vampires who might be shunned by the Sanctified in stricter countries instead bolster the church's membership in Mexico.

The older faction of the Acolytes — only lumped into the Circle in its opposition to the Sanctified church — is slowly gaining new power. Ancient vampires, born prior to the arrival of the Spanish, are quietly converting neonates and ancilla throughout Mexico. They perform bloody rites of sacrifice in ruins crushed beneath Mexico City, slaying mortals and Sanctified ghouls alike, to feed and strengthen their gods. They seek out the resting places of ancient Damned, dig them up and feed them offerings of Vitae, gradually resurrecting the old ways. When these so-called True Aztecs (a name concocted by modern Sanctified) gather enough vampires, they will wage new Flower Wars against the Church of Longinus and finally win their centuries-old guerilla war against the Spanish conquistadors.

The Ordo Dracul

The Order of the Dragon is an active covenant in a few Mexican cities, especially in resort towns along the Pacific and Gulf coasts. In general, however, it is not a major cultural or political force among the Damned of Mexico. In many cities, the Ordo Dracul is not represented at all.

It's seen as a strictly European institution by most Mexican vampires. In some cities it is passionately reviled as an artifact of the French intrusion into Mexico's history in the era of Emperor Maximilian. Though the Ordo Dracul actually came to Mexico via Spanish vampires in the 18th century, it was a noisy handful of Austrian Dragons residing in Mexico City in 1866 who came to characterize the Order in popular thought. Rumor has it that those Austrian vampires were burned to Final Death following the death of Emperor Maximilian, though an Austrian Dragon in Veracruz insists that's not the case.

The popular image of the Ordo Dracul in Mexico is that of tuxedoed and mustachioed European bureaucrats decorated with medals, sitting in secret circles of plush chairs beneath lush palaces. They pass around prepubescent Indian children as if they were bottles of brandy, sipping off them and wiping their mouths with their hands. Money slips down through the cracks of Mexican society into their secret parlor, dripping like molten silver, which they use to gild their havens while indigenous vampires sleep in the dirt.

Local Dragons may take offense at this outdated stereotype, but at the same time that they take offense they must also wonder how the idea got out — and who has leaked out their symbolic feeding rituals.

The Clans

Before the Spanish conquest, the clans were how Mexica vampires identified and allied themselves. The clans were families and social castes. If a mortal was to be Embraced, he would traditionally be brought before the eldest vampires so that a suitable sire (and thus clan) could be selected for him. The vampire-to-be was then laid out across a temple altar and sliced across the throat, sacrificed, his blood sent into the earth to feed the gods. In exchange, his sire's vampire blood was fed to him, a gift back from the gods to the new vampire. Thus was the curse of the gods bestowed upon him — the need to feed on blood to continue his existence, just as it was for the gods.

Mayan vampires put just as much emphasis on one's clan, but didn't ritualize the Embrace like the Aztecs did. To the Maya, the relationship between sire and childe was more intimate, much as it is with modern Kindred. Mayan childer were as likely to be lovers as apprentices.

The historical roles of the clans among Mexica vampires have faded in most Kindred domains, but not all. The lingering memory of the nights before the conquest continue to inform tonight's notions of what it means to be a vampire, to be Ventrue or Daeva, to be Nosferatu, Gangrel or Mekhet in Mexico. While vampires typical of the clans as described in Vampire: The Requiem can be found throughout Mexico, so can examples of the old Mexica interpretations of the Blood. More common than either of these extremes, however, is the unique pastiche of old and new that defines the Mexican Requiem for so many vampires.

The Strange Mythology of the Clans

Though the precise origin of the clans is unclear (see Chapter One), certain mythological associations link the clans to the core symbols of the Mexican cosmos. The clans are thought to represent the five previous incarnations of the world — the five cycles of existence created thus far by the gods — as described in Aztec legends of the Five Suns. Each clan was, according to legend, created during a different cycle of existence. As supernatural beings whose nature is to defy death, however, the clans have persisted through the destruction of previous worlds into the current one. This is only possible because the clans feed on blood, just as the gods do, and use it to replenish their strength continuously.

At the same time that the clans draw some of their self-identity from Aztec mythology, they draw another vital component of their mythic significance from the Mayan concept of the Sacred Tree, which grows at the center of creation like the axis of the world. Its branches sprawl through the heavens, forming the dome of the world. Its roots twist through the Underworld, reaching down to the bottom of the universe. Mankind exists on the ground between these extremes, and vampires dwell were the humans are.

The Sacred Tree is the center point of the world, from which the five cardinal directions can be derived. The Tree itself is the fifth direction — the center. Each direction has a symbolic, mythical significance and each clan corresponds to a different cardinal direction.

The strange intermingling of these myths — the Aztec cycle of worlds and the Mayan tree at the center of them all — creates an odd tension for tonight's vampires. According to the Mayan myths that Mexican vampires use to define their roles in Kindred and mortal society, the five clans and the five directions are fully represented. But according to the Aztec myth of the Five Suns and the cyclical destruction and replacement of the physical world, a new clan is created whenever the Earth is recreated. If the end of the current world is drawing near (as every generation always believes), then what role will a new clan play in the directional scheme of the Sacred Tree? Will a new clan replace one of the existing five or will the next world somehow expand in some new direction, exemplified by a new breed of undead monster?

Looking Through the Clans

As the only uniquely vampiric structure in vampire society during the nights of the Aztecs, the clans serve as a lens into the worldview and Danse Macabre of an age that is all but vanished. Regardless of which clan you choose to play, read them all. Hidden truths about Mexico's Damned, both tonight and in centuries past, lay within the clans. The old ways may have faded — may even be lost — but they still inform the ways that the World of Darkness feels tonight. Even if your Mexica Succubus' or Mayan Shadow's Requiem is modern and new, ancient bloodstains color his insides. He can never be fully free of what once was.

Daeva

When the conquistadors arrived in the New World, the Daeva were the priest-kings of the Mexica Damned. With the Ventrue and their supernatural predilection for dominance long-since vanished from the land, the Daeva led through instigation and implication. While European Ventrue were lording over their subjects, Mexica Daeva were insighting their followers to action. While Ventrue Princes were solidifying their power over Europe in the Middle Ages through the careful arrangement of cold laws, Daeva were cultivating loyal city-states in Mexico by raising and channeling the passions of the people.

The Daeva of the Aztecs were essential and glorified, like priests, but they were also rare and fearsome, like kings. Tonight's swollen ranks of Mexica and European Daeva are eyeballed (or spit on) by cautious elder Succubi as the illegitimate children of kings who've been fucking commoners during their exile. The Daeva, for all their stylish swagger and supernatural grace, have lost their sheen. Once they were ambassadors to the gods and counselors to kings. Tonight they are petty Don Juans and wannabe pop stars.

But a few untarnished lines of Daeva blood remain. A handful of powerful Aztec Incubi have returned to the world from their deathly sleep since Tenochtitlán fell, and they have Embraced pious and gallant new heirs to restore some prestige to the rule of the Aztecs-in-exile.

Mexica Daeva with an appreciation for the old ways should strive to remind their undead kin of this, say the elders: "Our cities have been taken but we have not. The Mexica remain, plainly. And we remain as grand emperors despite our lack of palaces. The invaders should not forget this."

The rulers of the Aztecs were called tlatoani, a Nahuatl word meaning "speaker for" but often regarded simply as the Mexica equivalent of emperor. The tlatoani, from Tenoch (the founder of Tenochtitlán, which now lies underneath Mexico City) to Moctezuma (the Aztec leader who fell to Cortés), were voted to their positions by the aristocracy of the Aztecs. Each had the religious authority of a pope and the temporal power of a president.

The Daeva were thought of as the familial pool from which the vampire tlatoani should be drawn. The supreme Daeva would then hold power that was a shadowy reflection of the mortal emperor's — as indistinct but solid as a temple in the dark. The vampire speaker was seen to be a lesser figure than the mortal tlatoani, however. When a living speaker died, the sitting Daeva's power came up for vote again.

In the strange, hybrid mythology of the Mexican Damned, the Daeva were regarded as the central clan, positioned at the center point of the Sacred Tree, which vampires seem to have inherited from the Maya. This reflects the notion that the Daeva — supposedly the clan created in the newest incarnation of the world — are the emotional heart of vampire society, most in touch with the mortal humans for whom the world was created. The color of the Daeva is green, from which they derive their Nahuatl nickname, Xoxocti.

Nickname: Seductoras, Los Magnificos. Also called tlatoani or Speakers.

Covenant: Tonight, the Daeva have slipped into every major covenant in the land. The stereotype of Indian Daeva automatically belonging to revolutionary Carthian movements or Aztec-descended Acolyte sects is both mildly offensive and based on truth. Vampires descended from Mexica Daeva sires can theoretically claim to be the heirs to Aztec vampire-kings, and this leads many of them to participate in covenants that respect their power (or at least celebrate their cultural significance).

Of course, the original power structure of Mexica vampires much more closely resembled the Invictus than the Carthian Movement, and this detail isn't lost on so many Daeva. The Invictus of many modern cities have adapted to welcome and support the political power of many indigenous Daeva — few living humans know that the nighttime world of their local cities are governed by thousand-year-old Aztec priests. Still, the popular notion among younger Kindred is that Mexica Daeva stick with the Carthians to overthrow "the Spanish Invictus," even though the modern Invictus in many cities are no more Spanish than they are Roman.

Few Aztec Daeva (meaning Mexica Daeva old enough to recall the nights of the so-called Aztec Empire) are genuine members of the Lancea Sanctum, but because of the vampire church's local adaptation to Mexican culture, neither are as many Daeva at war with the church as rumors might suggest. If anything, Aztec Daeva seek to turn the Sanctified establishment into just one fiber in the culture of Mexico's Damned, much as the conquistadors twisted Nahua culture to appease (and subjugate) local mortals. So, yes, a great many Aztec Daeva hold some level of token membership in the Circle of the Crone — but that covenant is often too splintered for the tastes of ancient Aztecs. The oldest Daeva consider themselves loyal priests to the Aztec cosmos above all else. Everything else is politics.

Appearance: Indigenous Daeva, like their European cousins, are typically drawn from the most charismatic mortals — living men and women capable of attracting a Succubus's attention. Many modern Mexican Daeva do tend towards traditional Mexican clothing from the colonial era: bright colors, woven fabrics and richly patterned clothes. European-descended Succubi who reside in Mexico, and Daeva Embraced in recent nights, are likely to favor modern European fashion and the sexiest current cuts drawing attention in tonight's discothéques. As in nights past, Daeva rule through magnetism, by setting trends and being coveted, not through rigid oversight.

Havens: Indigenous Daeva might dwell in stucco haciendas or mansions painted with classic Mexican murals. Some sleep in hidden chambers in Mexico City penthouses while others lay in a pile with their whores in the back of Tijuana brothels. Though some decorate their havens with relics and artifacts of the old nights, few are willing to sleep far enough from modern life to inhabit catacombs or ruins. Modern Daeva are building new things that honor the old ways, not hiding in rubble. Whether he's a thousand-years old or fifty, tonight's Daeva uses the magnificence of the ancient world and the modern in new ways to reclaim the passionate status and love from his people that Aztec vampires enjoyed long ago.

Background: The greatest difference between the ancient Mexica Daeva and the modern is the source of their progeny. Where the Mexica Succubi of old were drawn from the noble piousness of Aztec priests and holy folk, modern Daeva are pulled from the ranks of the most fashionable peacocks at the discotheque. Ancient or modern — Mexica, mestizo or European — the Daeva are still Daeva, lead by their hearts and their libidos. The glorious regalia of the ancient world's Aztec priests are all but gone, and many of tonight's Daeva learn in life to regard Indians as remote fringe folk. The true cutting edge of the world's social elite are always on the glittering, sharpened face of the city where new things are being made, tried and shown off. No matter what Mexica vampires do to animate the corpses of Aztec tradition, as the years go on the old ways fall further behind — this is the inescapable quandary of the Nahua vampire and it is no better represented than in the torn feelings of the Daeva.

So with every new Daeva Embraced the Nahua vampires become more like the modern mixed-blood pastiche and the Mexica ways become more diluted. So the Daeva always struggle with themselves over chasing what they want and being what they are.

Character Creation: Like European Daeva, Social Attributes and Skills are typically primary, for the sake of impressing and leading followers. Traditional Aztec Daeva are likely to favor Mental Attributes and Skills such as Academics and Occult over Physical prowess (which was historically seen as the purview of the Gangrel). Specialties focusing on religion are essential choices for Daeva who seek to fulfill the roles of their forebears. Re-styled Crúac rituals can be used to invoke the ancient magic of Aztec priests, whether honestly or as pro-Mexica propaganda.

Clan Disciplines: Celerity, Majesty, Vigor

Organization: Mexica Daeva traditionally organized into groups based on religious needs. The eldest, most prominent Daeva in the city-state would educate and direct all those beneath him, whether they were his own young childer or aged vampire-priests in their own right. This traditional arrangement is strictly enforced in only a few cities in modern Mexico, often regardless of how other local vampires regard their own Prisci. More often, tonight, the Daeva move in the same social currents as the local vampire (and mortal) culture — childer disobey their sires, wander off on their own hedonistic paths and stumble through their shamelessly secular Requiems in pursuit of the next high, the next lay, the next Vitae and little else.

Bloodlines: Platina (a small bloodline of wealthy silver barons who draw their members from a tithe of first-born sons from a single mortal family), Maxtla (Tlacopán-descended governor-priests), Malintzin (the cursed descendents of Dona Mariña), Murales (Aztec-styled communists and Diego Rivera wannabes who mystically coerce mortals through public art)

Concepts: Aztec priest, border-town prostitute, Diego-Rivera wannabe, discotheque predator, el Mariachi, Frida-Kalho wannabe, Jaguar warrior, Mexica king, porn recruiter, resort-town seductress, Soap-opera actor.

Stereotypes

Gangrel: Native or European, they have an understanding of the land we'll never fully appreciate.

Mekhet: Their blood, more than any other, is sure to blend with Spanish Vitae. Shadows are always the same.

Nosferatu: When the childer of Xolotl return, the Nosferatu will see what monsters are.

Ventrue: They say they're lords, but they're slaves to the madness of their cattle the same as us.

• • •

Lupines: Our allies in the dark. The cousins we love and hate.

Mages: Meddlesome, power-hungry troublemakers.

Mortals: Short-sighted and fragile, but the world's theirs, not ours.

Gangrel

The Gangrel stalk through the dark, sometimes prowling on all fours, sometimes dashing like pumas after prey. Since the earliest nights they have been the vampires in the dirt, pitting claws against bone and fangs against flesh without fear of man or animal. While Mexica sorcerers were said to be able to change their bodies by donning the skins of animals, the Gangrel are believed to change their skins by touching the animals within themselves.

In the nights of the Aztecs, the Gangrel were praised and prized as warriors. They fought against rival vampire groups in single combat, battling naked in the ball-court at night when the stands were filled only with the black shapes of vampires with glittering eyes. Their weapons were their teeth, their hands and their savage instincts. Stories are still told about Gangrel nobly facing werewolves they knew they could not defeat, for the sake of demonstrating the fearlessness of their people and their honorable willingness to fulfill the promises of their tlatoani, who agreed to give the Uratha annual sacrifices worth fighting for.

In this way, in the sense that they fulfilled the celebrated Aztec role of the warrior selected through combat for the honor of delivery to the gods through ritual sacrifice, the Gangrel were truly the warrior caste of the Mexica's undead people. The Gangrel took pride in enduring, in surviving against great odds — many still do. Unlike their undead cousins, who find meaning in damnation by accumulating knowledge or followers through eternity, the Gangrel of the Mexica and the Maya alike understood that Final Death was inevitable. The glorious power of the undead, then, was the ability to endure that much longer than a mortal body would allow. Survival was worthy of celebration. Every night past the length of a normal life was a small victory. Every foe outlasted, every challenge overcome, is one more than a mundane life would have been able to bear. It was the proud thrill of going beyond human limits that gave the Gangrel their might — and it still is.

Yet, practically speaking, most Gangrel weren't warriors. They were enforcers, more like police than soldiers. A rare, valuable Gangrel would be chosen to participate in ritual combat; most others were called upon to track or intimidate vampires at the edge of society. Others upheld the security of the Masquerade by murdering mortals who learned too much. Some were sent to put pressure on werewolf packs that have wandered outside their agreed-upon turf. These are what most Gangrel are tasked with tonight, half a millennium later, too.

Don't mistake ritual combat for theatrics, however. The outcome of ritual combat was not always a foregone conclusions. Slaves won on the battlefield sometimes earned their freedom by fighting off their enemy's greatest combatants. Sacred parts of a cherished combatant might be sent back to his people, so that both cities could gift his blood to the gods and gain their prestige. Whether the outcome is determined already or not or sort of beside the point to a Mexica Gangrel. What matters is how you act in the moment… and if you survive to see more moments.

The Gangrel clan is associated with the South, which puts them at the right hand of the Sun, where any king would keep his sword. Some of this southern connection may also come from the legends (potentially true) that some city-states south of the Aztec lands, in what would now be Central America, were actually controlled by Gangrel leaders. The sacred color of the Gangrel is yellow (like the Sun), from which they derive their Nahuatl nickname, Costi, and a reputation for fearless even in the face of unstoppable enemies (like the Sun).

According to Aztec vampire myths, the Gangrel were the clan created in the third incarnation of the world, about halfway removed from the Underworld and the animals of the earth, before they were inspired (some say domesticated) by the Daeva.

Nickname: Feroz, Salvaje

Covenant: Although Gangrel have a reputation throughout Mexico for doing their own thing and wandering at the edges of Kindred society, it seems that most so-called Savages don't count themselves among the unaligned. The idea of the Gangrel as the wanderer on the fringe more likely comes from the clan's hesitance to sink too deeply into any Kindred institution larger than their immediate experience. A Mexican Gangrel is much more likely to pursue and accept status in the hierarchy of the local domain than in any larger body that might make assumptions about his loyalties — like a vampire church or political party that assumes anyone with the same badge is an ally. Gangrel are loyal to Princes more often than Bishops, the Priscus rather than the Prefect. A Gangrel may be an essential part of a covenant and a loyal representative of its philosophies, but if she's smart she stays near the door so she can dash out when the fires start. You say this makes the Gangrel a traitor and a coward, but she says she's the one who'll bring blood back to your torpid corpse and resurrect you.

Appearance: The stereotype of Mexican Gangrel comes in two broad varieties: the Danny Trejo-style bad-ass with the sun-worn looks and dark, unknowable eyes or the gap-toothed rural poor with bare feet and strong arms. As with most stereotypes, the truth of the Gangrel runs the gamut.

Havens: Since the ancient nights of the Aztecs, the Gangrel have considered themselves bound to the land. A Mexica Gangrel doesn't consider herself anchored to one site, like a house, but to a territory, like a city or a stretch of road. For some Gangrel, this leads to low-rent Requiems spent in rusted mobile homes or big-rig trailers. For the rest, this means sleeping in dirt or sand. Look for wild dogs and odd, stand-alone ruins like a stone head or a carved stella in the middle of an empty lot or burned-out building. That's where the Gangrel are.

Background: Tonight's Aztec and Mayan Gangrel are not so unlike Savages anywhere in the world. Mexican Gangrel are often drawn from the poorest ranks of mortals, but those who are self-sufficient, survivors, capable of finding contentment, comfort and food through simple gaul and ingenuity. Still, the odds are best that mortals who may be found alone in the night, far from the nighttime lights of discos and dance floors, are most likely to be Embraced into the Gangrel clan: truck drivers, caballeros, hikers and divers, farmers and even factory workers and other urban essentials who dwell outside the sight of their richer neighbors.

Character Creation: Protean is essential to a Gangrel's survival, and they know it. Traditional Mexica culture associates the Savages with Physical Attributes and Skills, but Mayan Gangrel are as likely to be focused Social traits. All across Mexico, from the ancient nights to the present, Gangrel have also played the role of intelligence gatherers and envoys in the wild, ambassadors to jaguars and

werewolves. Modern Gangrel often fill similar roles, but with more of an emphasis on Resilience and Protean than Animalism. There are fewer wild lands to watch, after all, and the modern vampire's greatest worry isn't the loss of human cattle to animal predators or illness, but the loss of vampires to mortals, mages — and other vampires.

Clan Disciplines: Animalism, Protean, Resilience

Organization: Historically, Mexica and Mayan Gangrel formed into groups based on their skills and contacts and blood. They were as much a covenant of warriors and scouts as a clan. Tonight, Gangrel often still stick with their own, forming into coteries of vampiric relatives or feudal cohorts. They ride through the night in pick-up trucks, on motorcycles or on pounding, blood-fueled feet. They share the nasty camaraderie of soldiers and the quiet familiarity of brothers. They don't look at each other when they talk, they look out at the nighttime world, watchful and wary… but calm. They know the night is dangerous, and they know they're not invincible, but nothing is going to take them out or hurt their domain and not get scarred or killed in the process.

Bloodlines: Los Bucólicos (a bloodline of violent Hounds drawn from fatally wounded gangsters from the international Los Bucólicos gang), Chichimeca Muertes (trace survivors of a northern Mexican nomadic peoples said to have been "the dogs to werewolves"), Dead Wolves (a werewolf-linked bloodline supposedly descended from a would-be werewolf)

Concepts: Archaeological looter, Aztec warrior, caballero, drug-runner, envoy to the Uratha, farmer, homeless predator, human smuggler, predator of wilderness tourists, truck driver.

Stereotypes

Daeva: Ours are priests. Theirs are whores. They all stick their hearts where they don't belong.

Mekhet: Untrustworthy and invaluable, no matter where they come from.

Nosferatu: Let them roam the earth, so long as they're on our side.

Ventrue: They posture like Daeva but call it "thinking."

• • •

Lupines: Distant cousins.

Mages: Keep them down here where we can reach them.

Mortals: If you don't take them seriously, you're a terrible hunter.

Mekhet

They were sorcerers, spies and scholars, the detectives of the fire-lit Pre-Columbian world. They read men's souls, moved like smoke through the dark and stood unseen in the presence of living kings. As they saw it, the Masquerade was the cunning veil of secrecy that kept the living from seeing the undead, and they were the secret weapons that allowed the undead to look in on the living.

The Mekhet of the ancient nights were, by most accounts, selfish and cowardly master strategists who surrounded themselves in a shroud of lies and secrecy to make their methods seem more arcane and their schemes more delicately designed than they were. In effect, it seems that the Mekhet had created a kind of second Masquerade between themselves and their Gangrel and Daeva cousins. They described themselves as magicians, assassins and seers — and in truth they were all of those things — but their methods were probably no different than those known to tonight's Shadows. Legends claim that the Mekhet of the Aztecs knew spells and spirits that have since been lost, that they knew secret ways to capture the powers of werewolves and wizards in their own blood, but all of that is probably just echoing propaganda.

What is known is that Mexica Shadows kept certain blood-magic rituals hidden within their own ranks for centuries, even though some of these sanguinary spells would have been the proper purview of the Daeva back in those nights. Tonight, many of these rituals are commonly known as variations of Crúac's power, but of course stories persist that certain circles of Aztec Mekhet have been keeping rituals to themselves for a thousand years. Certainly some of the old rituals the Mekhet knew must have lost during the fiery nights of the Conquest — any Shadow in torpor since before the arrival of the Spanish might very well know rituals or Devotions otherwise lost to modern vampires.

But whether the Mekhet truly are keeping rituals secret from the rest of Kindred society is just an example of the core worldview of Mexican Mekhet. The point of legends about ancient magic and stolen mystic powers is that no vampire can ever be sure of anything she thinks she knows about las Sambras.

Mexica Shadows often formed coteries, more like covens, composed exclusively of their own kind. Though they were loyal to their mortal and undead masters, they seem to have maintained the integrity of vampire society the way that a general maintains the wall that surrounds his keep. The Mekhet of the Aztecs did not want any harm to come to the Gangrel and the Daeva who nobly exemplified vampire society, but neither did they identify very closely with them. The Mekhet thought of themselves, to some degree, as a separate people dwelling together with the Daeva and Gangrel for mutual protection.

Mayan Shadows, on the other hand, were better integrated with the other two clans, but did not associate much with their own kind. Mayan Mekhet were largely independent and typically isolated. Sire-childer pair seem to have been common, but domains with more than one or two Mekhet typically divided themselves into cells of individual or paired Shadows.

In the past two centuries, some Kindred have speculated that the Mekhet were not originally a Mexica breed of vampire, that perhaps their clan descended from the Maya or (in keeping with the symbolism of the Sacred Tree) some precursor civilization to the Aztecs, such as the Toltecs. Some modern Mekhet have latched onto the grandiose idea that the Mekhet of Mexico descend from vampires the Mexica found at Teotihuacán — thus the Mekhet were already present in the Valley of Mexico when the Aztecs arrived from Aztlán. Little if any evidence has appeared to support this claim, but several Mekhet in Mexico City insist the evidence exists and is being kept secret and safe by the city's Shadows.

The Mekhet are believed to be the clan created during the second incarnation of the world, as they are not as earthly as the Gangrel but not as unearthly as the Xolotli (Nosferatu). The Mekhet are clearly still beings of the Underworld, but they have also been graced with remarkable insight, suggesting that the gods favored them over the Xolotli.

The sacred color of the Mekhet is black (Pisti, in Nahuatl) and they are associated with the West — the direction of the Underworld.

Nickname: Enscombreceros, Las Sambras, Las Fantasmas

Covenant: As the archivists, spies and architects of the undead Aztecs, the Mekhet were like a covenant of their own. They kept tabs on the kine, kept count on the coffers and kept their eyes on all their supposed allies. Tonight, the Mekhet can be found in every covenant in Mexico. European Mekhet get into everything, falling like their namesake shadows into every crack, behind every door, as soon as the lights go out. Indigenous Mekhet are commonly found in the Circle of the Crone, acting as scholars and warlocks, or in the Invictus, serving as bookkeepers and strategists. In the eyes of even ancient Mexica vampires, however, the opportunistic Mekhet are the Kindred who have most abandoned the old ways and adapted to the modern night. This is good for the Mekhet, because Shadows like the security that comes with being important. This is good for Aztec vampires, because it means Aztec spies have gotten inside the Spanish ranks.

Appearance: Like Mekhet in other countries, Mexican Shadows are difficult to categorize by their looks. Indigenous Mekhet sometimes express themselves through symbolic jewelry and patterned ponchos or dresses to mark themselves as witch-doctors or medicine men, thus blending into the cultural background of mysticism that's all around them. They present themselves as seers, wise women and fortune-tellers to locals and tourists alike. Despite the jokes that many modern vampires make, these aren't the most common Mexican Mekhet. The truth is that a great many indigenous Mexican Mekhet go unseen, unnoticed by vampires from Laredo to Belize. They are more common — and much closer — than any vampire suspects.

Havens: As with European Mekhet, the Shadows of the Mexica change their priorities as they age. Younger Mekhet, regardless of their ethnic heritage, tend towards havens in lively, active locations. Often these neonate Shadows dwell in tiny but secure holes in the heart of Mexico's most desirable urban areas. Eventually, however, as a Mekhet accumulates more and more precious information, he gets more likely to withdraw from mortal society to a location where he can still monitor the Danse Macabre but can also protect his most valuable asset — himself. These Mekhet sacrifice location for size and retreat to larger, labyrinthine havens on the edge of urban areas, where they can see their enemies coming.

Background: The Mekhet are the slowest of the Mexica clans to reproduce. Whereas the Daeva Embrace through passion, intuition and naked lust, the Mekhet scrutinize, research and study a potential childer for months or years. Whereas the Gangrel curse siblings and compadres to form tougher, more formidable groups of Savages, the Mekhet cultivate resources they can utilize, investing in childer that can earn the Mekhet security and intelligence for decades thereafter. In theory, this means that the common thread running through the background of Mexican Mekhet is quality, capability or strategic value. In practice, this means new Mekhet come in one of two broad categories: those intended for short-term use and those invited for long-term participation. But a Mexican Requiem is unpredictable, and some Mekhet end up being worth something very different than expected.

Character Creation: Traditionally, it is the place of the Mexica Mekhet to look after the city's records and information. Thus, Mental Attributes and Skills are usually important for Mexican Shadows. In the modern night, Mekhet come in all flavors. Shadow assassins often rely on Physical Skills and Social Attributes. Mekhet spies pair Mental Attributes and Social Skills. As information-gatherers, Auspex is plainly valuable, but so are Contacts and Allies. A Herd or a Retainer is good for controlling one's environment (variables make plans murky) and for auditioning potential new assets. No matter what his age or ethnicity, a Mekhet is likely to prize the Haven Security Merit.

Clan Disciplines: Auspex, Celerity, Obfuscate.

Organization: Like all their Aztec kin, Mexica Mekhet honor their elders through custom and deference. A Mekhet Priscus is typically regarded as the most savvy Shadow, well suited to survival in a difficult world. A Mekhet elder who is plainly upstaged by one younger is ashamed, but so is the Shadow who upstaged him. Outside of this polite hierarchy of age, the Mekhet of Mexico are rumored, in some cities, to maintain a secret society, hidden even from their fellow Mexica vampires. This society meets monthly, on the darkest nights, often underground and usually protected by hybrid powers of Auspex and Obfuscate. The aim of these meetings seems not to be the overthrow or betrayal of any covenant or Prince (the vampires who attend these meetings aren't so trusting to participate in such grandiose plots with public enemies just because they share common blood), but the preservation and empowerment of the Mekhet clan in the gloom of a perilous nation. The Mekhet are not about to slip away like the ancient Nosferatu and Ventrue clans did in Mexico.

Bloodlines: Cuiatl (a slippery brotherhood of poisoners), Jade Skirts (Aztec funerary priestesses and rainmakers), Yoal (an ancient lineage of Nahua warlocks said to have power over shadows and nocturnal snakes)

Concepts: Archaeologist of vampire lore, black-market antiquities dealer, Catholic priest, drug designer, envoy to the Awakened, keeper of Aztec codices, professional kidnapper, servant of the old gods, village shaman.

Stereotypes

Daeva: Let them feel and sing and dance all night, provided they don't stop listening to us.

Gangrel: Admirable in all the ways we don't need to be.

Nosferatu: Our rivals in the night. Let them know fear themselves.

Ventrue: So heavy-handed. Why rule when you can control?

• • •

Lupines: Let them stand between us and what's worse, and let us have their backs.

Mages: If only.

Mortals: The world was made for them, but it will be our fault if it comes crashing down.

Nosferatu

They were the earliest of the Damned, more monsters than men. Shepherds of the dead who feasted on their own flock, they wandered the road between the living world and the Underworld, never truly in either. They are the childer of the Mexica psychopomp, Xolotl, half alive and half dead, immortal only in the sense that even their destruction will not grant them true death. The Xolotli, the cursed childer of Xolotl, are barred from Mictlan, the realm of the afterlife.

The legends of the Xolotli led many European Kindred to the conclusion that these supposedly extinct vampires were, in fact, the Nosferatu of Pre-Columbian Mexico. The appearance of the Nosferatu in Mesoamerica cinched it. Some vampires will tell you that when the Nosferatu first stepped onto Mexican dirt, the local vampires knew the Xolotli were back.

Xolotl was the grim reaper of the Aztecs, twin brother to the revered Quetzalcoatl, and the king of the Underworld. When the sun disappeared for the night, Xolotl was its escort through the darkness. The Xolotli, it is said, were his adopted sons, whom he found wandering on the path between life and death. They were meant to watch over the nighttime while Xolotl guarded the sun, but being unable to escape the tinge of death that haunted them, they spread illness and death as they collected blood for the Underworld. Eventually they were exiled from their service to Xolotl for being too monstrous and inhumane. Striving to ape (or mock) their godly father figure, the childer of Xolotl adopted their own childer from the ranks of the living, and so the curse of undeath began to spread by the Embrace.

In the legends of Aztec and Mayan vampires, the childer of Xolotl were thought of as fanciful horror stories — tales of monsters so horridly cursed that they could no longer dwell near the living. Truly, the tales of the Xolotli suggest vampires much more gruesome and sinister than the average Nosferatu, but the vampires of Mexico were quite sure that when they first met Europe's Haunts, they were meeting monsters of the same breed as the Xolotli. Some of tonight's vampires suppose that the Xolotli were a Nosferatu bloodline that wholly replaced its parent clan in the land before becoming extinct and, thus, taking the local Nosferatu clan with it.

One night, the truth may be known. Mayan vampires insist that some Xolotli still sleep beneath the earth at old religious sites or in the depths of black-watered cenotes. It's only a matter of time before one of these vampires awakes and collides with the modern Danse Macabre.

Meanwhile, Aztec vampires at the time of the Conquest believed that Xolotli could still be found in the distant north, possibly in Aztlán, the ancestral home of the Mexica. Nosferatu vampires were present among the Native American tribes of the Pacific Northwest around that time, but nothing suggests any connection between the Pacific Northwest and Aztlán, so this detail is inconclusive.

The story of the extinction of the Xolotli is wildly inconsistent. In some Mayan domains, the Xolotli are said to have vanished into the earth all together, where they are now trapped in Xibalba, the Underworld. Other Mayan stories claim a disease spread through the Xolotli that rendered them unable to gain power from mortal blood, and so they destroyed themselves in a war for the finite amount of blood they all possessed — only the handful of sleeping Xolotli represent the victors or the survivors, depending on your point of view. One Aztec legend, popular in the Valley of Mexico, claims that the Xolotli destroyed each other in a war of succession, to see who would replace Xolotl in the next incarnation of the world. An alternate version of this story has the Xolotli hunted to extinction by werewolves, which sparks the Mexica truce with the Uratha to spare other vampires in exchange for honoring the work of the Forsaken.

Whatever the disparities in the stories, they share a certain timeline. In almost every version of the Xolotli legend, these vampires predate every other clan, but die out early in the life of the current world, about the time that Teotihuacán and the Toltecs seem to collapse. Thus it's possible that the Nosferatu of the New World were the familial clan of the Toltecs, and that the dissolution of Toltec civilization caused the Xolotli their Requiems.

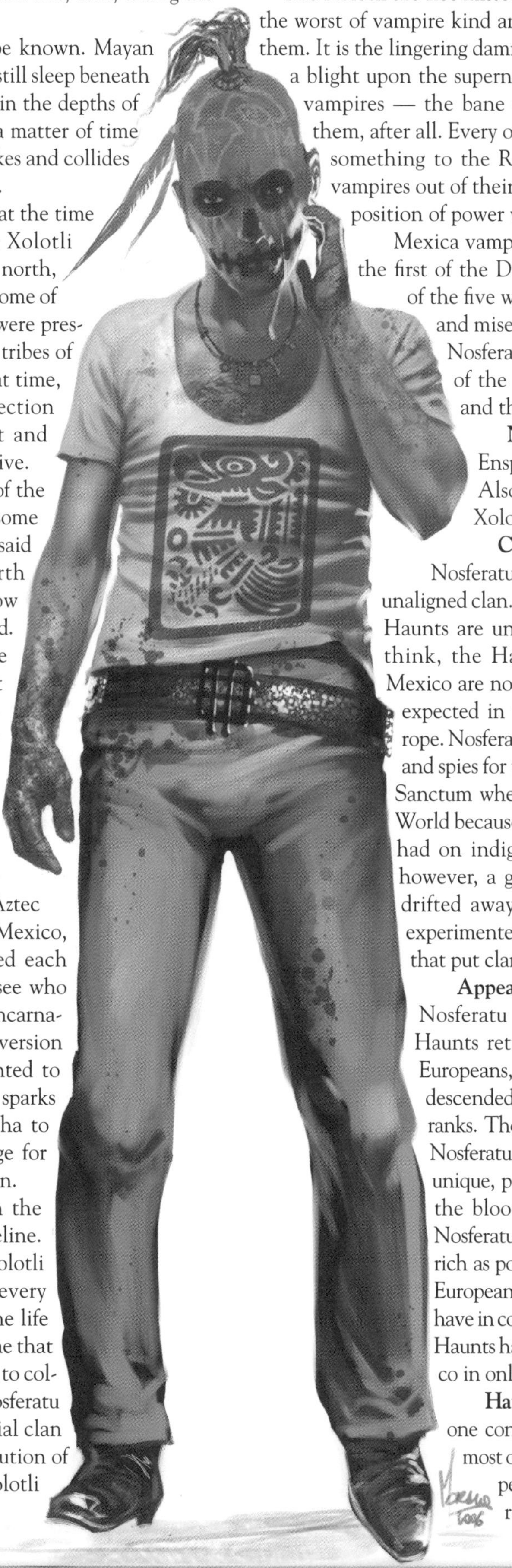

The Xolotli are not missed, however. They represent the worst of vampire kind and the curse that surrounds them. It is the lingering damnation of the Xolotli that is a blight upon the supernatural existence of modern vampires — the bane of sunlight was meant for them, after all. Every other clan has since brought something to the Requiem to gradually bring vampires out of their cursed suffering and into a position of power without damnation.

Mexica vampires consider the Nosferatu the first of the Damned, created in the first of the five worlds through misfortunate and misery. On the Sacred Tree, the Nosferatu are assigned the direction of the ancestral dead, the North, and the color white (Ichcati).

Nickname: el Extinguido, el Enspectros, el Perdido Muertes. Also: Xolotli or the childer of Xolotl.

Covenant: In Mexico, the Nosferatu are often seen as the great unaligned clan. Though not nearly as many Haunts are unaligned as many vampires think, the Haunts who have come to Mexico are not the ever-present monsters expected in the United States and Europe. Nosferatu became de facto enforcers and spies for the Invictus and the Lancea Sanctum when they arrived in the New World because of the fearsome effect they had on indigenous vampires. Tonight, however, a great many Nosferatu have drifted away from the covenants and experimented with cliques and coteries that put clan ahead of covenant.

Appearance: Tonight's Mexican Nosferatu are an odd hybrid. Since Haunts returned to Mexico with the Europeans, many Aztec- and Mayan-descended mortals have joined their ranks. The visual clue that marks the Nosferatu of Mexico is, thus, only the unique, personal features that reveals the blood of any Haunt. Mexican Nosferatu tonight are as likely to be rich as poor, urban as rural, Indian as European. What tonight's Nosferatu have in common, is their youth — new Haunts have been Embraced in Mexico in only the last few centuries.

Havens: Privacy is the number one concern for the Nosferatu, and most often privacy comes at the expense of proximity. Nosferatu reside where mortals won't, whether it's because of filth, disease, disgust or fear. As with Nosferatu elsewhere in the world, this often means forgotten urban pits and tunnels, ossuaries or catacombs, empty water-towers or derelict buildings. In the past two hundred years, a trend has arisen among the Nosferatu to find havens in Mexica and Mayan ruins, as a means of insinuating themselves into Aztec culture. Several coteries of Nosferatu have taken to dwelling in the isolated caves of old cenotés not far from Mexican cities.

Background: It is a strange fact of Kindred existence that the Nosferatu are considered European even though they may Embrace childer from the ranks of Mexica mortals, just as any other clan might. No custom exists to help a Mexica Nosferatu integrate into Kindred society — hateful indigenous elders will hate or pity him as a victim of Nosferatu spite while European racists will see only a non-white Haunt. Even away from the hate that comes from elders' remembrance of the Conquest, indigenous Nosferatu are unlikely to find a place among the clan-centered Mexica Kindred without proving themselves over many years. Meanwhile, some colonial Nosferatu strive to fulfill ancient Mayan or Aztec prophecies by "resurrecting" the extinct Indian Haunts by Embracing Nahua mortals. To date, all these mixed-blood vampires seem like just more mestizo Kindred, childer of colonial rape, rather than any boldly returned breed of monster.

Character Creation: A valuable Nosferatu has Attributes and Skills that let him maximize his value to whatever covenant, faction or Prince that governs his fate. Many Nosferatu are not so lucky as to be valuable. Because so many colonial Haunts damned their childer to the Requiem out of spite or malice, many modern Nosferatu struggle to find a place where their Skills can be put to good use. Some lovely mortals are given Nosferatu blood as a kind of sick punishment, cutting the benefits of their Social Attributes with the Nosferatu curse.

Clan Disciplines: Nightmare, Obfuscate, Vigor

Organization: Nosferatu that would scheme against one another in other countries might band together in Mexico. The common hell of being outcast by fellow Indian vampires drives indigenous Nosferatu to form coteries together for the sake of their own survival. In practice, these coteries often seem to be organized by age, but in truth the Nosferatu respect power above all else — it's just that elder Haunts are usually more powerful than their younger peers. Though these adopted "families" of Nosferatu are by no means common enough to warrant recognition by Mexica clans or colonial Kindred as anything other than miscellanea, the time may come when these vampires become numerous and organized enough to be taken seriously as a new culture of Nosferatu. When that night comes, the Mexica will have to seriously consider if these monsters represent the return of the extinct Xolotli.

Bloodlines: Heroinómana (heroin-addicted Haunts whose blood offers a unique and horrific high), Mezquinos (a family of faceless, hideous mestizos who stalk Mexico City's slums), Pit-Haunts (a scattered flock of bone-eaters that haunt cenotes and ruins)

Concepts: Beast of the cenote, drug dealer, haunter of Mayan ruins, hitman, homeless predator, kidnapper, tourist-eating border-town predator.

Stereotypes

Daeva: Control others through the gut rather than the brain? Not so different, are they?

Gangrel: It seems the farther you get from downtown, the farther they get from civilization.

Mekhet: Wherever you go, shadows are the same.

Ventrue: Either side can give the speeches, if it keeps them busy.

• • •

Lupines: This fucking close to living like dogs.

Mages: I don't want to know what they're hiding, but I don't want them knowing it, either.

Mortals: They're everywhere, unless we say otherwise. Fear is the ultimate fence.

Ventrue

Alien kings from a distant land, foreign invaders with an insatiable thirst nor for gold but for blood, the Ventrue are the iconic tyrants of Mexico. They symbolize the Spanish Conquest and embody the greed that drove so many living men and so many hungry corpses to ravage the lands of the New World. To some, they are glorious knights and dons whose ingenuity, guile and courage led them to victory and power. To others, they are monstrous oppressive murderers who ruined lives and obliterated irreplaceable monuments in the selfish, short-sighted pursuit of fleeting, earthly power.

Though Mexica and Mayan Ventrue do exist, the clan is seen as a distinctly European breed. Indian mortals who are Embraced into the Ventrue family are collaborators, tools or victims. Even while new generations of vampires learn to make their peace with the European covenants and the childer of those Kindred who burned Tenochtitlán, the Ventrue clan remains, on some level, stained by centuries of soot and blood. It quickly became the target of all Mexico's undead ire and the clan may never be dug out of the hate and bile that have been heaped on it for five hundred years.

Tonight, the Ventrue are a clan splintered by the pressure of its status against its self-image. Though a great many Ventrue have no fear of being hated as long as they are obeyed, newer Ventrue must face the realization that there may be no place for new, loathed rulers in Mexico. Established conquistador-kings have fortified their positions in the cultural and political landscapes of many cities, but these encrusted rulers not only keep subject Kindred in place, they block the path to power for newer Ventrue. Like a fetid lake of polluted waters, the Ventrue of old may be hated and immovable, but they are also seen as an inherent part of the landscape. Tonight's malcontents may not believe they can replace their polluted lake, but they have the confidence and the pride to stop new lakes from being tainted.

A clan not unlike the Ventrue existed in the foggy history of the Aztecs. The popular consensus among tonight's Damned is that this old clan, extinct in Mexico during the era of the Aztecs, must have been Ventrue, as it is the only of the five clans otherwise wholly unrepresented in the land. The Mexica and the Maya had no name for this clan, which they associated with pre-Mexica Teotihuacán and knew only as "the thirsty dead of the city where men become gods (Teotihuacán)."

Mortal scholars believed for many years that the mysterious builders of Teotihuacán were attacked and driven out of the majestic city by the Toltecs, who burned the place in the 7th century. More recent archaeological theories approach the story that vampires of the Mexica and the Maya have held to be true for more than a thousand years.

By the reckoning of Aztec vampires, the people of Teotihuacán revolted against their city's elite class, slaughtering their own kings and nobility out of spite. The city's rulers were held too tightly in the grip of vampire dominators who used their blood to control and enslave the city's most powerful living people. These vampiric puppet-masters ruled through a combination of force and fear, sweetened with lies. These vampires promised the people that they would become like gods, one night (presumably through the Embrace). Some Kindred claim that these vampire kings planned to Embrace mortals in Teotihuacán by the dozens, turning it into a city of the damned. This is what caused the mortals to revolt, burn the city to purge it of the undead, and flee.

That was the end of that tyrannical clan. In the eyes of the Mexica's Daeva, it is a cautionary tale. The previous world's clan very nearly managed to achieve the sacred place intended for vampires, as bloody intermediaries between men and gods. But those vampires became obsessed with their own cold power over the passionate grandeur of earthly existence. They strove not to excel in their place but to exceed it in pursuit of godhood. The price was the utter destruction of their clan… in this land.

But it seems the previous world's clan managed to lay claim of distant lands and entrench themselves as Lords. When Spanish vampires first arrived in casks of dirt from Europe, word spread quickly among the Aztecs that they were servants of the tyrant clan of the last world.

In many domains, the Ventrue are associated with Quezalcoatl and the Toltecs, but these are fuzzy relatives. The Toltec connection seems to be a confused or generalized acknowledgement of the Ventrue's place in the ancient nights before the Aztecs. The Ventrue association with Quezalcoatl is more insidious. Much as Cortés is said to have been considered a returning avatar of the god by some Aztecs (including, supposedly, Moctezuma himself), the Ventrue are associated with Cortés (despite no genealogical or historical connections of importance). This is almost certainly an invention of the invading Ventrue, however. Upon hearing tell of Quezalcoatl and his potentially prophetic link to Cortés, the Lords worked to connect themselves to absentee gods, too, in the minds of Mexica vampires. The Ventrue weren't invading, they were returning. Rhetoric or not, the connection has stuck. The Feather Serpent is now more commonly depicted in association with the Ventrue than the Daeva.

In the multi-world mythology of the Aztecs, the Ventrue are considered the fourth clan. They emerged in the previous world as an imperfect approximation of the passionate and genuine rule that would eventually come with the Daeva. In the myth of the Maya, the Ventrue are linked with the Eastern branches of the Sacred Tree, as well as the color red (Chilti).

Nickname: Los Patróns, Tiranos, Invasors

Covenant: In Mexico, the Ventrue connection to the Invictus has been even more exaggerated than it is in Europe and the United States. Many malcontent Mexican vampires see the Ventrue not as the in-born aristocrats of the Invictus, but the Invictus as the society of slavery and tyranny created by the Ventrue. Naturally, the truth is much more complicated. In some cities, Carthian Ventrue control Kindred Society like fascists. In other domains, Trotskyist Ventrue have created Carthian states utterly free of Invictus rule. In more than a few cities, even-handed Invictus governments are overseen by Daeva, Mekhet or Gangrel vampires. Modern Ventrue are as likely to rise through the ranks of the uniquely Mexican Lancea Sanctum as they are the rungs of the Invictus. In those cities where the Ordo Dracul can be found, the Ventrue make up no small percentage of the membership.

Appearance: The overwhelming majority of modern Ventrue in Mexico are white, Spanish- or American-born foreigners. As with traditional European Lords, Mexican Ventrue favor conservative, simple and somewhat formal outfits. In Mexico, however, this often includes decorative flourishes and red, white and green embellishments that American Ventrue would find flamboyant. Tonight's Ventrue can be said to fall into three general categories: those frozen in the wardrobes of the late 1800s, those frozen in the wardrobes of the 1920s and those trying to blend in by wearing the most severe, blackest suits and dresses of the season.

Havens: Ventrue who did not get rich off the backs of the mortals of Mexico got rich by inheriting funds from their betters — or are currently waiting to do so. Ventrue havens are often like urban haciendas, with private staffs and living cattle kept on the grounds. Tithes of blood or money (or goods worth good money) come in from satellite communities or sub-domains. Few colonial Ventrue dwell alone, however. Lords in Mexico need protection (or needed it once and are unwilling to part with it now), and that protection often comes in the form of ghouls, childer or Hounds.

Background: One clan stereotype is based in truth: the Ventrue rarely Embrace mortals of Indian blood. Certainly it has happened in the course of Mexican history, but even when it has been done, the Embrace has been a strategic move rather than some genuine expression of admiration or love. Historically, this discrimination has had more to do with the mortals who became Ventrue in the past 500 years. Nothing in the Ventrue blood makes a human being into a racist — mortals manage that on their own. In the nights of the Conquest, it was often not fair-minded Ventrue who were attracted to the New World, and the slow course of Kindred culture has hardly changed their minds. In the past few decades, however, as more mortals have been raised to avoid racism and, eventually, reach the ranks of the business and political elite, the colonial Ventrue have Embraced more open-minded childer. In time, as these Lords grow ready to take on their own heirs from the ranks of the digerati, the industrial sector and the drug cartels, more Mexica-descended mortals will be brought into the clan.

Character Creation: As with European Ventrue, Social traits are valuable for Lords who expect to rule well. Mental Skills can sometimes make up for a pedestrian intellect. It is, of course, money that attracted so many colonial Ventrue to the New World, so Resources are often high and often inherited from one's sire. Many Ventrue have fortified themselves in towers of Status, where they cannot be easily reached by street vampires. To rule from such heights, a Lord needs many Allies and Contacts and, often, a trustworthy Retainer.

Clan Disciplines: Animalism, Dominate, Resilience

Organization: The Ventrue of Mexico proudly trace their Damned ancestry back across oceans and centuries to Spanish dons. The most powerful Lords in Mexico maintain sprawling havens where generations of childer can reside in luxury and safety with them. Clan offices often translate into city positions — the Prince is often Priscus, the Primogen and Hounds are often Whips. The longer a Ventrue has been in the New World is often more important to his authority and Status than his outright age, however. Thus the traditional colonial term "first generation" has become a title of great esteem among the Lords of Mexico. (E.g., "My sire is a first-generation Ventrue, and he says it's not like that.")

It's been 500 years since the Conquest, however, so few first-generation Ventrue are still walking the earth. Some have been burned in the fires of revolution, others are sleeping away their hunger. Thus many of tonight's most powerful Ventrue are struggling to maintain rule in the absence of their first-generation leaders. Some are literally following the instructions left for them by their sleeping sires.

Bloodlines: Las Cocas (a handful of vampire drug lords whose blood has been forever altered by the cocaine addicts they became addicted to in the 1980s), Nahualli (see p. 78 of Bloodlines: The Hidden), Veracruz (a Sanctified bloodline that gains spiritual power by invoking the names of Mexico's Saints and Spanish conquistadors)

Concepts: Catholic abbot, corporate executive, drug lord, human trafficker, master of the hacienda, real-estate mogul, remote village mayor, resort-town director, silver mine owner, Spanish Conquistador, sweatshop lord.

Stereotypes

Daeva: They've done well enough in the absence of real authority.

Gangrel: Always the same animal. Only the stripes change.

Mekhet: Useful, when contained. They've been given enough rope to hang themselves with here.

Nosferatu: Our unique asset. Let them think what they want, so long as they keep the locals afraid.

• • •

Lupines: Any era of peace with them is just a pause between bloody misunderstandings. Watch closely.

Mages: Still so human. And here, so very much alone.

Mortals: The curse of the kine is that they are all so alike in ignorance and death, no matter what they do.

Havens in Mexico

Mexico has a First World heart with a Third World body: the country portends in many places to be a modern country with all the trappings of progressive life. This is true, to an extent, but to obtain those trappings, one must navigate a busted infrastructure, crooked officials, an unpredictable environment and enough red tape to hang a horse.

Vampires in Mexico dwell in havens, just as they do most other places. Of course, a haven isn't just a house, and requires a number of stipulations to make it both safe and useful. If the haven doesn't at least protect the vampire from the hot Mexican sun and give him easy access to prey, what's the point?

Cuidado!

The path to finding a proper haven is fraught with peril. Any vampire can kick down a door in the *barrio* of Mexico City and sleep under a ragged mattress or a handful of blankets — and, while some Kindred are forced to do that very thing, that doesn't make it a proper haven. Navigating the tribulations of procuring a haven isn't easy.

Red Tape

Renting or purchasing real estate in Mexico isn't a quick process. Same goes for getting phone service, electricity, television, whatever. Companies want to see proof of identification, proof of employment — and that's after one gets the company's attention via handwritten letters, phone calls or tracking people down on foot. Getting paperwork pushed through can take weeks or months. Obtaining phone service and electricity is nearly impossible in many of the small towns, but even in a big city like Mexico City, it can take anywhere from nine days to nine *months*. Of course, some Kindred have all the time in the world: they are, to a point, eternal. But when a vampire needs a haven immediately — as in, he has EPR rebels on his trail and he has nowhere to stay before the sun comes up in 12 hours — what's to be done?

Two solutions: first, Mexico is a cash economy. The smart people recognize this. Finding the appropriate parties and putting actual pesos in hand will go a long way toward getting things done quickly. Nearly everybody has a price — slicing through red tape is definitely possible, it just depends on how much the machete costs.

The second solution is simply to steal a haven. Many Kindred recognize the right haven when they see it — no windows, defensible position, near the *discoteca*. They can't just buy it. Instead, they *take* it. The haven's current occupants can find a new home (which might be in a shallow grave a few towns over).

Cell phones

Cellular service has grown by leaps and bounds in Mexico, and for that reason most of the country's occupants — including vampires — use cell phones. Cell service is still spotty at best, however, and only major areas of population can manage to make calls regularly. (Stranger still is the fact that some vampires, when using phones outside the metropolitan areas, *hear* something coming through the static and dead air. This electronic susurrus seems to be words, but not in any language they recognize.)

Still, most Kindred use *mensajero*, or couriers, to deliver their messages. Such messengers are usually ghouls or neonates, as regular citizens are too unreliable.

Isolation

Once again, Mexico is a land of extremes. Sure, Mexico City has a population of more than 22 million living in its metropolitan area — but Mexico also has large stretches of countryside and wilderness. Remote towns and regions are linked by unreliable roads and rail systems.

Vampires looking to travel to any of these remote areas — or *through* them on the way toward a larger population area — need to be wary. For one, the roads are terrible, ruined enough in spots to swallow the front end of a large car. Plus, seasonal rains in the spring can wash out entire chunks of road. A few vampires have found themselves stuck out in the open with only hours before dawn.

The worst hazards of travel are beggars, robbers and kidnappers. Beggars can mob a car outside tiny villages, asking for clothing, food or money. Robbers want the same things, except they don't *ask*. Kidnappers see a driver or traveler as a target. Somebody might pay some ransom (which may be a million pesos or just the code to an ATM card) to have the victim back. To these groups, a pair of headlights is an open invite.

All three of the above groups tend to manufacture homemade roadblocks out in the middle of nowhere. Such a roadblock might be a string tied across the road (sometimes fitted with heavy cans or sticks hanging from the cord) or a herd of animals hurried into the road so that passage is impossible. (Some vampires can use such roadblocks themselves, in an effort to secure food or money.)

Kindred, of course, fear the isolation found in Mexico: it's essentially a trap. Getting caught out in the middle of nowhere can mean getting caught under the sun. This is why most Kindred find havens in the city, and stay there when they do.

Crime

Muggings, home invasion, kidnappings, murder. Mexico's crime rate isn't particularly damning on paper, but at the street level, the country can feel like a war zone. The United States has a higher crime rate in many cases, but

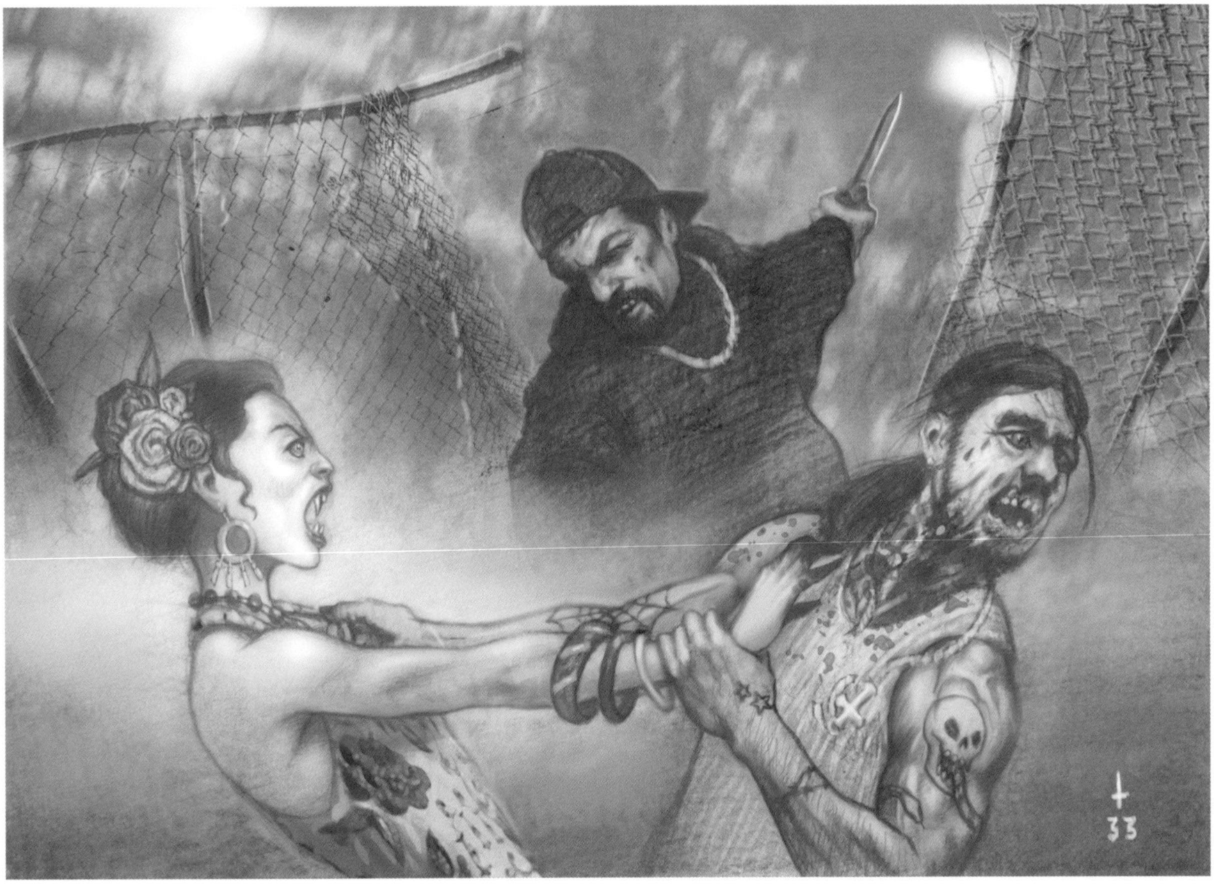

there, crime is walled off: the population can be as ignorant as it wants. Not in Mexico. Even the ritziest neighborhoods are only moments away from some crime, somewhere. It's like having a relaxing swim — amidst hungry sharks.

A vampire looking to establish a haven — or to protect it — has to be vigilant against those looking to take what she has. As mentioned above, some might want to rob her, others might want to ransom her. Even a vampire in an expensive condominium in the opulent La Condesa neighborhood of Mexico City has to worry about who might come and try to break into his place.

Corruption is endemic to the country. For a quick cash hand-off, doormen will open doors that shouldn't be opened, a security company will "have a malfunction" in a system and cops will look the other way. Not all cops are corrupt, to be sure, but they get paid a meager salary (and in many towns, have to purchase their own bullets). Most are corrupt enough to look the other way on small criminal violations (100 pesos gets you out of running a red light, 200 pesos for accidents or shoplifting), but some are willing to act as accomplices to major crimes for bigger payouts.

This means that no haven is safe. Vampires must rely on themselves to keep a haven secure (see "Haven Security," below).

Haven Location

When deciding on a haven, one consideration for a smart vampire is just how far the haven is from both a prominent and prudent food source. Prominent meaning, of course, that lots of humans gather somewhere at night. Prudent implying that the vampire can feed in relative safety and not under bright lights.

This is represented by the Haven Location Merit (see p. 100 of Vampire: The Requiem). In Mexico, this Merit doesn't differ wildly from how it functions in other Western countries. Points in this Merit may indicate proximity to the following:

• Nightclubs (*discoteca*), bars, strip joints. A vampire might make his home near the upscale Condesa, Polanco or Zona Rosa districts in Mexico City, or near the seedy Coahuila "red-light" districts of Tijuana.

• Touristy locales. Puerto Vallarta, Cancun, Acapulco. All make for good hunting, and therefore, good haven locations. Tourists go missing all the time. Moreover, the police seem less likely to listen to tourist complaints in certain areas (since tourist complaints usually leave with the tourists), giving the vampire an advantage. Whether the vampire stalks old Mayan ruins or hunts the shopping districts of Mexico City, she will surely find those who do not belong. Many vampires use ghouls to run scams offering "tours" to tourists, taking them, drugging them and making them food.

• Transportation hubs. Mexico City alone is home to Metrobús (city bus), as well as the Mexico City Metro and Xochimilco Light Rail (connected train lines serving more than four million passengers per day). Any spot along one of these arteries makes a good feeding ground.

• Choked urban areas such as the *barrios*. The population of the country swells year by year, and the infrastructure cannot keep up. Mexico City is home to crowded *barrios* and thousands of homeless (some estimate that the city is home to nearly 75,000 street children), all of whom can lie close to a vampire's nest.

Ills of the Blood

Mexico's overpopulation has a number of consequences, one of which is mounting disease. The populace is affected by such diseases as hepatitis, yellow fever, typhoid fever, malaria and rabies. Insects spread some infections, and Mexico City suffers from "fecal snow" (dried feces from sewage flats caught on the wind) that can spread others. Since many diseases are blood-borne, they can be spread via a vampire's bite.

One disease worth noting is onchocerciasis, or "river blindness." A largely tropical disease, the pathogen is spread by tiny black flies, who deposit micro-thread worms in the body — these worms (or microfiliarae) often attack the eyes, resulting in blindness. The flies can, and do, bite vampires. Moreover, a vampire who bites an infected victim may very well draw such tiny worms into his own undead crucible.

The worms seem to cause no harm to a vampire (few Kindred even recognize the infestation), but they can be spread via bite. (Some wonder what happens if the worms develop a taste for the undead Vitae. Would they consume a Kindred's blood? Or would such infected creatures become frighteningly resistant to treatment outside the vampire's body?)

Haven Security

Use of the Haven Security Merit in Mexico is, ultimately, not that different from anywhere else. In nicer parts of the cities, one can have a security system in place (monitored from on- or off-premises), with cameras and strong locks. Some vampires live in opulent hotels or high-rise apartment buildings, all of which feature layers of security by their very nature: countless floors, lots of locked doors, guards. Not every Kindred is so fortunate (or affluent) to have access to such accoutrements, however.

Outside the cities and large towns, security must be improvised. A haven hidden in an old mine, off water tunnels or simply behind a grove of trees or cluster of rocks might add a point or two. Some vampires maintain underground havens — dug-out cellars found beneath trapdoors (often concealed beneath colorful rugs and spare furniture). Some of the Damned live amidst Mexico's naturally obstructive features: in a cave beneath the lip of a dormant volcano, in a bunker hidden in the rainforest or in an abandoned mine out in the desert. While such isolated havens may add a few points to Haven Security (and Size), the isolation almost ensures that *no* points can be put into Haven Location because of the haven's distance from the human food source.

A number of vampires choose to — or are forced to — live in the slums of Mexico City. Those who choose to live there recognize it as the slaughterhouse that it is, fresh meat everywhere. Those who are forced to there are without money or influence. Regardless of how a vampire ends up there, his haven needn't be without some level of Haven Security. Those living in *barrio* hovels may secretly reinforce their doors away from prying eyes, or put up other types of improvised security (bear-traps, lots of padlocks, low-hanging razor wire). Some *barrio* Kindred don't even live in the closet-size tenement apartments or shanty-homes made of corrugated tin. They instead live in places one wouldn't even think to look: in the sewer tunnels beneath open-air markets, in church attics or in the back rooms of unregistered sweatshops (*maquila*).

One thing worth noting is that, for those who can afford it, a number of companies exist for the sole purpose of setting up home or hotel security for wealthy tourists. These are not "normal" security companies, and may even operate illegally (paying the local authorities for the right to exist unhindered). These companies consist commonly of American or European ex-military, who set up elaborate security systems and put in place personnel who will protect a home and its inhabitants by whatever force necessary. Many of these organizations are quite honorable — as long as the money is coming in, of course. A few, however, are merely false fronts for kidnapping gangs and robbers, all on the hunt for rich marks.

Communal Havens

Shared havens are quite common in Mexico. Years of chaos have given many Mexican Damned a level of trust unseen among the Kindred of other countries. Faith, blood and family bind many of these vampires, but above even those is the need for safety. Mexico can be a turbulent country, and its history provides constant example of this tumult. Uprisings, gangs, disease, poverty: vampires either stick together, or they go hungry and mad. The trust found in one another is far from absolute — many knives have stabbed many backs — but the prudent vampire knows how to walk the line and keep his eyes open.

Thus, shared faith and the need for safety allow Kindred to dwell together in havens. Often, Kindred of specific broods, bloodlines or covenants come together, allowing them access to havens more useful and secure than if they had been alone.

Sample Havens

Below are a handful of sample havens that can be taken by characters (with the appropriate Merit points).

Show Me the Pesos?

A Storyteller might consider also assigning a potential Resources value to the following havens. For instance, the silver mine might cost a vampire nothing — it is, after all, a pre-existing feature that the vampire can simply inhabit. Casa de Solana, however, isn't readily available to a Kindred without money (at least Resources 3). Certainly, players, they choose a haven similar to the ones below, should be encouraged to think outside the box — Resources is not the only way to get a hold of such a place (some literally steal such locations from their original human or vampire owners), and a good story can come out of how a character obtains and keeps such a haven. Resources isn't necessary, only one avenue of obtaining a proper haven.

Silver Mine

(Location 0, Size ••••, Security ••)

Mexico is littered with old, unused mines — some from as far back as the 16th century, when native miners braved the dangerous subterranean passages to dig out the country's hidden riches. While many of these mines are now tourist attractions, many remain hidden or simply superfluous, and an astute vampire can make use of one as his haven.

Most mines provide lots of space and some level of obstructionist security: cramped tunnels, fraying rope ladders, rickety bridges over yawning chasms. Some mine entrances are hidden in hard-to-climb mountain passes, and even require use of old cable cars to reach (many of which don't work reliably). This can make a troublesome journey for those looking to sneak into the vampire's haven — though it can be pretty problematic for the vampire himself, as well.

More worrisome is a mine's proximity to people. Rarely is a mine close enough to the human herd; those Damned residing deep in the mines must make the long and occasionally dangerous journey to feed nightly, or must instead kidnap mortals to keep nearby in the dark depths of the old tunnels.

Casa de Solana

(Location ••, Size •••, Security ••••)

Modern Mexican architecture often features stark contemporary edges paired with the deco sensibilities of the '30s and '40s. Casa de Solana is a good example of progressive architecture, and for its Kindred inhabitant, is also a tough nut to crack.

The house, located in the San Angel district of Mexico City, is surrounded on all sides by cobblestone roads (and beyond them, small garden parks). The house itself has smoky windows on all sides, moored by concrete and a slate roof. The sun shines brightly through the windows during the day — but the Kindred within sleeps inside the house's central core. The middle of the house is literally a concrete fortress (though a comfortable and luxuriant one) hidden behind a steel door.

An independent, on-premises security system monitors every room from within the center fortress. The glass is bulletproof. The front door is locked with three deadbolts. While not impenetrable, the house remains duly protected.

The San Angel district is oddly peaceful in the crowded, polluted throng of the city. With expensive mansions, old monasteries and open-air markets, the neighborhood draws a number of tourists — all of whom are potential prey for the Kindred who makes this house his nest.

Priorato de la Resurrección

(Location ••, Size ••, Security 0)

This church — the Priory of the Resurrection — sits on the edge of the ever-spreading *barrio*. The chapel is not large, and sits disused with cracked paint, cold candles and fractured windows of colored glass. The Kindred within may exist as a local figure to those few humans who dare to visit him within the darkened church. He offers them quiet benediction, and they tithe him blood in return.

The vampire who dwells here has reasonable access to the slum-dwellers, who haunt the streets and buildings and remain crowded into nearby shanties and tenements. The chapel offers no security from prying eyes, however: it is as public as a haven can get, so the Kindred must be prepared to handle whatever contingency approaches.

Barrio Hovel

(Location •••, Size 0, Security 0)

The hovel is a ramshackle house whose cracks and fractures are covered over with duct tape, rotten wood and pilfered street signs. The house sits in the middle of the 72 blocks of impoverished slum-land that is Mexico City's *el barrio bravo* — the vampire is just another of the nameless and faceless inhabitants of this place (called *gente pobre pero honrada*, or the "poor but decent people").

The advantage is, of course, that for the predator, the slum is never without food. Not only are the locals prime-picking (with a new victim every night), but the neighborhood is also home to a video piracy ring where "merchants" sell pirated tapes, DVDs and software from underneath dark canopy tents. Those who come here seeking such illicit goods make for easy meals.

The Hacienda

(Location •••••, Size •••••, Security •••••)

The hacienda — a plantation — went out of style in the late 1800s, but many of Mexico's Kindred still keep the traditions of the hacienda alive. The plantation itself is a large chunk of land that operates as a farm for livestock and agriculture. Once, these plantations were connected to the larger economy, offering low yield and high prices. The Kindred have taken the hacienda system and maintain it separately from the economy and society of Mexico. The people and function of the hacienda are utterly isolated, and in fact the hacienda's only purpose is to keep itself running.

It works similar to a medieval fiefdom: a single vampire acts as *patrón* (or lord) of the hacienda. Up to 50 *peóns* work the land: these workers are likely mortals, though they might be ghouls or in rare instances, even other vampires. The workers never leave the hacienda. They are born there. They die there. Often, several families reside on the hacienda grounds, mating together, holding weddings and *fiestas* and forming isolated cultures all their own.

The *peóns* are indebted to the *patrón*. They are all paid the same rate (meager wages) and must pay the vampire for food, privileges and any celebrations they wish to hold. Most pay with money, but those aware of the vampire's nature also pay in blood. Many hold blood debt to the lord of the hacienda — and all debt is passed to the children once the parents die.

The populations of individual plantations are incredibly insular: many of the workers have *never* seen life outside the hacienda's borders. Certainly some escape, but most are made to believe that everything they need is within the hacienda — family, food, life. To go outside the plantation betrays the family and the *patrón*.

Haciendas are not without religion. While many of these farms and manors are lorded over by vampires of the Invictus, most haciendas are in some way connected to the Sanctified. Midnight mass is held every week at most haciendas, and the workers are quite religious. (This also creates yet another level of dependence upon the vampire: they look to the *patrón* for spiritual fulfillment.)

As of late, the system has begun to break down. Encroaching populations and an unstable environment has lead to breaches. Other vampires pilfer the workers, or in some cases, the workers (suspecting that more exists outside the hacienda walls) revolt and destroy the vampire lord in a bloody coup.

Also worth noting is that haciendas do not always farm in traditional ways. Some Kindred have taken the process to a new level: some farm blood (from human "livestock"), some create vicious sweatshops (producing and selling goods to big American companies) and others run small criminal empires (drugs, usually).

Campesino Family

Many of the haciendas of Mexico are connected (and, in fact, the vampire lords often form distant broods of their own). Some of these lords maintain a number of ghouls, and history has seen the birth of several thrall bloodlines.

One of these bloodlines — the humbly-named *campesinos*, or "farmers" — are prized for their tough bodies but pliable minds. Each ghoul of this particular lineage gains a +1 to Stamina automatically, but suffers a –1 penalty to Composure and an additional –1 penalty on any Composure roll meant to resist a vampire's supernatural wiles. This bloodline is not tied to any one clan, and many of the *patrón* Damned share the ghouls with one another as favors. Unfortunately, as of late, the bloodline has suffered a number of odd congenital defects: shriveled limbs, weak hearts, missing noses. Defective specimens are kept around to perform the most revolting or difficult tasks, but they are often castrated or genitally mauled so that they may not further pollute the bloodline.

Disciplines

The Kindred of Mexico have a very strange relationship with their own powers. Many believe that their Disciplines are a gift from the manifest gods or saints above, and the Disciplines' applied success depends entirely upon the qualities of the vampire himself, not the relative weakness of his intended target. Those traditional vampires set in the ancient ways of the domain are assured by their sires that the old gods of the peoples of the region are both testing and favoring them, providing them with the power to move the world — or destroy themselves. Only purity of heart and honest virtue allows them to survive the exploitation of their mystic energies. More modern Kindred are taught a modified version of this story, adopting the ancient imagery of their predecessors and merging them with the Catholic saints of the conquistadors. Many are Christian themselves and simply accept the notion of patron spirits as a comfortable extension of their religious beliefs. Others come to understand that the ideal of each Discipline is embodied in these notional influences, and prefer to treat them as empowering constructs of the imagination.

As a result, a startling majority of Mexican Kindred behave as though they are taking part in an ongoing relationship with the gods or saints of their faith and spend a significant amount of energy analyzing their successes and failures, so that they may better understand the path of their Requiems. It is not unusual for a vampire to pay tribute to his patron saints before and after a dangerous or otherwise important endeavor. Prayer is common as well, and many carry marks or trinkets intended to please the gods. It is worthwhile to note that even those Kindred who would not consider themselves religious have a tendency to pay lip service to the notion of "sainted gifts," and many are surprised to find themselves uttering a serious prayer in times of extreme stress.

Some of the younger, more skeptical Kindred of the domain will occasionally point out that asking for aid from beyond or wearing the symbols of the saints just serves to telegraph a vampire's intended strategy, making it easier for their enemies to outwit them. While certain believers would argue that one's foes need not witness the declaration, most have a simpler answer: the price of proper conduct is small when compared to its benefit. A vampire who truly carries the blessings of his faith can only be defeated if he is unworthy.

Optional Rule: Strength in Faith

The superstition of Mexican Kindred is a double-edged sword. While the tendency to credit adherence to faith or outside influence for one's strength can bolster confidence, giving so much credit to one's faith can also work to undermine one's confidence. Storytellers running a game themed around deep-seated beliefs may wish to make use of a "placebo" mechanic that enforces both its positive and negative aspects: whenever a character attempts to make use of a Discipline, she must first assure herself that she has the blessing of a relevant god or spirit. That assurance can take many forms: kissing a small medal, kneeling quickly before an altar and whispering a quick prayer or making some kind of sacrifice. Once the proper obeisance is performed, the player may add a +1 bonus to dice pools that relate to the Discipline's use for the scene in question. If, however, the character fails to pay proper tribute before the attempt, a –1 penalty is applied instead.

Example: *Julio, a Nosferatu, has been taught, and fully believes, that San Miguel has the power to strengthen Kindred who fight with honor and clarity of purpose. Julio wears a medallion of the angel around his neck, and he always kisses it, puts it to his forehead and whispers "San Miguel aid me" before entering battle. When he does so and activates Vigor, the Storyteller allows Julio's player to add one die to his combat rolls for the scene. However, one night Julio is surprised by a foe who rips the medallion from his neck before he can prepare himself. Since Julio has benefited from his belief for so long, he cannot function at full capacity when it is taken advantage of. If he activates his Vigor for the fight that follows, the Storyteller rules that his player must remove one die from all combat rolls for the scene.*

Storytellers who want to emphasize the role of faith in the supernatural powers of Mexican vampires might grant no bonuses for tributes, only penalties for missed tributes. This implies either that the faith of these monsters has real power, or that all Mexican Damned suffer from a degree of the Power Fetish Obsession derangement (p. 191, Vampire: The Requiem). Whether the bonus or penalty is a result of actual outside interference or simply the manifestation of the character's faith in herself is a matter of speculation. Whatever the case, the modifier is just as effective.

Animalism (Instinto)

Traditionally, the Discipline of Animalism was associated with the animal totems of the ancient world. It was said that those vampires who exercised Animalism' power were gifted with the language of the spirits, speaking not directly to the animals in the material world, but rather to the powers that guided them. The creatures of the wild bent themselves to the will of the Kindred, not because of forceful dictates, but because the spirits were convinced by demonstrations of the proper respect, and approved of the vampire's intended purpose. The vampires who approach the Discipline this way always mimic the sound of animal speech in addressing the creatures and make a serious effort to avoid showing anger or frustration when an animal fails to accede to their wishes. To these vampires, the creatures of the wild are not "lesser spirits," but equals.

Those who believe in the spirits will often show an affinity for a single wild breed, believing that it falls within the purview of their personal totem spirit. A Gangrel whose totem is the owl, for instance, will find that dealings with owls are easier and more comfortable than any other applications of the Discipline. He may go so far as to refer to the owls as his "brothers and sisters," and focus his ken on them.

Modern Kindred (and, most notably, the Ventrue of Mexico), tend to see things differently. To them, the creatures of the earth and sky are lower beings, ideally to be shown the love of all God's creation, but not to be elevated beyond their station. These vampires will speak to the animals in human tongue, and take a failure to assume command of the animals' will as a weakness in themselves or their purpose, not reticence on the part of the target or any guiding spirit. These Kindred rarely develop any special empathy for a single type of creature, and argue that those who do are verging on obsessive mania in service to an outdated system of beliefs.

The patron saint of Animalism is San Francisco de Asís, who is customarily portrayed in a simple robe, preaching to a tree full of birds. Among the Mexican Kindred community, variations of the image replace the birds with local fauna: jaguars, coyotes, owls, bats and even scorpions.

Sample Tributes: Painting or drawing animal images, punishing a mortal who mistreats a beast, scattering food or seed for animals, visiting a nesting site or sanctuary, wearing a tattoo of a Nagua totem symbol

Auspex (Claridad)

The power of sight and knowledge is sacred to its practitioners, and not without good cause. The secrets of the world unfold themselves before the Kindred gifted with God-given clarity, and the devastating potential of the stark understanding that follows can prove more potent than any sorcerer's curse. Truth is like a fire — what it touches can never be fully restored to its previous state.

Those who carry the teachings of an earlier age believe that Auspex is bestowed upon vampires by Quetzalcóatl, the wise creator and god of the skies. His sign is the feathered serpent, and many of his adherents speak of the effects of Auspex in terms of "feathers" — Aura Perception (Auspex ••) is described as the unfolding and turning of multi-hued wings behind the subject, for instance, and those Kindred powerful enough to engage in Twilight Projection (Auspex •••••) tell tales of flying on the great back of the serpent himself, manifest in the world beyond the material realm. Telepathy (Auspex ••••) is represented as an unraveling of tightly coiled thoughts, revealing the true shape of a subject's mind.

Rather than deny the ancient view, most modern practitioners of the Discipline incorporate the old god into their outlook, mashing him in with Christian angels and heavenly vision. It's often difficult to tell whether they believe Quetzalcóatl is a manifestation of the archangels or vice versa.

There is an alternate Auspex ••• power for Mexican Kindred: The Feathers' Flight. It replaces The Spirit's Touch, and is mutually exclusive — a player must choose one or the other when purchasing Auspex •••, and cannot subsequently buy the other.

The patron saint of Auspex is San Gabriel, the archangel, who is usually depicted in flight, with a shining bird overhead, carrying white lilies or with trumpet in hand. Many modern Mexican Kindred believe that every image of San Gabriel sees what happens before it, and will take pains to give one prominent place in their havens or Elysium sites as a means of declaring that they have nothing to hide.

Sample tributes: Acknowledging a painful truth about one's self, kneeling before an image of San Gabriel, praying under an open sky, wearing or growing a white flower

••• The Feathers' Flight

Whereas most Kindred seek to pick up impressions from specific objects, the seers of the ancient Mexican vampires developed their powers differently. After learning to view the halo of shining feathers that compose a subject's aura, Kindred begin to develop the ability to track the path of those feathers back through time.

The power manifests as visible tracks of color through the air, representing the path of the individual, and spots of color on anything the target has recently touched. The tracks will give some residual impression of the target's emotional state at the time (from the hue itself, as with aura perception), and will grow brighter with proximity to the present. A knife held last week in anger might carry a dim red glow, while one brandished just minutes ago would shine a brilliant crimson. The vampire using the power need not have the subject in sight at the time, so long as he is acquainted with her. Thus, the power may actually be used to track a friend or foe whose current location is unknown

— provided that the vampire using the power knows at least one place the person recently visited.

Using this power requires some concentration, limiting the activity of the vampire making use of it. He may walk and speak quietly, but is unable to engage in any strenuous activity or respond to any strong emotional stimulus. If he does so, the power fades and will not re-activate until he can return his full attention to it.

Note that the use of this power does not reveal the exact time of the subject's presence — just a relative estimate based on the brightness of the track. It's difficult to say if a half-dim track means that a subject was present three days ago or five days ago, for example.

Cost: –

Dice Pool: Wits + Investigation + Auspex

Action: Instant

Roll Results

Dramatic Failure: The vampire perceives a tangle of illusory paths around the true one, making it impossible to track the subject properly. It's highly likely that any further attempt this scene will yield a false result, leading the vampire in the wrong direction.

Failure: There is no discernible path. If the subject is present, the failure is apparent. If not, it simply seems as if the subject has never been in the current location.

Success: The path of the subject (up to a week old) appears as a spectral ribbon of color, floating in mid-air. Anything in the area that the subject has recently touched is "painted" with this light as well. The color of the light indicates the basic emotional state of the subject at the time. If a location is well traveled by the subject, it will be immediately apparent to the vampire using the power, who will see tracks running back and forth through the area.

Exceptional Success: An exceptional success provides an extended view of the subject's path, allowing the vampire to track the subject back for a month. Every object, creature and person the subject touched in that time will be marked, and the emotional state of the subject at the time will be laid bare.

Suggested Modifiers

Modifier	Situation
+2	Power is turned on a vampire with whom the user has a blood tie (see p. 162 of **Vampire: The Requiem**).
+1	The user has recently read the subject's aura using Auspex •.
–	The subject has been in the area or handled the object examined in the last hour.
–1	The subject was last in the area recently, but not less than an hour ago.
–2	The subject was last in the area a few nights ago.
–3	The subject was last in the area a week ago.
–4	The subject was last in the area more than 8 nights ago.

Celerity (Velocidad)

Traditionally, the Discipline of Celerity is associated with the scouring winds of the Mexican deserts, and is overseen by Ehecatl, an aspect of the great god Quetzalcóatl. Kindred who employ Celerity are said to be creatures of the air as much as they are of the earth, letting themselves be carried across the soil by the currents of the skies. The teachings of elder vampires explain that the use of Celerity is less an active effort to increase one's speed and more a relaxation into a divine gift of lightness and flight. As a result, most who engage in the traditional teachings show little effort when moving at supernatural speed — they almost seem to become less aware of their actions, "floating" through their movements in a dreamlike state. Strangely, when several Mexican vampires all move together with Celerity, they do seem to follow a mutual path in motion, and they are all likely to deny choosing the direction. Observers tend to liken these groups to flocks of birds or flights of arrows loosed by a rank of archers.

Modern Kindred deride these views, taking more responsibility for their personal power and choosing to believe that the speeds they achieve are a demonstration of skill. Those who break with tradition adopt the symbolism of San Sebastián. To them, arrows and birds are to be dodged with skill and grace, not embodied.

The patron saint of Celerity is San Sebastián; he is usually portrayed as a young man, tied to a tree and shot with arrows.

Sample tributes: Being shot, carrying an arrow or arrowhead, praying under a tree, wearing or carrying a feather, whispering into the wind

Dominate (Domine)

The signature power of the Ventrue is the only Discipline that is not associated with any of the old gods of Mexico. Almost every member of the clan makes a point of dismissing the "primitive" traditions of their counterparts, and many point to Dominate itself as evidence of their superior intelligence and will. That's not to say that Modern Kindred don't treat the Discipline with just as much superstition as others — it's just that their tributes are exclusively Christian in flavor.

Elder Mexican Kindred are especially fearful of Dominate, knowing how effectively it was put to use during the Spanish invasion centuries ago. Some will go to great lengths to avoid private discussion with Ventrue, while other Kindred react with violent anger whenever they suspect manipulation, even if there is no actual power in use. More than one serious, decades-long vendetta has been launched by accusations of exploitation via this power.

Old Mexican Kindred with access to the Discipline have traditionally kept it a secret from their counterparts, choosing to believe that Dominate served as evidence of their own divinity, not a gift from beyond. Those who admitted to this belief were reviled by the other Kindred of their time, and retain the habit of concealing their talent even now.

The patron saint of Dominate is San Expedito, depicted as a roman soldier holding up a cross and standing on a dead crow. The cross is labeled HODIE (Latin for "today"), and the word CRAS (Latin for "tomorrow") emerges from the dead bird's mouth.

Sample tributes: Carrying a sheathed weapon for display only, killing a crow, speaking the phrase "today, not tomorrow," wearing red

Majesty (Majestdad)

There is a long and storied tradition of Majesty among Mexican vampires. Practitioners of the power of temptation, associated equally with sweet desire and filthy degradation, believe that they are exercising the gifts of Tlazolteotl, the great goddess of temptation and excrement. The application of Majesty is not restricted to beautiful things — many a victim finds himself grubbing in diseased environs to please the object of his desire. In Mexico, Majesty is not just a means to win the love and cooperation of the weak-willed — Majesty is also a demonstration of earthly desire's price.

The classic image of a traditional Mexican Daeva is a terrible, gore-spattered beauty, standing over the steaming guts of her still-sighing sacrifices. While modern Kindred take great pains to soften the appearance of their power, it does seem to many that the old interpretation is closer to the truth — no matter how pretty a face you put on it.

There is an alternate Majesty •••• power for Mexican Kindred: Barring the Bone Gate. It replaces Summoning, and is mutually exclusive — a player must choose one or another when purchasing a •••• Majesty power, and cannot subsequently buy the other.

The patron saint of Majesty is San Valentin, who is often associated with red roses. Those Kindred inclined to incorporate the imagery of Tlazolteotl often include a single red snake somewhere in pictures of the saint as well, paying heed to the dark side of Majesty. A common shorthand adopted in modern nights simply depicts a small serpent curled up within the petals of a rose.

Sample tributes: Collecting gore or excrement in a bowl, having sex, holding a red gem in the mouth, touching a tattoo of a sacred heart, wearing or growing a red rose.

•••• Barring the Bone Gate

This potent power, developed by the ancient high priests of the Mexican Kindred as a demonstration of divine favor is both awesome in its display and terrifying in its implications. A vampire, by exerting his will, can delay the death of any mortally wounded being so long as she remains in his presence. Priests would make use of this power to hold their human sacrifices at the edge of death until exactly the right moment, showing their still-beating hearts to the ceremonial crowds. Warrior kings would stand above their subjects in battle, keeping their deaths at bay until the fight was won.

The subjects of this power are hardly given a pardon. Those who are at the brink of death are held at its edge for the duration, feeling the pain of their wounds and the rattle of their final breath again and again. Unable to escape, they are caught in a strange rapture that centers on the vampire using the power, feeling the power of his presence unto their last moment. The subject of the power is immediately aware that the vampire is responsible for keeping him alive, and that he will die as soon as he is released. As soon as the power is relaxed, affected subjects die instantly.

Barring the Bone Gate cannot be used on a character who is not mortally wounded — the character's Health chart must be marked full with lethal damage. However, the power can be directed at a character any time during a scene in which the vampire believes the character will die — it will activate at the moment of her death.

Example: *Maria, a Daeva, draws her sword, preparing to do battle with Domingo, a ghoul. Before they clash, she activates Barring the Bone Gate, hoping to hold him at the moment of death if he falls. Later in the scene, she strikes hard enough to fill all of the Health boxes on his sheet with lethal damage. At that moment, her Majesty activates and the player makes a Presence + Subterfuge + Majesty roll in an attempt to hold him.*

This power's effects may last as long as an hour or an entire night, depending on the strength of the vampire using it, but the power always ends immediately at dawn. If the power is successful, the vampire may choose to cut it short at any moment before it elapses normally. Mortals who are dying from a loss of blood may be Embraced at any time during the use of the power.

Cost: 1 Willpower per scene

Dice Pool: Presence + Persuade + Majesty – the subject's Resolve

Action: Instant.

Roll Results

Dramatic Failure: The subject's death is not delayed, and the vampire attempting to use the power is momentarily transfixed as the power of death overwhelms her. She is incapable of action for one full turn following the failed attempt, and may not use this power for the remainder of the night.

Failure: The subject's death is not delayed.

Success: The vampire holds the subject at the brink of death for the remainder of the scene. At the end of the scene, the vampire may attempt to use this power again, so long as the sun has not yet risen. The subject is able to function at a penalty, suffering all of his wound penalties on all rolls, but does not need to roll to remain conscious or active.

Exceptional Success: The vampire holds the subject at the brink of death all the way until dawn, if she wishes. The subject no longer suffers the effects of wound penalties on his dice pools, but is still mildly disoriented and visibly wounded.

This power may be used on more than one individual at a time, so long as all of those affected can see and hear the vampire with their own eyes (not through a camera or monitor). In the case of multiple subjects, the highest Resolve of the group serves as the penalty to the vampire's activation roll. Potential subjects are affected based on their Resolve dots — those with the fewest dots in Resolve are affected first.

Example: *Diaz, a Mexican Daeva, is attempting to rally a group of thugs to fight off a police squad long enough for Diaz to escape. There are six thugs present, and the highest Resolve in the group has three dots. Diaz's Presence + Persuade + Majesty dice pool is 10, minus Resolve 3, for seven dice. Diaz wants to minimize the penalty to his activation roll, so he decides that he'll attempt to affect just five of the thugs. (Hopefully, he thinks, the sixth will stick around just because the others do.) This penalizes his dice pool by another –3, for a total of four dice. Diaz scores just one success, but because he took on the dice pool penalty that's all he needs to affect five subjects. Of the six thugs, the five with the lowest Resolve ratings are affected. In this case, it means that one thug with three dots of Resolve is the only one unaffected. He chooses to flee and fight another night.*

Suggested Modifiers

Modifier	Situation
–	Character attempts to maintain a hold on one subject.
–1	Character attempts to maintain a hold on two subjects.
–2	Character attempts to maintain a hold on three subjects.
–3	Character attempts to maintain a hold on four to five subjects.
–4	Character attempts to maintain a hold on six to 10 subjects.
–5	Character attempts to maintain a hold on 11 to 13 subjects.

Nightmare (Pesadilla)

The coming of the Nosferatu to the New World brought the terrible power of Nightmare, previously thought forgotten to the point of near-total absence, to the forefront of Kindred conflict. Associated by older, more traditional vampires with the power of the underworld, those who wielded Nightmare quickly found it convenient to tie themselves to the old gods of death in the region, significantly amplifying the effect of their will on the locals. Mystic opportunism mingled, in some places, with legitimate belief, and tradition took root. These nights, it's difficult to discern which vampires were taught by the old native powers and which adopted and cloaked themselves in the attributes of local fear for a strictly psychological advantage.

The patron saint of Nightmare is Santa Dymphna, depicted as a young woman carrying a book. Some of the images carried or displayed by Kindred take pains to hide a tiny bat or spider somewhere within the folds of her dress.

Sample tributes: Drinking blood tainted with hallucinogens, eating a spider, feeding meat to a bat or owl, spitting blood on the ground, wearing or carrying bones

Obfuscate (Ofusque)

Traditionally, the Discipline of shadow and stealth is associated with Tezcatlipoca, the Smoking Mirror, the shadow-twin of Quetzalcóatl and co-creator of the world. Darkness and mist curl at the edges of Tezatlipoca's domain, and vampires draw this fringe about themselves, concealing their actions and identities from the denizens of the mortal world. The vampires in the region often speak of Obfuscate as "the smoke" or "the mist," likening the use of the Discipline to clothing one's self in these substances. Those who vanish from sight under direct observation with the Cloak of Night (Obfuscate •••) sometimes seem to actually dissolve in a curling haze, and many have found that all of the powers of the Discipline are a bit easier to do in smoky environs.

The patron saint of Obfuscate is San Antonio, the Catholic guardian of lost things and missing people. He is depicted holding a baby Jesus, and Kindred artists will normally portray him in foggy or smoky surroundings.

Sample tributes: Blowing smoke, carrying a map, extinguishing light, gazing into a mirror, leaving something of value in a crowded place

Protean (Cambio)

Ever fluid, ever changing, the Kindred who made use of Protean in the old nights of northern Mexico were said to be children of Iztaccihuatl and Popocatepetl, the lovers who were transformed into mountains by the gods. These vampires, free to change while their ancestors were frozen in place, haunted the jungles of the region, running wild with the beasts and stalking their human cousins. Those in the south were said to be blessed by the Balam (or to be Balam themselves), the jaguar gods of the Mayan people.

The patron saint of Protean is San Raphael, the archangel, who is normally depicted standing and carrying a staff.

Sample tributes: Helping a lost traveler get to his destination, praying in a remote location, sleeping under the earth, walking a great distance, wearing or displaying the image of a butterfly

••• The Jungle's Sting

Upon activation of this power, the vampire instantly grows a patch of thin, greenish-black tendrils from his head, back, abdomen or arms. The tendrils are rubbery and fragile, and are only vaguely prehensile. However, at the slightest contact, they discharge a liquid toxin that burns even undead flesh. Some liken them to the stinging tentacles of a jellyfish, while others note their resemblance to certain poisonous creepers found in the jungles of the Yucatán.

Cost: 1 Vitae

Dice Pool: This power involves no roll. The location of the tendril's growth is chosen by the vampire at the moment of activation.

The added danger of contact with the tendrils imparts a +1 bonus to the vampire's attack rolls in unarmed combat. If the vampire successfully strikes the opponent with the tendrils, the damage normally inflicted by the attack becomes aggravated. If the tendrils are touched without an active attack (for instance, an unsuspecting opponent simply grabs hold of them), they inflict one level of aggravated damage. In addition to the combat bonus, the tendrils impart a +2 stealth bonus in the jungle, because of their resemblance to the parasitic vines in the region.

••• Shape of the Beast

Do vampires draw their animal forms from the land around them? From the blood of their ancestral Kindred? From the unique character of the Discipline they learn? No one knows for sure. What's clear, though, is that a great deal of variety exists in the Blood.

The natural forms assumed by vampires in Mexico are not necessarily the wolf and bat. Depending on the Kindred's mystic heritage — his sire and/or the vampire who taught him the Discipline of Protean — his bestial self may manifest in the forms of different animals. When the character's first dot of Protean is purchased, the player or the Storyteller must determine which of the following animal sets will be inherited from the vampire's sire or mystic teacher.

Coyote and Bat: This pairing seems to be the most common among the Indian Kindred of Northern Mexico, where coyotes and vampire bats live naturally. (Supposedly, native Kindred from the Western United States adopt coyote and vulture forms, rather than these.) Use the benefits described in Vampire: The Requiem as usual.

Serpent and Eagle: These animals are in the blood of native Mexica Kindred from the region around Mexico City. Each animal form conveys a separate host of benefits. *Serpent:* Size 1, +2 Defense, +1 Dexterity, Strength becomes 1, +2 bonus to perception dice pools involving smell or vibrations. *Eagle:* Size becomes 2, fly at Speed 25, +3 bonus to perception dice pools involving sight, beak and claws inflict lethal damage.

Jaguar and Condor: This pair of animal forms is much more common in South America, but Kindred of this ilk can be found in a few domains in Northern and Southern Mexico, too. *Jaguar:* Size becomes 4, Speed is doubled, teeth and claws inflict lethal damage and add +1 bonus to attack pools, +2 bonus to Stealth dice pools. *Condor:* Size remains 5, –1 Strength, +2 Stamina, +1 Defense, fly at Speed 18, +3 dice to scent-based perception pools, vampire may gain 1 Vitae for every 3 points of Size of a carrion corpse for up to 12 hours after its death (+2 on feeding dice pools) — this doesn't enable the vampire to feed on creatures below the needs of his Blood Potency.

Resilience (Resistencia)

Where Celerity freed a traditional Mexican vampire to the caprice of the wind, Resilience inured the vampire to it. Tales abound of ancient Kindred with bodies covered in scars and patches of torn flesh, rising from a hail of arrows or shaking off the clubs of the strongest warriors. Some made a show of their Resilience, using it to demonstrate their divine nature. Others simply refused to fall on the battlefield, sparking legends that remain in the modern nights. One such tale, that of "the Jaguar who would not turn from the Spanish guns" has become something of an apocryphal tale among Mexican traditionalists, told to inspire their brethren and underscore the boundary between the native bloodlines and those of Europe. Gold is the color of Resilience to the native Kindred — the gold of the Jaguar's fur, and the gold of the flayed god Xipe Totec's body beneath the flesh.

Resilience is everywhere among modern Kindred in the region. Nomads find Resilience particularly useful, sharing it with those coterie-mates to whom it does not come naturally. Ventrue and Gangrel sport Resilience in their clashes, echoing the lengthy, difficult, age-old battles between the native Kindred and the European invaders.

The patron saint of Resilience is San Judas Tadeo, the Christian guardian of lost causes. He is depicted as a green-cloaked man with a flame over his head, holding a sacred medallion. The flame in Kindred artwork is always gold in color.

Sample tributes: Burning one's self, flaying a victim, kissing a gold medallion, refraining from feeding, wearing leather

Vigor (Fuerza)

For a region so wracked with war, it is no surprise that Vigor has played a major role in the development of Kindred society. Passions run hot in Mexico, and politics often spill out into the streets from the halls of diplomacy. Ancient Aztec vampires, dedicated to Huitzilopochtli, the hummingbird god of war, were said to have crushing the steel armor of the Spaniards with their bare fists. The European invaders brought their own force to bear, shattering stone idols and tearing mortal warriors limb from limb in their fury. The Kindred of old would roar their fury to the skies, stone-hard muscle rippling under their bloodstained flesh.

In modern nights, Vigor remains the warrior's gift. Pitched battles are still fought on the streets and in the deserts of Mexico, and steel and stone still crumble beneath the blows of raging Kindred. Contemporary vampires mark themselves with hummingbird tattoos and blazing sword patches, advertising both their strength and their willingness to do battle.

The patron saint of Vigor is San Miguel, the archangel, who is typically portrayed with sword in hand, standing on the head of a dragon or devil. The image of San Miguel is so popular among Mexican Kindred as to be nearly ubiquitous in their domains. Older vampires accept him as a representation of Huitzilopochtli without a need to alter the image at all, and younger ones like to display their *machismo* by associating themselves with the sword-bearing symbol of strength.

Sample tributes: *Bearing the image of a sword and a hummingbird, sharpening or cleaning a weapon while praying, soaking in a downpour of rain, stepping on a downed foe, willing the scars of battle to remain on one's flesh*

Bloodlines, Lodges and Legacies

Calacas

Listen to me, cabron. *I know what you did. I know where the bodies are buried, and I know what they'd do to you if they found out. By the way, your wife says hello.*

On *el Día de los Muertos* in Mexico City in 1902, a chapter house of the Ordo Dracul embarked on a bizarre experiment in an attempt to understand the Day of the Dead and its occult origins. The Mexico City Dragons had a theory that, to a limited extent, the laws of life and death worked backwards during the Day of the Dead. They held that the shades of the dead did not want to return to the world of the living, but that some compelling force drew them back from the Underworld just as surely as it normally drew the souls of the deceased to their eternal rest. The Dragons further hypothesized that, just as some souls were able to resist that force by remaining on the earthly plane after death, some souls might also be able to resist the spiritual "low tide" and remain in the afterlife through the Day of the Dead. By studying both those ghosts who remained in the material realm and those who clung to the Underworld, the Dragons thought to achieve a greater understanding of the forces that anchored the Kindred soul in its state of perpetual stasis.

The Dragons gathered in their chapter house shortly before midnight on November 2, 1902. There were five researchers present to catalog the results of the experiment, which was to be conducted principally by Hector Luíz Guerrera, a Nosferatu elder who had been a medium in his breathing days, and another whose identity was never recorded — popular theory holds that this other was a mortal necromancer. At precisely midnight, when tradition dictated that the souls of the departed began to return to the world, Guerrera and his associate conducted a ritual that was supposed to conjure a ghost from the Underworld, which would be channeled into Guerrera and use the Nosferatu as a mouthpiece. The ritual appeared to work, but the ghost's strength of will proved stronger than the Dragons had expected. Guerrera, apparently under the ghost's control, killed his associate and three of the researchers, then fled the chapter house. The surviving Dragons reported that Guerrera's previously unremarkable face had been transformed into the likeness of a skull, giving him the appearance of a living *calaca* mask.

Hector Guerrera disappeared from Kindred society after that unfortunate event, and popular consensus was that the possessing ghost, not realizing its new body was that of a vampire, did not seek shelter from the sun and was killed a second time the next dawn. Then, in 1928, a Kindred with a face like a *calaca* mask presented herself at the Mexico City chapter house of the Ordo Dracul. She claimed to be the childe of Hector Luíz Guerrera, and said that her sire had mastered the ghost that possessed him and learned much about the "tidal forces of life and death." His childe, Rosa, had been sent to guarantee that no retribution would come upon Guerrera for the deaths of the three Dragons more than a quarter of a century before. Rosa was assured that Guerrera would be welcomed back with open arms, as long as he would share his insights with the order.

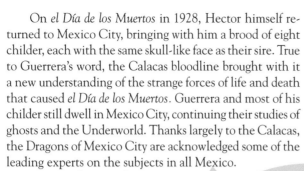

On *el Día de los Muertos* in 1928, Hector himself returned to Mexico City, bringing with him a brood of eight childer, each with the same skull-like face as their sire. True to Guerrera's word, the Calacas bloodline brought with it a new understanding of the strange forces of life and death that caused *el Día de los Muertos*. Guerrera and most of his childer still dwell in Mexico City, continuing their studies of ghosts and the Underworld. Thanks largely to the Calacas, the Dragons of Mexico City are acknowledged some of the leading experts on the subjects in all Mexico.

Parent Clan: Nosferatu

Nickname: Bones (used collectively for the entire bloodline as well as for a specific member)

Covenant: Most Calacas belong to the Ordo Dracul. In fact, the bulk of Calacas in modern nights have no direct blood lineage with Hector Luíz Guerrera at all, having been inducted instead by Guerrera or one of his childer acting as Avus. Those Calacas who leave the order usually remain Unbound, but some have been known to fall in with the Circle of the Crone. Less mystically inclined Calacas tend to favor the Carthian Movement over the Invictus. To date, there has been no verifiable record of a Calaca joining the Lancea Sanctum, but that is likely due more to the Ordo Dracul's prejudice against the Sanctified being fed to fledgling Calacas rather than any specific disinclination toward the teachings of Longinus.

Appearance: Most Calacas are of Mexican heritage, but they range across the spectrum from almost-pure Spanish blood to 100% Zapotec. They tend to dress in reserved, subdued clothing befitting an academic, though some young Calacas deliberately take an opposite tack, dressing in brightly colored, elaborately decorated traditional dress, making themselves look like the calaca decorations mortals put up for *el Día de los Muertos*.

As part of assuming the Calaca bloodline, all members' faces become exceptionally pale and distorted, with small eyes sunken in deep sockets, vestigial noses and thin lips that show the prominent outlines of their teeth. Their appearance is not blatantly supernatural, and most humans who see them assume that they suffer from some deformity or birth defect, but a Calaca's bizarre appearance will certainly draw attention.

Haven: Most of the Calacas in Mexico City lair at the Ordo Dracul's chapter house in that city rather than maintaining havens of their own. Those who do maintain havens, or members traveling abroad, often claim cemeteries or old, abandoned mortuaries as havens. Others prefer the traditional Nosferatu standby and lair in the sewers or storm tunnels.

Background: When a Calaca Embraces, she almost always chooses a mortal with some sort of psychic affinity for ghosts. Whether this is simply out of respect for their founder or because mediums have some ineffable quality that survives the Embrace and makes the bloodline's studies of the afterlife easier has never been revealed outside the bloodline. Naturally, as members of the Ordo Dracul, Calacas also look for a keen intelligence and a desire to question and ultimately understand the world around them.

Currently, however, the bulk of the Calacas bloodline comprises ancillae and, rarely, particularly gifted neonates who were not Embraced into the bloodline, but who have spent years studying ghosts and mapping Haunts and have advanced the order's understanding of these subjects sufficiently to impress Hector Guerrera, or one of his childer. These notable scholars are offered membership in the bloodline, with one of Guerrera's original childer (or, in rare cases, Guerrera himself) serving as the prospective member's Avus. Some Nosferatu have traveled from as far as Yucatán or even the United States to receive this honor.

Character Creation: Most Calacas are of a scholarly bent, and not terribly well adapted in social situations (unsurprising, given their parentage). Ghosts don't always congregate in easily accessed public places, and Calacas must sometimes investigate crumbling Aztec ruins or hazardous mountain passes to conduct their research; as such, Mental Attributes tend to be primary, with Physical secondary and Social lagging behind. Likewise, Calacas tend to focus on Mental Skills and Merits, with Occult and Eidetic Memory being the most common, respectively. Physical Skills are useful for exploration and self-defense, but many Calacas prefer to make Social Skills their secondary category in order to have a broader palette to draw from when dealing with recalcitrant ghosts. Buying a second dot of Blood Potency is a good idea, or else the character is just a Nosferatu applicant hoping to be chosen for the bloodline.

Bloodline Disciplines: Auspex, Nightmare, Obfuscate, Vigor

Weakness: The Calacas are not a pretty bunch. Their parent clan's flaw manifests in a unique and specific manner, making them resemble the *calacas* decorations popular on the Day of the Dead. As for all Nosferatu, Calacas do not gain the benefit of the 10 again rule on Presence- and Manipulation-based rolls, and any 1's rolled in those situations subtract from the character's total successes.

Furthermore, the Calacas' frequent close proximity to ghosts and haunted Dragon's Nests (and, if rumor is to be believed, the unique circumstances of the bloodline's creation) means that ghostly phenomena are drawn to these vampires like iron filings to a magnet. This typically manifests as random cold spots, ethereal breezes or faint, barely audible whispers around the character. This effect is deeply unnerving, even to those accustomed to it, and seems to get worse as the Calaca's Humanity erodes. For this reason, Humanity acts as a cap on *all* the Calacas' dice pools for social interaction (not including Intimidation or rolls to activate Nightmare powers), not just when they interact with mortals.

Organization: The Calacas are still a fairly small bloodline, and though they are mostly centrally located, they are surprisingly loosely organized. Individual members are free to pursue whatever line of research they feel is relevant, as long as they share their findings with the rest of the bloodline and, ostensibly, the Ordo Dracul (in reality, Hector Guerrera decides which of the bloodline's findings are passed on to the order at large). If a member's work is considered frivolous, dangerous or otherwise detrimental, a simple majority vote of Guerrera's childer can proscribe a Kindred from continuing. Guerrera himself can veto his childer on these votes, and occasionally does so.

Character Concepts: Ghost hunter, Kindred medium, ley-line mapper, Ordo Dracul troubleshooter, Underworld-obsessed researcher.

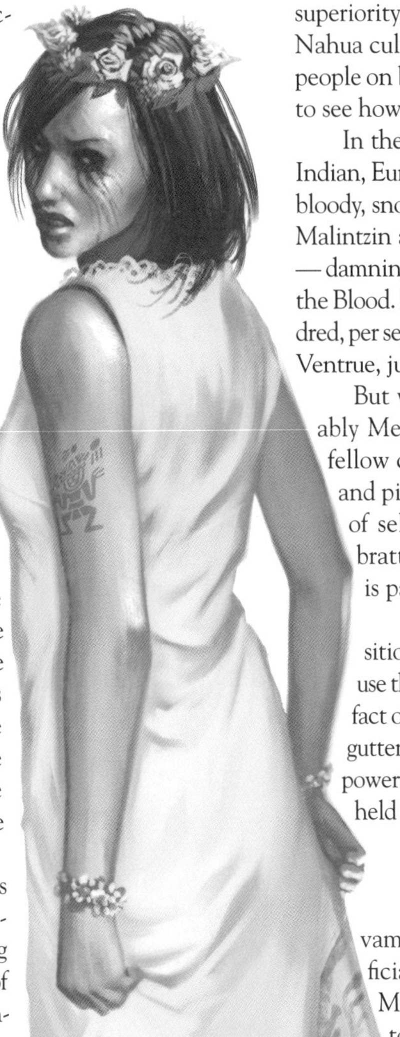

Malintzin

"To the victor go the spoils. Then his children inherit."

The Malintzin are a vampiric manifestation of wealthy mestizos, the mixed-blooded traitors and collaborators who joined the ranks of the Spanish conquistadors and delivered Mexico into their hands. The name Malintzin is even derived from the iconic betrayer of the Aztecs, the Nahua woman who served Cortés as translator and eventually became his wife: La Malinche. To the Spaniards she was known by the noble name of Doña Marina. To the Nahua, she was Malintzin.

Tonight, La Malinche remains a complex character. She is a vilified traitor, responsible for aiding the Spanish in the destruction of the Aztecs and hated for her abandonment of her own people. At the same time, she is seen by many as an icon of Nahua victimization — if she had not been at Cortés's side, she would have fallen under his sword like so many of her people.

La Malinche may be responsible for the survival of Aztec culture beyond the death of its rulers and capitols. Her marriage to Cortés may be symbolic of her betrayal, but the birth of their son represents the creation of a new hybrid culture blending Indian and European ways. She was a woman who had once been traded as a slave from the Aztecs to the Maya to the Spanish. Can it be surprising that she would have no love for the empire that enslaved her?

The vampires who took her name represent the worst of the mestizos stereotype. They see themselves as noble realists who have risen above the "noble savagery" of their Indian blood to join the ranks of the winning team. "The victory of the Spanish reveals their superiority," say the Malintzin. To them, the preservation of Nahua culture is charity, a merciful gift given to a defeated people on behalf of one of their own, who was savvy enough to see how the conquest of New Spain would end.

In the minds of most other Mexican Kindred, whether Indian, European or mestizos themselves, the Malintzin are a bloody, snobbish manifestation of turncoat colonialism. The Malintzin are said to have been Embraced by Spanish greed — damning in its own way — as all Kindred are Embraced by the Blood. Malintzin are often not even regarded as being Kindred, per se, by Mexican vampires. They are neither Daeva nor Ventrue, just as mestizos are not quite Spanish or Indian.

But while any mixed-blood Mexican is still undeniably Mexican, still able to be loved and respected as a fellow compatriot, the Malintzin are typically despised and pitied. A Malintzin with power is an embodiment of selfishness and betrayal, a moronic sell-out or a bratty fop. A Malintzin with no power (a rare thing) is pathetic trash who got her comeuppance.

And yet the majority of the Malintzin remain in positions of power, protected by the colonial Damned who use them as figureheads or regarded as a simple, despicable fact of the Requiem by those vampires who survive in the gutters beneath them. The Malintzin are supernaturally powerful leaders — their formidable mystic powers have held revolutions are bay for five hundred years.

Parent Clan: Daeva

Nickname: Malinchismas or Traitors

Covenant: The vast majority of Malintzin vampires belong to the Invictus. According to the official line of the bloodline's sole formal Avus, called Malintzinita, any non-Invictus vampire that claims to be a part of her line is either a liar or a spy. The Malintzin take pride in their roles as symbolic heiresses to the conquistadors and Spanish colonials. They hold prominent (if often ceremonial) positions within the First Estate because they believe that stability is the best way to govern. The constant cycles of revolution that have plagued the mortals of Mexico only prove their point, to their minds.

Appearance: The very small number of Malintzin makes it easy to generalize their appearance. The girls who attend to the Lady Malintzin herself dress themselves in traditional pre-Colombian Aztec or Mayan garb, often coming across as re-enactors or some kind of old-fashioned wedding party. Their male counterparts dress in more modern clothing on most nights, but decorated for formal functions with accessories that evoke the Conquest: swords, breastplates and knotted, silken sashes. It's worth noting that every male Malintzin active tonight grew a beard in preparation for their Embrace.

Haven: Most Malintzin reside in the sprawling hidden palace of Malintzinita, the bloodline's founder and Prince of her own city. Those Malintzin that aren't a part of the founder's retinue nest in similar places: penthouses, lavish vaults and gilded subterranean suites mixing Spanish architecture with Aztec frescoes and indigenous Mexican plants. Gold and silver are common themes in Malintzin havens, as are animal skins and bright textiles like blankets and tapestries. Security is always of primary importance, however. Many Malintzin nest in small, luxurious havens that are hidden from common Kindred and locked to would-be rivals.

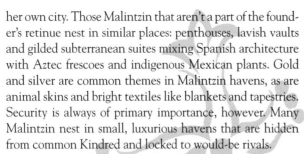

Background: To date, all Malintzin have been beautiful mestizos. Beyond that, they have only one trait in common: the affection of Malintzinita, whether as sisters, comrades or lovers. All but a few Malintzin (possibly as few as two) are young women between the ages of 16 and 21. Most were wealthy, or heirs to wealth, in life, but not all.

Character Creation: Social Skills are essential to one's existence as a Malintzin, but those can be learned. What's truly vital is one's appearance: Social Attributes must be good enough either to catch the eye of Malintzinita or to compel one of her previous petitioners to risk her wrath. In practice, dots in Covenant Status: Invictus are necessary to even get an audience with the bloodline's Avus, though clever vampires (and Storytellers) may find ways around that. A vampire with the right mindset for a Malintzin's Requiem should already have dots in Herd and Retainer. A Malintzin should almost certainly be of mixed Indian/European blood, though going against that assumed rule could make for an interesting character concept.

Bloodline Disciplines: Celerity, Dominate, Majesty, Vigor

Weakness: The Damned descendants of La Malinche suffer the curses inherent in the blood of both the Daeva and the Ventrue clans. In addition, a Malintzin must have at least one dot in Herd, Retainer or Fame to maintain her sense of identity and confidence. Without a dot in one of these Merits, a Malintzin must spend a Willpower point to awaken each night, in addition to Vitae.

Malinztin who suffer derangements tend towards severe afflictions of self-doubt and anxiety. Melancholia, Megalomania, Paranoia, Anxiety and Delusional Obsession are all likely derangements for these vampires.

Organization: The Malintzin bloodline descends from a young vampire woman known only as Malintzinita ("the Little Malinche") tonight. She is said to have been the daughter of Hernán Cortés and Doña Marina, born in secret before the son that history remembers as theirs. Cortés wanted an heir that he could present as the First Son of Mexico (though his own greed eventually overshadowed his son's importance), and at the time when his first-born daughter was conceived, Doña Marina was not yet recognized as a worthy woman by Cortés's priest. So this daughter, one of the first mestizos, was hidden away.

Tonight, that daughter is the sole recognized Avus of the Malintzin bloodline and a much hated Prince in Mexico. She claims that she was cursed with undeath by God himself, but many of her subjects claim she was cursed by the betrayal of her mother and the greed of her father — that she was damned since birth to never walk beneath the Mexican sun as an adult. Any Kindred who joins the bloodline either accepts the hatred of the Malintzin in exchange for power or simply has no care for the thoughts of her fellow Damned.

Malintzinita keeps the majority of the Malintzin bloodline in her direct employ as spies, aides and advisors. A small number of vampires — possibly only one — have been given the Malintzin blood to take with them to other cities as a symbol of royal descent from the self-appointed First Daughter of the Mexica. These posturing fops are typically token mestizos vampires kept on the arm of Ventrue Princes as a means of showing their connection to "the native Kindred."

One other vampire is said to be passing along the Malintzin bloodline: a Nahua Incubus who was supposedly once Malintzinita's concubine. The rumor goes that he fled her city in 1911 to find some way to escape the Malintzin line, but ended up joining the ranks of some Carthian revolution in Northern Mexico.

Concepts: Evil queen, insidious scheming heiress, Mexican Marie Antoinette, party monster, Prince's little girl, spoiled brat, traitorous step-mother, wicked step-brother.

Dead Wolves

"Look at that moon. It's gonna be a good night."

The fates of vampires and werewolves in Mexico have always been tangled. Whereas, in some lands, the Kindred and the Uratha maintain a cold separation from one another, here they are likely to be allies as enemies. Perhaps nothing represents the centuries of cultural contact between the Forsaken and the Damned better than the Wolves of Blood.

The story of the first so-called Dead Wolf is well known by werewolves and vampires of Mexico. But this story does nothing to explain the metaphysical circumstances of the bloodline's creation.

According to legend, the first Dead Wolf was a young man named Juan Colmillo, who lived in Northern Mexico around the time of the Mexican-American War (1846–48). Colmillo was born a werewolf, but before his First Change he was Embraced by a Gangrel vampire hunting displaced families in the Texas territory. Just why this Gangrel damned Colmillo varies depending on who's telling the story — some say Colmillo was planning to take his family to Texas and start new lives as Americans, others say Colmillo's wife had once been the Gangrel's wife when he was alive. Most stories agree, though, that Colmillo was made immortal so that he could witness America's eventual suffering and defeat on its Mexican border.

Heartbroken over Colmillo's fate, one his werewolf cousins came to him in the night and tried to undo the vampire's curse. The werewolf bit him, stuck him with silver and even gave Colmillo some of his blood in an effort to rouse his primal rage to overthrow his vampiric blood. Desperate to save his cousin, the werewolf provoked Colmillo into a bestial frenzy in the light of a full moon, hoping that Colmillo's inner wolf would slay his vampiric Beast. Instead, says the legend, Colmillo killed the werewolf and drank him to dust.

Colmillo was never the same. Though nothing could free him from the damnation of the Requiem, his blood did change to reflect his familial connection to Father Wolf and Mother Moon. The Dead Wolves bloodline was born that night, with the death of one werewolf for the sake of his fallen kin.

What truth there is in this story is questionable. The vampire called Juan Colmillo was destroyed by a French wizard in the 1860s, though even that may just be a continuation of the legend. Some Dead Wolves do remember Juan Colmillo personally, though none can say for sure if that was ever a real name. (Colmillo means, roughly, "canine tooth.")

The Colmillo legend seems to be a parable illustrating how werewolves should be willing to give their lives for the sake of the Damned and how vampires should be willing to adapt to make peace with their cousins, the Uratha. The legend is also held up by many diplomatic Uratha as a reminder that the Kindred are not necessarily, in their nature, blood-sucking monsters. Many of them were in the midst of other lives when they met with damnation, and many of them did not ask for it. Werewolves should consider each vampire as an individual, not as a breed.

As for the purpose of Colmillo's damnation, many Indian and mesitzo Forsaken and Kindred maintain that the Gangrel's prophecy has not yet come to pass. America will suffer ruin along its border with Mexico — a ruination that will benefit the Mexica and their descendants. Juan Colmillo may not have survived to witness that night, but his blood continues on so that one night some Wolf of Blood will do what Colmillo was damned to do: witness the end of Texas.

Parent Clan: Gangrel

Nickname: Bloody Wolves, Wolves of Blood, Wolf-Blooded. The confusing similarity between the Wolves of Blood and the wolf-blooded mortal relatives of the Uratha is the subject of jokes, but it's also meant as a reminder that the Kindred of this bloodline are honoring the spirit of Juan Colmillo, who truly was wolf-blooded.

Covenant: Modern Dead Wolves can be found in virtually any covenant, though few reach meaningful levels of authority in any. Wolves of Blood are more likely to serve a Kindred Prince as Hounds or Heralds, carrying their laws or their words to the Uratha and to rural, unaligned vampires. Because of their animistic beliefs, Dead Wolves often get lumped in with the Circle of the Crone, even though this bloodline's spiritual beliefs have less to do with any religious philosophy and more to do with nightly business. Sanctified Dead Wolves are not uncommon. When possible, Dead Wolves attach themselves to Kindred society through the de facto hierarchy of the court, rather than picking sides between political covenants. These vampires have enough to balance between their werewolf and vampire allegiances; they don't need to be dragged into Carthian/Invictus schemes, too.

Appearance: These rustic, rough vampires care little for their appearance to modern mortals. Many are the kinds of wild-haired, long-bearded, howl-at-the-moon madmen that local folks mistake for drunken, delirious lunatics. Most Wolf-Bloods dwell in

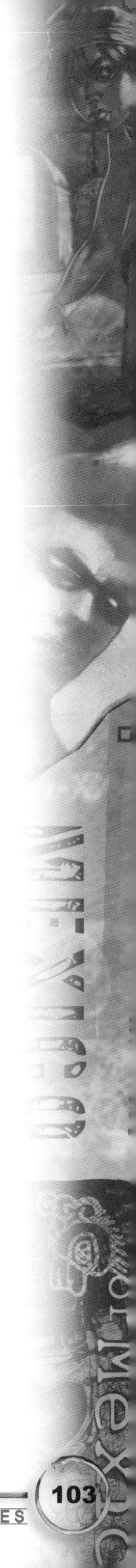

the dust and dirt of rural, northern Mexico and look like it. They wear worn denim, scarred leather jackets and flannel shirts, except for those Wolf-Bloods who predate such things, and sport simpler clothes that appeal to their dated, fur-trapper sensibilities. Since so many modern vampires in the Wolves of Blood family are also thugs for local Princes, shotguns, axes and mining picks are often in hand.

Haven: Few Dead Wolves maintain havens of any significance. Through the powers of Protean, they dwell in sand and soil, concrete and water. Dead Wolves who maintain tight relationships with a werewolf pack may nest near the pack's totem or private den, though its unusual for even a Wolf of Blood to sleep under the same roof as an Uratha cohort. Most Dead Wolves do reside within friendly werewolf territory, though, where they can expect a certain amount of informed awareness during daylight hours. Having a ghoul watch your nest in the daytime is one thing, but having a battle-ready werewolf shaman patrolling nearby is a whole other thing.

Background: Dead Wolves come to the bloodline through a connection of some kind to the Uratha, whether that connection was formed before or after the Embrace. Most Dead Wolves are therefore the kinds of people who can relate to werewolf concerns like territoriality, spiritualism and the resonant consequences of everyday actions. It happens to be true that most Dead Wolves are either Nahua or mestizos from central or Northern Mexico, but quite a few white Gangrel from Texas and Arizona have come to the bloodline in the past forty years, too.

Character Creation: Despite their close ties to both Kindred and Forsaken societies, Dead Wolves need to be self-sufficient. The Survival Skill is important, as is Stamina and as many dots in Disciplines as you can muster — it's often the shared exposure to the world's frightening strangeness that helps Dead Wolves and werewolves bond. A Wolf of Blood needs to have something to offer to local Uratha if he wants to be more than acquaintances. Uniquely vampiric powers are one option. Contacts, Allies, Resources and valuable Skills are just a few other options.

Bloodline Disciplines: Animalism, Protean, Resilience, Sublunario

Weakness: In addition to the inherent weakness of the Gangrel clan, Dead Wolves suffer from a vulnerability of their blood. Any damage inflicted on a Wolf-Blood with a silver weapon deals an additional point of damage — lethal for silver daggers, bashing for silver bullets, and so forth. This additional damage is added as an automatic success after a successful attack against the vampire, it does not increase attack pools against him.

In addition to the bloodline's vulnerability to silver, the Dead Wolves are somewhat affected by the phases of the moon. On nights of the full and new moons, a Dead Wolf must spend additional Vitae to stay awake and active. Vitae must be spent as normal for the vampire to awaken, and an additional Vitae must be spent a number hours later equal to twice the vampire's Stamina dots. Additional Vitae must be spent every time this same interval passes until sunrise.

Organization: As a bloodline, the Wolves of Blood have no real organization of their own. They plug into vampire and werewolf societies rather than create their own. Still, one long-standing tradition persists through Dead Wolf culture. Any Dead Wolf may welcome another vampire into the bloodline if that vampire can get a werewolf to vouch for him three times, on three different nights of a full moon in three different months. Only after a single Uratha has vouched for a petitioner three times will a Dead Wolf welcome the new vampire into the bloodline and vouch for him to other werewolves.

Concepts: Embraced wolf-blooded kin, Envoy to the Lupines, Kindred overseer in the pack, Lupine-hunter, vampire bounty-hunter, would-be Uratha Embraced before the First Change.

Sublunario

The unique supernatural properties of a Dead Wolf manifest in a Discipline they call Sublunario. What, exactly, gives Sublunario its power is unclear, even among members of the bloodline. Some say a wolf-spirit sleeps within the vampire's Vitae, using his hollow heart as a spectral den. Others insist that the power could only be possible through the consumption of a werewolf, and these Lupines must assume that every Bloody Wolf is a predator of the Uratha. This may have been true of the first Dead Wolves, but it is easily disproved by modern Wolf-Bloods like the agents of Prince Castillo (see p. 156).

Sublunario grants a Kindred a degree of power from the influences of Mother Moon, the great spirit that helped to create the Uratha. This power is not bestowed by her, but soaked up from her ambient grace by the power of a Dead Wolf's blood.

Cost: 1 Vitae per scene (for most effects)

Dice Pool: Most Sublunario powers require no dice rolls to activate. Rather, this unique Discipline augments the vampire's intuitive understanding of the world and creatures around him. The Discipline grants the following mechanical benefits:

• The mystic resonance of Sublunario in his blood allows him to contribute to the Uratha bond with select spirits. The vampire may contribute dots in the Totem Merit to a werewolf pack (see p. 79 of Werewolf: The Forsaken). Each dot of Sublunario grants the vampire one dot in the Totem Merit, which is only effective when shared with a werewolf pack. The vampire may share in any benefits of the totem-spirit's sponsorship that are not werewolf-specific. For example, the vampire may gain a bonus to Skills or Attributes, but can never use Gifts. According to legend, a vampire's Sublunario connection to a totem spirit can never be changed unless the spirit is broken from the pack. Thus, if the vampire falls out of favor with his honorary pack, he cannot use his Sublunario-granted Totem dots unless his old totem spirit is either destroyed or driven to abandon the pack.

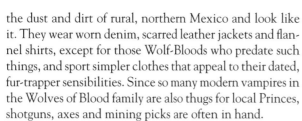

• The vampire must select one of the five phases of the moon when he purchases this Discipline: full, gibbous, half, crescent or new. Under that phase of the moon, the vampire is able to "ride the wave" (see p. 181 of Vampire: The Requiem) without any cost in Willpower. The vampire's Sublunario dots serve as a bonus to the Resolve + Composure dice pool to goad the Beast in this way. (At the Storyteller's discretion, additional phases of the moon may be "purchased" by the character for five experience points each.)

• The vampire may roll his Sublunario dots once per scene to gain a bonus on Empathy, Persuade, Intimidate and Socialize dice pools made with or against werewolves. Each success on this roll grants the vampire a bonus die to dice pools using those Skills. Note that while the vampire's instinctual behavior is spiritually informed, these bonus dice do not represent any mystic coercion of the werewolves the vampire interacts with — this Discipline affects the vampire, not werewolves.

• The vampire may divide his Sublunario dots as bonus dice between the two "insight Skills" linked with the phase of the moon under which he activates this power. All of the vampire's Sublunario dots may be placed into a single Skill, if he likes. To re-allocate these bonus dots within the same scene, the vampire must spend another Vitae. As the month progresses and the moon cycles through its phases, the vampire's insight Skills change.

Action: Instant

Insight Skills

Full Moon (Warrior): Intimidation, Survival.
Gibbous Moon (Visionary): Expression, Persuasion.
Half Moon (Walker Between): Empathy, Investigation.
Crescent Moon (Spirit Master): Animal Ken, Occult.
New Moon (Stalker): Stealth, Subterfuge.

Devotion: Wolf-Man

(Protean •••, Sublunario •••)

With this power, a Dead Wolf can transform himself into a state partway between man and beast. Visually, the vampire appears very much like the archetypal wolf-man: a hairy, feral figure with a hint of a snout, a slit nose and a mouth full of wolf-like teeth. This form, coupled with the vampire's own ferocity, makes for a terrifying creature.

Cost: 1 Vitae

Dice Pool: None. This power activates only when the vampire rides the wave of the Beast and spends a Vitae to activate it. While in this form, the vampire gains a +2 bonus on all perception-related dice pools, a +2 bonus on Intimidation dice pools and a –3 penalty on any dice pools requiring speech. Anyone attempting to identify the character by his appearance suffers a penalty equal to the vampire's Protean or Sublunario dots, whichever is higher.

While in this bestial form, only people unfamiliar with werewolves would mistake the vampire for one. The Kindred's appearance most resembles that of an Uratha in its near-human form (Dalu).

Action: Reflexive

This power costs 15 experience points to learn.

El Sacrificio (Lodge of the Sacrifice)

The story as the Aztecs knew it was this: the world has been created and destroyed four times. In each, the world perishes differently — a flood drowns the people, the mantle of the Earth shudders and spits magma, disease sweeps across the populace or red comets descend from the heavens and burn everything. The end, however, is always the same. The sun burns out, the people die. This is the fifth world, now, and the gods have stayed the hands of destruction, but do so only at a price. That price is human sacrifice.

The werewolves of El Sacrificio don't necessarily believe in the Aztec story, not wholesale. Certainly some do. Others believe it is a metaphor for the collapse of the paradise lorded over by Father Wolf. What these werewolves *do* know is that the old beliefs of the Aztecs (and the Toltecs and Mayans before them) have given life to very real spirits — or, the spirits gave life to those ancient beliefs. Regardless of the details, this lodge recognizes that the old gods still exist, hidden outside of sight but still communicating with the world in small ways. These old spirits are powerful and hungry. With the flick of an ephemeral wrist, plagues are born, tectonic plates shift and monstrous ocean waves stir and gather.

And so, the werewolves seek to placate these old gods. The Lodge of the Sacrifice offers humans to one particular god, the lord of all the old spirits, a being called Xiuhtecuhtli. This entity is the *patrón* of light and darkness, with a blood-red face and a yellow wolf painted on his chest. Through his spirit-servants, he demands that this lodge, having existed for centuries, helps continue the contract that humankind had with the spirits. Humans have broken the contract, and thus the world should again be destroyed — but the old spirit has given these werewolves the chance to take up the cause.

He promised them some level of reward for honoring him with sacrifice. Xiuhtecuhtli also promised that if they did not honor him accordingly, he would shake the humans from this world like a wolf shaking water from his fur.

Proof of this came in 1985. The werewolves of El Sacrificio — whose ranks had already thinned due to a local upsurge of Pure attacks — decided that they could no longer in good conscience continue the human sacrifices. And so they neglected to do so, and instead chose to enter the Shadow and hunt Xiuhtecuhtli in an effort to destroy him.

They could not find him, and his answer at having been dishonored was swift: an earthquake measuring 8.1 on the Richter scale shook Mexico City. More than 4,000 people died according to official records, though the true numbers were four or five times that. Ten times that were left injured, many permanently. The old spirit sent messengers to the werewolves, explaining that the earthquake was only *un gesto pequiño*, a "little gesture." Worse would come if they did not give him what he wanted.

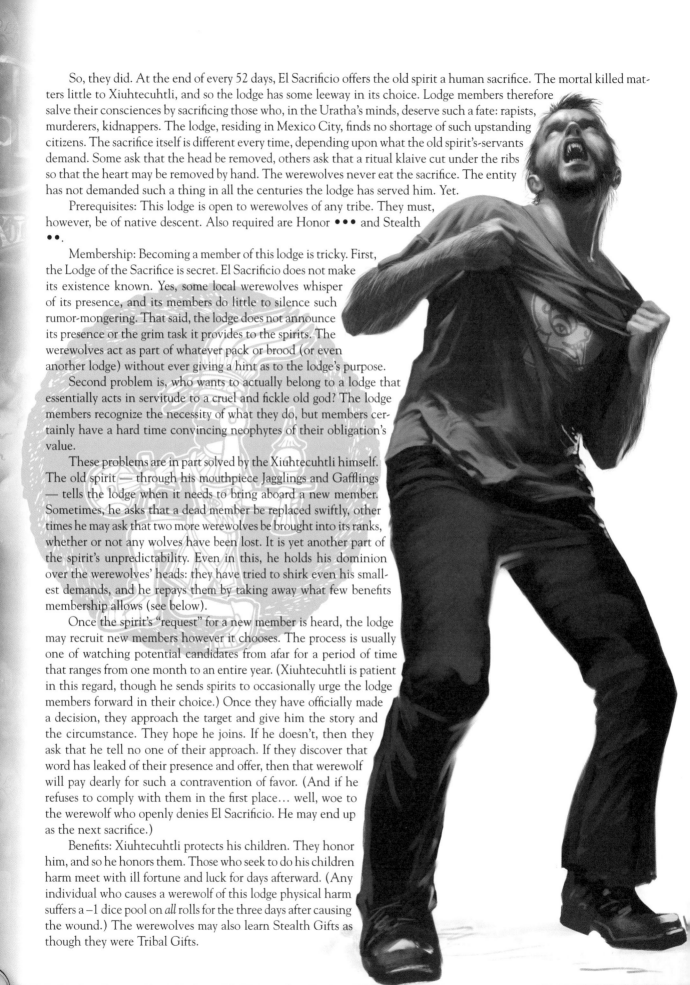

So, they did. At the end of every 52 days, El Sacrificio offers the old spirit a human sacrifice. The mortal killed matters little to Xiuhtecuhtli, and so the lodge has some leeway in its choice. Lodge members therefore salve their consciences by sacrificing those who, in the Uratha's minds, deserve such a fate: rapists, murderers, kidnappers. The lodge, residing in Mexico City, finds no shortage of such upstanding citizens. The sacrifice itself is different every time, depending upon what the old spirit's-servants demand. Some ask that the head be removed, others ask that a ritual klaive cut under the ribs so that the heart may be removed by hand. The werewolves never eat the sacrifice. The entity has not demanded such a thing in all the centuries the lodge has served him. Yet.

Prerequisites: This lodge is open to werewolves of any tribe. They must, however, be of native descent. Also required are Honor ••• and Stealth ••.

Membership: Becoming a member of this lodge is tricky. First, the Lodge of the Sacrifice is secret. El Sacrificio does not make its existence known. Yes, some local werewolves whisper of its presence, and its members do little to silence such rumor-mongering. That said, the lodge does not announce its presence or the grim task it provides to the spirits. The werewolves act as part of whatever pack or brood (or even another lodge) without ever giving a hint as to the lodge's purpose.

Second problem is, who wants to actually belong to a lodge that essentially acts in servitude to a cruel and fickle old god? The lodge members recognize the necessity of what they do, but members certainly have a hard time convincing neophytes of their obligation's value.

These problems are in part solved by the Xiuhtecuhtli himself. The old spirit — through his mouthpiece Jagglings and Gafflings — tells the lodge when it needs to bring aboard a new member. Sometimes, he asks that a dead member be replaced swiftly, other times he may ask that two more werewolves be brought into its ranks, whether or not any wolves have been lost. It is yet another part of the spirit's unpredictability. Even in this, he holds his dominion over the werewolves' heads: they have tried to shirk even his smallest demands, and he repays them by taking away what few benefits membership allows (see below).

Once the spirit's "request" for a new member is heard, the lodge may recruit new members however it chooses. The process is usually one of watching potential candidates from afar for a period of time that ranges from one month to an entire year. (Xiuhtecuhtli is patient in this regard, though he sends spirits to occasionally urge the lodge members forward in their choice.) Once they have officially made a decision, they approach the target and give him the story and the circumstance. They hope he joins. If he doesn't, then they ask that he tell no one of their approach. If they discover that word has leaked of their presence and offer, then that werewolf will pay dearly for such a contravention of favor. (And if he refuses to comply with them in the first place… well, woe to the werewolf who openly denies El Sacrificio. He may end up as the next sacrifice.)

Benefits: Xiuhtecuhtli protects his children. They honor him, and so he honors them. Those who seek to do his children harm meet with ill fortune and luck for days afterward. (Any individual who causes a werewolf of this lodge physical harm suffers a –1 dice pool on *all* rolls for the three days after causing the wound.) The werewolves may also learn Stealth Gifts as though they were Tribal Gifts.

Trail of Hearts and Heads

The Lodge of the Sacrifice provides a rather gory story hook for any who want it, leaving behind human sacrifices that are sure to draw the attention of all manner of creature: mortal, mage, vampire and even other werewolves.

What if the victim were a vampire's ghoul? Or a mortal's brother? Or an actual *mage* connected to a powerful local legacy? Does the sacrifice have ramifications in the Shadow, such as summoning spirits of misery that disrupt the activities of other local Forsaken?

What happens when the members of this lodge grow uncomfortable with their task? If they decide again to hunt the old spirit, can they trick him and find him before he decides to bring some other horrendous disaster against the people of Mexico?

Fetish: Cuchillo de Hueso (•••)

Some of the werewolves in El Sacrificio make klaives from the bones of their victims. These klaives are small, like paring knives, and often feature blades of obsidian, flint or stone bound to a human bone with dried tendon. When using this blade against another living being, the activation of the fetish causes the victim to suffer terrible numbness all over his body (provided that the werewolf causes at least one lethal point of damage with the knife at the time of activation). This numbness results in the victim losing half of his Speed and half of his Defense (round up) in addition to any damage caused. The werewolves use these knives to help slow and subdue potential victims of the sacrifice. The klaive inflicts damage as a normal knife (see p. 167 of the World of Darkness Rulebook). Such klaives are empowered by any venom-bearing spirit (snake, spider, bee, etc.).

Action: Reflexive

Dreamers of the Black Sun

One of the most feared and reviled among the Pandemonium-fueled Legacies of the Mastigos, the Dreamers of the Black Sun are an active force of chaos and pain in the mortal world. Merciless, fanatical and consumed by fear, their presence is said to herald the deaths of hundreds. Some believe that the Dreamers are corrupt victims of their own mystic energies, drawn helplessly to calamity and forced to inure themselves to the pain they witness. Others, however, know the Dreamers better: these mages are appalling engineers of disaster, slowly immolating themselves in the same fires that consume their victims. Power plant explosions, tunnel collapses, airplane and train crashes — all are projects of the Dreamers, and all are organized to empower their malicious works.

Founded in the dark days of the bloody Aztec Flower Wars, the Dreamers of the Black Sun are the priests and directors of a mystic organization now known as the Black Sun Cult. Spawned by the disillusioned, cynical instruction of a 13th-century Mastigos named Tochel, their teachings are a mishmash of Aztec and Atlantean lore, twisted by imperfect interpretation and willful misdirection. Members of the Black Sun Cult believe that the mortal world is warped and corrupt by design — a misbegotten, chaos-laced creation built by hubristic, degenerate gods. In these mages' eyes, perversion is implicit in the design of every earthly object and inhabitant. A paradise once existed, they argue, and it was torn apart to provide the base material for the ruinous human world. This paradise is identified with Tamoanchan, the mythical Aztec world of Itzpapalotl, the great and terrible Obsidian Butterfly. The only survivors of its destruction are the demonic Tzitzimime, distorted spirits of vengeance bent on the annihilation of Earth. Trapped in the sky and hidden by the sun, they await the day of unending eclipse when they will drop to Earth and visit the righteous fury of their forgotten world on all of humanity.

The influence of the Black Sun Cult extends throughout northern Mexico and the southwestern United States. The cult members' presence is concentrated in urban centers, with little or no membership in rural or other, less populous zones. If reports are to be believed, though, individual cells have begun to travel outwards, appearing recently in surprising places: Brazil, Barcelona, even Tokyo. Whether these emergences indicate an expansion of the cult or a dispersion of existing membership is unknown to observers.

The Dreamers often communicate with spirits they identify as Tzitzimime, hearing their whispers from the rippling chaos of Pandemonium. To empower the agents of Tamoanchan and better receive their guidance (or even encourage their manifestation in the mortal world), the mages of the Black Sun Cult work to provide sacrifice on a grand scale, sabotaging structures and transport systems in an effort to murder dozens or hundreds of souls at once. These sacrifices are ritually prepared and carried out so as to channel energy to the Tzitzimime, providing them with the strength to slip their bonds and come to Earth. Eventually, the Dreamers hope, the energy gathered will be sufficient to bring about the day of unending eclipse and end the pain of life.

Black Sun magic makes use of the raw power of fear, ritually occluding conscious thought by immersing the practitioner in base terror and opening a conduit for the energies of Pandemonium to pass through. They call this "opening the bone passage," a practice that puts considerable physical strain on the mage. To help stimulate the effect, Dreamers often subject themselves to threatening circumstances with little or no guarantee of survival, trusting their own power to preserve them. Many actually remain at the site of a planned sacrifice (for instance, sitting as a passenger in an airplane that has been sabotaged), allowing themselves to participate in the tragedy and risk becoming its victims. The heightening of fear that precedes the event often provides them with enough power to survive once it begins — but not always.

Their pursuit of fear is not always fueled by magical study, though. Some of the members of the Legacy become addicted to the sensation so essential to their workings, noting that they become bored and listless without the extreme stimulus they are accustomed to. Many turn to masochistic practice, pushing themselves further and further into the world of self-inflicted pain in an attempt to chase the adrenal high of panic.

The Dreamers were once a minor Legacy with relatively little influence in the mortal world. Among the Aztecs, the Dreamers were a death cult without the power to match their rivals, constantly at risk of complete destruction. Even in modern nights, their numbers are too few and their practice too dangerous to allow functional long-term organization. Turnover is frequent in the cult, and on average, the Dreamers lose members faster than they gain them. Only the dedication of a few surviving tutors has kept the Legacy alive at all. However, the advents of mass transit and modern weaponry have made it relatively easy for smaller numbers to have a greater overall impact. Even with a dwindling membership, the cult is achieving larger and more frequent sacrifice, leading to thousands of mortal deaths in recent years. To lend some perspective to the threat they now embody, enemies of the cult have noted that energies harvested by the Black Sun mages during the last 10 years may well surpass those gathered during the whole of the preceding century.

Because of the mages' activities, the cult's enemies often make a point of hunting down and neutralizing the Dreamers of the Black Sun. The practices of the cult are abhorrent to outsiders and cannot be tolerated in good conscience. While the Dreamers don't make a policy of seeking conflict with their own kind, individual members can become quite enthused about the battles that come their way, finding great satisfaction in deadly magical conflict.

It's true that the Dreamers are not entirely unredeemable. Individual cases of repentance and rejection of the values of the Black Sun Cult have been reported, lending hope to those who seek a peaceful means to end their crimes. Former members often become great crusaders against the actions of their Legacy, working tirelessly to end its murderous activities. The cult itself cares little about losing members, and makes no effort to pursue its former adherents.

And yet, the organization still survives. One by one, new mages add their power to the Black Sun cause, regardless of the dangers involved. The tutors of the Legacy find disenfranchised students, drawing them into the teachings of Tamoanchan. The Dreamers may be few, but their fervor is intensifying, as if distilled. The fewer there are, the harder they are to find and the more dangerous they become.

Parent Path: Mastigos

Nickname: Saboteurs

Appearance: The Dreamers of the Black Sun are damaged by their frequent exposure to emotional stress, and often appear gaunt, nervous or otherwise unhealthy as a result. The more powerful they become, the more they suffer — and the worse they look. Many of their ritual oblations can entail close brushes with death, and most of the more experienced members of the Legacy bear the disfiguring marks of their practice. Long, ragged scars are common, as are gnarled or arthritic limbs.

In general, the Dreamers make an effort to appear unremarkable or "normal," often dressing in cheap, generic clothing to avoid standing out in a crowd. At the site of large sacrificial workings, they often make an effort to masquerade as victims (tourists in a plane crash, sports fans at an arena collapse) to allow them to remain in proximity without evoking suspicion. Dreamers often make their escape from crime scenes huddled under emergency blankets or lying in the back of ambulances.

Background: The Saboteurs almost always emerge from failed or painful backgrounds — often sufferers of mental illness or neglect, they are people who feel they have reason to believe that the world has gone wrong (or should never have been), making them logical candidates for the revelations of the Black Sun Cult. Many engage in escalating self-abusive or even suicidal behavior before joining the cult and suffer the effects well into their service.

Organization: Every Dreamer is a Mastigos, awakened to the Watchtower of the Iron Gauntlet. Each is initiated as a priest in the Black Sun Cult and instructed by a tutor within the organization. In general, initiates are assigned positions of status in the cult and responsibility for a number of mortal agents. Most make little or no effort to communicate with mages outside their cell and will often go out of their way to avoid contact except when searching for a student of their own.

Almost every member of the Legacy ties herself to a specific demon, working to energize her patron with regular ritual sacrifice. Some have specific dates or locations reserved for their activities, and will practice their works on a set schedule.

A number of Black Sun cells have actually located ancient vampires who are traditionally identified as Tzitzimime on Earth. Most of these Kindred are deep in the long sleep of torpor, and they become a ritual focus for the members of the cult. They are secreted away in the sanctums and hollows of the Legacy, positioned at the nexus points of the gathering energies therein. If one of these Tzitzimime awakens while in the possession of the cult, the mages feed it willingly and unleash it upon the living world.

Suggested Oblations: Witnessing or surviving a catastrophic accident, standing out in the open air under a solar eclipse, leading a number of mortals to their deaths, experiencing a moment of true terror

Concepts: Apolitical mercenary hit man, cult-inspired thrill-killer, fanatic terrorist, priest of the Black Sun Cult, receiver of nightmarish visions, self-destructive masochist, suicidal warrior

Quote: *"The bones of our misbegotten race are stolen from the glory of Tomoanchan. We must return them to their rightful owners and let paradise be rebuilt."*

Attainments:

Dreamers of the Black Sun concentrate their studies on the Mind Arcanum, along with basic principles of the Death Arcanum. To successfully channel the energies of their Attainments without going mad, their minds must be strong enough (Resolve 3+) to endure the significant strains involved. With the second Attainment and higher, these mages must also have a solid base of understanding in matters of mortal fear (Intimidation 3+ or Science (Psychology) 3+).

The nimbus of every Dreamer is twisted by the energies of the Black Sun practice, suffusing the nimbus with a chaotic, dark mist. Mage Sight will reveal that Dreamers expel a black vapor when performing their works — some seem to exhale it from their nose and mouth, while others give off wisps of tainted steam from their flesh. Those Dreamers who choose to reveal their nimbus to observers may gain a +1 bonus to a single act of Intimidation.

1st: Harbinger of Fear

Prerequisites: Gnosis •••, Mind ••, Death •, Intimidation ••

The mage opens a small conduit to the nightmarish alien realm of Tomoanchan, shocking himself into an adrenalin-soaked state. His body reacts immediately to the self-imposed distress: he shakes and sweats, and blood drains from his face. Those who observe him become disquieted by his proximity, finding their own mood colored by doubts and fears. Most will instinctively seek to put some distance between themselves and the mage, thus dimming the effect — but those who cannot or will not leave the area are inspired to a heightened state of aggression.

To activate this Attainment, the Dreamer performs an instant action; no roll is required. Those who wish to remain in close proximity to the mage must succeed on a Resolve + Composure roll, and even the ones who succeed will feel agitated or uneasy. The effects last for up to one hour.

2nd: Horrifying Spasm

Prerequisites: Gnosis •••••, Mind •••

The Dreamer inspires a moment of terror in an observer by twitching and jerking his body in an unexpected and disturbing manner. Any target who is in the midst of an action that requires concentration or coordination will find his efforts disrupted by the effect, and may be in danger of causing a catastrophic failure. This attack is instant, and requires a Resolve + Intimidation + Mind roll opposed by the subject's Resolve + appropriate Ability. If successful, the victim's action fails.

Example: *Pedro is driving his truck, a normal action that requires no roll. As he rounds a corner, he is confronted by the sight of a Dreamer of the Black Sun who uses Horrifying Spasm on him. The Storyteller makes a Resolve + Intimidation + Mind roll for the Dreamer, and Pedro's player makes a Resolve + Drive roll. The Dreamer gains more successes than Pedro, so Pedro momentarily takes his hands off the wheel, causing the truck to careen off the road.*

Optional Arcanum: Death •••

If the mage also has Death 3, he can cause the victim of this Attainment to make a mistake that actually does damage to any inanimate object she is currently using. The added effect is similar to the Death 3 "Destroy Object" spell (see p. 139 of Mage: The Awakening). If the Attainment roll is a success, apply damage to the object as described in the spell.

3rd: The Scream of the Dying Sun

Prerequisites: Gnosis ••••• ••, Mind ••••

When this Attainment is activated, the energies of Tomoanchan momentarily flood the mage's body with terrifying force. He responds immediately with an involuntary, uncontrollable scream of pain and fear, letting the chaotic power issue forth. While the scream itself puts great stress on the mage's body and mind, the scream is devastating to anyone who witnesses it. While all in the immediate area are shaken by the release, suffering a temporary penalty on their actions, one target (as chosen by the mage) is struck blind and overcome with terror for the remainder of the scene. This Attainment is an instant effect, requiring a Resolve + Intimidation + Mind roll and opposing the chosen target's

Resolve + Composure. The Dreamer must be in physical contact with the chosen target — either by successfully grappling her, or by otherwise initiating touch.

Roll Results

Dramatic Failure: The Dreamer fails to release the scream properly, and it damages him on the way out. While all observers (including the target) still suffer the –2 effect on actions that round and the next, the Dreamer himself is struck blind for the remainder of the scene and cannot invoke any more Attainments until his vision returns.

Failure: The Attainment's energies do not accumulate properly, and the mage cannot release them. She will not scream unless she chooses to, and the sound will have no unusual effect.

Success: The scream builds within the mage and escapes him. All witnesses within 10 yards suffer the –2 penalty on their actions in that round and the one that follows it. The chosen target is immediately blinded, and will remain so for the rest of the scene. She suffers a penalty (see "Fighting Blind," p.166 of the World of Darkness Rulebook) on all actions until her sight is restored, and will almost certainly fail any tasks that rely on sight alone.

Exceptional Success: The Scream of the Dying Sun issues forth with such overwhelming force that all witnesses in the immediate area suffer a dimming of their sight, suffering the –2 penalty on all actions for the remainder of the scene. The chosen target is blinded for a day, suffering the penalties listed above for the duration.

Optional Arcanum: Death ••••

If the Dreamer also has Death 4, the energies she releases can actually scorch the victim's eyes, dealing actual physical damage to them and rendering him blind until the wounds can be healed (by normal means or otherwise). The added effect is similar to the Death 4 "Rotting Flesh" spell (see p. 144 of Mage: The Awakening), but it relies on the Attainment roll described here instead of that of the spell. If the Attainment roll is a success, apply the damage to the target as described in the spell.

When the Dead Return

In Spanish, it is called *el Día de los Muertos*, the Day of the Dead. Lasting from November 1st to November 2nd, this holiday is quite possibly the most widely known, quintessentially Mexican holiday familiar to the rest of the world, even if it is often poorly understood at best. Those unfamiliar with the holiday often see the skeleton decorations and the visits to graveyards and equate the Day of the Dead with Halloween, but that is a gross oversimplification (and in the World of Darkness, gross oversimplification can get you killed).

To the mortals of Mexico, *el Día de los Muertos* is a holiday that celebrates the love and the remembrance of those who have passed on. It is a time to reminisce about departed friends and family members, to remember that they are still looking out for their earthly relations and celebrate their lives. Day of the Dead has also become a popular tourist attraction, drawing curious visitors from other countries (particularly the United States) in much the same way as Mardi Gras or Carnivále. Meanwhile, in the shadowy underground of the supernatural, the Day of the Dead draws tourists of an altogether different sort. Curious scholars of the Ordo Dracul skulk the streets by night, mapping the abnormally large number of haunts that spring up during the nights. Lupine shamans from the Bone Shadow tribe lurk on the far side of the Gauntlet, studying the spiritual causes and effects that allow the long-departed to return. Necromancers on the Path of Doom scour the graveyards and ancient, forgotten tombs, hoping to glean long-forgotten knowledge from shades returning from the Underworld.

Theme: Superstition and Religion

El Día de los Muertos is a day when many old folk superstitions come to the forefront of Mexican life. People leave offerings of food drink, and flowers for the dead, and in some cases wait up by the graves of their loved ones all night, hoping to meet the departed souls of friends and family. At the same time, a strongly traditional Catholic religious element balances the old superstitions, with family members constructing altars for the departed, decorated with crucifixes and images of the Blessed Virgin Mary. The living spend time praying for the souls of the departed, whether in church or at the altars they make at home. This counterbalance of pre-Christian superstition and Christian faith is a common theme throughout Mexico, but comes into sharpest focus during the Day of the Dead.

Mood: Hope

The Day of the Dead is a celebration of hope for the mortals of Mexico, a fervent, sometimes desperate hope that the Hereafter is a better place than the Here, and that the family and friends who have gone on ahead are still watching over their loved ones. For the poor, life in Mexico can be a desperate, fierce struggle for survival, and if the departed shades of your loved ones are looking out for you, then maybe, just maybe, you'll survive the crime and the drugs and the poverty for another year. Even the wealthy and prosperous honor their returning ancestors, perhaps hoping that the spirits will put in a good word for them in the afterlife, perhaps just hoping that Abuelo José won't become angry and curse them with bad luck for the coming year.

A History of the Day of the Dead

Festivals honoring and venerating the dead have existed in Mexico for at least 3,000 years, and quite possibly longer than that. The indigenous peoples of Central and South America, among them the Aztec, Maya, Purepecha and Nahual peoples, commonly kept skulls both as trophies and as symbols of life, death and rebirth. Few records of the earliest of these ceremonies survive, having been wiped out by the conquistadors in their efforts to convert the natives to Christianity, and the practices of the native tribes at the time of the arrival of Europeans may have been quite different than the earliest festivals.

The celebration that would form the basis of the Day of the Dead was originally a month-long festival honoring the Aztec goddess Mictecacihuatl, the Lady of the Dead. It fell during the ninth month of the Aztec solar calendar (near the beginning of August in the Gregorian calendar), and was dedicated to the celebration of children as well as the remembrance of the dead. When the Spaniards arrived in the 15th century, as part of their efforts to convert the Aztecs to Christianity, the conquistadors moved the festival to the first two days of November to correspond with the Catholic festivals of All Saints and All Souls' Day. Ironically, this is a case of double-syncretism, as All Saints was moved to November 1st in the 8th century to correspond with the Celtic festival of Samhain. This blending of pagan tradition and Catholic ritual eventually evolved into the present *Día de los Muertos* festival. Although it is commonly thought of as a Mexican holiday, the Day of the Dead is celebrated in many countries, including the United States (especially in areas with a high Mexican immigrant population), Brazil and the Philippines.

The Wrong Day?

The current placement of the Day of the Dead at the beginning of November is a relatively recent invention, at least as it compares to the festival of Mictecacihuatl. So if the Day of the Dead was only moved to its current date as a religio-political power play to usurp traditional holidays, what does that mean for the mystical symbolism of the day? Here are a few possible answers to that question:

• Fashionably Late: The original Aztec festival, roughly corresponding to the month of August, is the true "Day" of the Dead. During this month, the dead can return from the Underworld for a time, and the Day of the Dead is largely mortal superstition and tradition. However, since a ghost can regain Essence by being remembered by the living, the festivals of *Día de los Muertos* still draw the shades of the departed, which may explain why even the supernatural denizens of Mexico commonly believe in the festival's mystical significance. If only they would start looking a few months earlier, they might see the full impact of the Day of the Dead.

• The Power of Belief: In this theory, it is not the date that is significant, but the belief of the people that allows the dead to return. There is no mystical alignment of the spheres on a particular date that opens the doors to the Underworld, only the power of human belief and emotion. Werewolves and some mages point to the dramatic impact human belief and emotion can have on the Shadow; it only stands to reason, they say, that the human mind can have a similar influence on the Underworld. This theory might also explain why the peculiar happenings of the Day of the Dead tend to be restricted to regions where the holiday is celebrated: Mexico, the Philippines and Mexican American communities in the United States, for example.

• Same Shit, Different Day: The Church chose the first two days of November for *el Día de los Muertos* festival to syncretize it with All Saints and All Souls' Day, which were themselves put there to absorb the Celtic New Year and festival of the dead. Samhain is marked by a similar belief that, from October 31st to November 2nd, the dead would return to the world of the living. For whatever reason (perhaps some strange mystical alignment of the stars and planets, perhaps the power of human belief, perhaps some even more esoteric reason), the beginning of November has always been a time when the dead could return to the world of the living. Whether the original Aztec festival of the dead is also such a time or whether the priests of Mictecacihuatl were off in their calculations is left to the Storyteller.

• It's All a Hoax: Of course, there is always the possibility that there is *no* occult significance to the Day of the Dead at all. As mentioned previously, the increase in ghostly activity caused by the shades of the departed flocking to their families' remembrances to gain Essence could easily account for a belief, even among the supernatural denizens of the World of Darkness, that the dead are able to return even from the Underworld on these two days. In this case, of course, it doesn't matter when the original festival was versus the currently accepted dates, because there is nothing going on beyond a festival to honor and remember the dead.

Practices of the Day of the Dead

For most people, the observance of *el Día de los Muertos* begins on October 31st. In preparation for the return of the deceased the next day, families spend this day cleaning and sprucing up the graves of their departed relatives. Depending upon the state of the grave, this could range from simply clearing off weeds and laying some flowers on the plot to the purchase of a new headstone. Wealthy individuals with family mausoleums often have the crypts repainted or add new decorative flourishes to them.

November 1st is commonly referred to as *el Día de los Angelitos*, the Day of the Little Angels, and tradition states that this is the day when the souls of departed children return. It is customary to leave *ofrendas*, or offerings, of small toys and candies out for the returning souls. Depending on the region, these offerings may be left on the grave or on the family altar.

The following day is the day properly known as the Day of the Dead, and this is when the souls of adults return to the world. Predictably, the offerings left on this day are usually cartons of cigarettes, bottles of *tequila* or *mezcal*, and similar libations enjoyed by the deceased. Traditionally, a large feast is held in the early morning hours of the 2nd, but in most major cities this has been largely replaced by a family dinner with special dishes, such as *pan de muerto*, in a tradition not entirely dissimilar to an American Thanksgiving dinner.

Throughout the festival, families formally welcome the dead into their homes and visit the grave sites of their relatives, often having picnics there. In addition to offerings at the graves and family altars, many families prepare dinner for the departed and leave the food out overnight. Gifts are also given to the living, commonly in the form of sugar-candy skulls or small trinkets with a death theme.

Ofrendas

One of the traditions of the Day of the Dead most familiar to non-Mexicans is the leaving of offerings at the grave or at the altar. These *ofrendas* can be nearly anything that honors the memory of the dead: a favorite food, a high school diploma or a beloved toy. A few kinds have become traditional, and are discussed below.

Food

These offerings are among the most common. Any sort of food the deceased enjoyed is appropriate, as are sugar candy skulls, cookies and *pan de muerto*, "bread of the dead," a kind of sweet egg-bread commonly baked into the shape of a skull. In Oaxaca, *pan de muerto* is baked in the shape of a burial shroud, with a face imprinted on one end while the bread is still hot. Comestibles are usually eaten by the living after the festival, but the folklore holds that the spirits of the dead consume the spirit of the food, and thus it has no real nutritional value to the living.

Story Hook: Pan de Muerto

In the small town of Juchitán de Zaragoza, Oaxaca, a local bakery has shut down all of its normal operations during *el Día de los Muertos* in order to focus exclusively on baking *pan de muerto*. The bread is baked in the traditional Oaxacan style, but the faces pressed into the bread are disturbingly lifelike, sometimes seeming to change expression when no one is looking at them. When the characters (or one of their friends or relatives) purchase a loaf of the bread, they recognize the face of one of their departed relatives — someone who has never been to Oaxaca.

Drink

Alcoholic beverages (traditionally of Mexican manufacture) are popular *ofrendas*, as are traditional drinks such as *atole* (a hot, cornstarch-based drink with vanilla and cinnamon) and *champurrado* (similar to *atole*, but with chocolate). Comestibles are usually eaten by the living after the festival, but the folklore holds that the spirits of the dead consume the spirit of the food, and thus it has no real nutritional value to the living.

Food, Drink and the Dead

According to the folklore surrounding the Day of the Dead, the food and drink left out as *ofrendas* are spiritually consumed by the dead. The physical remains of the food are held to have no nutritional value, but occasionally the *ofrendas* may convey a more esoteric benefit. By virtue of its connection with the Underworld, the food or drink left out for the dead may give a mortal who consumes it an increased affinity for perceiving ghosts.

At the Storyteller's discretion, consuming *ofrendas* after the Day of the Dead festival is over may grant a mortal character the benefit of the Unseen Sense Merit, pertaining to ghosts. The character may also be able to see ghosts that are not manifested. There is no roll for seeing ghosts; the Storyteller decides when or if it is dramatically appropriate. These benefits last until the first new moon after *el Día de los Muertos*.

Flowers

Many cultures place flowers on graves as a sign of remembrance and a symbol of life. On *el Día de los Muertos*, the custom is to decorate the graves of family members with large, vibrant bouquets to show that they are still remembered. Marigolds (called *flor de muerto*, "flower of the dead," because the blooms are thought to attract the deceased) and chrysanthemums are the most popular, as are any flowers the deceased was particularly fond of.

Calaveras y Calacas

One of the more unusual traditions of the Day of the Dead is the *calavera*. *Calavera* is a colloquial term for a skull, but in the context of the Day of the Dead, this means a short poem, written as a mocking epitaph for a (still-living) friend or family member. In smaller towns, *calaveras* may simply be written and give to the recipient, but in larger cities they are often published in newspapers or written in graffiti. *Calaveras* satirizing public figures are predictably common, and published *calaveras* are often accompanied by a cartoon skeleton drawn in the style of Mexican engraver José Guadalupe Posada.

Calacas are skull- or skeleton-themed decorations, masks often worn in parades or figurines made of wood or clay. In keeping with the holiday's hopeful, celebratory theme, *calacas* are usually depicted in festive garb, dancing or playing musical instruments. In keeping with Aztec traditions, they are often shown with marigold leaves. The abundance of *calacas* decorations is likely one of the main reasons why *el Día de los Muertos* is equated with Halloween in the United States.

Story Hook: Calaveras Malvados

In a major Mexican city (perhaps Mexico City or Tijuana), the local newspaper publishes the best *calaveras* sent to them by the paper's readers, lavishly and often humorously illustrated, over both days of *el Día de los Muertos*. This year, one of the *calaveras* published on the 1st stands out from the others: it is poorly written and barely literate, and rather than the usual jocular mockery, it depicts the death of a man named Ernesto in rather graphic detail. That the newspaper even published it is startling enough, but at midnight that night, a man named Ernesto Ruíz dies in exactly the manner described in the poem. The next morning, there is another *calavera* in the same broken verse, this time describing the death of someone with the name of one of the players' characters.

Día de los Muertos and the World of Darkness

Up to this point, this section has discussed *el Día de los Muertos* in a relatively mundane, non-supernatural sense. Apart from the story hook sidebars, the preceding section depicts the Day of the Dead more or less as it occurs in the real world. But what happens in the World of Darkness, when the dead can return considerably more often than once a year, and in many forms, often with less virtuous intentions than watching over their living relatives?

The Day of the Dead is a significant event for many of the supernatural denizens of Mexico. Obviously, ghosts are affected the most dramatically and directly affected by the Day of the Dead, but the peculiar effects of these two days in November draw the curious and the scholarly from the shadows in droves. Many are natives, who have devoted their (sometimes unnaturally long) lives to understanding *el Día de los Muertos*, while others are immigrants or tourists, drawn by the rumors of strange happenings in Mexico during the festival.

Ghosts

Through mechanisms unknown, *el Día de los Muertos* brings with it major, albeit temporary, changes to ghostly existence. For two days out of the year, the shades of the departed find that they can almost be with their loved ones as they were when they were alive, and sometimes even interact with them. During *el Día de los Muertos*, ghosts find it easier to be near their loved ones and manifest before them. The ghosts can even consume food and drink left as *ofrendas*, almost as though they were alive again. Of course, the atmosphere of remembrance for the dead means that an ample supply of Essence is available for those two days.

For most ghosts, just as for most mortals, *el Día de los Muertos* is a time of hope and joy, however fleeting. Even the weakest ghosts have a chance to appear to their loved ones, and particularly strong-willed ones can even converse with their families. *Ofrendas* offer a chance to remember what it was to eat and drink, and for two short days, the cold, pale existence of the ghost seems just a little warmer. Of course, that only makes it that much crueler when the calendar rolls over to November 3rd, and all that is snatched away again. Some ghosts that retain enough self-awareness to recognize the brevity of the Day of the Dead are driven mad by it, and use the ease of manifesting to terrorize mortals out of sheer spite or, worse yet, find a host to possess. Ordinarily ghostly possession is strictly short-term, but some occultists surmise that the nature of the Day of the Dead might make it possible for a strong-willed ghost to drive out the soul of a living mortal and claim a new body for itself.

¿Solo en México?

Even though it is celebrated in several Latin American countries, the Day of the Dead is considered a primarily Mexican holiday. But what about the rest of the world? Do ghosts in Detroit and Beijing suddenly and inexplicably acquire remarkable freedoms for two days in November? As with many things, the answer lies with the Storyteller. Depending upon your chosen interpretation of the nature of the Day of the Dead, it might be restricted to communities where belief in the holiday is strong (if, for example, *el Día de los Muertos* is caused by a powerful surge of human emotion and belief), or it might be a global phenomenon (if the Day of the Dead is a cosmic alignment of Earth with some other realm).

Obviously, if *el Día de los Muertos* is a global phenomenon, it makes it easier to use the supernatural elements of this section outside of Mexico, but it does lessen the incentive for a group of characters to travel to Mexico from wherever their home base is to investigate the mystery. Use whatever answer best suits your chronicle.

Día de los Angelitos y Día de los Muertos

Popular tradition in Mexico dictates that the day of the festival, properly known as *el Día de los Angelitos*, is when the souls of departed children return, while the second, the day properly called *Día de los Muertos*, is when the adults retun. If you want to use that particular piece of folklore, simply allow the ghosts of children to benefit from the effects described below on November 1st, while the ghosts of adults get the benefits on November 2nd. This is an optional rule; use it if you want to incorporate more elements of the traditional Day of the Dead folklore into your chronicle.

Effects of Día de los Muertos on Ghosts

During the Day of the Dead festival, ghosts are endowed with considerably more freedom than they ordinarily enjoy. Their anchors are loosed, connections with their families strengthened and their ability to manifest is greatly improved. In some cases, ghosts long since banished to the Underworld can return to the lands of the living during *el Día de los Muertos*. From midnight on November 1st until dawn on the 3rd, ghosts receive the following benefits:

- A ghost may wander away from its anchors freely, regardless of its Power. The ghost may still spend one point of Willpower to instantly jump to one of its anchors, but it is not obligated to remain within 10 yards per point of Power it possesses. If a ghost is outside its maximum radius at dawn on November 3rd, the ghost is automatically teleported to its nearest anchor and loses a point of Willpower.
- All living members of a ghost's family become anchors for the duration of the Day of the Dead. This has no major effect on

the ghost, because of the above benefit, but does allow the ghost to instantly jump to any family member's location by spending a point of Willpower. These temporary anchors vanish at dawn on November 3rd; if the ghost is near a family member who is *not* one of the ghost's actual anchors, the ghost immediately jumps to its nearest anchor and loses a point of Willpower. Note that family is not strictly biological in this sense: what constitutes "family" varies from ghost to ghost; the ghosts of individuals who grew up in a traditional, large Mexican family might have a dozen or more parents, grandparents, siblings, aunts, uncles, cousins and even in-laws who count as *familia*, while the ghost of a child who grew up with only his older brother to take care of him might only count that brother as family, even if his parents and other siblings are still alive and well.

- All rolls made to manifest gain a +2 bonus, and failed manifestation attempts do not cost a point of Willpower.
- Ghosts do not suffer the –1 penalty per decade since death to Finesse rolls made to communicate with mortals without the appropriate Numen.
- Ghosts in the Underworld may return to the physical realm by succeeding on a Power + Finesse roll, as if manifesting. All appropriate modifiers based on the location of the ghost's manifestation apply (see p. 210 of the World of Darkness Rulebook). In addition, this roll suffers a –3 penalty above and beyond the usual modifiers. The normal Day of the Dead manifestation bonuses (+2 to manifestation rolls, failed manifestation attempts don't cost Willpower) do not apply to this action. Returning to the Underworld is a reflexive action and requires no roll. Ghosts risen from the Underworld *must* return of their own volition by dawn on the 3rd. What happens to those that don't is a mystery, but those few mages powerful (and foolhardy) enough to explore the Underworld have hinted that the unfortunate dead caught at daybreak vanish from the Underworld completely — whether destroyed utterly or transcended to another realm, none can say.

In addition to these documented effects, rumors persist of other, unverified side effects of *el Día de los Muertos*, both beneficent and baneful. One story claims that ghostly possession can be made permanent if the ghost Rides a mortal for the full duration of the festival. Another claims that, if those who truly loved the ghost in life will pray and fast by the graveside for the duration of the holiday, God Himself will reach down from Heaven and raise the deceased back to life. Still others tell that the ghosts of the wrongly murdered are given special powers of vengeance during the Day of the Dead with which to punish their killers. The details vary from region to region.

Story Hook: Miracle Church

Popular legend states that, by passing through the crucifix above the altar of the *Iglesia de Maria y Todos Angeles* in Tehuacán, Puebla, a ghost may receive forgiveness and pass on to Heaven. This year, as the Day of the Dead approaches, those ghosts with the remaining sentience and capacity to travel have begun to congregate in the neighborhood around the church. Some have come through happenstance, following an anchor that was brought to the city, while others are natives of Tehuacán and still others have used Numina to bully or frighten mortals into bringing one of their anchors to the church.

The sheer number of ghosts hovering around the church is creating a pool of death-resonant Essence that may, in time, develop into a powerful locus. (Loci are described in both Werewolf: The Forsaken and Mage: The Awakening; players without access to those books may simply treat them as Dragon's Nests.) That would be bad enough, but all hell *really* breaks loose at midnight on November 1, when the first ghost passes through the crucifix — and nothing happens.

Ofrendas and the Dead

As described earlier, *ofrendas* are offerings left out in memory of the dead, usually in the form of food or drink. During the *Día de los Muertos* holiday, ghosts are actually able to consume this food and drink, at least spiritually, and for a fleeting moment remember what it was to be alive. Other *ofrendas* are not as readily ingestible, but still count as moments of *memento mori* that allow a ghost to regain Essence (see p. 208 of the World of Darkness Rulebook). The following chart can be used as a guideline for how much Essence a ghost can regain from various *ofrendas*.

Ofrenda	Essence Regained
Food or drink	1*
Flower	1†
Toy or other memento	1*†
Minor maintenance to grave	1*
Prayer for the dead	2
Major maintenance to grave	2*
Night-long vigil at grave	2
Complete renovation to grave	3*
Recognition of manifested ghost	3

* Regain one additional point of Essence if the *ofrenda* was something the ghost loved in life (e.g., a favorite brand of tequila, paintings of the sea on the mausoleum of a girl who loved the beach).

† If the *ofrenda* is left on the grave rather than an altar, regain one additional point of Essence.

Story Hook: La Fantasma de la Venganza

In the slums of Juárez, the drug dealers and cartel soldiers tell stories about *La Fantasma de le Venganza*, the Spirit of Revenge. Said to be the ghost of a murdered policeman (in various stories killed by the cartels, by his corrupt partner or by a crazed junkie),

La Fantasma stalks the streets of Juárez, still bleeding from the gunshots that killed him, watching over the city and protecting the victims of drug violence like a vengeful angel. For most of the year, the stories say, he is content to act indirectly to disrupt drug trafficking and prevent drug-related crime (conjuring up the lights of a phantom police car, for example, or manifesting visibly to a would-be rapist as a well-armed bodyguard escorting the potential victim). But on the Day of the Dead, La Fantasma is thought to be able to manifest as a physical, earthly presence, whereupon he goes on a bloody rampage through the ranks of the Juárez cartel, killing as many of its members as he can find in those two days.

Crime reports in Juárez are spotty at best, and sifting out dead drug runners from the innocent victims of the citys murder rate can be difficult, but there *does* seem to be a spike in cartel-member killings around the beginning of November going back seven years. Needless to say, the drug lords of Juárez tend to spend *el Día de los Muertos* behind locked doors, praying.

Vampires and the Day of the Dead

The native Kindred of Mexico have always considered the festivals of the dead, in the different forms they have taken over the years, to be "their" holidays. Before the coming of the Europeans, Mexico's Kindred often hid amongst the priesthood of Mictecacihuatl, the Lady of the Dead. Therefore, it was their duty to conduct nocturnal ceremonies to their goddess throughout the solar month, guiding the souls of the dead back from *Mictlan*, the Underworld. Less-pious Kindred sometimes, in flagrant violation of the Masquerade, ruled openly over smaller villages as avatars of Mictecacihuatl or her husband, Mictlantecuhtli, the Lord of the Dead. Presiding over their own bloody festivals of the dead, these vampires used the month-long festival of the dead to demand *ofrendas* of blood from the cowed populace. It is generally believed that the conquistadors wiped out the vast majority of such pre-Christian blood cults, but it is possible that, in some isolated village far from the modern urban areas of the country, sanguine "gods" still extract yearly tribute from a population of blood dolls that still practices the ancient Aztec faith.

"Immigrant" Kindred (and this label is often applied to any vampire, regardless of ancestry, born after the arrival of the Europeans) tend to have less possessive attitudes about *el Día de los Muertos*, though it doesn't take a master satirist to recognize the irony in a holiday which celebrates the dead returning to take nourishment from the living. Many Kindred still celebrate the holiday as they did during their breathing days, visiting the graves of relatives and praying for their souls at homemade altars. In some domains, it is considered a major social faux pas to recognize one's mortal life during *el Día de los Muertos*; instead, *ofrendas* of Vitae are left for Kindred who have suffered Final Death. In at least one domain in Chihuahua, the Prince has instituted a tradition that, for the two days of the festival, Kindred leave their usual havens and sleep the day away in places of death: crypts and coffins are most common, but some daring vampires have been known to use mortuaries or funeral homes. Although many businesses close on the Day of the Dead, it is not an official holiday, and so the Kindred who sleeps the day away in a place of business risks discovery or worse.

Predictably, a number of superstitions about the Day of the Dead have arisen among the Kindred of Mexico. One of the most popular holds that a vampire's mortal relatives can clearly see her reflection during the Day of the Dead, and can even recognize her in photographs or videos that were taken during *el Día de los Muertos*. Another superstition holds that the blood of family members is especially potent during the Day of the Dead, yielding *two* points of Vitae per point of lethal damage inflicted. Some Kindred who have committed the sin of Amaranth have reported strange, torpor-like dreams of their victims gaining revenge in horrible ways while the vampires sleep. Since few Kindred are willing to admit to the practice of diablerie, it is difficult to gauge whether this might be an effect of *el Día de los Muertos* or simply the paranoid Kindred psyche at work.

The Carthian Movement

Among the vampires of the Carthian Movement, *el Día de los Muertos* is generally regarded as no more or less significant than any other major holiday. In some domains, the Day of the Dead is ignored entirely, along with anything else that might distract the Carthians from the fiery rhetoric of its charismatic leaders. In others, as in mortal society, the Day of the Dead is an excuse to throw a party and unwind. Carthian Day of the Dead celebrations are typically more energetic than those of other covenants; in one domain near the California border, the Carthians lay claim to an entire city block in the Rack for the duration of the festival. As far as the mortals know, it's one hell of a party, probably organized by local nightclub owners. The Movement uses the general chaos and confusion of the teeming mass of mortals as a cover for the covenant's more clandestine operations: everything from back-room deals with the city's power players to assassinations have occurred while the bass pounds and the mortals dance away their lives.

The Circle of the Crone

The Acolytes, more than any other covenant, cling to the oldest traditions of the Day of the Dead. Most celebrate the festival of Mictecacihuatl during the month of August, and either ignore or pay lip service at best to the modern holiday in November. In most domains held by the Circle of the Crone, it is taboo to feed from children during the festival, and even in cities controlled by other covenants, Acolytes usually restrict their own from feeding on the young. Those Kindred with the ability to see or converse with ghosts often make a point to seek out the spirits of the dead and glean what wisdom they can from the ghosts. The Circle of the Crone eschews the modern practices of *ofrendas* and remembrance, instead focusing their veneration on Mictecacihuatl, whom the Acolytes see as an aspect of the Crone. Spiders, owls and bats are sacrificed with obsidian blades in dark sepulchers unlit by even the dimmest light. As the 11th hour was deemed sacred to the Lord and Lady of Mictlan, many Acolytes consider it auspicious to begin a new task sometime during the hour between eleven o'clock and midnight.

The Invictus

As with most holidays, the Invictus treat *el Día de los Muertos* not as a religious occasion or a time for veneration but as an excuse to show off the covenant's wealth and power. Lavish, spectacular Day of the Dead celebrations are *de rigeur* in Invictus domains, and the Kindred who can put on the most lavish and impressive display is accorded a great deal of respect among the social elite. Death is, of course, the common theme, but the parties themselves may be anything from staid, reserved affairs with the guests dressed in funerary garb to wild, Vitae-soaked orgies in cemeteries or frenetic dances for guests dressed in *calaca* masks and vibrant *traje de charro* costumes. Invictus Princes often hold court in cemeteries or cathedrals during the two nights of *el Día de los Muertos*. In Invictus-held domains with a strong Sanctified presence, *el Día de los Muertos* is often a traditional time to reaffirm the traditional allegiance between the First and Second Estates. The Prince and his officers attend the Lancea Sanctum's services and receive the Bishop's blessing to continue ruling over the city's Kindred, and in some domains the Prince might even conduct a special Mass himself.

The Lancea Sanctum

The Sanctified came to Mexico with the conquistadors, and just as those Spanish warriors, the Sanctified still tend to see the whole *Día de los Muertos* affair as vaguely blasphemous. Younger members, Embraced after the Day of the Dead became syncretized with Roman Catholicism, are more accepting of the holiday, but the covenant's elders still remember the old festivals of Mictecacihuatl and refuse to have anything to do with it. In domains where the Sanctified celebrate *el Día de los Muertos*, it is considered the ultimate taboo to leave *ofrendas* for relatives from one's mortal days. Doing so is seen as a rejection of Longinus' teachings, defying the injunction that the Kindred are Damned monsters, wholly separate and apart from the run of humanity. Instead, the Sanctified leave *ofrendas* of Vitae (usually no more than one or two Vitae) for the shades of sires, grandsires, childer and broodmates who have met Final Death.

The Ordo Dracul

The Order of the Dragon doesn't care about silly peasant superstitions or backwards zealotry, and the Dragons pay only lip service at best to games of politics and social standing. What fascinates the Dragons about *el Día de los Muertos* is the occult truth behind the holiday. Certainly the order's mystics have observed a trend toward a greatly increased number of hauntings during the Day of the Dead, and members of the covenant who map the course of ley lines across Mexico have consistently reported an explosion of short-lived Haunts springing up at the beginning of November, but the order, at least on the whole, hasn't figured out *why*. Chapter houses across Mexico become a flurry of activity toward the end of October as the Dragons ready their experiments and prepare themselves to observe the most minute details of *el Día de los Muertos* in the hopes of finding the truth. These experiments sometimes yield strange fruits; one such attempt to divine the truth behind *el Día de los Muertos* resulted in the creation of a new bloodline, the Calacas (see p. 99).

The Day of the Dead and Other Supernaturals

Vampires aren't the only supernatural creatures with an interest in *el Día de los Muertos*. Though the Kindred may not understand the werewolves' actions, it is clear that the Lupines have a keen interest in the festival as well. Mortal magicians, too, seem to use the Day of the Dead to contact ancient ghosts and recover long-lost knowledge. The powerful emanations of the Day of the Dead are a potent lure for many of the denizens of the World of Darkness, and a wise individual, Kindred or not, steps lightly for the first two nights of November.

Werewolves

Mexico is a wild, dangerous place for the Uratha, and the Day of the Dead is often the peak of that danger. The returning ghosts, as a general rule, aren't much of a threat —members of certain specific cults among the Lupines might pay the ghosts special attention, but for the most part they are ignored — but the sudden influx of ghosts and attendant death-resonant energies has a tendency to create a large number of potent loci with potentially hazardous consequences. The sudden, rapid shifts that occur in the mystical landscape cause sweeping changes in the Shadow, and even though the mortals celebrate *el Día de los Muertos* as a joyful time of remembrance, the spirits spawned by such an abundance of death-resonant Essence are rarely so benevolent. Urban packs especially have their hands full dealing with a sudden overabundance of death-spirits, all struggling to find a source of Essence by any means necessary. Similar to any predator confronted with an overabundance of prey, the Uratha typically spend much of the month of November culling the herd, so to speak, thinning out the numbers of death-spirits before their combined influence spills over into the physical world in the form of a killing spree, plague or some other source of mass death and destruction.

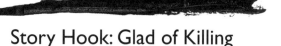

Story Hook: Glad of Killing

El Día de los Muertos is a festival of the dead, but it is also a festival of joyful remembrance of those who have passed on. Outpourings of joy and festivity happen just as frequently as thoughts of death and the afterlife, but it is the nature of happiness to be fleeting (especially in the World of Darkness), so these spirits rarely grow beyond motes. This year, though, a newly spawned death-spirit, desperate for a source of Essence, began consuming these joy-motes. The spirit has become *magath*, a freakish hybrid of two different kinds of spirit, calling itself Glad of Killing. The spirit, now representing the perverse joy of ending another's life, has found a way across the Gauntlet and joined with a lonely young man named Juan Vega. For now, the spirit is only Urging Vega, but the urges are growing stronger every day. Last week, Vega hit a little girl with his car — and realized he had enjoyed it. If Glad of Killing is allowed to fully Claim Juan, there's no telling how much death he could cause before he's caught.

In some ways, rural packs have an easier time on the Day of the Dead, as fewer mortals concentrated in the area means less-drastic changes to the spiritual landscape, but that same emptiness of population can have its own drawbacks as well. The surge in death-resonant energy is not solely the result of human emotion, but also comes from whatever force causes the dead to return from the Underworld. Most of the time, the energy fades and dissipates shortly after *el Día de los Muertos* ends, but every once in a while that energy lingers, pooling in some location with a pre-existing resonance of death. In the vast, empty stretches of desert, this cycle can repeat for many, many years, and a pack that does not diligently patrol its territory can end up with a frighteningly powerful death-spirit that seemingly came out of nowhere.

Ancestor-Spirits and the Day of the Dead

Werewolves are creatures of spirit and flesh, with a fundamentally different metaphysical make-up from humans. Uratha do not leave behind ghosts when they die (usually), but some old and especially potent lineages of Uratha are watched over by ancestor-spirits, spiritual representations of the entire family line and the bonds of loyalty that unite a family. While not strictly speaking the returned dead, these spirits do enjoy some benefits during *el Día de los Muertos*, in much the same way that ghosts do. Throughout the Day of the Dead, *Imria Hithim* enjoy the following benefits:

- +2 on all dice pools for Numina relating to crossing the Gauntlet or affecting things on the other side of the Gauntlet (including, but not limited to, Gauntlet Breach, Material Vision, Materialize and Reaching).
- The ancestor-spirit only loses one point of Essence every two hours the spirit spends in the physical realm without finding a fetter or a living host.

• If the ancestor-spirit does not already have the ability, the spirit gains the Possession Numen for the duration of the Day of the Dead. The spirit can only use this Numen to possess members of the family the spirit watches over (those members may be Uratha, wolf-blooded or ordinary humans).

Mages

If anything, mortal magicians are even more of an enigma to the Kindred than the Lupines. The Ordo Dracul and, less frequently, the Circle of the Crone may run into mages from time to time, usually in conflict over a mystically significant site that both want to control, but their goals and methods remain mysterious at best. Nevertheless, vampires who know how to recognize a wizard have frequently reported that there seem to be an unusual number of foreign mages coming into Mexico around the time of the Day of the Dead. Few of them stay in the cities, though; and as most Kindred don't leave their gilded cages, there is considerable uncertainty as to just what all those willworkers are up to.

The truth, surprisingly, is less sinister than the more paranoid Kindred believe. According to various histories and fragmentary accounts, some of the earliest refugees from the Fall of Atlantis sailed west from the island continent and landed in Central and South America. Many mages, particularly those of the order called the Mysterium, believe that the aboriginal cultures of the Americas, especially the Aztec, Inca, Maya and Olmec civilizations, were either founded by or heavily influenced by Atlantean mages during the cultures' formative years. Even the greatest of those ancient mages is presumed to be long-dead by now, but the Day of the Dead affords a unique opportunity to seek out and learn from the ghosts of those first emigrants from Atlantis without the usual hazards that come along with a journey to the Underworld. *El Día de los Muertos* is, for the Awakened, a treasure-trove of potential knowledge of the Mysteries — many mages spend the two days of the festival crawling through ancient, ruined temples and tombs of long-forgotten sorcerer-kings, evading devious traps and mystical wards in the hopes of meeting the ghost of a willworker who looked on Atlantis with his own eyes.

Story Hook: The Journey to Mictlan

Somewhere in Oaxaca, there is a cabal of Scelesti: perverse, corrupt mages who sold their souls to the denizens of the Abyss for unholy power. According to rumor among the local mages, this cabal has an annual tradition on the Day of the Dead called the Journey to Mictlan. According to Aztec mythology, when a soul left its body behind, it wandered for four years before finally finding its way to Mictlan, the afterlife. The Scelesti's Journey to Mictlan doesn't take quite as long, but mages still fear it, and rightly so. In the Journey to Mictlan, a victim (sometimes a mage, sometimes a Sleeper) is kidnapped on October 31st and prepared for the ritual. At dusk on Halloween, the cabal conducts a potent ritual that rips out the subject's soul and casts it into the Underworld. If the victim manages to find her way back to her body by dawn on November 3rd, she is restored and offered a place of prestige within the cabal (even Sleepers are offered this position; they typically either Awaken or go completely mad and die in short order). If the "ghost" does not return by the time the sun is fully over the horizon on the 3rd, the victim's body is cremated and disposed of, trapping the ghost in the Underworld permanently.

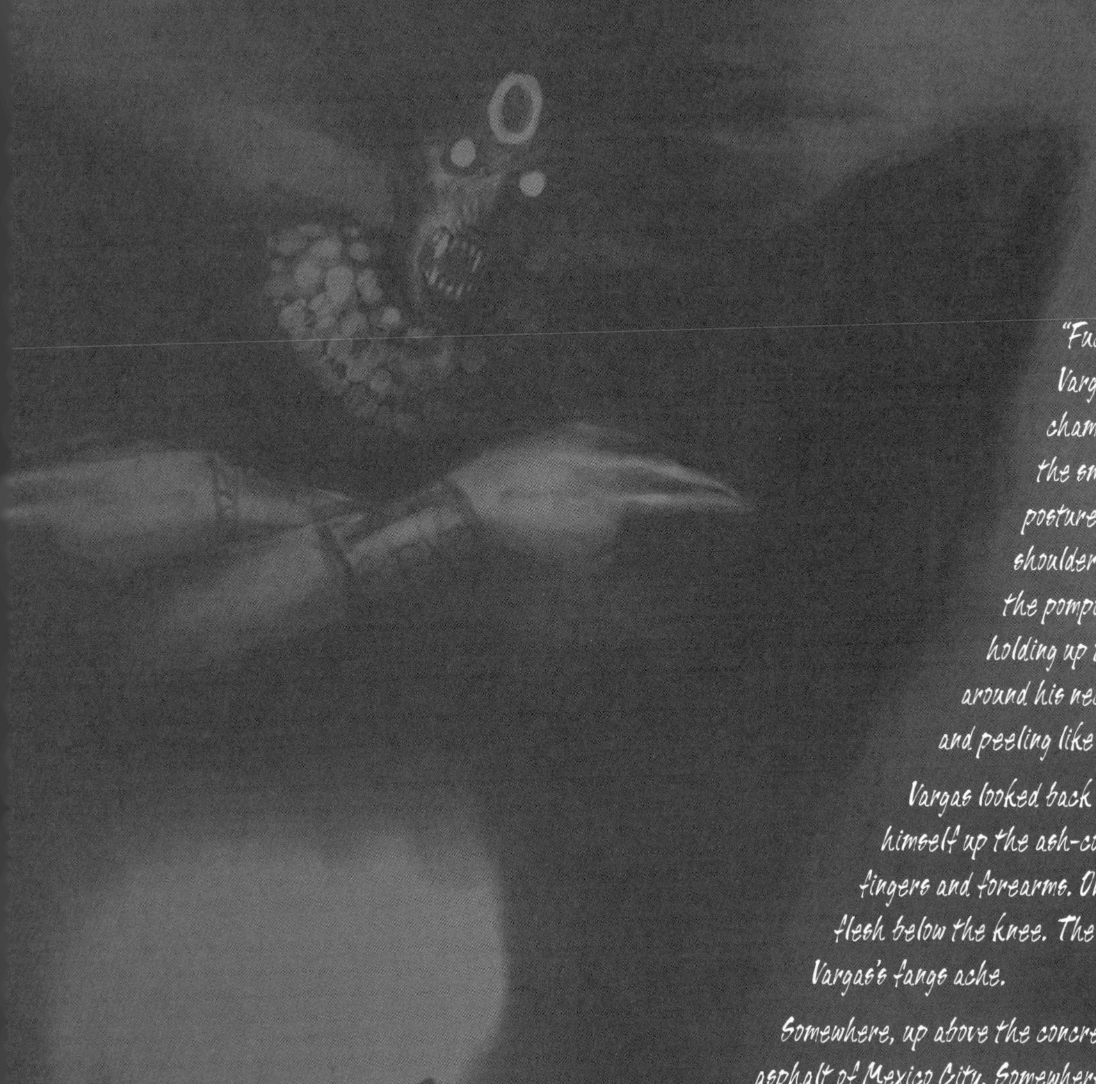

"Fuck you, you ancient wannabe!" Vargas yelled into the dust-choked chamber. The thing at the top of the smashed stone stairs had the posture of a muscular man — its shoulders were hoisted back with the pompous poise of someone used to holding up the weight of the gold draped around his neck — but its flesh was dry and peeling like old plastic.

Vargas looked back at Brubaker, who was pulling himself up the ash-covered, broken steps with his fingers and forearms. One ripped leg trailed dangling flesh below the knee. The smell of exposed blood made Vargas's fangs ache.

Somewhere, up above the concrete and rebar, was the modern asphalt of Mexico City. Somewhere up there, the weight of rushing cars made the room rumble. Somewhere up there was the bastard who had dropped them down here.

But the stairs led into gritty like chalk dust and black like tar.

"We'll go through you if we have to!" Vargas's fingertips split as he forced claws out of his bones. "You're no fucking god!"

"I am the gods' mouth. I am their teeth." The mummy-priest's voice came out of the blackness behind its fangs with living clarity, as if it had lips or breath.

Vargas shook as the thing grew, it fingers stretching into needles. In its belly was a colorless glow vaguely the grainy, milky texture of the night sky.

"This is what men once meant when they said 'god.' Not just me, but this place and your blood and the sacred work we do tonight, taken together. It is a great honor to be a part of me."

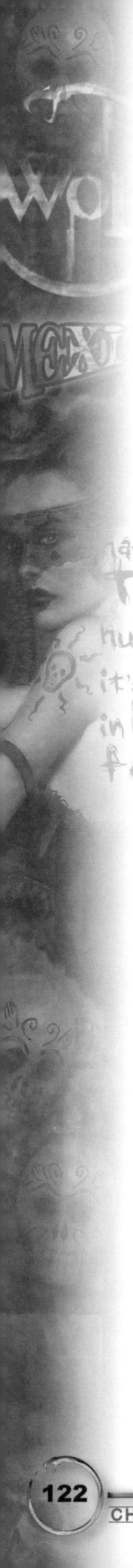

Chapter Three Storytelling

> "In Mexico you have death very close. That's true for all human beings because it's a part of life, but in Mexico, death can be found in many things."
> – Gael Garcia Bernal

The Atmosphere of Mexico

One of the most dangerous and unpredictable regions in all of the World of Darkness, Mexico has an ambiance that is unique. Drenched in bloody history and shot through with corruption and strife, the setting is violent, desperate and toxic. Unnatural blight and fierce virtue clash in sharp contrast, tearing holes into one another in permanent struggle. Some believe that the whole of the region is a lost cause, worthless as anything more than a simple, devastating demonstration of the potential disaster that looms for the world at large. Others swear that the battle is far from lost, holding the possibility of a bright future in their hearts until the very last.

There are five major features in the thematic landscape of Mexico in the World of Darkness: ancient influence, superstition, bleakness, modern defiance and lawlessness. Each dovetails with the next, forming a complete picture of the hidden battle that rages across the nation each night.

Ancient Influence

Old gods and old ways haunt the domains of Mexico, buried beneath a thin shell of modern culture. In some places, the ruined temples of the ancients literally exist under the towns and roads, and the dead things interred within still whisper to the world above. Vampire priests of the Olmec age slumber in torpor, ready to rise in the modern nights. Those who have already awakened bring their bloody ways back into the world of humans, reviving the practices and worship of their long-dead culture. The ghosts of vanished civilizations wander the dusty plains, feeding their rage and frustration to unsuspecting highway travelers. Darker spirits curl among the flora of the jungle, waiting to unleash their primeval, inhuman passions upon the mortal developments at their borders.

Everything in Mexico is somehow touched by these elements. Every structure, every living creature, is nearer to corruption by ancient forces than the mortals could ever imagine. Somehow, some part of the modern world that stills these voices in other lands just doesn't exist here. Perhaps the old ways are too strong here, fueled by the bloodshed and fury of centuries. Perhaps the will of the locals is weak, bred out of them by the forward-looking vampires and spirits through generations of culling and manipulation. Whatever the reason, this is a corner of the world threatened constantly by the darkness of ages past.

Imparting the sense of ancient influence to your players is a matter of descriptive text: make sure that everything seems tainted, somehow, no matter how new or artificial, by the tendrils of the past. Instead of depicting simple decay, make sure to illustrate that something else lurks below the surface of every modern development, waiting to emerge again. Nothing is built on a vacuum, and in Mexico, nothing vanishes completely. Paint peels in the heat of the midday sun, revealing stained, centuries-old stone beneath. Power hums below the pavement, suggesting hidden thunder. A feather ground into the dusty roadside shines with a slick, unnatural color, hinting at unseen creatures beyond modern sense or reason. Nothing new seems to work completely right in this land, in the presence of the monstrous powers of old.

Elder vampires and spirits seem utterly alien to visitors with contemporary sensibilities. The old ones' culture is one long destroyed, and there has been little to no integration of their beliefs into those beliefs that have supplanted their culture. Basic systems of thought such as mathematics, affairs of state and ethics are derived from assumptions different from those commonly accepted today. Sexual politics, slavery, the role of the individual in society — all of the views likely to be held by an elder of the region are going to clash with modern ideals, and they are enforced by the power of the ages. How does a neonate relate to ages-old Kindred who believe that the sun rises and sets based on a 52-year cycle of ritual negotiation with the gods above, signed in the blood of thousands of mortals? How do neonates begin to unravel the complicated rules of service and bondage held by the elders as too basic to require explanation? The young ones cannot. The two forces, young and old, are in permanent opposition, and the future of the land and all of its inhabitants may depend on the outcome.

Rejecting the Invader

Storytellers wishing to underscore the corruptive effect of the undying ancients may choose to adopt an optional mechanic that weakens the trappings of the modern world in proximity to their influence. Every time a character attempts to make use of reasonably up-to-date technology in the presence of an ancient power, the Storyteller can apply a penalty of –1 to –5 dice (depending on a roll of the creature or spirit's Resolve or Resistance Attribute) to the operation of the equipment. The penalty will underline the atmosphere of stubborn obsolescence and will heighten tension if the characters tend to rely upon their equipment.

Equipment that doesn't require a roll to use may still fail or perform poorly. When determining how affected any piece is, the Storyteller may wish to make a roll using the ancient creature's Resolve (or, in the case of spirits, Resistance). If success is achieved, the equipment suffers a minor malfunction. Exceptional success would indicate a complete shutdown.

Example: *Beatriz, a young Nosferatu, keeps feeling as if somebody is watching her. Growing fearful, she pulls out a cell phone and dials the number for a coterie-mate. There is an extremely old vampire very near to Beatriz, having recently awoken from torpor, and he finds the technology she holds abhorrent, rejecting it instinctively. The Storyteller rolls four dice (the elder's Resolve), for a 5-8-8-1: two successes. The phone works, but static noise fades in and out over the voices. After she hangs up, Beatriz draws a sawed-off shotgun, just in case. If she tries to fire it, the Storyteller decides Beatriz will suffer a –2 penalty on her rolls, as the elder's power " rejects" the shotgun as well.*

Superstition

While the living aren't exactly conscious of the old powers that encroach upon their world, they are aware that some-

thing supernatural (or unnatural) is inextricably tied to their environment. Their response is one of heightened credulity and tendency to seek protection, in one form or another, from those forces. As a result, the population of Mexico in the World of Darkness is more religious and more superstitious than the country's real counterpart. People are more likely to respond to an unexplained occurrence with a fervent prayer or habitual mystic tribute than rational denial in this setting. Anything is possible to them, and everything is to be feared.

Strangely, the Masquerade of vampires is no less powerful under these circumstances. In the atmosphere of strong belief, even mundane coincidences and natural events begin to take on fearsome significance. Actual supernatural events are often masked in the "noise" of everyday happenstance, taking on no more and no less significance in the eyes of the mortal population. Very few mortals are quick to guess that any specific event is the work of Kindred unless the mortals have had dealings with vampires in the past. In general, a sickly relative is assumed to be the victim of vague "bad spirits" or "curses," and the solution suggested is supplication at the altar of a saint or an application of herbal remedies, not a sharpened stake. However, those who do learn of the actual existence of vampires are quicker to arm themselves, and more likely to find support here than elsewhere in the world.

The homes and business places of mortals in the setting are littered with the detritus of belief: statuettes, candles, portraits and medallions of saints and angels, images of the deathly Santa Muerte and the skeletal figures of Los Dios de los Muertos and any number of crosses, charms or other protective devices against evil influence. Churches are full of worshippers at every Mass, and the *haciendas* of the rich and powerful have small chapels of their own built on the grounds.

To foreign characters, the superstitious nature of both the mortals and their supernatural counterparts may seem unusual (or even laughable) — but to the denizens of Mexico, it is a very serious matter. Skeptical outsiders are the ones who may find themselves mocked and pitied in this domain, and they will quickly learn that they present a preferable target to the unholy creatures of the land.

Storyteller's Option: Faith as Armor

In most places in the World of Darkness, the articles of faith have little effect on supernatural creatures unless they, too, are believers. However, in this superstition-heavy environment, it makes sense to assume that most of the mystical agents of the region would be just as swayed by belief as their mortal counterparts. Storytellers may wish to enforce this effect with a mechanic bolster to those mortals hoping to fend off supernatural creatures with their articles of faith. A simple +1 bonus to Composure or Resolve when holding or presenting a symbol of faith (or standing in proximity to an altar or religious artifact) can illustrate the effect without overdoing it.

Example: *Paulo the vampire is in the middle of feeding when one of the locals wanders by. Before she can flee, he grabs her and locks eyes with her, determined to Dominate her mind and erase the memory of the encounter. Unable to escape his grip, she instead reaches up to her rosary necklace, grasping it tightly in her hand. When Paulo's player makes the Wits + Persuasion + Dominate roll for The Forgetful Mind, the Storyteller will apply a +1 bonus to the victim's Resolve for the purpose of Resistance.*

Bleakness

The constant threat of ancient powers and their subconscious acceptance by the modern mortal population has lead to a widespread sense of oppression and hopelessness. Even when the people are celebrating, there is an undercurrent of sadness, a silent acknowledgement that any happiness is fleeting, and must be embraced before it vanishes. There can be no hope for the future in a land that is teetering on the brink of a rapid slide into the past. Where modern technology and philosophy fail, the old ways awaken and drag all of the living down into a world that is darker, more demanding and more dangerous. Where superstition reigns, advances in thought and culture are hindered by sloth and prejudice. The people of the land have learned to live in the environment of permanent decay, and many of them have stopped trying to repair the damage. In some territories, color and passion are leached away by the grinding influence of hidden forces. Everything is bleached a sandy, off-white and pitted with age.

Many of the settings in Mexico may serve the atmosphere of bleakness well: desert plains, brushed dry by scouring winds, make a great spot for an encounter. A ghost might haunt a ruined courtyard amidst walls tumbling into a garden overrun by parched cactus. Characters might find themselves wandering into a vast shantytown at the edges of a great city, observing the sad, filthy faces of the destitute inhabitants.

Large-scale attempts to fight off the bleak undercurrents of the region can never succeed unless the plan involves eliminating the age-old influences that source them. New developments, economic initiatives and social movements are all worthwhile efforts (assuming they're sincere), but they will eventually fail without a hard-won battle fought directly against the supernatural forces concerned.

The Paradox of Oppression

You may find that the dreariest, most depressed parts of the region are useful for supporting the horrors of the World of Darkness, but that's not the only part these settings can play in your story. In the deepest gloom, the Virtues of your cast will have a great opportunity to shine forth. Where is Charity more welcome, for instance, than a village of folk in desperate, dire straits? Where can Hope and Faith find their greatest victories but in the most forlorn circumstances? An unforgiving terrain is a test of Fortitude in disguise. A community held fast in the depraved grip of an elder vampire is one begging for Justice.

This is the paradox of Mexico: amidst the bleakness and despair of the environment, the greatest examples of virtue arise. Tempered by harsh circumstances, their exercise seems even more powerful, more significant than anywhere else. Make sure the players in your game are aware of this and give their characters the chance to make the very best of their situation.

Modern Defiance

But that battle is being fought, and not just by the mortals of Mexico. There are modern creatures among the supernatural population as well, and many of them do not believe the forces of the ancients are beneficial. Unlike the mortals, who operate under the hazy pressures of the Masquerade, some of these creatures are fully aware of the oppressive powers at work, and are proposing to put an end to them.

That defiance has a tendency to be reflected up and down the scales of power and life, showing itself in many ways. Lush, uncontrollable floral growths invade the edges of a dust-swept village. Colorful celebrations and parades arise, seemingly out of nowhere, on the filthy roads of the most depressed communities in the country. Miraculous visions of angels appear to a wandering drunk, giving him the hope and strength to change his ways and to preach the same to his neighborhood.

Meanwhile, young, nomadic vampires plague the countryside, seeking out their slumbering elders and attacking them in their sleep, claiming the territories of old for themselves. A war is unfolding between the old and the new in the Kindred world, and the violent, occasionally liberating effects are rippling out into the living populace.

Rebellion's Fire

The friction caused by natural resistance to the hidden forces in Mexico is all the more powerful because of the strength of those forces. When rebellion grows strong in the population (whether mortal or otherwise), a strange, unpredictable effect sometimes follows. Passions are inflamed artificially, and for a moment entire neighborhoods can be swept up in the excitement, even if those who dwell within are not aware of the cause. Simple disagreements explode into violence. Sweet affection becomes undying love. Jealousy becomes a murderous rage.

If the pressures of a scene involving ancient powers seem to be spiraling out of control, it may be appropriate for characters who are nearby *but not involved* to make a Resolve + Composure roll to resist becoming a temporary outlet for the emotional overflow. Those who fail will experience an overwhelming amplification of their current emotional state for the remainder of the scene. Those who succeed are not affected. Those who are already involved in the pressure situation will not feel or notice the effects personally, since the energies are directing themselves away from the source.

Nobody knows exactly why these emotional flares happen, but some of the more astute mortals are starting to clue in. Vampires and mages have noted that they are not exempt from the effect, and are not likely to remain comfortable with the situation unless they can find a way to take advantage of it.

Lawlessness

The battle of ancient and modern forces has thrown the natural order of Mexico into chaotic disarray. Many of the mortals chafing against the stagnant influence of the old spirits cast about for a concrete enemy to fight, often mistaking the government and police forces for the enemy. Others are dissatisfied with the inability of the law to protect them from the unnatural predators of the night, choosing to band together in vigilante groups and neighborhood gangs for defense. Some outlaw gangs grow immensely in power, developing into funnels for money and influence as their strength outstrips that of their law-abiding neighbors.

The Kindred world is no better. Neonate vampires are questioning the rule of their established governments with more and more frequency, emboldened by the regular violent incursions of Nomad coteries into their domains. Elders in some territories, frightened by the bloodthirsty behavior of the Nomads, have all but declared wholesale war on the younger vampires of the region. Law and tradition are collapsing in a rapidly escalating battle for supremacy.

The relative assignment of right and wrong is easily confused in this setting: good citizens turn fugitive, running from corrupt lawmakers. Violent, anarchic forces invade the homes and neighborhoods of innocent people, fighting desperately to release them from a powerful parasitic influence. Small injustices explode into full-blown riots, suspending morality in favor of a temporary outlet for the justified frustrations and fears of the people.

The lawlessness that plagues the region is no less powerful than the bleakness that inspires it, and no more likely to be erased by mundane initiatives unless they target the supernatural forces that inspire it. Social programs and tougher law enforcement can help stem the tide of chaos, but the real root of the problem lies beyond their reach.

Knowing the Territory

Many of the domains of Mexico are extremely dangerous, and much more so for characters who lack the Streetwise Ability. Kidnappings for ransom occur in the hundreds each year, and robbery, assault and murder are commonplace. Those who don't know the territory are immediately obvious to the local population and are likely to be targeted by the criminal element (or a supernatural one masquerading as a criminal).

It's advisable that players in any story set in Mexico assign some dots to Streetwise, even if their characters aren't extremely savvy — if they live in the region, they're sure to have heard some warnings. If they don't, the ability to come off like a local might be the most effective defense option available to them.

Of course, not everybody wants to avoid trouble. There is a common hunting style among Mexican Kindred who pretend to be naïve, wealthy mortals lost in a bad neighborhood just to attract would-be criminals for feeding.

Running Mexico Anywhere in the World

The themes and motifs of a Mexican game need not be restricted to the borders of the country as it stands today. Much of the American Southwest was once a part of the Mexica nation, and can be affected by all of the factors discussed here, if the Storyteller so desires. Aztec, Maya or Olmec museum pieces anywhere in the world could be tainted by the energies of ancient Mexico, and the effects could spread outwards into any city. Illegal trade in artifacts could do the same — or a tourist could "pick up" an ancient curse or entity and bring it home unawares. The buried world of Mexico in the World of Darkness is scratching at the modern surface above, eager to rise again. These old influences will take any opportunity, even if it is thousands of miles from their native territory.

The atmosphere that comes with those old influences is a reflection of the effect they have on the living world above. Over time, anyone, anywhere in the world will begin to react unconsciously just as the Mexicans have done. The bleakness and lawlessness of the region are not factors of Mexican psychology — they are reactions to the power that presses itself upon the people. With the right push, a story anywhere in the world can take on the flavor of this region.

The Mexican Wild

Vast, varied and largely unconquered, the Mexican wild provides a range of great settings for any story. Distinctive scenery and dangerous locales are readily available to support any theme and provide a serious challenge for any character's skill sets. Each of the environmental types represented in the following examples creates a different atmospheric opportunity and provides alternate choices for backdrop that can add depth and difficulty to a plot. Depending on the characters' familiarity with the territory, the setting a Storyteller chooses can represent an antagonistic or supportive force, enriching the story.

It's a good idea to examine the tone and difficulty of your plot before selecting a setting, so that you can make a choice that best creates the effect you're looking for. A search for a hidden enemy would be complicated by a feature-rich environment such as a mountain range or the deep jungle, intensifying the mystery and focusing on a stealthy hunt, while a relatively open setting such as a seashore or a desert plain would simplify the search and direct the focus to strategy and the mechanics of direct confrontation.

Sierra Madres

The Sierra Madres are vast, wide stretches of mountainous terrain, linked around and across all of Mexico and full of potential havens and hiding spots for those hardy individuals who can make themselves comfortable with the rocky countryside. The peaks of all four ranges (the Occidental, Oriental, del Sur and Eje Volcánico Transversal) are home to huge pine-oak woodlands and a vastly diverse ecology of flora and fauna. There is no shortage of food for the skilled survivalist (either mortal or Kindred, assuming the blood of animals still sustains them), and the nearly incomprehensible array of diversions and obstacles presented by the forested canyons allow for the perfect retreat, if necessary.

Many of the mountains in the Sierra Madre ranges are very steep, with a buildup of deep soil along the incline, where the great forests take root. Rainfall and temperature fluctuate along the mountains with changes in elevation and positions on the rock faces (those facing coastlines tend to see more rainfall and less extreme winters, while those facing away from the coasts are drier and more extreme). The higher peaks are covered in snow year-round, while the lower ones experience frequent melts or never see snow at all.

Of course, no territory is unclaimed. Vampire Nomad coteries make frequent use of certain mountain lands as retreats, tactical or otherwise. Uratha packs roam unhindered through the wild, and old spirits dwell deep within the mountain passes, waiting patiently for unwary trespassers. The Sierra Madres are wickedly dangerous, most especially for those who are ill-equipped to understand the depth of the threats that lie within.

Some of the mountains play host to holdout tribes of native peoples. Some mountains are home to more devious

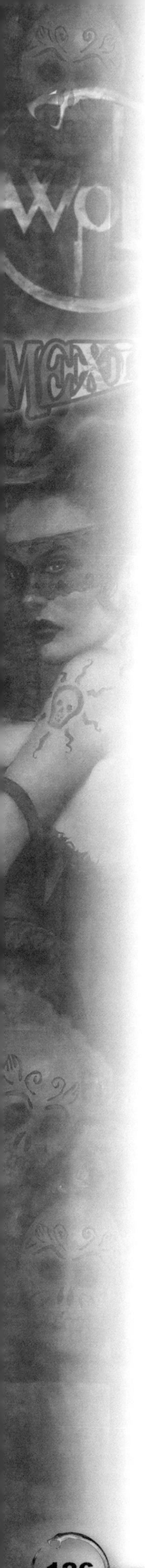

mortal groups: reclusive cults and fugitive criminal bands will occasionally clear out a cave somewhere along the rocky cliffs of a range, making it their own.

The dizzying heights and wide vistas of the mountain ranges make an excellent backdrop for stories with themes related to an uncertain future. Characters might lose themselves in the forested slopes, working to discard their pasts and move ahead, or they may be chased into the mountains, fleeing a dogged pursuit. The twisting terrain and dark reaches of the forest easily translate into a labyrinthine set piece, and the progress of a story can follow an ascent up a mountain, ending in an panoramic view at the top.

For survivalist characters, entering the mountain territories can also represent a reversal of fortune: an environment that is unforgiving to most becomes a powerful base of operations for those who know the lay of the land.

Flora: Abundant. Mixed stands of pine, fir and oak trees. Grasses, shrubs, flowering plants, mosses and some cacti.

Fauna: Abundant. Parrots, hummingbirds, owls, finches, turkeys, eagles, gray wolves, grizzly bears, chipmunks, squirrels, mice, coati, rattlesnakes, spiny lizards and barking frogs.

Sightlines: Obstructed at ground level, where forests and rocky outcroppings interfere. Cover is abundant and easily accessed. Wide vistas are available at altitude, where characters have a good vantage over the rest of the terrain.

Ability Specialties: Science (Geology), Athletics (Climbing), Drive (Hairpin Turns), Survival (Mountaineering, Camping, Trapping, Hunting, Foraging), and Animal Ken (individual species)

Sample Setting: Citlaltépetl, the Storming Peak

Home to the highest elevated point in the country, Citlaltépetl (also known as Mount Orizaba) is an extinct volcano in southern Mexico, between Mexico City and Veracruz. The mountain is more than 18,000 feet high, and capped with snow year-round. A part of the Sierra Madre Oriental range, Citlaltépetl shares a pine-forested base with several mountains in the area.

Climbing the mountain rapidly becomes difficult. A relatively tame slope suddenly rises to steep, icy, smooth rock before the halfway point. Handholds vanish under snow just as the temperature falls drastically, multiplying the problems in ascent. To make things worse, there is a supernatural agency at work on the peak, set in place to prevent intrusion.

Over 400 years ago, an elder vampire chose Citlaltépetl as her resting place, knowing that the sleep of the ages was coming upon her. Calling upon the power of the dark gods above, she wove powerful magicks into the face of the mountain so as to better protect her resting place, a carefully hidden alcove near the summit.

If anyone climbs within 500 feet of the cave (a wickedly difficult feat even on its own), the rituals of the old vampire activate, wracking the side of the mountain with a windstorm that precipitates a small avalanche. The insidious ritual is such that the dislodged ice and snow will fall in a directed manner, duplicating and scrambling the landmarks on the mountainside and rendering it almost impossible to maintain one's bearings. Many an unsuspecting party has been caught in one of these storms and ended up completely lost on the mountainside, eventually starving or dying of exposure to the elements.

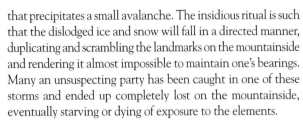

Mortal trespassers need not be aware of the vampire's existence to get caught up in one of her storms — the ritual is indiscriminate, and does not require conscious intrusion to activate. The setting could play host to a story about mountaineers caught in a crisis beyond their ken just as easily as one about intrepid vampire-hunters.

Kindred characters may be aware of the elder's existence, and may be attempting to climb the mountain either to revive or destroy her. Nomads in search of an elder's blood might hear a rumor of the slumbering power on Citlaltépetl and head that way in hopes of finding an easy target.

Mages and Uratha would easily understand that Citlaltépetl's deadly storms are not entirely natural, and may choose to investigate. The spirits of the mountain itself are being warped by the presence of the powerful vampire, and may be calling for release.

Deserts

The Sonoran and Chihuahuan Deserts stretch across the northern region of Mexico and extend into the southwestern United States, divided by the canyon cliffs of the Apache Highlands. Both deserts are sun-baked wastes, scattered with low dunes over parched volcanic earth. The environment is harsh and unforgiving: even the most skilled survivalists are hard-pressed to find food, water and shelter, especially if they find themselves lost without equipment designed to arm and protect them against arid conditions.

The lands of both deserts are relatively flat and featureless, interrupted by the occasional gulch or cliff rise. Rainfall is extremely rare, and quickly vanishes into the ground when it does fall. Droughts often last for a full year, sometimes as long as two or even three. There are a few rivers crossing through the Chihuahuan Desert, but they run muddy and are unlikely to provide potable water without proper filtration.

There isn't much in the way of activity deep in the two deserts of Mexico: life is just too difficult, and feeding is scarce for Kindred and mortals. Occasionally, small bands of fugitive or otherwise reclusive individuals will camp somewhere in the arid wastes, hoping to escape scrutiny. Encounters are likely to be rare unless characters are on one end of a chase.

There are some small towns near the borders of the deserts, collections of dusty, windblown one- and two-story adobe buildings. The citizens tend to be uncommunicative, wary folk, burned one too many times by wandering Nomad vampires. The inhabitants are unlikely to trust strangers, and some will get violent as soon as they sense a threat.

The flat, nearly featureless landscape of the Mexican deserts lends itself well to stories with themes of isolation or loss. The silent, unforgiving wasteland reflects both hopelessness and calm with stunning simplicity. Characters who can go no further, in a moral sense, might find themselves at the edge of a literal desert, looking forward to a future of desolation and difficulty.

Flora: Rare. Scrub bush, tall Saguaro cacti and ironwood trees.

Fauna: Rare. Roadrunners, fringe-toed lizards, king snakes, bighorn sheep, tarantulas, butterflies, fire ants and mountain lions.

Sightlines: Extremely clear. Flora provides little in the way of cover, and the landscape itself is extremely flat. At night, moonlight is rarely obscured by clouds.

Ability Specialties: Medicine (Heat Exposure), Drive (Desert Terrain), Survival (Finding Water, Camping, Shelter, Foraging), and Animal Ken (individual species)

Sample Setting: El Camino del Diablo

The dreariest, hottest and arguably deadliest environment in all of the region: El Camino del Diablo, the long stretch of desolate salt-pan desert at the northern quarter of the Sonoran Desert. In the summer, even late at night, the air of El Camino del Diablo is hot enough and dry enough to wick the moisture from the flesh of the living. Every year, dozens of hopeful illegals are claimed by the desert, dying of exposure on the 70-mile trek between the nearest source of water and the United States border. Deadly rattlesnakes curl in the creosote bushes throughout, and the drag roads of La Migra, the well-armed border patrol, crisscross the arid land roughly every 20 miles.

What's worse, the desert is haunted by a number of ghosts, pathetic remnants of those who fell in their attempts and must wander aimlessly forever, seeking passage that they can no longer see or understand. Many still believe that they thirst for water and will attack mortals in a futile attempt to steal their canteens. Other ghosts stagger from one unmarked grave to the next in search of their bones, their woeful keening audible for miles across the flat land.

Nomad vampires occasionally hit the drags as well, knowing that the desperate mortals who make the run will be weakened by their trek and relatively easy to hunt, not to mention incredibly simple to dispose of. Desiccated bodies are nothing unusual out in El Camino del Diablo and are unlikely to be reported.

A wide range of story opportunities are presented by the desert crossing. Mortal characters may be attempting the run themselves, may be searching for the remains of a friend or relative who was lost to the scorching sands or they may be officers of La Migra who happen to find themselves in the wrong place at the wrong time.

Kindred Nomad characters could encounter a rival coterie on the road or find themselves face-to-face with a malicious spirit. Law-abiding vampires might be tasked with locating and punishing a Nomad coterie that's been running the drag route, indiscriminately taking down mortals in their path.

Mages and Uratha could get themselves involved with mortals attempting to cross the border for one reason or another. They may have truck with the spirits that haunt the desert, looking to heal or destroy them. The sands of El Camino del Diablo could serve as the setting for a duel of ideals, far removed from witnesses so that the opponents can unleash their full talents without fear of discovery.

Jungle

The Maya Forest is a large jungle territory covering more than six million acres at the southern tip of Mexico, along the Caribbean coast and extending into Central America. The forest is wet and dense, forming an unbroken canopy of green over much of its breadth. Food and water are abundant, as are dangerous species of animal life and stinging insects. Characters who stray from established paths and roads are quickly going to find themselves lost in a tangled, impenetrable mass of flora and thick, soft earth.

The topography of the jungle is relatively flat, easing the difficulty of foot travel but making navigation even more difficult. Hundreds of plant varieties flourish in close proximity under frequent rains. The jungle edges out all the way to the Caribbean shore, and is dotted with small streams and stagnant pools. Drinking water is easy to find, although that taken from the ground may be tainted with parasites.

There are a number of mortal tribes and cults hiding within the Maya jungle, as well as the occasional illegal compound, where any numbers of large-scale criminal enterprises are organized. Kindred coteries move with the mortal blood supply, and a number of Nomad coteries crisscross the territory in their wanderings, making travel through the wood extremely dangerous. There are some Uratha packs willing to push deep into the forest, seeking the powerful spirits that dwell in and around the ruins hidden within.

There are some legal mortal settlements dotted around the edges of the jungle, including a couple of resort towns. Business is slow at most of these retreats though, harried as they are by the creatures that dwell within the forest.

The claustrophobic, variegated environs of the Maya forest make a good setting for stories with themes of mystery or primal power. Every choked path and curling shadow suggests a hidden threat or undiscovered promise. Curiosity or greed can drive characters further and further into the deep clutches of the tropical green, and they may not have any idea of what really awaits them within.

Flora: Abundant. Xate palm, rubber tree, chicle, allspice, ferns, mango, parasitic vines and mosses, algae, psychotropic mushrooms, tropical grasses and flowering plants.

Fauna: Abundant. Anteaters, howler monkeys, jaguars, pumas, ocelots, storks, vultures, parrots, iguana lizards, poisonous centipedes, army ants, leeches, mosquitoes and cockroaches.

Sightlines: Extremely obstructed. An interlaced network of thick flora blocks view in all directions, and characters will often have less than five feet of clear sight unless they are in an artificial clearing or on an established path.

Ability Specialties: Academics, Medicine or Science (Medicinal Plants), Athletics (Swimming), Survival (Jungle Terrain, Insect Repellant, Shelter, Foraging) and Animal Ken (individual species)

Sample Setting: Amiqui-atl, the Long Drop

Just a short drive from San Cristóbal de la Casas in Chiapas, Amiqui-atl is a stunning natural waterfall more than 50 meters high, emptying into a deep pool at its base. The falls are surrounded by jungle, but a recent rise in tourism has necessitated the construction of a single road leading to the attraction. Small vendors' stalls are stationed at the parking area near the pool, and there is a small structure to accommodate parks officials and a restaurant. Limited space is provided for camping, which must be arranged at the parks office.

Despite the brisk tourist trade, many of the locals are not happy with Amiqui-atl's discovery by the world at large. There is a dark tale about the falls, and it is one that they are not eager to share. Most refuse to even translate the name properly, claiming that it means "long falls" or "long drop." In actuality, the name means "thirsty water."

Legend has it that the pool at the base of the falls is magical, and will grant vast powers to anyone who drowns herself in it — vast powers that will last for one night and then vanish, leaving her dead. According to the local stories, the pool first conferred these powers on an unsuspecting woman who threw herself from the falls after discovering that her husband had begun an affair with another local girl. That night, the drowned woman was seen walking the streets of her hometown, dripping wet and whispering to herself. Just after dawn, her husband and his lover were found in bed, decapitated. The woman herself was discovered in her own garden, dead of drowning despite the absence of a nearby body of water.

Several mortals have made use of the falls over the last century. The nature and extent of the powers they are granted are unknown — in every case, their enemies meet with some terrible violence, and then the satisfied avenger is found drowned.

What empowers the waterfall is also unknown. Mortal characters who hear of the legend may choose to investigate, hoping to understand the source of its power. Wandering Kindred may stumble across the tourist site and accidentally drown a mortal there, witnessing the rise and return of a vengeful spirit bent on the Kindred's destruction. Mages may track a mystic power source to the bottom of the deep pool with intent to harness its energies for their own purpose.

Coastlines

The Ocean Shores of Mexico range from isolated strands to resort settlements. The soft ground gives way to loose sands in most areas, hardening into flat plates in some locations. The ocean coasts are dotted with mangrove growths and lagoons, most especially along the Yucatán Peninsula in the south. Fishing and foraging are relatively easy for a skilled survivalist.

The most popular tourist destinations in Mexico are all along the shores, and many formerly destitute towns are thriving now, building their business around vacationers from the north and across the seas. Huge resort hotels, condo communities and vacation villas are springing up all over the shores, playing host to millions of visitors each year. Characters with the money can arrange extremely comfortable accommodations for themselves without difficulty.

Both the Gulf and the Pacific waters are warm year-round, and teeming with life — from small fish and crustaceans to larger deep-sea varieties. The waters are relatively shallow in most places, dropping off drastically about 30 or 40 yards from the shore. The sand is soft, but the majority of the shores are littered with shell fragments and small stones.

While tourist towns are abundant food sources for the Kindred population, most foreigners are relatively safe as long as they stay in their hotels. Even the vampires are careful not to ruin a good thing, avoiding the blood of the vacationers unless the Kindred feel they have no choice. The bustling towns that spring up around resorts are more than adequate to feed even the most demanding Kindred.

Away from the tourist settlements, conditions on the beach are surprisingly desolate. There is little in the way of food for vampires, and nothing to protect the mortals who do show themselves.

The stark contrast between the artificial, exclusive paradise of the resort communities and the barren, empty shores beyond is an excellent source of atmosphere for a story. The setting invites explorations of themes of subjugation, envy and ignorance on the divide between the world of plenty and its bleak surroundings.

Flora: Middling. Tropical grasses and palms giving way to sand scrub. Resort gardens are rich and varied, but usually fenced off and artificially maintained.

Fauna: Middling. Marlin, tuna, sharks, groupers, barracuda, jellyfish, crabs, gulls sand finches and lizards.

Sightlines: Clear. Most of the land is relatively flat sand, and the waters are usually unmuddied. There is little in the way of cover unless characters take advantage of artificial structures or create their own.

Ability Specialties: Athletics (Swimming, Scuba), Survival (Fishing, Camping, Finding Shelter), Socialize (Tourists)

Sample Setting: The All-Inclusive Mangrove Resort

Puerto Vallarta, Acapulco and Cancún may be the most popular tourist destinations in Mexico, but that popularity means crowded beaches, noisy hotels and trampled scenery. There is a new wave of resort villages cropping up along the Mexican shores, catering to rich clientele who don't want to share their beaches with thousands of other guests. The Mangrove Resort, recently constructed on the southern Gulf shore, at the edge of the Yucatán Peninsula, is just one of the new offerings, and is rapidly garnering acclaim. Situated on a white sand beach near the edge of the jungle and well removed from towns and tourists, the five-star facility offers each suite a sizable balcony overlooking the ocean. Twenty-four-hour bars, refreshment stands and world-class meals are included with the price of the room, and two large swimming pools, four tennis courts, a nightclub, a spa, parasailing and deep-sea fishing services are provided to keep the guests entertained. The Mangrove Resort offers the best of the best, and its guests are never left unsatisfied. "Peace, privacy and perfection" is the sales pitch, and it delivers.

But the Mangrove is about to suffer a blow to its reputation. A hungry coterie of Nomad Kindred has been circling the area for some time, chased further and further away from civilized land by the more established vampires in those territories. At the very edge of starvation, they have stumbled across the resort and its guests. A violent attack is imminent.

There are several stories that could be told in this scenario. The Nomads themselves could be the characters, and must wrestle with their own hunger as the easy pickings of the hotel are waved in front of their faces. Mortal characters could be guests at the hotel during the inevitable assault, or they could be locals who stumble upon the aftermath. The characters could even be local Kindred who have been carefully feeding upon the guests and staff of the resort and must fend off the ravages of the Nomad gang.

Mayan Ruins

Nestled among the dense rainforests, Mayan Ruins dot the Mexican south. Pitted with age and covered with elaborate hieroglyphic designs, these stone structures rise from their surroundings with a distinctly organic feel, like huge teeth set in the body of the land. Most are water-worn and crumbling, and many are teeming with life — plants growing through cracks in the stone and insects, birds and other creatures nesting in the crooks and alcoves throughout the structures.

The cities of the Maya were built around mystic gathering points, not commercial ones, so the focus of each terraced structure is clearly religious. The markings indicate the attentions of ancient gods and powers, and almost every ruin bears the location of an identifiable ritual temple. Aqueducts delivered water to some buildings, and elaborate tombs are built in proximity to many of the ritual spaces.

Drenched in ancient mystic workings, many of the ruins are both dangerous and irresistible to seekers of knowledge. Some ruins re haunted by vicious spirits of old, still hungry for vengeance against the conquistadors and their kin. Other ruins serve as tombs for elder vampires who have lain undisturbed for centuries. Certain cults make use of some of the sites, drawing power from the supernatural energies that still echo within their temples.

Kindred of the Ordo Dracul (and, of course, many mages) are known to make investigative pilgrimages to ruin sites, searching for information on the ways and means of the classic, pre-Conquest vampires. These investigative trips are notoriously difficult, and usually require a large retinue of mortals for feeding and support. Some coteries of the Circle of the Crone actually make their home within the ruins of their ancestors, relying on the constant presence of archaeological teams and tourists for feeding.

Strangely, the structures that are most well-known make up less than 50% of the actual ruins in existence. Many remain undiscovered, hidden in the jungle mass or sunk into one of the many small lakes that dot the countryside. To those who have a true understanding of the abundance of veiled temples and tombs, their startling tendency to remain undiscovered can only be explained by conscious intervention. What they cannot say is what the source of that consciousness may be, or why it would seek to conceal these particular formations and allow others to be exposed to modern investigations.

Mayan ruins provide an atmospheric backdrop for stories involving themes of mystery, old crimes and their consequences or hidden motives. In a secret ruin, characters may come face to face with ancient, unacknowledged truths, or the characters may be the first to discover a powerful threat to the modern world.

Flora: Abundant. Jungle growths invade the ancient structures of the Mayan ruins: Xate palm, rubber tree, chicle, allspice, ferns, mango, parasitic vines and mosses, algae, psychotropic mushrooms, tropical grasses and flowering plants.

Fauna: Abundant. Anteaters, howler monkeys, jaguars, pumas, ocelots, storks, vultures, parrots, iguana lizards, poisonous centipedes, army ants, leeches, mosquitoes and cockroaches.

Sightlines: Obstructed. The twists and turns in collapsed structures provide an abundance of cover, and encroaching jungle flora interferes with sight as well. Some ruins sport open terraces or cleared spaces that are less difficult to observe.

Ability Specialties: Academics (Mayan Civilization, Linguistics), Occult (Mayan Religion), Science (Archaeology), Athletics (Climbing), Survival (Camping, Foraging), Animal Ken (individual species)

Sample Setting: The Sunken Tombs

Deep in the forests of Tabasco, under a canopy of vine-wrapped palms, there is a strange, undiscovered wonder.

The ruins of a great temple to the Mayan lords of death are half-buried there, surrounded by a network of shattered stone tombs. The shards of the crypts that once encircled the temple are sunk into the loamy ground and covered with dark mosses, making them seem like little more than lumps in the earth when seen from a distance.

The temple itself, adorned with carvings of skeletal gods, collapsed into the ground during a powerful earthquake at least a century ago. The building is tilted at a precarious angle, its north face now completely underground and overgrown with dense foliage. The walls are severely cracked, and the building itself is bent at an angle in the middle, where the earth dropped away violently during the quake.

Entry to the temple is now impossible through the main door, which was on the north face. There is a stone slab hidden in the jungle floor near the west face that can be lifted to provide access via a small tunnel, but there are also two large cracks in the wall that can be squeezed through. Because of the tilt in the floor, climbing to the main chamber of the temple is quite difficult — there's a significant slope, and little in the way of handholds in the middle of the room. However, treasures await those characters who can make it to the temple: a small codex of writings related to the underworld of the Mayan people and prayers made to invoke the favor of the lords of death, as well as a number of valuable carvings and hieroglyphic wall-stones.

The tombs that surround the temple are, for the most part, empty. There are no treasures to be found in them and — no bodies. Whatever once rested there now walks the jungle, seeking inhuman comfort for the rude awakening of decades past. What, exactly, the bodies that were once interred there have become is up to you. They may be ghosts, the walking dead or even vampires. Whatever the case, the beings scour the jungle now, and any living wanderers who happen across the creatures' path are in serious danger.

Mortal characters in this story might be searching for the ruins as a follow-up to local legends, or just because they're treasure-seekers on a hunch. Kindred or mage characters might come in search of the powerful knowledge that may remain in the temple's codex, and Uratha would likely respond to the disruption of the spirits thereabouts.

The Extinction Crater

Hidden for eons, the Extinction Crater on the Yucatán Peninsula is a setting that deserves its own, distinct entry. Roughly 65 million years old, the crater is half-filled with the waters of the Caribbean Sea. The crater's rim is so smoothed over by age that modern geologists failed to notice the crater until 1978, when a petroleum company's magnetic survey led to the discovery of a huge, circular mineral anomaly approximately centered on the town of Chicxulub, Mexico.

The impact crater of Chicxulub is so large (roughly 185 miles wide) and so old that many scientists believe it may mark the collision of a meteor that caused the extinction of the dinosaurs. The immense cloud of dust that this meteor strike would have caused may have blocked the sun's rays for several years, drastically reducing global temperatures and spawning massive shifts in both air and water currents.

On land, the edges of the crater are marked by a ring of depressions, now mostly overgrown, but traceable by the preponderance of sinkholes (locally referred to as "cenotes") on the perimeter. Many of these freshwater holes are connected by a network of natural subterranean passages and caves, most of which are unmapped because of the danger and difficulty in exploring them. Many divers have been claimed by the buried caves of Chicxulub, and local guides will usually refuse to participate in an attempt to enter the passages.

Underwater, the perimeter is practically undetectable by the unaided eye. Sand and coral have filled or grown over many of the depressions and projections that mark the outside edge of the crater, and seismic shifts in the sea floor have erased many of the visible features of the site. Magnetic data and gravity-anomaly maps clearly reveal the boundaries of the crater though, and are often used by explorers.

In addition to natural data, however, those sensitive to more esoteric energies have noted that the crater has a distinct and altogether unpleasant atmosphere to it — it's almost as if the crater has marked the spirit of the Earth as severely as the physical face. While the wildlife is no less abundant there than in surrounding territories, some astute observers have noticed that plants, animals and even mortals seem shorter-lived within the crater's bounds than without. It's as if death itself is more concentrated within the extinction crater, harder to resist. Illnesses and injuries that might not be life-threatening elsewhere have a tendency to become critical there, without explanation. Accidents seem to occur more frequently, and even the spirits there are subject to a withering force.

All of the mystic Kindred covenants are interested in the Chicxulub crater, but each has its own explanation for the energies found there. Expeditions, however, are rare because of the heightened sense of danger — most vampires aren't willing to risk their unlives for concrete gain, much less a mystery, no matter how great.

An atmosphere of otherworldly or otherwise unfamiliar danger is well-served by the extinction crater setting. Characters in Chicxulub may face high-risk challenges they don't understand (or never expected), and Storytellers are not limited by normal earthly bounds in explaining the circumstances there.

Flora: Abundant, both on land and in the sea. Fast-growing species dominate the area — low ferns, palms, vines and mosses are clearly in the majority. Old-growth trees are rare, and those that remain are hardy survivors, marked with the scars of illness and parasitic attack. Underwater, weed growth seems normal, but a skilled observer will note that fast-growing species dominate there as well.

Fauna: Abundant, both on land and in the sea. On land, howler monkeys, jaguars, vultures, parrots, iguana lizards, poisonous centipedes, army ants, leeches, mosquitoes and cockroaches are most abundant. Skilled biologists will notice that poisonous varieties are a little more dominant here than in most parts of the jungle, and that there is an unusual incidence of fatal injuries and illnesses among all species. In the water, coral growths are abnormally abundant, but the reefs are somewhat underpopulated by other forms of life. Skilled marine biologists will notice that the coral tends to die faster than is normal, contributing less to the growth of the reefs with each generation than should be expected.

Sightlines: Obstructed. Thick jungle growth on land impedes vision, and the irregular outcroppings of reefs under the water provide ample cover.

Ability Specialties: Academics (Geography), Medicine (Forensic Pathology), Occult (Spirit Energies, Death Magic), Science (Archaeology, Biology, Cartography, Geology, Marine Biology), Athletics (Diving), Survival (Jungle, Ocean)

Sample Setting: The Subterranean Ring

Local Kindred of the Circle of the Crone have known about the crater for much longer than the mortals. Those vampires who dwell in or near Chicxulub tell stories of the impact in their litanies, painting it in metaphorical terms. They speak of the crater as a "great scar" on the planet, and recite reverent tales of the catastrophic winter it must have caused. Some refer to age-old covenant prophesies that suggest "a working in a great Circle" that will blot out the sun and allow Kindred to walk the days as they do the night.

The Hierophant of the Circle has gained a limited understanding of the warped spiritual energies that remain at Chicxulub, and believes it is possible to encourage an "echo" of the original event, mystically encouraging a release of energies that will once again darken the skies. He and his followers are preparing a great ritual to realize his vision.

Mortal Retainers, under the instruction of their Circle masters, are striking out to the edges of the crater and placing ritually prepared stones (each carved with a ritual incantation and weighing a little over 400 pounds) within the network of underwater caves on the perimeter. Twelve stones need to be placed before the ritual can begin — and many of the missions to position them have already claimed the lives of the mortals involved.

The characters in the story may come from nearly any background: mortal investigators, Kindred of the Ordo Dracul or Lancea Sanctum, mages with a sensitivity to the death energies of the crater or Uratha who have observed the spiritual effect of the region. They may discover the activities of the Circle (probably by coming across one of the placement teams) and eventually uncover the mad plans of the cult in Chicxulub.

Attempts to prevent or disrupt the placement of the stones will require exploration of the sinkhole network under the jungle floor — in cramped, dark, dangerous conditions with the threat of opposition from the Circle retainers.

Any story that unfolds within Chicxulub crater will be more dangerous than the norm — and that might be exactly what some players are looking for. Make sure to discuss whether or not they want to participate in a high-risk story before jumping into the setting, and run a prologue that illustrates the extent of the threat.

Kindred Society in Mexico

The potentially lethal environments of the Mexican wilderness are matched, if not surpassed, in dangerous possibility by its urban centers. The mortal population, squeezed as it is by the supernatural influences that bleed up from history's depth, is troubled by violent urges and monstrous demands. Only the most devilishly advanced or wickedly amoral of predators could survive in the midst of these passionate people — and thus the Kindred of Mexico are best described. Fierce and ruthless, they form societies that would absolutely terrify the casual observer, if such a creature could exist. As one influential vampire of Mexico City famously stated at one Elysium meeting, "to know us is to be destroyed."

Vicious intrigues are the norm in Mexico. Balanced rule is a rarity, and many of the cities play host to constant battles for ascendance. Princes rise to power and fall to civil war with startling regularity. Cycles of rebellion and vengeance are frequent, often supported by shadowy forces and elder warmongers determined to prevent modern Kindred from establishing anything like a comfortable social hierarchy. Those few domains that seem immune to violent uprising are ruled with such rigid control that they remain unassailable only as long as the stress-laden vampires responsible for them manage to hold onto their sanity.

Those vampires who do pass their Requiems in the halls of Mexican Elysium are social warriors par excellence. Strategists and politicians without peer, they endure the constant assault of their competitors. In Mexico, the Danse Macabre is a ferocious, fast-paced affair for all parties. Virtue withers with every step. The blood of participants spatters the marble floors with each turn. Nobody is safe. Nobody is calm.

The Meeting of Worlds

In the Elysium sites of Mexico, the dynamic of Kindred relations is extremely complicated. Philosophical and political differences are just outer layers in a composite burden that every vampire carries with him, a burden that include history-laden lineages, racial and religious prejudices, inherited territorial disputes and interwoven mortal ties.

Within the covenants, individual bloodlines (whether established as entities on their own or not) are often named and considered representative features as strong and relevant as any visible characteristic. Behavior is reflected up and down the ladder of blood, constantly adjusting the reputation of every walking member of the line. Even those covenants that do not traditionally engage in ancestral tracing have adopted the practice in most Mexican domains, each for reasons of its own. Many simply wish to keep

themselves abreast of factors that are likely to influence the decisions of historically minded competitors. Some maintain their records as a means of exclusion, ensuring that their membership is not "tainted" by some undesirable quality, actual or imagined. Some are concerned to prove that their line is exclusively native or exclusively European, perpetuating the conflict that began with the Spanish invasion of the 16th century.

Mortal race is more of a factor in Mexico than in many regions, underscored as it is by the relatively common practice of exclusive Embrace and exacerbated by constant fear of native elder influence, hidden but not destroyed. European Kindred, eager to erase the influence of the ancients, can never be sure if a native vampire is recently Embraced or newly arisen from centuries-long torpor. Modern native Kindred, aware of the suspicion of the outsiders, feel an understandable frustration with their situation, while true devotees of the ancients undermine their efforts to discard the stigma. In truth, the influence of the ancients makes itself known among the European vampires as easily as it does with those of native stock — but the descendants of the invaders comfort themselves with a system of shared denial.

Racism as Madness

At its core, racism is a delusional prejudice and reliance on the oversimplification it embodies is a harmful impediment to interpersonal relations in a mixed society. Storytellers wishing to highlight its insidious, destructive power may choose to assign it to certain characters as a derangement with the following details:

Compulsive Bias (mild): Your character irrationally associates a certain distinctive "type" (race, nationality, religion, gender, vampire clan or other general umbrella attribute) with undesirable qualities, and is unable to overcome his bias through normal rational or logical means. He will assume that all individuals of the chosen type embody the qualities he focuses on, and will likewise assume that any behavior typifying those qualities must be credited to individuals of that type.

Effect: Any time the character deals with individuals of the chosen type, he suffers a –2 penalty on Social rolls, and has difficulty concealing his distaste. The character reacts naturally with fear, contempt or revulsion when discussing or interacting with the type.

Example: *Clara is a Spanish-born elder Daeva of the Invictus. She was Embraced in Barcelona, and traveled to Mexico in the first 50 years of her Requiem. Her early nights in the region were traumatic, and she bore witness to several violent assaults led by Mayan Kindred on the Spanish settlers she kept as a herd. One night, she personally fought off an attacking Gangrel, slaying* *him with her bare hands. Ever since then, she has suffered from the Compulsive Bias that all native Kindred are ugly, brutish and coarse. Now, whenever she deals with a pure native vampire, she suffers a –2 on all Social rolls because of her barely-concealed dread and disgust.*

If a racist or otherwise prejudicial outlook grows into a full-blown derangement, it can only be overcome by a reclamation of Morality (or, for vampires, Humanity).

Deep-set religious influences also contribute to the mix in Mexican Kindred relations. The legacy of Catholic invasion bleeds into modern thought, forming a foundation of conservatism or rebellion in each mortal (depending on their personal experiences and character) that is rarely shaken when she makes the transition to a vampire's Requiem. Religion itself may be abandoned or, as is more likely, dramatically altered by the Embrace, but the core of faithful fervor or stubborn denial tends to remain.

Ties to home territory and mortal family further complicate the relationships of Mexican vampires. While these ties are no more or less powerful than those of vampires anywhere else, the interplay of ancestral, racial and religious variables tend to amplify the potential dilemma embodied in mortal connections.

Thematic Keywords: Blind loyalty, conquest, crusade, festering hatred, history, honor and duty, inherited rage, stubbornness.

Sample Plots: Fight for recognition in a domain ruled by a racist outsider. Try to maintain faith and virtue in the midst of a vicious battle between Kindred lineages. Work to eliminate the influence of antagonistic lines in the domain. Assassinate a vampire who once dishonored your ancestor. Help a recently arisen elder masquerade as a modern neonate.

Ability Specialties: Academics (Genealogy, Kindred Lineages), Investigation (Mortal Civic Records), Politics (Diplomacy), Empathy (Body Language), Subterfuge (Cultural Indicators)

Romance and Vendetta

The many lines drawn by the prejudices and predilections of Mexican Kindred only serve to intensify ordinary emotional interactions. Romance is often complicated, if not an outright transgression, and simple disagreements always threaten to ignite (or re-ignite) long-standing grudges. The complex interplay of factors in a vampire's history and personal makeup contributes to the escalation of passion in all cases.

Many of the Kindred in Mexico fill their time with amorous dalliances, and each domain has its own legendary loves. Ambitious neonates whisper tales of social elevation in romance, perpetuating the myth (or overestimating the probability) of the possibility of forging a direct, powerful connection to the movers-and-shakers in Kindred society. Politically shrewd Kindred note the destructive potential of love, occasionally finding themselves vulnerable to it as an unexpected, irrational result of their constant worry.

In 19th century Mexico City, a fierce romance between a lowly devotee of the Circle of the Crone and a Meister Player of the Invictus created ripples that are still felt in the domain today. The affair was initiated against the instruction of the Hierophant, who disapproved of the Invictus vampire's pure European heritage, and the affair continued despite the growing outrage of Kindred in both covenants. In the midst of controversy, facing threats of disownment and shame, the two left the domain and became notorious Nomads, criminally defiant of the laws of their compatriots. Their names were thenceforth stricken from the records of the domain by order of the Prince, and discussion of their activities forbidden from Elysium. They still run free, according to popular rumor, and their devotion to each other is an inspiration to emotional Kindred who dream of escape even now, despite the efforts of their pragmatic leaders.

Running a Romance Story

A romance plot is likely to involve intense politics and social play, providing the characters with a number of personal challenges. Love can intersect with loyalties or traditional social barriers, forcing those under its sway to defy orders from superiors or behave unpredictably. With so many of these barriers in Mexican Kindred society, it is more likely that a romance will invoke the disapproval of characters' compatriots. Many of the Virtues and Vices of Kindred are inspired in the presence of love: Hope and Fortitude play a strong part in any forbidden affair, and participants (and observers) can easily become enmeshed in Lust and Envy. The play of attraction and amorous involvement is common in Elysium, but the appearance of all-consuming, true love is rare and compelling.

Those closest to the characters in a romance plot often become antagonists, working against the union because they are unwilling to accept it. These villains, malicious or otherwise, make a great addition to any story because of the difficulties they prevent. Characters are unlikely to want to destroy their own friends and blood relatives, so they will be forced to find non-violent solutions to end the interference. Appeals to humanity and manipulation of emotion come into play, allowing the Storyteller to present the themes of the game from an unusual angle.

Romance itself can be a manifestation of the atmospheric elements common in the region. Ancient influence can guide a union between modern descendants or participate directly in the form of an awakened elder. Neonate lovers can express modern defiance in their refusal to restrict themselves to traditional roles. Love itself is a lawless emotion, transcending the bans and barriers of society.

Vendetta, on the other hand, is likely to entail extreme physical conflict. Characters are embroiled in a long-term feud that explodes into violence, creating a survival challenge on all sides. Everyone in the domain is forced to declare his or her loyalties, polarizing disagreements and raising the overall feeling of tension: those who support the losing side are bound to suffer, so vampires are well-advised to put their all into ensuring victory. Those who cross traditional boundaries in declaring their loyalties are bound to invoke the disapproval or outright animosity of their closest blood relations.

A domain can be completely destabilized by a vendetta. Throughout the 18th and 19th centuries, the city of Xalapa in Veracruz played host to one of the longest-running and most ferocious Kindred blood feuds in the region. Thanks to the inherited animosity between Tepeu, a native Gangrel elder, and a Spanish Ventrue by the name of Hector de Rivera, two factions in the city involved themselves in a series of bloody conflicts that resulted, over the passage of time, in the destruction of nearly 50 Kindred. The vendetta continued even after de Rivera's destruction in the early years of the 19th century, and only came to a close when the last member of his faction was eliminated in 1882. In the period of most intense conflict, no official decree could encourage enough restraint: vampires on both sides would seek excuses to initiate a battle whenever they encountered their opponents. The Elysium of Xalapa has never been the same since — memories of the conflict are fading, but every member of the old court who remains still fears a return to hostilities.

Running a Vendetta Story

Unlike a romance, vendetta focuses on a physical conflict and is likely to entail a serious threat to the characters' safety. If they are drawn into the unfolding battle, they may be forced to take it to its conclusion: kill or be killed. If not, they will have to face the derision or disappointment of their compatriots — a humiliating circumstance that might draw them into violence whether they like it or not. Similar to romance, vendetta plots will often involve a test of will and self-control, but with a much stronger potential for inhumane behavior. Vendetta is an amoral exercise, pressuring normally charitable and prudent characters into destructive action. Pride and wrath threaten to take precedence in a vendetta story, presenting the characters with a spiritual threat that is easily as perilous as the physical.

The antagonists in a vendetta plot will be clearly separated from the characters, although the division can be along any number of lines. Those who are provoking the action are likely to be overtaken by Wrath or Pride while the rest are dragged helplessly along in their wake. Characters who participate in the battle will be risking Final Death, while those who attempt to end the hostilities may end up making enemies of both sides.

Similar to romance, vendetta underscores several of the atmospheric elements of Mexico. The bearing and feeding of a grudge is one of the defining elements of a poisonous ancient influence, and a history of warfare is sure to contribute to both the bleakness and the lawlessness of a domain.

A combination plot allows the best and worst of both story elements to come together. A forbidden romance in the midst of vendetta (or one that causes a vendetta to resurface) will place the lovers in mortal danger while presenting other characters with a multi-layered dilemma.

For best results, it may be effective and enjoyable for a Storyteller to establish a history of both extremes in a domain. Characters should feel that old romances still haunt the Elysium and that forgotten vendettas are just waiting to resurface. A complicated political balance shot through with tense passions is a perfect base for almost any vampire story, especially if the characters feel that they may get swept along with any flare-up — giving them a reason to provoke or prevent one, depending on their needs (and the preference of the players).

Thematic Keywords: Desire unleashed, desperation, duels of honor, forgiveness, insult, undying passion, walking the razor's edge.

Sample Plots: Defend the love of two Kindred from warring factions. Try to put a stop to a decades-long vendetta between vampire lineages. Seduce a prominent vampire among your enemy's ranks. Defy an injunction against fraternization with the descendants of a despised elder. Undermine and destroy a pair of outlaw lovers.

Ability Specialties: Brawl (specify enemy), Weaponry (Dueling), Empathy (Matters of the Heart), Persuasion (Inspiring Mercy), Socialize (Discouraging Inhibition), Subterfuge (Concealing Emotions, Seduction)

The Undying War

The struggle for the conquest of mortal Mexico may have ended almost 500 years ago, but in the Kindred world, forces native to the land still wage war in an effort to maintain control of their domains. Adherents of the old ways maintain political strongholds all over the region, edging out European sensibilities with no less ruthless totality than that of the conquistadors. In those cities that are ruled by Kindred of Spanish origin, the threat of torpid vampires rising to re-ignite the battle is ever-present. Attempts at peaceful compromise in some domains have only given rise to an environment of subtle warfare. Vampire lines, inheriting their imperative causes nearly as tangibly as they do Disciplines or weaknesses, work incessantly to seize political and social prominence even when they are forbidden to destroy or exclude the opposition. Convoluted plots of social sabotage are omnipresent. Those hoping to avert open conflict put intricate systems of etiquette in place, but these systems grow more and more byzantine as the lawmakers struggle to keep up with the Kindred who find ways to circumvent or pervert the boundaries to serve their ends.

The war is a self-feeding process. Every personal slight and injury adds fuel to the long-burning fire, and in some places the battle has so much momentum that it almost seems to exert a will of its own, dragging all of the participants along with it. Attempts to slow or stop the cycle of grievance and recrimination are opposed by the inexorable drive of accumulated history. For nearly every vampire in the land, escape seems impossible and the eventuality of destruction at the hands of an inherited enemy seems unavoidable. Only the real long-term thinkers can even imagine a realistic end to the complicated hostilities of Mexican Elysium, and of those rare Kindred, only a few can muster the self-confidence to predict a favorable outcome.

In some domains, the lines of intrigue are woven so tightly that many Kindred can't even be sure whom they're working for. The Elysium of Guadalajara in the early 20th century was an extreme demonstration of the confusion that can result from the machinations of the undying war. Lines of heritage, lineage, political and religious loyalty became so tangled that nearly half the vampires in the city were double- and triple-agents for different factions, splitting their loyalties and masking their true intentions so finely that some were driven mad by the strain. The intricate and staggeringly malleable lines of communication changed so quickly that a significant contingent of Kindred abandoned the struggle completely, falling into torpor or otherwise retreating into reticent isolation. Diplomatic relations among the covenants were badly damaged, and several decades of dedicated effort were required to reopen talks. Not a single vampire was destroyed in the intense and confusing struggle for supremacy, but some Kindred still aren't sure who won the domain.

Stories set in domains subject to the vagaries of the undying war are excellent for running characters through high-stakes social challenges. Long plots might involve bringing the hostilities to a close (one way or another), while shorter, less ambitious ones could use the constant dodge-and-parry of politics as a potentially explosive backdrop, greatly increasing the tension felt by the characters.

Thematic Keywords: Confusion of loyalties, political minefields, pressure, sensitive information, struggle for supremacy, subtlety, veiled threats.

Sample Plots: Advance the traditional cause of your line in disobedience to the Prince. Attempt to rescue a vampire caught in a snarl of political blunders. Represent your faction at a pitfall-riddled Elysium gathering. Plan and execute the overthrow of a politically entrenched opponent. Risk offending close friends and allies by enforcing an unpopular edict of the Prince.

Ability Specialties: Politics (in Elysium, Backroom Dealings), Stealth (Hand Signs), Intimidation (Subtle Warnings), Persuasion (Sowing Doubt, Inspiring Loyalty), Subterfuge (Doublespeak)

Conveying the Complexity

Running a story in the midst of the undying social war works best if the complex interactions between Kindred are difficult to unravel, making it more likely that a careless character could stumble into a bad situation. The sense of danger

in a tense milieu is enhanced by a thorny diplomatic problem — any statement could offend the wrong vampire, leading to serious diplomatic snarls (or worse, a call for revenge).

There are three simple ways to convey the complexity of an Elysium embroiled in a social war. First, by game mechanics: have players roll Intelligence + Politics or Wits + Politics if they wish to understand another vampire's place in the domain, their own place in relation to another's or their disposition with respect to a certain faction or covenant. If politics are volatile enough, these checks will have to be frequent — circumstances can change from night to night or week to week, and nobody wants to be caught operating on outdated assumptions.

Example: *Isidro the Carthian Mekhet is in a volatile Elysium. He is greeted by Miguel, a Daeva of the Invictus with notoriously racist views. Isidro's first instinct is to snub Miguel, but he thinks for a moment. Isidro's player rolls Intelligence + Politics and gets a success, so Isidro remembers that Miguel, although distasteful, is currently considered an asset to the Carthians because of his recent willingness to ally against troublesome elements in the Ordo Dracul. Isidro nods warmly, narrowly avoiding offending and alienating a valuable collaborator.*

Second, with the requirement of qualifying knowledge: a faction might communicate costume requirements to its trusted friends before an Elysium gathering in order to facilitate identification, or may pass around a coded phrase that is to be spoken upon introduction. The more specific and unusual the demands, the more the players will understand the taxing expectations that are placed on their characters. If proper behavior is established correctly, characters will begin scrutinizing everything that is said and done in their presence, wondering if they are missing a coded message or if they have mistaken an invitation to identify themselves as an ally for a simple, innocuous statement.

Third, with descriptive text: make sure the players are aware of the layers of communication in Elysium. Describe the careful attention Kindred pay to every statement, or the clear staging of some of their postures and remarks. Inject significance into apparently accidental events, taking the time to point out the ease with which a character could interpret the event's "choreography." If the players take up the challenge, they may start arranging "unplanned" demonstrations of their own instead of speaking directly.

The Plague of Nomads

For many Kindred who are young or otherwise inferior in power, there is only one escape from the turmoil of social conflict: the road. The domains of Mexico boast a greater proportion of Nomad vampires than those of any other region in the world, and the last 100 years has seen a tripling of their numbers. Some are disaffected Kindred looking to shrug off the chains of inherited animosity and flee the suffering imposed on them by the mistakes of their elders. Some break away from oppressive domains, hoping to find a more favorable home and forced to wander until they do. Some are simply frustrated by the complicated politics of Elysium, choosing to exist as a solitary band in the wild.

Then there are the wanderers tasked with a more definite goal: to crusade on behalf of their side in the undying conflict, lending strength to their compatriots and striking a blow against their enemies wherever they go. Indigenous vampires and their descendants stalk the highways in search of "fallen" domains, those ruled by "invaders" to make war on. Conquerors and their inheritors roam the countryside in search of slumbering elders to destroy and native Kindred to destabilize.

For vampires on the road, there is no way to predict the sympathies of strange Kindred. Encounters between coteries often begin and end with violence. In the constant struggle for resources, the political convolutions of stable Elysium sites are exchanged for the simpler physical battle for survival. Because of their surprising numbers in Mexico, a coterie on the road rarely goes more than a few weeks without encountering competition — and unclaimed blood is growing more and more scarce with time.

To the Kindred of stable domains, the last century's steady increase in Nomad population is a serious problem. Devoting a force to repelling Nomad incursions is necessary, but often turns the attentions of policing Kindred outwards, weakening the internal structure of the domain. Hunting the Nomads is impossible without employing a roving force of one's own, and that usually requires negotiation with a coterie of undesirables.

Furthermore, the presence of nearby Nomad coteries can completely skew a domain's political balance. In Hermosillo, Sonora, the need to defend against near-constant incursion in the 1970s militarized the Kindred of the city, empowering a reactionary assembly of Invictus vampires and diluting the influence of their more tolerant competitors. Every time a successful strike drained resources or threatened damage to the Masquerade, those in favor of a tactical, organized government gained support. Eventually, the city fell to a rigid dictatorship of the Invictus, resulting in a bloody purge and pitching the domain into a decade-long war with the wandering outsiders. Against expectations, the ranks of the Sonoran Nomads swelled in those nights — a number of coteries Embraced unlucky mortals to keep their numbers up, exiles from the city formed their own units and new groups that wandered into the range of the Invictus Knights were drawn into conflict. By the end of the 20th century, the landless Nomads in the desert were estimated to outnumber the stable Kindred of Hermosillo, two to one. The situation is dire, and many believe it will never be fully resolved.

Nomad Cycles

Observant Kindred have noticed that all but the shrewdest (or most paranoid) Nomad coteries eventually fall into a wandering pattern, visiting familiar territory and reliable feeding grounds again and again over the years. If they aren't careful, they become relatively easy to predict, making them simpler to confront or avoid than their more creative competitors. Crusaders or stable domain security forces will pay a high price for reliable information about an enemy coterie's wanderings so that they can plan a coordinated ambush or disrupt their source of vitae.

Investigators watch closely for reports of cyclical symptoms of weakness or unexplained violence in small mortal communities, knowing that these occurrences might indicate the establishment of a habitual Nomad path. Rumors of mortal villages that begin to understand what is happening to them and arm themselves against future vampire incursion are common — the Kindred in stable domains often refer to the threat of a mass breakdown of the Masquerade, as news spreads outward from these alleged hunter communities, as justification for eliminating Nomad coteries.

Some coteries come to rely on these cycles for trusted communication and exchange of goods, attending scheduled meetings with other wanderers at the intersection of their respective paths. Occasionally, three or four coteries will meet at once, forming a temporary domain and disbanding it soon after.

The preponderance of Nomad coteries in the Mexican region opens up a wide range of story styles. Guerrilla-style conflict provides an intense physical and diplomatic challenge for characters on both sides. Pursuit plots are intellectually and physically engaging for characters as well, and relatively simple for Storytellers to run because they have clear criteria for success or failure: either the Nomads are located and engaged before a time limit is run out or they aren't. Finally, the temptation to become Nomads is itself a compelling addition to any plot — as an escape option, it may seem attractive to characters and could lead to a struggle for survival on the road.

Thematic Keywords: Competition, defending territory, dispossession, fierce individualism, invasion, lawlessness and loyalty, limited resources.

Sample Plots: Repel a Nomad incursion into stable territory. Strike out into the wild in pursuit of Nomad enemies. Broker negotiations of peace between the representatives of your domain and a wandering coterie of Kindred. Flee a restrictive domain and try to survive in the wild. Unify a number of Nomad coteries and stage a coup.

Ability Specialties: Investigation (Indications of Kindred Presence), Drive (Pursuit), Firearms (in motion, Sniper), Stealth (Covering Tracks, Shadowing), Survival (Tracking, specific terrain)

Historical Settings

A wealth of flavors and situations are available to Storytellers willing to run characters through historical settings, especially in a region that has undergone such radical changes. Flashback scenes can help establish the behavior of Kindred in modern nights (or leave players with a better understanding of their elders' quirks), as well as laying the groundwork for the long lines of conflict and aggression common in Mexico.

Five sample historical periods in Mexican development are detailed below, each with a number of potential story hooks, setting details and notes about potential pitfalls and advantages of their use.

The Island City

During the dark nights of the 14th and 15th centuries, the great city of Tenochtitlán (Teh•NOTCH•tee•tlahn) rose above the salt waters of Lake Texcoco, overlooking the range of the Anáhuac valley. The city was the prize of the Aztec civilization, a maze of temples and gardens arrayed over a complicated system of intricate canals. There, the elder powers of the region ruled as gods, worshipped by human and vampire in a bloody tradition of sacrifice and appeasement.

Setting a story at the apex of Aztec civilization can provide a real opportunity to explore the horrors of faith gone wild and the motifs of ancient power, blood as currency and the madness of permanent war. In these early nights, the ancient influence of pagan Kindred is unchallenged by modern fashion.

The setting of Tenochtitlán is rich for flashback imagery as well. The details of the scenery can be incorporated into the hazy visions of torpor for modern characters, or a quick image might escape from the thoughts of an elder under the effects of Auspex.

Setting Details: Tenochtitlán was situated on a wide plateau, surrounded on all sides by the marshy, salty, snake-infested waters of Lake Texcoco. At night, the edges of the lake would vanish into darkness on all sides, intensifying the isolation of the city. Four constructed causeways were placed to allow access across the black waters, crossing a series of dams and canals that were built as systems of water filtration, transportation and defense. Wooden bridges were placed across these canals in the daytime, and removed at night.

The terraced temples of the Aztec religion dominated the skyline, some with dozens of towers rising all around the flat-topped center. Thousands of torches lit the streets at night, pouring smoke and dripping oil constantly. Floating gardens were built on sculpted mounds of earth, anchored in place by the roots of the trees growing within. Nopal cactus and its prickly fruit were everywhere.

The Aztec empire was ethnically diverse, and a wide range of tribes and fashions were represented in their great city. Trade was brisk and constant, and tributes to the nobility and their religion were extravagant. There were no pack animals, so all ground paths were designed for travel on foot. All roads were guarded, and were relatively safe.

Constant human sacrifices were made to guarantee the return of the sun each morning, and the Flower Wars were conducted without pause in order to ensure the capture of potential victims. Slaying enemies in battle was never preferred — it was always best to take them alive, delivering them to the temples for proper use.

At the sacrifices, victims were painted with blue chalk and led to the top of a great temple. They were laid on a stone slab at the top, where a priest would cut them open with an obsidian blade and remove their hearts. Assistants threw the bodies of victims down on the steps, where they would later be removed. Their heads would be saved and added to the *tzompantli*, a wall of skulls within the temple.

Every night at midnight, trumpets were sounded from the temple roofs to indicate the time. There were soundings five times in the day as well: at sunrise, mid-morning, midday, mid-afternoon and sunset.

The vampires of Tenochtitlán were divided into two distinct groups: on the one hand were the god-nobility, presenting themselves to great herds of frenzied worshippers as emissaries of the gods above (or, in some cases, as gods themselves) and gathering their tributes in good faith. Many truly believed the vampires' tales — very few would consciously deceive their people, and anyone who suggested that they were not what they claimed would face a wild rage unparalleled. On the other hand were the feeders: lowly vampires who took blood wherever they could find it, living as thieves in the streets of the city. After a great sacrifice, many of the feeders would emerge from the shadows to lick clean the temple steps or steal a headless body for draining.

Story Concepts: Elevate a lowly feeder to the status of a minor god. Discover the false rule of a god-noble who cares nothing for his people and depose him. Run with the soldiers of the Aztec in a Flower War, seizing victims for the great sacrifices of your people. Dwell as feeder thieves in the canals of the city, preying upon the citizens and hiding from the god-nobles above.

Storytelling Advice: If a setting as exotic as dark-ages Tenochtitlán has a single overriding drawback, it is that players will have a difficult time relating to the culture portrayed therein. Players may tend to make an effort to demonstrate their characters' "superiority" (i.e., relatively modern outlook) to prevailing attitudes of the Aztecs, or players may feel forced to simplify those attitudes to the point of caricature.

Talk to your players before setting a game in Tenochtitlán, and make sure they're comfortable playing in the setting and you're comfortable with their interpretation of play. If it doesn't look like it's going to work out the way you hoped, it's best to think about another approach to your story. Can it be told as a series of flashbacks, experienced by modern characters through a flood of memories or borrowed consciousness? Can it be constructed as a shared dream or illusion meant to demonstrate the old ways to modern characters?

Tenochtitlán is a perfect setting for illustrating a sense of hopelessness for characters. The Aztec people are caught up in a practice of perpetual warfare, feeding the demands of their bloody religion without the possibility of satisfaction. The players will be well aware (even if the characters are not) that the culture is doomed: the invasion of the Spanish conquistadors looms in the future, after all, and the great achievements of the city will soon fall into shadow and decay.

The Clash of Cultures

The 16th century saw the arrival of the European Catholics and the conversion of Mexico into a Spanish colony. As the great Chichimeca wars waged in the north, the cities of the south were emptied out, razed and rebuilt in the image of the foreign conquerors, ushering in an age of persecution. The temples and texts of the old gods were destroyed in an attempt to erase their worship. The people were ground under the machinery of their conquerors, forbidden to read or write and decimated by smallpox, typhus and the rigors of forced labor.

Setting a story in the period between the 16th and 19th centuries allows you the freedom to run characters through an ongoing war for territory and resources. The subtlety of modern nights is not entirely necessary — savagery and brutality ruled the day, so it went largely unnoticed in the night. The horrors of invasion and cultural genocide are wide open for the telling in this setting, as are the varied moral dilemmas presented by the atrocities of the mortals.

Flashbacks to the wars of conquest can establish the long-term behavior of Kindred in Mexico, as well as explain the inherited animosities that filter down through the bloodlines and clans in the region.

Setting Details: In the mortal world, many of the women were married to Spanish invaders and produced *mestizo* (mixed) offspring, who found themselves subjected to a stratified caste system based almost entirely on their physical features. Spanish-born whites (*peninsulares*) ruled at the top of the hierarchy, followed by Mexican-born whites (*criollos*), then mixed Spanish and natives (*mestizos*), mixed Spanish and blacks (*mulattos*) and, at the bottom, natives.

In 1521, the city of Mexico was founded on the ruins of Tenochtitlán. Lake Texcoco was drained, and the white churches and houses of Spanish design were built. The viceroyalty of Spain made their home in the new city, and soon attracted all that comprised the nobility of the colony. The city then was a bastion of hope and decadence — a place for the conquering European forces to plant their banners and make a home. There, the great capital of the Aztec empire was crushed to powder beneath the armored boots of proud, bloody-minded conquistadors.

Obsidian weapons were shattered by steel. Leather shields were shredded by gunpowder. Stone edifices were blown to pieces. The great sails of the Spanish fleet appeared all along the Gulf coast, the crosses they bore blazing in the sunlight behind clouds of cannon smoke.

A shadowy war was waged then, in the deep, dark nights beyond the understanding of the mortals. European Kindred rode the sails with their mortal counterparts, striking into the heart of the conquered nation like so many burrowing spiders. The god-nobles and feeders rose up to do battle, but the Europeans hid behind the cleansing fires of the Spanish Church, letting their great temples and havens burn so that they could pick up the pieces afterwards.

Ventrue stood then, in polished armor, with steel flashing in their hands, accompanied by the terrifying Nosferatu.

European Gangrel clashed with their native brothers and sisters, wolf crashing into jaguar in the wet blackness of the jungle. Daeva faced Daeva. Mekhet faced Mekhet. The time was one of aggressive chaos and bloody succession, with the whole of the region hanging in the balance. Nothing was settled yet, and no future was clear.

Mortals were laid low by the thousands, overridden by disease and despair. They would collapse in the streets, delirious with pain and fear while the crosses of the European faith were mounted atop new churches. The elaborate villas of the new nobility were built on the ruins of temples, hosting victors' celebrations on the former sacrificial grounds.

Story Concepts: Join the battle to repel the conquistadors. Arrive with the Spanish fleet to claim the Mexican territory for your clan and your line. Seek a median between the old Kindred and the new, hoping for a peace that the humans cannot find. Rise up against the old god-nobles as feeders looking to win power for themselves. Work feverishly to ease the suffering of the mortals while the engines of conquest grind on all around you.

Storytelling Advice: The conflict between native and European forces dominates this setting utterly; it is almost impossible to play characters in this time and place who don't involve themselves in the battle. If your players are not enthused about playing a war (or if they're not comfortable with the themes of subjugation involved in this particular war), you may wish to avoid the setting.

If they are enthused about it, they may find the setting extremely exciting — they will be presented with options that are not usually available in the modern world. Be careful to avoid a "supersoldier" approach, though — vampires aren't heroes, after all, and even when they do good deeds, they must fuel their works with the lifeblood of human beings.

One approach that might work to provide challenging play is to run a series of historical scenes involving the murderous clashes between Kindred in these nights, down through the generations. Every session, players could take on different characters further and further down the line of ages as they meet again and again in bloody conflict with their enemies. Some nights, they will emerge victorious, and some nights they will be the victims of wholesale slaughter. The frustration and futility of Kindred war could be illustrated as a sort of prelude, bringing the players to a point where they begin with their "real" characters — ones that the players will play indefinitely. They will be likely to understand the innate rage of their characters and simultaneously wish to avoid the fate that awaited their ancestors.

Following the First Mexican Empire

After the war of independence and the ill-fated formation and rapid collapse of the First Mexican Empire, the nation of Mexico was bankrupted by a series of poor choices in diplomatic concessions to Spain and distribution of internal resources. Land grant initiatives were put in place in the north, providing property to families who agreed to emigrate from the United States and assume Mexican citizenship (and convert to Catholicism). Before the new territories could contribute significantly to the nation's base of power, the Mexican War of the 1840s erupted, resulting in the massive reduction of Mexican territories.

Setting a story in this time period allows characters to participate in the formative days and nights of a fledgling nation, witnessing the infinite possibilities and enduring the many disappointments of the process. A more modern veneer of gentility and refinement is slowly forming, even as the heat of war burns beneath. Characters of all types must define themselves along a series of axes: civil or violent? Forward-looking or nostalgic? Nationalistic or territorial?

Flashbacks to this setting might help to establish the fear of chaos and sense of looming disaster that many of the ancillae of Mexico seem to experience on a nightly basis. To those who experienced the upheaval of the early 19th century, no peace can ever be assured and no declaration ever considered permanent. Allegiances and diplomatic ties were shifted, severed, repaired and realigned with such speed during those nights than many have never fully recovered, and the court of some domains still reflect that instability in modern nights.

Setting Details: A nation in chaos. Poverty and depression were counterbalanced by the pride of the recent achievement of independence from Spain and the fierce nationalist rhetoric of the war with the United States of America. Undersupplied and underfunded, the military put out constant calls for enlistment. The territories of Texas and California attempted to secede and have themselves recognized as independent republics, cutting a line down the middle for families who lived on both sides of the border.

Political upheaval threatened Mexico City constantly. Following the collapse of the failed empire of 1821 and the then-current attempts to rebuild the national economy while caught in the midst of a war, the republican government faced frequent threats of rebellion. Federal officials and their would-be opponents both courted influential citizens, creating an atmosphere of intrigue unparalleled in the nation's history.

The halls of Kindred power were no less affected. The triumphs of the Spanish vampires in expunging the influence of their native counterparts were threatened by political upset in many domains. Unlikely sympathizers with the old ways began to make themselves heard even as upstart Nomads from America threatened to colonize the cities, forcing the Spaniard Kindred to assume the role of defenders of the land. Reversals and upset seemed to rule the night, driving more than a few vampires into frustrated slumber or unleashing them from their home territories, forcing an upswing in Nomad population.

The formulation of a national identity gave rise to a series of idealistic declarations, many of which were doomed to failure in the face of real circumstances. Unification of diverse elements under the Mexican flag was necessary under the threat of invasion, and resultant pride was both a natural defense mechanism and a balm against the pain of military humiliation. Many Kindred became disillusioned with the notion of mortal dedication, noticing how formerly bitter enemies were willing to abandon their ideals in a desperate bid to repel their mutual enemy. To them, the humans of the region seemed fickle and confused, and never more so than at this time.

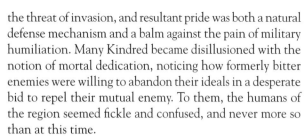

The relatively unpopulated territories in the Mexican north (most notably the modern states of California, Arizona, New Mexico and Texas) were subject to an influx of migrants from the south and immigrants from the United States. War broke out because the immigrants wanted the land but didn't wish to subject themselves to Mexican law — exacerbated by the ban on keeping slaves, which proved extremely unpopular with former American citizens. A number of Kindred, hoping to carve out a niche for themselves, moved north with the Mexican hopefuls (and later the military), establishing new feeding grounds in the fledgling cities of Los Angeles, Tucson and San Antonio. To them, the struggle to seize control of new domains proved difficult and dangerous, but those who survived would reap benefits well beyond their expectations.

Story Concepts: Claim a mortal colony as a feeding source, defending it from Nomad raiders. Invade an established feeding ground, wresting it from the grasp of Spanish vampires. Take the opportunity of the conflict to revive an ancient elder so that he can make a bid for power. Stalk enemy soldiers in the northern territories. Struggle for power in the disorganized halls of Mexico City's Elysium. Establish a new domain in the war-torn north.

Storytelling Advice: Players should have no trouble connecting with the means and motives of characters in a 19th-century Mexican setting. The social mores and technology are nearer to modern understanding, and the struggle of various political factions may provide them with an opportunity to play out a formative conflict without shoehorning it into an established, modern city.

However, Storytellers must avoid the temptation to allow players to run wild just because the backdrop is in the past. For flavors of open war, an earlier setting may be more appropriate — in the 19th century, the Kindred of the city are in the process of settling upon their (hopefully) permanent arrangements and are growing weary of combat. Mexico's 19th century offers a fantastic opportunity to explore the battle fatigue that so many ancillae experience as they begin to look to their futures and become less and less willing to risk their existence.

Characters in a Nomad story might flash back to the conflicts of the 19th century as a way of illustrating the beginnings of their tradition. Perhaps their sires were once influential political players, established in one of the bustling cities of the region before they were cut loose by an unexpected turn. Maybe they were former denizens of the northern territories, expelled by American Kindred eager to stake new claims.

El Milagro Mexicano

The 20th century began with violent revolution in Mexico, collapsing the rule of established dictator Porfirio Díaz Mori and paving the way for a drastic change. The Partido Nacional Revolucionario, a unified force of revolutionary generals, seized power in 1929 and reversed many of the traditional policies of the government. For 40 years, the PNR (changed in 1938 to the PRM [Partido de la Revolución Mexicana] — and then again in 1946 to the PRI — Partido Revolucionario Institucional) presided over the most successful economic period in the history of the nation. Business and trade flourished and money poured into the country, largely due to the government's annexation of foreign oil interests on Mexican soil, a program of widespread workers' unionization and directed distribution of land packages to lower-class citizens.

The PRI governments during the period of El Milagro Mexicano (the "Mexican Miracle") enjoyed unprecedented popularity, and rarely faced serious opposition. To many of the people of the nation, it seemed that Mexico had finally come into its own, and would take its rightful place on the world stage. The economic collapses of the latter half of the century were yet to come, and hopes were high.

In the mid-'50s, the first of the nation's several 20th-century economic collapses brought El Milagro Mexicano to an end. Strangely, the incidence of elder reappearance roughly coincided with the end of the prosperous era, forever connecting the two in the minds of many Kindred. Those who were Embraced during the preceding decades proved most vicious in opposition to the native elders and their dedicated followers, witnessing the rapid decline of mortal living conditions and blaming it on their ideological enemies.

Setting Details: A period of exceptional prosperity. Communities that were destitute only a few years earlier enjoyed unprecedented levels development and affluence. Celebrations were frequent, and nationalistic hopes were at an all-time high.

For the Kindred, El Milagro Mexicano was a time of abundance as well. The mortals were finally at peace, easing the feeding situation and allowing many vampires to enjoy a reliable surplus of Vitae for the first time in their Requiems. Elder native Kindred rarely rose in those nights, whether by accident or design. An atmosphere of peace prevailed, and many shortsighted vampires allowed themselves to believe it would last forever. The Elysium gatherings of the period were lavish and exuberant, reflecting the mood of the young vampires therein (despite the warnings of older European Kindred, who failed to convey the capricious nature of mortal finances and fates).

Many of the citizens of Mexico, both mortal and Kindred, took the developments of El Milagro Mexicano as indication that they were reaping the benefits of proper conduct — religiously, politically or socially — laying the unfortunate groundwork for the disillusionment brought on by the collapses of the late 20th century. New business developments and civic structures were being raised in the nation's cities, illustrating the hopes of the people. A network of highways and roads were laid down in anticipation of growing transit demands.

Story Concepts: Attempt to plan for the long term while Kindred around you insist on allocating your resources to wasteful celebration. Try to protect your mortal family from the vagaries of economic fluctuation. Accept the responsibility of caring for a hidden elder in torpor while your enemies search for evidence of his existence. Take advantage of the period of prosperity to conspire against the domain's overconfident Kindred government.

Storytelling Advice: Setting a story against the backdrop of El Milagro Mexicano affords the Storyteller the opportunity to establish a counterpoint to the mortal conceit that they are experiencing forces unique in history. Elder Kindred will well recall the nights that seemed endlessly prosperous to them — whether as priests of the Aztec and Mayan empires, or as conquering Spanish invaders, just as they will recall the periods of violence and deprivation that followed each. Neonates unwilling to heed the admonitions of their elders will soon learn the lesson: everything repeats itself, and they must either plan for the inevitable or get swept away in the tides of change.

Many of the elder and ancilla vampires alive in present nights will remember El Milagro Mexicano well — most of them were awake for the first half of the 20th century. Running a flashback story in this setting can help players understand the motives of their elder siblings and sires (or elder enemies). A few sessions in previously prosperous domains could establish an interesting outlook for Kindred who entered torpor before the collapses of the '50s and '60s, giving players the opportunity to play shocked and disappointed Kindred waking into horribly poor conditions in modern nights.

The Great Earthquake

On September 19, 1985, a catastrophic earthquake struck Mexico City, killing tens of thousands of citizens and destroying the homes of at least 10 times as many. Billions of dollars of damage was caused in a sudden, shocking display of natural power, as the city was literally torn open. The event left an indelible mark on everyone, mortal or otherwise, who experienced it.

The city was woefully unprepared for an earthquake. Under-built foundations cracked, collapsing long-standing structures and motorways. There was little in the way of an emergency plan for the city services, and those organizations that survived the initial shock lacked preparation and equipment, leaving most of their representatives struggling to meet the overwhelming need of the populace. In the absence of official response, ordinary citizens banded together to form search and

rescue parties, scouring the rubble for signs of their friends and loved ones. An aftershock of the quake, nearly as powerful as the first, followed less than two days later and damaged or destroyed many of the makeshift emergency facilities that were set up to handle the massive influx of injured civilians.

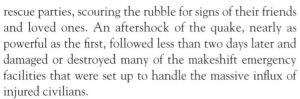

The psychic impact of the quake and its aftermath cannot be overestimated. The devastating blow to the faith of the people — both in their government and in the powers that be — combined with the sudden creation of hundreds, if not thousands of ghosts, set the stage for a city-wide plague of cynicism and spiritual decay.

Setting Details: A scene of total destruction. Many of the great, modern structures erected during or just after El Milagro Mexicano were destroyed in mere moments, bringing the hopes of millions down with them. The city streets cracked and buckled, revealing ruined stone beneath. In some places, fragments of ancient Tenochtitlán actually punched through the surface, rising into the blood-strewn rubble of the modern world.

Kindred havens across the city were torn to pieces, exposing those lying within to the morning sun. Within moments, a dozen prominent vampires met Final Death, and the night that followed saw the explosion of conflict between several rival factions, taking advantage of the chaotic aftermath of the quake to settle their differences. By the time the dust settled, roughly a third of the city's vampire population was unaccounted for and assumed destroyed.

Additionally, the upheaval realigned the city's mystic energies, disrupting the work of the Ordo Dracul and certain elements of mage society. Investigations and experiments that had been accumulating data for centuries were interrupted and, in many cases, completely annulled.

More mundane systems were damaged or destroyed as well — businesses, churches and residential feeding grounds all suffered the effects of the quake, forcing the local vampires to rapidly redraw boundaries that had remained in effect for centuries. The conflict over redefined territories in the city continued through to the end of the 20th century, and may be expected to carry on for some time.

Story Concepts: Survive the exposure of your group haven as the quake tears the walls open. Search for a coteriemate in the rubble of a collapsed feeding ground. Participate in heated negotiations to redraw territorial borders before the full count of dead and missing is received. Fend off the attacks of opportunistic enemies in the aftermath of disaster. Try to keep a pinned, injured mortal alive until emergency services can get to him.

Storytelling Advice: Running a story in with a large-scale calamity as backdrop allows you to bring the Man vs. Beast conflict of vampires into sharp focus. By all rights, the predatory Kindred should feel little in the way of concern for the mortals (or fellow vampires) in the domain, taking the opportunity instead to feed indiscriminately and destroy their weakened foes. The human side of characters cannot help but be moved by the tragedy, however, and will cause characters to behave more selflessly — attempting to rescue others, comforting the dying and so forth. The gravity of the situation isn't hard to convey, and may provide an intense and unexpected climax for stories of another type. A vendetta could be interrupted by the disaster, for instance, allowing the characters involved an opportunity to reconcile.

If you run the Great Earthquake as a flashback, it can help to establish the fears and grudges that define some of the villainous characters in a piece, or lay the groundwork for the development of characters who were otherwise altered by the experience: finding religion among the rubble, perhaps, or a reclamation of noble obligations brought on by witnessing the pathos of the victims.

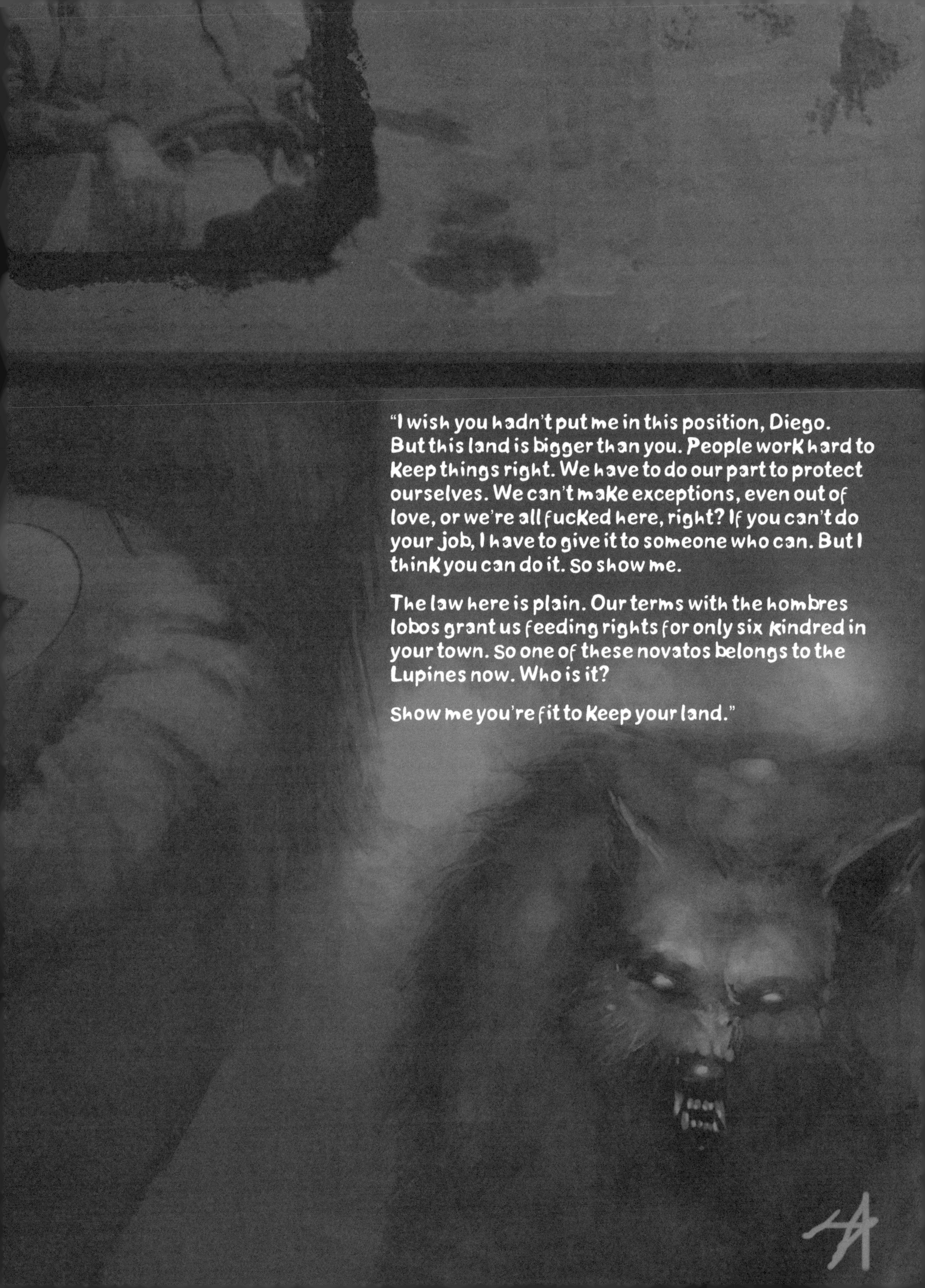

"I wish you hadn't put me in this position, Diego. But this land is bigger than you. People work hard to keep things right. We have to do our part to protect ourselves. We can't make exceptions, even out of love, or we're all fucked here, right? If you can't do your job, I have to give it to someone who can. But I think you can do it. So show me.

The law here is plain. Our terms with the hombres lobos grant us feeding rights for only six kindred in your town. So one of these novatos belongs to the Lupines now. Who is it?

Show me you're fit to keep your land."

Chapter Four: Local Powers

> **"When Mexicans no longer believe in anything, they will still hold fast to their belief in two things: the National Lottery and the Virgin of Guadalupe. For both have been known to work, even for those of us who believe in nothing."**
>
> **— Octavio Paz**

Princes

What if you want to set your chronicle in Mexico City, but you don't want the cozy blend of religious ideologies pitted against modern crime that was presented in Chapter One as the backdrop for your stories? What if you want to set your chronicle in Puebla or Oaxaca, but you don't know what the Prince is like there?

The following four Princes are your solution. The Prince of a city goes a long way to defining the mood of the city and what goes on there from one night to the next. By pairing one of the following Princes with the information you dig up on your chosen city, you have a setting for your Mexican chronicle. Put the Prisoner Prince in Mexico City, if you want, and turn your chronicle into an organized-crime epic with a truly monstrous villain. Put the Daughter of Conquest into Mexico City to focus your chronicle on two axes of class struggles in Mexico: rich vs. poor, Indian vs. Spanish.

Each of the following Princes was designed to be easily transplanted into the city of your choosing — even if that city's not in Mexico. Make Don Castillo the Prince of Los Angeles in your chronicle to create a delicate neo-feudal metropolis where Kindred and Lupines work together to keep mages and mortals under control. It's that easy.

Remember, too, that the players' characters don't have to be high-powered supernatural types to get close to most of these Princes in play. You could build a chronicle around the Prisoner Prince's nomadic messengers, the lady Malintzinita's retinue of socialite Harpies or Don Castillo's youngest new werewolf enforcers. These are your characters now. Plug them into your World of Darkness and go where the stories take you.

Alejandro Hurones, the Prisoner Prince

From a mortal life of criminal penury to the very apex of Kindred power, Alejandro Hurones is a Prince who has climbed the ladder of hardship, rising to conquer his domain so fully and so viciously that none dare to oppose him.

Embraced out of a life of thievery to provide his Carthian sire with a strong, trustworthy right hand, Hurones brought the lessons of 19th-century organized crime to the covenant. A veteran of street warfare and prison politics, he proved invaluable in matters of internal conflict, helping to unify the voice of the local Carthians. Within years, he formed a coterie of physical powerhouses, running it like a gang and fighting to protect his compatriots against the incursions of outsider Kindred. His gang's activities interlaced rapidly with mortal criminal enterprise, and the gang seized control of living operations, recruiting the most promising agents and working to exclude enemy interests. Flying largely under the radar of the then-Prince, a decadent, politics-obsessed Invictus traditionalist, Hurones' gang built a staggering base of power before attracting her displeasure.

By the time she ordered the application of restraint, Hurones and his cohorts were deeply entrenched in their territory. The Carthian Movement was targeted as a whole and attempts at diplomacy were undermined by Hurones' violent response. Two Invictus vampires were beaten into torpor and ransomed in the nights that followed, sparking the call for a purge. Prepared for the eventuality of persecution, Hurones upped the stakes and led his coterie to open war, throwing many of the ruling party off-balance and dragging the Carthians in his wake.

After months of intense battle, Hurones was captured and his coterie all but destroyed. His sire was punished with Final Death, and the territories of the Carthians were divided among the faithful servants of the Prince. For years, Hurones himself was held captive in the city's Elysium site, tortured and humiliated in an ongoing public display meant to cow the remaining members of the Movement. Despite the appalling circumstances of his imprisonment, the young Nosferatu refused to bend to the Prince. Time and again, Hurones was subjected to violent mistreatment and presented with an opportunity to submit. Time and again, he refused. Instead of demoralizing the Carthians, his example inspired them and they organized another violent revolt, freeing him and murdering the domain's Sheriff.

Hurones became both the leader of the revolution and the embodiment of its cause célèbre, re-injecting the movement with his dual ethos of strength and the inviolate loyalty of a downtrodden warrior. For years, he and his Kindred agents fought a pitched battle against the established Invictus rule, grinding away at it (and making use of rapidly growing mortal interests in their own revolution to undermine the ruling Kindred power base). Finally, after decades of unrelenting warfare, Hurones appeared at the Elysium before a shocked and horrified mass of Kindred, throwing the bloody ashes of his persecutor to the floor. The pristine walls of the hall were stained crimson that night, and every loyal member of the Prince's court was sworn to honor Hurones' rule or be destroyed on the spot.

True to form, the rule of terror that he established was even more oppressive than its predecessor. The Carthians assembled around him, dwelling within the domain as favored enforcers in a domain of Hurones' absolute law. No activity was permitted without his approval. No gain was made without tribute to him and his organization. No disrespect or dispute was tolerated.

In time, he began to understand that his rule of might would inevitably lead to a counter-revolution. While his Kindred were set to the task of uncovering and destroying dissenters, he turned his attention to building himself an impenetrable fortress. Taking inspiration from the unabated activities of his mortal allies in prison, he chose to move into a maximum security facility just outside town, running all operations from within.

Masquerading as an imprisoned crime lord, Hurones took control of the facility rapidly and easily. Within weeks, the guards, wardens and fellow prisoners were all in his hands. Free to come and go as he pleased, he enforced his will with fist and tooth, reshaping the prison in his image. His organization, now by far the largest and most powerful cartel in the domain, ran the building as a base of operations. The corrupt officials in charge funneled power to Hurones himself, allowing him to choose prisoner placement, giving him free reign and full access to all wards and turning a blind eye to the increase in beatings and murders within the walls.

In modern nights, regular visits from his mortal and Kindred lieutenants keep Hurones informed with respect to the night-to-night operation of his domain. On occasion, the Prince leaves the prison freely, walking the city streets or visiting the rare Elysium gathering.

For decades now, his hard-line rule has been unchallenged. His followers wiped out the last vestiges of real resistance some time ago, and those vampires who remain do so at his pleasure. He cares little for the complexities of covenant relations — all that matters to him is that Kindred of the domain pay their respects to him and deliver a "cut" of their power to his cartel every month. Hurones and his organization have made agents of the both the local police department and criminal element, using them to keep tabs on both mortal and Kindred interests (and to enforce rule, if necessary). His spies are everywhere.

It is considered nigh impossible to reach Hurones himself unless without being dragged before him. His prison haven is a labyrinth of windowless concrete and steel, populated by his mortal and undead servants and those who are more than eager to please his organization. Kindred who appear unexpected risk capture or destruction, and several are said to remain in long-term solitary confinement even tonight. Many people never see Hurones except through a barred sheet of bulletproof Plexiglas, and most never see him at all.

Description: Hurones is an imposing physical presence, thick-limbed and writ with the ragged marks of personal war. His leathery flesh is seamed with the deep puckers and scoring of long-healed injuries, each kept as a demonstration of his enduring strength. It is said that he maintains these scars as a memorial to his fallen foes: the more extensive the blemish, the greater his respect for the one who inflicted the wound.

His dark, steely eyes shine with devilish shrewdness, undimmed by age. Those who speak directly with him are struck by the sense of great experience and wisdom, fringed with an ever-present threat of explosive force. The deadly power of his physical strength is forever apparent — his muscles seem permanently knotted in preparation to unleash, and only his abiding intellect keeps them at bay.

Storytelling Hints: Alejandro Hurones is a veteran of poverty, cruelty and revolution. He knows perfectly well how the subjects of a misguided or selfish ruler can suffer, and yet cannot resist using the brutal tactics of his former oppressors in maintaining order. It is as though, despite intentions, he is forced to rely on the limited example of his domain and repeat the horrors of its past. Hurones is blind to the irony of his rule, and he works so hard to prevent another war of succession that even the worst crimes of repetition can be rationalized.

He is fiercely loyal, and rewards his faithful agents with familial treatment, protecting and honoring them as close compatriots. He will tolerate no accusation against the trusted elite of his domain, and shows clear favoritism to those who serve him honestly. On the flip side, the worst of his rage is reserved for traitors and betrayers — those who allow him to believe that they are dedicated to his service and his vision for the domain, then prove otherwise.

Hurones feels a conquering warlord's sense of duty to the domain. He fought for it, after all, and wants to make sure it stays worthy of his efforts. He promotes a philosophy of order and honor, encouraging his Kindred to avoid disrupting the lives of the living whenever possible. Violence between vampires is tolerated, so long as it falls within the regimented lines of organized arenas and Elysium dueling rings, but the stern Prince frowns upon those who toy with fragile mortals.

In personal dealings, Hurones is gruff and quiet, choosing his words carefully. His speech is spare and slow, as if he is attempting to communicate with a

minimum of sound. To him, words are all but meaningless, little more than a necessary bridge to provoke action. When moved to act, though, he is absolutely without hesitation.

Hurones' Purpose

Alejandro Hurones is designed to serve as a major antagonist to characters in a chronicle. No right-thinking vampire with a Humanity rating of 4 or higher should be able to dwell comfortably under Hurones' rule, but he is so deeply fixated and so frequently overcome with paranoia that resistance is extremely difficult. Carthian characters, specifically, might note that he's slammed the lid on the Movement's philosophy, forcing the covenant into a flawed modern reflection of the Invictus tyranny they claimed to be against.

Because of his intrusive style of rule, Hurones is not well suited as a background feature in peaceful, introspective stories. He is an obstruction, really, and his compatriots make a habit of harassing anyone who is not part of their organization.

Challenging Hurones' inhumane rule can lead characters into a long and difficult battle, testing their wits and skill in a high-tension chronicle. Any approach is possible

— warfare, espionage, seduction — but all are likely to be risky. Only a prolonged, carefully executed and ingenious plan is likely to reach the Prisoner Prince and unseat him.

Ruling Style: The Prince is supported by an elite body composed of those Kindred who aided him in the revolutionary overthrow of the domain. His rule is a ruthless criminal oligarchy, inspired by the operation of mortal cartels in the region. Only those who prove themselves in battle can ever really earn Hurones' esteem, and only those who risked their Requiems at his side will ever be fully trusted. These "veterans" are his *familia*, honored and respected in a way that more timid vampires can never be. Some are his childer, but most are unrelated Carthians. Only those who have risked Final Death in defense of the domain are granted the right to Embrace, and only they are allowed to serve as Primogen advisors. Newer Kindred may join this trusted inner circle, but only if they throw themselves into battle on the Prince's behalf — something that is becoming less and less necessary as his rule grows further and further entrenched.

Those Kindred who are not part of the trusted *familia* dwell in terror, knowing and fearing the swift and merciless treatment that enemies of the Prince are subject to. Many will do anything to prove their loyalty; bribery and other acts of servitude are common. Defiance is incredibly risky, and even whispered dissent is accompanied by frightened glances over the shoulder. There are rumors of a counter-revolutionary cell at work among the Kindred population, but most are too fearful to voice support for the idea, and many are convinced they are actually maintained by the Prince so that he can justify the neutralization of any vampire who displeases him.

Hurones is a firm believer in corporal punishment as both a deterrent against and a penalty for disobedience. Those who commit minor offences are either brought to his prison for painful confinement or thrashed in the streets. Those who actually invoke his wrath are frequently beaten into torpor or dragged into the sun.

Domain: Any domain ruled by Alejandro Hurones suffers under his tight, totalitarian control. The two thematic words that would apply to any story involving his rule would be *terror* and *immobility*. He is the ultimate nightmare Prince, allowing Storytellers to underscore the horrifying potential for stagnation in the curse of undeath. Thanks to Hurones, everything in the domain is frozen in place, held fast in his iron grip. He is like the vicious Beast lodged in the core of every vampire's heart, locked into his habits and demanding absolute obedience. Even the Prince himself is stored behind steel and concrete, housed in a great, inert compound that is as much a tomb as a fortress.

Because of Hurones' appreciation for soldiers and his inability to truly respect anyone who doesn't risk their Requiem in battle, his domain is tainted with violence. Intellectual Kindred fall by the wayside, and obedient physical powerhouses rise through the ranks. Crime is pervasive, but focused by the Prince's mortal allies. Police are corrupt accessories to the rule of Hurones' *familia*, and defiance in any form is met with brutality. The culture of bloodshed is such a defining feature of the domain that it seems impossible to fight it with anything but more of the same. Once again, a sort of immobility is presented: one cannot defeat the Prince without resorting to his tactics. It is the curse to which he succumbed many years ago, and one that he will likely pass on to his successors in the future.

Every character in Hurones' domain is pressured to throw in with his *familia*, and is sure to be asked to prove her loyalty with acts of violence. Attempts to remain pacifist or humane are considered indication of intellectualism or arrogance by the power elite and are treated accordingly. Humanity is difficult to maintain under Hurones' direction — and it seems that he wants it exactly that way. Storytellers wishing to underscore the challenge of maintaining Humanity in trying circumstances might find this Prince especially appropriate, using him to create a wartime atmosphere even in relatively peaceful surroundings.

When the Prince is pleased, the domain runs smoothly and most Kindred are able to go about their business as usual, so long as they make regular efforts to appease the Carthian *familia* and donate a portion of their gains — money, blood or influence — to Hurones' organization. The Carthians will throw occasional fetes in Elysium, most notably marking the day of the Prince's accession to the seat of power and destruction of his predecessor. These parties are lavish, boisterous and calculated to demonstrate the superiority of the Carthian elites in the domain. Stories run during these "good times" further support a focus on the Beast/Man conflict in every vampire. Characters who accept the system of rule have a relatively easy time, but must confront the damage complicity with the regime does to their Humanity.

When things are not going well, the Prince fears betrayal and the forces of the *familia* move hungrily from territory to territory, scouting for evidence of sedition. Kindred are pulled at random into interrogations and confinement within the walls of the Prince's haven. A story run during one of the Prince's paranoid phases presents a difficult physical challenge to characters, and may shift the setting to the inside of Hurones' fortress, allowing Storytellers to explore themes of confinement, isolation and endurance.

Story Concepts: Earn your membership in Hurones' *familia* by destroying your own sire on his orders. Attempt to infiltrate the Prince's haven stronghold and rescue an imprisoned Kindred ally. Hide from Hurones' enforcers and search for a way to appease the Prince after learning that he is angered by your activities in his domain. Attempt to shake Hurones' Carthians out of their close-minded mode of operation via political means. Locate and befriend a hidden cell of counter-revolutionary Kindred in the city so that you can choose either to take up their cause or betray them and earn the Prince's favor.

Clan: Nosferatu
Covenant: The Carthian Movement
Embrace: 1808
Apparent Age: 32
Mental Attributes: Intelligence 4, Wits 3, Resolve 5
Physical Attributes: Strength 6, Dexterity 3, Stamina 6
Social Attributes: Presence 3, Manipulation 2, Composure 4
Skills: Crafts 2, Investigation 4, Politics 4, Athletics 2, Brawl (Overbearing) 4, Stealth 4, Survival 3, Weaponry 3, Intimidation 5 (Alone with a Victim) 5, Streetwise (Criminal Gangs) 5, Subterfuge 2
Merits: Allies (Drug Cartels) 5, Allies (Prison Guards) 3, Allies (Police) 3, City Status: Prince 5, Covenant Status: Carthian Movement 5, Haven Size 1, Haven Security 5, Herd 4, Resources 3, Retainer 4
Willpower: 7 (reduced by Embrace, twice)
Humanity: 3 (Paranoia; 6)
Virtue: Fortitude. Alejandro has endured battles and tortures too numerous for mortals or neonates to comprehend. His strength only seems to grow with tribulation.
Vice: Greed. Power is Hurones' currency, and no matter how much he gets, he always wants more. He dreams of nothing less than the absolute destruction of all resistance and domination over every aspect of his domain.
Health: 11
Initiative: 7 (8)
Defense: 3
Speed: 14 (28)
Blood Potency: 6 (15/3 Vitae/per turn)
Disciplines: Obfuscate 3, Vigor 4, Nightmare 5, Resilience 3, Celerity 1

Monica Paez de Roa, The Gardener

Embraced more than 350 years ago for her heartbreaking beauty and soothing, shy voice, Monica Paez de Roa was a favorite of the Daeva in her city for decades. The half-Spanish daughter of a conquering warrior, she seemed infused with an innocence and earthly calm that was as circumstantially improbable as it was impossible to resist. Inducted into the Circle of the Crone by her sire, she practiced the worship of old gods in new masks, transposing the Catholic saints onto representations of Aztec divinity and teaching her compatriots the symbols and names of her father's people.

The domain of Monica's early nights was one of violent strife, reflecting the conquest of the mortals in the battle between native elders and the newly arrived Kindred of Spain. She watched vampires clashing in furious battle, literally tearing one another limb from limb, and yet she remained untouched. None could bring themselves to attack her — not the elder natives, to whom she spoke so endearingly, and not the invaders, who were confused by her European ways and often mistook her for one of their own.

In the midst of war, Monica found love with a Gangrel invader named Juan de Amaya. Their affair was conducted in secret, away from the prying eyes of Monica's native Circle and Juan's European Prince. For three short years, they experienced real bliss, forgetting the evils of vampirism in one another's arms. Inevitably, they were discovered and forbidden to continue their affair unless one or the other agreed to betray their Kindred. Neither would bend, and the two were forcibly separated. Juan was ultimately destroyed in battle, and Monica slipped into a miserable lassitude, eventually falling into a torpor that lasted throughout the 18th century.

When she woke again, she found her home domain completely changed. The invading Kindred had taken over, destroying or driving out most of their native counterparts in the process. Some remained and integrated themselves into the new society, choosing a Requiem of peace over dedication to the old ways. Monica herself was forgotten, and her awakening was a surprise to the Kindred of the city, who assumed she was of European lineage and welcomed her with open arms.

For nearly a century, she dwelled in sadness, mourning the loss of her Juan. None could console her, and she became a fixture of silent melancholy at Elysium. Dozens of Kindred threw themselves at her feet in the passage of time, desperate to bring happiness to this achingly beautiful, pitifully grief-stricken vampire. Every effort failed — but her kindness and patience with each earned her the admiration and love of many. She befriended many of her would-be lovers, walking with them in her gardens and dreaming of a world long gone. A new Circle of Acolytes formed around her, and she taught them her enduring ways.

Conflicts came and went, rarely approaching her, but often eliminating those more powerful. Two coup attempts shook the Elysium in the early decades of the 20th century, and the upper echelons of Kindred power in the city collapsed. Monica was surprised to find that her attempts at a quiet, unassuming Requiem had left her in a position of prominence: unparalleled in personal power and surrounded by a network of dedicated, able allies. She resisted the call of leadership, but her Circle grew in standing, and her network of supporters began interpreting her advice as official declarations — enforcing policies that she believed in but never intended to apply outside her own garden.

In 1932, the Kindred of her domain declared Monica's accession to the title of Prince, won without bloodshed and almost unanimously applauded. Since then, her rule has been imperfect but popular — she makes the errors expected of a vampire who never learned to lead, often erring on the side of personal experience and judgment over pragmatic necessity. Support for her remains strong into the modern nights, though.

Despite her rise to power and the comfort it brings, Monica is still unhappy. She has never loved since Juan was taken from her, and she believes she never will again. The huge garden she tends (and sleeps in) is a great memorial to him, sown with the flowers he would bring to her in their first nights together. There is nothing she wants for but reunion with her love — and that is an impossibility.

Description: Monica seems to be a teenage *mestizo* girl, somewhere around 15 or 16 years old. Her skin is naturally ash gray, but turns a light chocolate brown

when she is infused with fresh Vitae, and her eyes are large and dark. She wears her jet-black hair in two long braids, often tying them up in elaborate loops and pinning them with turquoise brooches. She is achingly beautiful, drawing astonished stares whenever she chooses to venture among the mortals of her domain. The perfumes of her garden often seem to attach to her, and she brings the fresh scent of summer blooms with her wherever she goes.

She almost always wears a simple, gauzy white summer dress and little else. She is always barefoot, and adorns her fingers with understated silver rings. Many have said that her uncomplicated approach to clothing reflects the virtue and vice of her observers: those who know themselves to be indulgent see a critique of their habits in her plain satisfaction. Those who are at peace with themselves aspire to her apparently easy minimalism.

Storytelling Hints: There are two major forces driving Prince de Roa at all times. On the one hand, the tragic experience of her first attempt at a Kindred Requiem has imparted the necessity and importance of patient calm to her. In all things, she prefers to construct an environment that works in her favor — the garden she dwells in is a great indicator of this habit, as are the subtle and grandiose traps she constructs for her enemies. There are entire bloodlines in her domain that are forever indebted to her because of her foresight and careful assistance through the decades. Monica will never react to an offensive challenge with overt hostility, but she also makes no effort to appease. Instead, she indicates displeasure with a cold silence, following it with indirect attack and passive-aggressive tactics designed to provoke self-destruction on the part of the opponent.

On the other hand, she is a dedicated and helpless sensualist. The truth behind her simple garb is less noble than most Kindred imagine. She wears a thin dress so as to better experience the breezes that blow through her garden and the textures of the plants all around her. She feeds frequently and beyond satiation simply to enjoy the warmth and taste of Vitae. Her mortal victims are drawn into her Discipline-sweetened clutches like insects to a spider's lair, and she wraps herself around them in languid, hours-long feeding sessions. When she is pleased, de Roa seems to slow down even more than usual, absently drawing her fingertips across nearby surfaces and creatures.

Prince de Roa is deeply intelligent, but she prefers to let other Kindred do most of the talking in personal interaction. As it is with her choice of dress, her tendency to passive conversation tends to reflect itself in her company's emotional state. Those who are already feeling guilty seem to assume that she's aware of their crimes and, if they are weak-willed enough, often confess without prompting. Those who are true allies of the Prince normally feel relatively comfortable in her taciturn presence.

She prefers to conduct personal, one-on-one meetings with Kindred in her extensive gardens, strolling slowly through the grounds. If someone behaves aggressively in her presence, she invokes Sovereignty without hesitation, and has no regrets about steering them towards her Retainers, who serve as dedicated bodyguards as well as companions.

De Roa's Purpose

Monica de Roa is a stable Prince whose rule promotes harmony and tolerance, even while demanding sacrifice. She is meant to serve as a pacifying force in any story, eliminating (or greatly complicating) a violent physical strategy on the part of the characters. Through her, the Storyteller can encourage social problem-solving.

Because of her history and the familial relationships she encourages, Prince de Roa and her rule create a great backdrop for emotional plots, most notably those involving romance, melancholy, nostalgia and vengeance.

Characters playing among the dregs of de Roa's Kindred society may see her and her extensive support network as antagonists. A plot of revolution against Monica could be interesting, bringing serious questions about freedom and safety into play. Any character who destabilizes her rule must understand that they run the risk of tearing the domain wide open and releasing the Kindred denizens of the obligations that keep them from one another's throats. Dwelling among the disfavored, though, illustrates the great sacrifice that certain Kindred are expected to make to allow an atmosphere of comfort and peace to be maintained for the favored majority.

Ruling Style: Prince de Roa rules with the assistance of deeply ingrained loyalties and a tangle of emotional connections among the Kindred of her domain. Many feel genuinely indebted to her because of past or present support and inspiration from personal dealings, while others are drawn into her service by ties of hereditary guilt. Because of these emotional bases for loyalty, and because it is nearly impossible to avoid feeling positively disposed in her presence because of her beauty and her Majesty, conspiring against Prince de Roa is extremely difficult. Kindred working against her rule are often betrayed by their trusted compatriots with little or no encouragement from the Prince herself. As a result, the rule of the Prince is relatively peaceful, precluding the need for heavy-handed tactics of enforcement.

De Roa hosts a large Primogen Council, including the Priscus of each clan in her domain as well as a trusted representative from each covenant. There are no taboos in discussion on matters of rule, but the word of the Prince is final law. Issues of debate are allowed to run their course at the council table, and when de Roa speaks, the discussion ends and is not raised again without her invitation. In addition to the benefits of direct access to the Prince, every member of this council is gifted with a feeding ground, gaining access to the precious (and thin) resource of blood in the domain.

The language of Prince de Roa's official proclamations makes it clear that she considers her self and her domain to be inextricable elements of one another: to love one is to love the other, and to damage one is to damage the other. Rumors that de Roa enjoys some preternatural connection to the land, feeling every shift and touch as if it involved her own flesh are prevalent among local Kindred, and have never been denied.

Prince de Roa believes that vampires carry more than just the Disciplines and features of clan in their blood. In her eyes, obligations and insults are likewise inherited — shared between childe and sire both up and down the line. Many a vampire has found herself suddenly tied to an obligation because of the foolish mis-step of a blood relation with little recourse but to encourage its fulfillment as quickly as possible. Those who enjoy the Prince's favor, reveling in the reflected glory of their close relatives (or the benefits of sharing their own glory), are happy to reinforce the system.

Domain: Similar to her gardens, any domain ruled by Monica Paez de Roa is both *complicated* and *resource-hungry*. Intricate and long-established relations between the Prince and her Kindred subjects make it very difficult for newcomers to understand the potential benefits and pitfalls of any political strategy. Dedicated and time-consuming research into the backgrounds and inherited obligations of every vampire in the city may be necessary — and since most Kindred aren't willing to undertake such a daunting task (or aware of the necessity), mistakes are often made. Complicating affairs further (and serving as a defining feature in its own right), the demands of the Prince and her tendency to "overstock" as a means of ensuring her satisfaction have resulted in a territorial shortage among her subjects. While the Prince enjoys the lion's share of good feeding grounds, her loyal subjects suck up the relatively scarce remainder, leaving everyone at the bottom of the predatory ladder in the lurch. Neonates and outcasts are often forced to feed on inferior sources such as animals or diseased mortals, or to trade services for sustenance. While many of those at the bottom end are less than satisfied with the situation, they are usually scolded for voicing their displeasure and instructed to consider the Prince's sizable demand fair payment for the peace and prosperity of the domain.

Political intrigue between familial lines is strong in Prince de Roa's domain, encouraged by her policies of shared responsibility and inherited regard. Members of individual lines are constantly working to ensure that their entire family stays in good standing. Competing families jockey for favor and the attendant access to resources, doing battle within the structure of the city instead of against it. Since those who please the Prince are empowered by territorial gains and policy-making opportunities, they work to maintain the system without the need for her direct guidance.

As a means to maintain her system, Prince de Roa takes great pains to ensure that violence is minimized under her rule. Those who seek to remain in her favor can best do so by promoting an atmosphere of peace and safety and discouraging bloodshed. The result is a self-sustaining environment of lawful Kindred citizenry — it is in the best interest of the power-players to refrain from overt conflict, and it is much easier for lowly vampires to please their betters than it is to fight them.

The Circle of the Crone benefits from de Roa's leadership in that the covenant's members are free to pursue their religious pursuits without prosecution, but, in truth, the covenant is suffering. The concept of tribulation has fallen by the wayside under the Prince's direction, and many of the members of her Circle are softening. If there is a threat to her rule, it will likely come from within the Circle itself — if one or more of the members are inspired to subject themselves to the real tests of their faith and cry out against the easy existence de Roa has arranged for them.

Story Concepts: Defuse rumors of Juan de Amaya's return before they drive Prince de Roa mad. Shake the stigma of a family obligation before you collapse into torpor for want of adequate feeding grounds. Neutralize a battle for favor between two Kindred families before it turns violent. Lead a group of starving neonates on a raid to steal blood from one of de Roa's favored allies. Seek the Prince's protection for two vampires in love, denying the sanction of their traditionally hostile sires.

Clan: Daeva
Covenant: Circle of the Crone
Embrace: 1644
Apparent Age: 16
Mental Attributes: Intelligence 4, Wits 4, Resolve 5
Physical Attributes: Strength 2, Dexterity 4, Stamina 3
Social Attributes: Presence 6, Manipulation 3, Composure 6
Skills: Academics 4, Crafts (Gardening, Flower Arranging) 5, Medicine (Natural Remedies) 4, Occult 5, Politics 3, Larceny 2, Stealth 2, Animal Ken 3, Empathy (Kindred) 5, Expression 3, Intimidation

(Blithe Appearance) 4, Persuasion 6, Socialize 3
Merits: City Status 5, Covenant Status (Circle of the Crone) 5, Haven Size 5, Haven Security 4, Haven Location 4, Herd 3, Retainers 4, Striking looks 4
Willpower: 9 (reduced through siring)
Humanity: 4
Virtue: Hope. Monica's serene presence and apparent virtue have a marked effect on those around her, and she takes pleasure in drawing others to a tranquil sense of optimism.
Vice: Gluttony. The curse of the Daeva overruns Prince de Roa with a strong urge toward sensualist pursuits, and she often occupies herself with sensation instead of sustenance. She drinks far more blood than she needs, and draining so much means that other Kindred are forced to go without.
Health: 8
Initiative: 10 (15)
Defense: 4
Speed: 11 (66)
Blood Potency: 6 (15/3 Vitae/per turn)
Disciplines: Animalism 2, Celerity 5, Majesty 5, Protean 2, Crúac 4
Crúac Rituals: Blood Witness, Rigor Mortis, Barrier of Blood, Deflection of Wooden Doom, Song of Blood, Willful Vitae

Castillo, the Kingpin Prince

Quote: *"You thought you could hide your guilt by slipping away? Every soul, living and dead, within a hundred miles pays tribute to this court. Where did you think you were going to go?"*

The man he was in life is long since gone. Tonight, Don Castillo is the self-made Prince of a domain he raised up out of the dust.

He was Embraced in the middle of the 19th century into the heart of a conflict between independence-minded Carthians and traditional Invictus vampires in Mexico City. Within a few years, he had a savvy understanding of the Danse Macabre. He was determined to become the Prince of his own domain and create a place of stability and respect among the Damned.

150 years later, Don Castillo sits in a wicker chair in a lush Spanish-style courtyard lit by white Christmas lights, sniffing an unlit cigar and offering his vampire vassals a seat by the pool. He travels across his domain in an armored car to attend a recital by a pair of talented young ghoul guitarists. He stands on his balcony in a linen shirt, feeling the chill desert air

pass over his dead flesh. He almost feels alive.

Castillo made his fortune by creating and selling drugs. Tonight he is in business with the most powerful and ruthless cartels in Mexico. He maintains a quiet influence over smuggling and gun-running operations. Thousands of mortals earn their wages, in one way or another, serving his empire.

Description: He's got the face of a soap-opera star and the eyes of the devil. With his rugged, *caballero* good-looks and his honeyed tongue, he is the spokesman for his own authority. He sells his utter control over the days and nights of Kindred, lupines and mortals within his cities, and the people buy it. He's a model for the dangerous, sexy Latin kingpin, exaggerated through the power of the Blood and poised to perfection. He'll seduce you, control you, scare you and kill you. And you'll love him for it.

Storytelling Hints: Castillo is a forward-thinking idealist. That means that any man, woman or child who gets in the way of his bigger picture can be replaced. No single being is more important to the stability and survival of the domain than Castillo himself.

Castillo truly believes that his little section of Mexico is better off with him in charge. He thinks of himself as something of a benevolent dictator, a Prince of the people, who has climbed his way to a position of authority and responsibility through perseverance and guile. He has little respect for the office of Prince — he has seen enough selfish, empty rulers waste their nights on the throne — and he does not expect his subjects to celebrate the title, either. Rather, Castillo wants his citizens, his people, to respect him personally, by addressing him as Don Castillo. Thus his role as the Prince isn't just something to be coveted and filled by some usurper or promising pretender. Castillo himself is the essential part of the role. It is not his job, it is his place.

The loyalty Castillo expects from his people gets returned to them. He rewards hard work, obedience and innovation. He understands that not everything happens as he wishes it did. He knows that people will let him down. This isn't some action-movie drug lord who executes henchmen for failing at difficult tasks. Castillo can't afford to gamble on replacements — he selects his agents for the long haul, to train them and raise them up to be better than they once were.

Castillo isn't willing to gamble with his fortunes or his domain, either. If he's betrayed, he makes an example of his betrayer. If he's disrespected, he responds with humiliation and torture. If he has to choose between the good of the domain or you, he chooses the domain every time. He scrapes off the shit, cries over the loss of one of his people, and then moves on.

Castillo's Purpose

Don Castillo is the essential, successful Mexican Prince. He maintains a lavish kingdom for the Damned and peace with the Lupines, and he pays for it with the blood of unknowing mortals. He kills, he addicts, he ruins lives and Requiems for the sake of those who fill their roles in his domain.

Some Princes are easy to hate, instantly creating a black-and-white conflict ripe for revolution. Don Castillo raises more complex questions. For what price, peace? How far can Castillo go — how badly can he hurt the characters — before they'll turn on him? With him, you can gradually dial up the tension to find just the right point, where characters and their players form different opinions about the same issues.

Castillo is meant as an example of a Prince who forges a domain not out of raw fear, tyranny or supernatural power, but out of savvy and cunning. Castillo's lordly authority comes from his social connections, his careful networking and his brilliant grasp of politics. Any character who chooses to go against Castillo must plan carefully to outwit him.

The conflict in this domain comes from two places: the outside and the center. Foreign vampires (meaning those from the nearest domain), nomads, unfriendly Lupines, looting mages, mortal witch-hunters, DEA investigators and rival cartels can all supply story fodder from without. Castillo supplies it from within. Earning and maintaining Castillo's favor is every tenant's full-time job here. If the characters are mortal drug-cartel operatives, werewolf enforcers or Kindred land-lords underneath Castillo's rule, whatever happens in their corner of the domain is their responsibility, and they have to answer to him.

Ruling Style: Don Castillo's rule is above challenge, but it is not absolute. Castillo believes the feudal-society model is the best way for the Damned to organize and survive eternity. He shares his rule with those Regents under him, imposing his inviolate authority only when problems aren't sorting themselves out to his satisfaction. That is his role as Prince, to settle all disputes beneath him and maintain the eternal sovereignty of the domain.

Castillo's philosophy is simple: Feudal systems afford the most capable individuals the ability to look after the less capable and, in turn, profit from their labors. Infeudation grants everyone their own small plot of ground, their own place in society, where they are lord, be it a city or a farm or a shack. One's worthiness to oversee others must be measured by the highest power in the land — the Prince. This is where feudal systems collapse among the living: kings die. Rule must pass on, and it is always succession that tears open the seams in any society. Kindred rise above this handicap. Castillo will always be the best informed, most invested and most experienced Prince for the domain. He will always be around to settle disputes between vassals.

Tenants and subjects of Don Castillo understand him to be a fair but brutal figure. The first night, he lays out the rules. The first time you screw up, he tells you what you did wrong and what to do to make it right. Go too far, though, and he'll cry red tears as he exiles you, lops off your hand or stakes you to the cracked desert ground.

Castillo's laws are simple:

- The Masquerade is the law.
- Tribute is inviolate.
- The siring of childer is forbidden.
- Harming peers and betters is forbidden.
- Harming another's property or vassal is forbidden.
- Trespassing is forbidden.

Any law may be broken if Castillo permits it, before or after the fact. Castillo, for example, maintains a non-traditional definition of the Masquerade. In his eyes, Kindred and Lupines and mages and ghouls and mortal servants are all a part of one select and secret culture — the citizenry of Castillo's rule. In practice,

There are two kinds of kine under Castillo's law: those who know and those who must not. Any mortal that serves Castillo and knowingly contributes to his tribute is considered to be "on this side of the Masquerade." Any mortal man, woman or child that does not need to know about Kindred or werewolf society is considered to be on "the other side" of the Masquerade. If a mortal should cease to be a part of the domain's feudal hierarchy or otherwise find himself exiled to the other side of the Masquerade, he's dragged away in the night by huge, brown wolves.

Domain: Castillo's territory is assumed to be large, even vast. It's a uniquely Mexican domain, spread out across several sizeable towns and wide stretches of desert or scrub, all orbiting Castillo's ranch, all moving his careful authority. The relatively low vampire population in each individual town center produces fewer competitors for Castillo's position at the top of the feudal pyramid.

Everyone has a job in Castillo's domain. Some jobs are essential, some are luxuries. One job is common to all the tenants in Castillo's domain, however: tribute.

Every vampire, ghoul, werewolf, mage and informed mortal owes tribute to the lord above him. That lord in turn pays tribute to Castillo. If you hold up your end of the bargain, providing blood, labor, intelligence, transport, money or time to Castillo, he holds up his end of the bargain. Let him down and he lets you down, denying you protection, repossessing your land or exiling you from the domain.

The jobs most Kindred are given are: to keep Castillo informed about what happens in his domain, to stay fed and feed tenants, and to protect the borders and the secrets of the domain. The tribute most vassals are charged with paying is blood. Mortals are the soil the locals till and Vitae is their crop. Ghouls drive pick-up trucks full of mortals into Castillo's hacienda, where they are quietly fed upon by their secret Prince and his coterie before being returned to their homes.

Castillo is owed a tribute of service by the werewolves who live within his domain. Long ago he and they came to the understanding that the Masquerade was in the best interest of Kindred and Uratha alike, but that werewolves were better suited to enforcing it. In Castillo's eyes, he has forged a vital alliance with those who might otherwise be his most dreaded enemies. In the werewolves' eyes, they have been given the authority to keep vampires in check without riling up the local Prince.

Clan: Mekhet
Covenant: Invictus
Embrace: 1845
Apparent Age: Mid-thirties
Mental Attributes: Intelligence 4, Wits 4, Resolve 4
Physical Attributes: Strength 2, Dexterity 3, Stamina 3
Social Attributes: Presence 4, Manipulation 4, Composure 3
Mental Skills: Academics (Business, History) 3, Computer 2, Crafts (Carpentry) 2, Investigation 1, Medicine (Pharmaceuticals) 1, Occult (The Blood, Uratha) 3, Politics (Domain management) 5, Science (Pharmaceuticals) 1
Physical Skills: Athletics (Running) 1, Brawl (Beat down) 2, Drive 2, Firearms (Automatic pistols) 2, Larceny (Locks) 4, Stealth (Shadow) 4, Survival (Urban) 1, Weaponry 1
Social Skills: Animal Ken 1, Empathy 4, Expression (Guitar) 2, Intimidation 4, Persuasion 4, Socialize (Host) 4, Streetwise (Drugs) 4, Subterfuge (Spot Lies) 5
Merits: Allies (Federal Government) 4, Allies (Drug Cartels) 5, Allies (Local Police) 5, Allies (Smugglers) 5, Common Sense, Contacts 5 (Federales, local merchants, shipping companies, the Catholic church, the press), City Status: Prince 5, Covenant Status: Carthian Movement 3, Haven Size 3, Haven Security 5, Herd 4, Resources 5, Retainer 5, Status: Lupines 4, Status: Drug Cartels 3
Willpower: 7 (reduced by Embrace, twice)
Humanity: 4 (Narcissism at 5)
Virtue: Charity. Castillo is a generous host and a firm but giving ruler. In his mind, an iron rule of fear, like those of the mortal drug lords he deals with, would be more secure. But in his heart he believes that by appealing to the loyalty and na-

tional pride of his subjects, he can solidify respect and prosperity for mortals and monsters in his little corner of Mexico. Note, however, that peace and freedom are not essential to his goals.

Vice: Pride. Castillo is all about respect, and believes others should be, too. When he is charitable, he should be praised. When he is merciful, he should be loved. When he must punish, his judgment must be respected. If others had the good sense and good grace that he has, the world would be a better place and his domains would be stable and prosperous.

Health: 8

Initiative: +6

Defense: 3

Speed: 10

Blood Potency: 5 (14/2 Vitae/per turn)

Disciplines: Auspex 4, Celerity 2, Obfuscate 4, Majesty 3

Devotion: Knowing the Stranger

Malintzinita, Daughter of Conquest

Quote: *"I think tonight we should go dancing. Have the Harpies bring in some kine to dance with us. We'll hold court tomorrow."*

Slave. Noble. Traitor. Victim. Wife. Mother. La Malinche was the translator and mistress of Hernán Cortés, conqueror of New Spain. To the Mexica, she was Malintzin, an embodiment of treachery and betrayal. To the Spaniards she was Doña Marina, invaluable ambassador and diplomat. Without her, the Spanish conquistadors would have had just one way to communicate with the native people they encountered: bloodshed.

Malinztinita, the Daughter of Conquest, claims to be La Malinche's child by Hernán Cortés. As she tells the story, she was cursed with undeath "in the night, by a god I never saw, whether Christian or Nahua." Thus she places herself in the same historic rank as Dracula and Longinus. By her reckoning, her damnation is meant as an eternal reminder of what fate must befall the Mestizos, those born of European and Indian blood.

Unlike Dracula and Longinus, however, no cult of followers studies the teaching of Malintzinita. She has written no manifesto or holy book, no guide to the Requiem. She has subjects only in so far as she has advisors who rule in her name.

Or so the Kindred on the street believe.

The Requiem of Malintzinita is gossiped about throughout the domain. She was Embraced — few believe she was cursed by any god — at a young age. Her enthusiasms are forever those of a teenaged girl. Though she has managed to modernize herself over the centuries, she seems to have learned very little in the lifetimes she has spent in the world. Inside her palatial haven, she throws parties for Kindred of every station. She attends private clubs and *discotheques* to be among mortals. She and her coven of "ladies-in-waiting" play dress-up all day in precious stones and antique gowns. Her existence is an eternal holiday.

Or so it appears to the vampires on the ground.

The truth is that Malintzinita has carefully constructed her Requiem to facilitate her almost complete removal from the Danse Macabre. Where once she truly was the puppet ruler of Invictus and Sanctified vampires, tonight she is a subtle, conniving and masterful manipulator. Many Kindred in her court believe she is feckless, though they do whatever she asks to maintain their status and hers. She controls her handlers like a spoiled daughter controls her parents, and it is exactly as Malintzinita wants it.

Her reputation as an ignorant playgirl affords her cover. When even 200-year-old undead *politicos* underestimate her, she enjoys an incredible freedom. She flits about the gilded, church-like halls of her subterranean estate chatting with her entourage of giddy vampire girls, but she isn't listening to them, she's listening to the Ventrue Priscus who thinks he can scheme against her in her own house.

Malintzinita has been the target of countless assassination attempts. She appears to be a weak ruler and an easy target — whoever destroys her may well win the loyalty of Indian vampires — but no Kindred survives for 450 years as an easy target. Ghouls have crept hooded into her haven in the daylight, with torches and pitch. A Gangrel Acolyte and warlock once brushed his blood on her at court, thinking she would rot and die. A Succubus petitioner for her bloodline slashed her throat with a straight-razor when she rejected him. Malintzinita isn't going anywhere.

Description: Both her flesh and her fashion seem selected to uphold her story — that she is the Damned daughter of La Malinche and Hernán Cortés. She is half-Spanish and half-Aztec, and beautiful as only legends can be. Forever frozen on the edge of womanhood by the power of the Blood, she has the fresh authority of an heiress and the vital invincibility of youth. Her clothes are a mix of modern high-fashion and antiquated Aztec finery. Only her mouth — a nasty array of needle-like teeth — betrays her cursed heritage. She is a magnificent succubus.

Storytelling Hints: Malintzinita wants two things above all: Power and bliss. To her mind that means the authority to do whatever she likes and the freedom to do nothing at all. She has both.

Malintzinita, unfortunately, is a paranoid coward. For 450 years she has been hiding behind the mask of a silly girl who doesn't understand why "the peasants" hate her so. For half a millennium she has pretended that power comes easily to her and that she has no fear of her own kind. In truth, she is terrified of her own kind. If, in fact, she was Embraced by a vampire, she doesn't know who did it or why — or if that vampire will return. She has no memory of that night, and only slight memories of any night all those centuries ago. She never wanted to be a vampire and she doesn't know why this happened to her.

So Malintzinita has carefully created a closed world for herself, where she can hide from the hate and the blood outside and enjoy the benefits of power. She has surrounded herself with a few trusted coterie-mates — her advisors and her so-called ladies-in-waiting — and otherwise strives to avoid contact with strangers for more than a few minutes. She arranges and attends elaborate parties and raves because she's desperate to feel like a part of some society, but every party ends the same way for her: she wipes blood from her lips with her thumb and wishes she had the courage to die.

But, of course, she cannot die. She couldn't do that to her domain. To her people. For all that they think she is a silly child, she is also a symbol of their past, a thread of Mexica culture stretching all the way back to last nights of the conquest. Her damnation, whether it was performed by a vampire or not, must be the will of the gods who battle for possession of her soul.

An ordinary person's soul is worth one lifetime's worth of deliberation, of battle, between the Christian God and the Aztec gods. But Malintzinita is trapped on earth until the heavens can finally win her. She's meant for something important on earth, in her domain. She's sure of it. Some night she'll do something great. Something historic. She'll fulfill her role on earth and change Mexico forever. Some night.

Malintzinita's Purpose

Malintzinita represents two of the core conflicts among Mexico's Damned: Rich vs. Poor and Native vs. European. She freezes the mindset of the collaborative Mexica in time, allowing modern characters to judge her however they like — to tell off, combat or join the Spanish conquest, as it were.

The obvious use of Malintzinita is as a spoiled royal Princess to overthrow with a great, old-fashioned Mexican revolution. She is shamelessly antiquated and unapologetic in her superiority. An interesting way to challenge players, however, might be to let them play members of the domain's court. Will they attempt to usurp or undermine the Daughter of Conquest, thinking they can beat her at her own game? Or will they enjoy their station and help her quash a Carthian uprising?

Ruling Style: Malintzinita surrounds herself with two loyal groups, each consisting of just three or four vampires. The first is her entourage of vampire-sisters from the Malintzin bloodline, whose only job is to be loyal to Malintzinita the girl. The second group is her Primogen, a handful of Sanctified and Invictus advisors who appear to control her but, in fact, conspire with her. Their only job is to be loyal to Malintzinita the Princess.

In practice, the Primogen has a great deal of autonomy. In nights past, Malintzinita exercised much more control over the domain, but for the last few decades things have been running as she likes them, so she has relaxed her authority. Still, she and her retinue watch the Primogen from behind curtains and through the eyes of dominated servants, to ensure their loyalty.

Malintzinita has little regard for those Kindred who do not attend court. She has parceled out land within the city only to her Primogen and the very oldest vampires — no more than seven or eight Regents operate beneath her authority. Those Regents are forbidden from granting their own territories to others. It is Malintzinita's city — other vampires simply lurk in it. That neonates and unaligned vampires struggle and suffer and meet their ends without her knowledge is just fine with her. Suffering is unavoidable, but she doesn't have to bask in it. Better that she just looks away.

The Primogen bring matters of the domain before Malintzinita for her consideration. "The kine are building again in Bartolo's territory," one says. "The Carthians are trying to arrange a census, to show how many Kindred get no help from the court," says another. "Lupines seem to have slain a Ventrue near the park," says a third.

"Is the Ventrue a Mestizos?" she asks.

"No, señorita," the Primogen replies. "A Spaniard."

"Send messengers to the pack to collect damages, then pay the money out to the sire or childe or whoever remains," Malintzinita says, thumbing through a magazine.

"How much should we—?"

"However much," she says. "Just so they don't fight. Are we finished?"

Domain: Malintzinita's domain is gold relic jutting from the mud. At the top are the care-free and wealthy Kindred who have the Princess's ear. At the bottom are the paupers and peasants from whom she receives tribute in blood. Only rumors and gossip trickle down from the top of the domain to the bottom, making the mud. Money, power and authority stay at the top.

On the ground, the domain is a chaotic mess of petty Regents enforcing Invictus law only when they can be bothered. This poacher goes unchecked, that one gets staked for his crimes. An Invictus neonate skirts the Masquerade, he gets lectured. A Carthian neonate does the same, he gets scarred. In the words of one local Carthian, "the smart play in this town is to stay unaligned and out of sight."

Havens are only secure if potential thieves or assassins are afraid of the owner's friends. Herds are only respected if they're protected with fang and nail. Ghouls go missing, get ransomed and turn up dead.

To a certain, coincidental extent, local werewolves help the Princess maintain her status quo. As long as they keep their paws off the property of important vampires, they can enjoy free reign through the official turf of uncounted neonates and the unbound. "Let the Queen have her tower," says one pack leader, "if it clears up the traffic on the streets."

Status is the ultimate currency here. And without Spanish blood, the most prestigious status is difficult to earn. Though Malintzinita is Mestizos, she believes that the rule of Mexico is the right of its conquerors. The great blessing of La Minche's work, in Malintzinita's eyes, is that she saved as many Aztec lives as she did. Without her at Cortés' side, the Mexica would have gone the way of so many other Amerindians.

Mixed-blood Kindred are welcome at court, but Indian vampires had best mind their station.

Story Concepts: Gather 40 or 60 mortal party-goers to populate an event for Malintzinita. Dispose of the bodies and dissuade any mortal investigation when two of those party-goers turn up dead. Escort one of Malintzinita's ladies-in-waiting to a clandestine meeting with local Carthians, who try to kidnap the Princess's aide and ransom her back. Compete for a place among the Primogen. Assassinate Malintzinita.

Clan: Daeva
Bloodline: Malintzin
Covenant: Invictus/Lancea Sanctum
Embrace: 1550-1560
Apparent Age: 15-17
Mental Attributes: Intelligence 4, Wits 5, Resolve 4
Physical Attributes: Strength 2, Dexterity 5, Stamina 3
Social Attributes: Presence 6, Manipulation 6, Composure 2
Mental Skills: Academics (Mexican History, Catholicism) 3, Crafts (Pottery) 5, Investigation 2, Medicine 1, Occult (Aztec ritualism) 4, Politics (Court) 4, Science 1
Physical Skills: Athletics (Swimming) 4, Brawl (Bite) 1, Larceny 2, Stealth (Eavesdrop) 4, Weaponry (Dagger) 4
Social Skills: Animal Ken (Snakes) 4, Empathy 5, Expression (Singing) 4, Intimidation 4, Persuasion (Seduction) 5, Socialize (Court) 4, Subterfuge (Lie) 4
Merits: City Status: Queen 5, Clan Status: Daeva 5, Covenant Status: Invictus 3, Covenant Status: Lancea Sanctum 3, Covenant Status: Circle of the

Crone 1, Haven Size 5, Haven Security 5, Haven Location 2, Herd 5, Mentor 4, Retainer: Ladies-in-Waiting 3 (x3), Retainer: Bodyguards 4 (x2), Retainer: Advisor 5, Status: Kindred Legend 3, Striking Looks 4
Willpower: 5 (reduced by siring childer)
Humanity: 4 (Megalomania at 5, Paranoia at 6)
Virtue: Faith. Malintzinita believes the conquest of Mexico was Spain's destiny and that it was God's mandated fate for the Aztecs to be destroyed. This extends into her belief that her Damnation is the result of a divine battle between the agents of Heaven and the Aztec gods for possession of her soul.
Vice: Sloth. Though she is also stunningly arrogant, it is Malintzinita's cowardice that truly cripples her. She is terrified of venturing out into her domain, where the Danse Macabre is at its bloodiest, because she believes warlocks and assassins of the Mexica — whether ghosts or vampires — lurk out in the darkness to destroy her.
Health: 8
Initiative: +7
Defense: 5
Speed: 12
Blood Potency: 8 (30/7 Vitae/per turn)
Disciplines: Animalism 3, Celerity 3, Dominate 5, Majesty 5, Resilience 5, Theban Sorcery 2, Vigor 2
Theban Sorcery Rituals: Vitae Reliquary, Liar's Plague
Devotion: Veridical Tongue

Broods

Throughout the World of Darkness, the covenants of Kindred society take many forms. In some domains, they are wholly distinct, plotting against each other like warring states. In other domains, they are separate but allied, dividing the duties and prizes of Kindred society between each other while they defend the city against a common threat. And in some domains, the covenants intermix in surprising ways, reflecting philosophies and loyalties inherited from mortal culture or adapting to endure against unusual threats.

When two or more covenants recombine their memberships and practices into a single group, it's called a *brood*. Sometimes the brood is the only representation of a covenant within the domain, sometimes it's little more than a glorified coterie.

The Catholic church's adoption of certain pre-Christian practices and beliefs in Mexico is a great example. While Sanctified vampires in some other countries consider the Virgin of Guadalupe to be heretical, in Mexico she is a bridge between the Lancea Sanctum and the Circle of the Crone. In some domains, Acolytes and Sanctified are hateful enemies. In Mexico City, Acolytes are welcome at Sanctified mass.

Broods can even include werewolves and mages, in much the same way that a covenant can be said to include a member's human retainers or herd. In the domain of the vampire Prince Castillo (see p. 156), for example, Kindred and Uratha conspire to protect the domain from the threat of mortal awareness.

In the following pages, you'll find a handful of Mexican broods. Substitute characters with those from your own chronicle, such as the players' characters' Allies and Mentors, as you see fit. Use these as models for creating broods in the domain where your stories are set. Much more about the formation, operation and design of broods will appear in future Vampire books.

Los Fiel de Cuernavaca

Those without faith are not welcome here.

The small city of Cuernavaca sits about 50 miles south of Mexico City, but is nothing like its larger patron. Known as the "City of the Eternal Spring," Cuernavaca is unusually temperate, helping contribute to a slower, more relaxed pace. The city acts as something of a historical junction, important to the old Aztec faith as well as the more recent Roman Catholicism. Here, Aztec kings came to bathe in the holy springs near the city, and to marvel at the nearby volcano, Popocatépetl. But Cuernavaca is also home to a magnificent cathedral, once a gilded Franciscan monastery and still a pillar of Mexico's Catholic faith. Cuernavaca is a city where these two faiths meet — a syncretism that is not lost on its Kindred.

The city is home to a number of Kindred, many of whom belong to the Lancea Sanctum or the Circle of the Crone. These faithful vampires number 12 specifically — six who pray to Longinus, six who honor the old devouring mother, Coatlicue. Unlike in some areas, however, the disparate Damned do not wage a quiet war against one another. Their faiths are different, they claim, but not incompatible. The Kindred of this city are wise enough to know that paring away one another's ranks may help to salve one's selfish righteousness, but would also weaken their hold on this glorious domain. Mexico City to the north is perceived to be a nest of the criminal and corrupt;

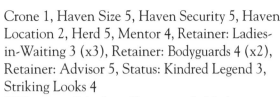

diminishing Cuernavaca in any way will only invite such chaos to spread.

These 12 faithful Kindred believe it paramount to remain vigilant in the face of chaos, regardless of contrary religions. This decision did not come easily, or without some measure of sacrifice. The alliance was born not out of a peaceful time, but out of an incursion from the north: sensing the weakness born of two conflicting covenants, agents of the Invictus came sniffing around. They bought property. They made friends in high places. They quietly turned or murdered some of the 12's existing allies. In a matter of months, the invasive First Estate had managed to root its claws deep in Cuernavaca's soil.

It was almost too late. The 12 discovering the Invictus' penetration, sought to undo the harm that was done. The vampire faithful temporarily discarded their feud and set out to convince the trespassers that this city was not theirs, and would never be. Setting aside differences wasn't easy for all — some of the Circle threatened to betray the Sanctified "monsters," even if that meant acting as traitors to their own coteries. They were convinced — not without spilled blood — to remain true to their own.

The struggle was long, with both sides gaining and losing ground as the months and then years went on. The power of the Invictus, backed by seemingly inexhaustible resources, threatened to overwhelm the faithful.

It culminated with *la Noche del Exilio*, or the Night of Exile. Tired of the relentless give-and-take, the 12 Kindred refused to play passive games of dominance any longer. They set out with retribution on their minds, and they got it. They found and abducted several of the Invictus powerbrokers, and dragged them in the pouring rain to the Grutas de Cacahuamilpa (an extensive series of grottoes outside the city). There, the 12 Kindred beheaded the Invictus and let the greasy ashen remains wash away in the underground river. Both covenants offered the ash to their saints and gods, and went home.

To their surprise, the alliance between the two groups did not diminish. They decided to forgo the repetitions of history and avoid the old mistakes. The 12 Kindred now comprise a single brood: *Los Fiel de Cuernavaca* (the Faithful Ones of Cuernavaca).

Nickname: Los Religiosos

Covenant: Faith gives these Kindred a common bond: six belong to a small cult of the Crone (Coatlicue), and six are Sanctified. They are unlikely to allow coteries of other covenants into the brood without a great deal of effort on the part of the eager Kindred. The members do have friends among the Ordo Dracul of Mexico City, however.

Appearance: By and large, the members of this brood dress as they wish: the Acolytes prefer clothing that is wild and unkempt, whereas the Sanctified dress in more somber, relaxed garb. During some ceremonies and meetings, the members of Los Fiel wear dark brown robes and masks made of corn husks and terracotta. All of this brood are of native descent.

Havens: The Acolytes accept a single communal haven: the closed-down train station just southwest of the Tlahuica ruins of Teopanzolco (old Aztec pyramid and plaza). As a single coterie, the supplicants of Coatlicue also inhabit tunnels that connect the old station and the ruins. They have allies among the Cuernavaca Archaeological Society, thus allowing them access to the ruins' more sensitive areas, where they tend to perform their blood-soaked rituals (Crúac).

The Sanctified do not share havens with one another. Most of them live in small apartments or homes surrounding the hill upon which the city's Catedral de Cuernavaca rests. Most live moderately, with few amenities. The Bishop of the brood, Father Ernesto Reyes, lives in a small unexceptional home not far from the Palace of Cortés. His haven is the epitome of ascetic: he sleeps on the hard floor, covering himself with dried palm fronds, and has no decorations besides a few saintly icons scattered throughout.

Organization: Seventy-five percent of the time, the vampires of the two covenants do not meet or deal with one another. They hold their own religious ceremonies away from each other. They each maintain control over varying parts of the city and its populace, with very strict lines understood as a long-standing accord (called the *Solidaridad*).

The two groups cannot exist entirely dependent of one another, however. They hold meetings monthly, with all members in attendance (and presided over by both Father Reyes and the Hierophant of Coatlicue, Itotia). Vampires air their grievances, which are resolved either by the coterie leaders or through games of skill (chess, feats of athleticism, hunting). Most meetings take place at the Palace of Cortés in the middle of the city: this location was once sacred to Aztec kings, a fact Cortés recognized when he built a palace atop it.

The brood also comes together several times a year for national and religious holidays — each covenant alternates control (and thus the nature) of these celebrations. The Sanctified prefer more solemn and spiritual observance, while the supplicants of Coatlicue are far more wild and unbound with their festivity. Usually a fine balance is struck for both parties, but occasionally one side goes too far, potentially insulting the other. Members of the brood do their level best to avoid violence when this occurs — similar to above, grievances are aired and then settled with some air of nobility and solidarity. Usually.

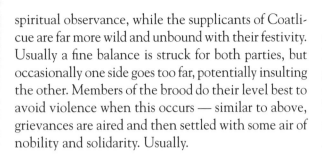

New Devotion: Chains of the Spirit

(Majesty •, Obfuscate ••)

Religious and spiritual disagreements are common amongst the Kindred of this brood, even among the vampires of a single covenant. Such arguments can easily escalate to violence — dead blood can suddenly run very hot, indeed. When used, this Devotion helps a vampire of the brood project an aura of blessedness; the impression given is that she possesses an obvious spark of the divine, thus calming those who look upon her. (This is perceived differently by each vampire: one may see that she has faintly glowing eyes, another may witness a halo around her head like sun glare.)

Cost: 1 Vitae per scene

Dice Pool: Presence + Survival + Obfuscate – opponent's Composure

Action: Instant

If the Devotion is successful, the vampire appears beatific and holy to those viewing her. First, this negates the effects of Predator's Taint (the vampire herself may still suffer those effects, but those viewing her do not). Second, any vampires within a number of yards equal to her Blood Potency have difficulty frenzying. When resisting frenzy (which they must do, as they cannot "ride the wave" if this power is active), a nearby vampire gains a number of bonus dice upon the "resist frenzy" roll equal to the caster's successes on the activation roll. This power remains active for the rest of the scene.

This Devotion costs nine experience points to learn.

Society and Culture

The Kindred of Los Fiel understand that they are not alike, but the reality is this: Mexico is a land of extremes, and at time those extremes collide and bring chaos. The two covenants here can either crash into one another, thus breeding disorder and weakness, or they can maintain a suitable coexistence. They have, for the last few decades, chosen the latter.

It hasn't been easy to reconcile the two faiths into one group, and it remains troublesome to this night. Most, though not all, of the brood have come to a grudging respect of one another's religions. The leaders on each side (Father Reyes and Itotia) go above and beyond mere respect, however, both believing that there is more to one another's faith that links them. As late, both have become entranced (some would even say obsessive) about the ideas of sacrifice, a notion intrinsic to both groups' ideas. The Sanctified offer small offerings (*milagros*) to the saints, and the Acolytes leave gifts for Coatlicue.

The myths and stories of both sides are not entirely incompatible, either: Coatlicue became pregnant as a virgin, and of course Christ is the child of a virgin birth. Longinus stabbed the savior and was changed by the blood, whereas Coatlicue was beheaded by her children — and the head became the moon, and the blood the stars. Both Itotia and Reyes recognize the sacredness of blood in both stories, which is further exemplified by both Theban Sorcery and Crúac. Neither have yet attempted a syncretism of those two covenant-specific sorceries — but they have discussed that possibility.

Of course, Coatlicue is a far more barbaric figure than Longinus or the saints. She is certainly a strong mother figure, but she is also a brutal figure of death, with claws for digging graves and a necklace threaded with human hearts. The Acolytes themselves do not perform human sacrifice (though some Crone cults in Mexico certainly do), instead preferring small offerings of blood and prayer. Still, the Sanctified whisper about such blasphemy and horror, and wonder if they have bedded with serpents.

In the end, most of the brood are civil to one another — some, like the two respective leaders, are even quite friendly. Others dwell quietly with distrust and discontent. The shared aims and common enemies of the two covenants keep the bond from breaking, however.

Characters

Here are a few sample characters who belong to the Los Fiel brood.

Father Ernesto Reyes (Ventrue)

Father Reyes, Bishop of Cuernacava's two Sanctified coteries, is a sober, solemn man who lives a nearly ascetic lifestyle. He believes strongly in the precepts of sacrifice and suffering, though these don't make him a belligerent torturer — no, rather, those two concepts merit discussion over action, and apply more directly to spiritual matters than physical ones. He is a small man with light coffee-colored skin and dark eyes. He is often seen rubbing a small silver bracelet: his Saint Isidro pendant, the patron saint of farmers (speaking to Reyes' original origins as a farmhand nearly a century ago). Reyes secretly harbors a desire to bring the pagans of Cuernavaca to Longinus and God. He dares not speak this aloud.

Itotia (Daeva)

Itotia is wild, unpredictable, with a tangled mane of black hair trailing her wherever she goes. She is the Hierophant of Coatlicue, watching over the five other Acolytes and helping them beg for the Crone's love and power. Itotia is prone to wild mood swings — swaying from fiery elation to anger born with bared teeth and blood-caked fingernails. To calm herself, she tends to the ruins nearby the Acolytes' shared haven, tending to wildflowers, wandering up the steps to the pyramid, praying to the goddess and spilling her own blood on the stone. Much to her own surprise, she believes herself falling in love with Father Reyes. She does not agree with his faith, but understands what brings him to it.

Ángel (Mekhet)

A dark distrust festers inside Ángel's dead heart. He is one of three Kindred belonging to the Sanctified's second coterie in Cuernavaca, and acts as its priest. He recognizes on the surface the practical wisdom of pairing with the heathens as opposed to against them, and yet lately he has wondered: if their true concern is spiritual and not physical, as Father Reyes claims, then why stoop to worry about such base matters as safety? The Lancea Sanctum does not need to control Cuernavaca — in fact, an influx of outsiders would give them a new herd that could be brought to the glory of God. While he has no proof, Ángel knows what the heathens do at their fallen temple: murder, incest, perversion for the sake of blasphemy. For now, he'll allow it. But he knows that motions must be made in secret to anticipate the changes when they come. A tall man, skeleton-thin, he can be seen prowling the Palace of Cortés on many nights, seemingly lost in thought.

Broken Plume (Bone Shadow)

Broken Plume is a werewolf belonging to a pack of Bone Shadows that calls itself the Flowers of Quetzal. He is a cripple, one leg withered and thus shorter than the other, and he serves as the emissary between his pack and the Los Fiel brood of vampires. The pack has a deal with the brood, predicated on the same pragmatism that keeps the disparate Damned together: mutual protection. The werewolves want to maintain the spiritual sanctity of Cuernavaca, and that means keeping things as calm and normal as possible. The brood doesn't want to make waves — if they keep the Masquerade, then the Kindred won't draw the attention of others who come sniffing around for weakness. Both sides work toward common goals, though not always knowingly. The brood helps keep order, and the pack helps the brood with protection when necessary. From time to time, one group will also help clean up the other's "messes." Broken Plume is looked down upon by his own pack, but he is given unusual honor among the Acolytes of Los Fiel, who almost consider him a supplementary brood member. Whether they find him a fascinating curiosity or a truly holy creature remains to be seen.

Adaptation

This brood is based on the pragmatism born from a common enemy, and as such, can be adopted for use in nearly any city or story you find necessary. The players can remain the same or can be of covenants different from the ones listed — it matters little. What matters is that, in a given domain, two or more disparate groups are able to look past their obvious differences and forge a bond. This bond needn't be perfect and without conflict (such conflict is, in fact, expected), only that the trouble isn't enough to dismantle the alliance.

C.V.

We will find time to pray only when our work is done and the blood on our hands has finally dried.

"C.V" stands for *Chicos Víriles*, or roughly translated, the "Red-Blooded Boys." This brood, located in and around the Tepito *barrio* district of Mexico City, is a gang of thugs consisting of about six separate coteries. Most were born on the streets, made immortal on the streets and still hunt the streets to this night.

Some of its members have wormed their way into the upper echelons of Kindred culture, wear nice silk suits and make good money — pesos that eventually get pumped back into the brood's criminal activities.

The C.V. gang pretends to be about democracy and freedom — gang members claim that the oppressive monsters who rule Mexico City were born with silver spoons up their asses, and it is the gang's job to rip out those spoons out their mouths and take control of the whole city. And yet, despite all the talk about oppression and a lack of freedom, the brood itself hangs on strict central leadership, with every member bending to the will of their charismatic leader, Amato Colon.

Colon and his cronies (planted throughout the various coteries) have managed to convince the Kindred of this gang that their very presence threatens the tyranny of the city's vampire lords, and that one day they shall have the resources to move in and take control. The reality is, for Colon at least, this is a secondary goal — the primary goal is grow fat with blood and money.

He and the rest of the brood are criminals, first and foremost. Some are thieves, setting up roadblocks and street-traps that allow them to steal and run, whereas others are kidnappers, extortionists and murderers. Some vampires of the C.V. recognize this directly, that any effect they are having on the so-called oppressive autocracy is ancillary. Others buy into the fact that, by creating and encouraging crime, they are thus bringing chaos to the city, which only hurts the repressive "stability" of the ruling regime.

Nickname: Bangers, Bloodbangers, "The Boys"

Covenant: C.V. has representation from the Invictus, the Carthians, and even some Acolytes. At present, no members of the brood belong to either the Lancea Sanctum or the Ordo Dracul — that said, Colon and the brood members do not as a rule reject those covenants or their members. Whispers suggest that they actually have a few hidden allies among the Sanctified of neighboring broods.

Appearance: The majority of the Boys' vampires were, at one time, gang members in the *barrios*. Therefore, they tend to look like bangers, with various gang tats and urban wear. There is no brood "uniform," however — some members wear the false military outfits common among guerrillas, while others might be seen wearing rags or even expensive suits.

Havens: Most, though not all, of the brood possess havens in and around the Tepito district of Mexico City. Some within individual coteries maintain connected, though not necessarily communal, havens. Connected havens might be several small apartments inside a given building (with many of the walls busted out between apartments to make larger quarters). The district is also home to several warehouses, and below it runs several unused subway tunnels, of which are used by the coteries of the Boys.

Tepito is a stretch of 70-some blocks with approximately 150,000 human inhabitants. It is a *barrio* consisting of several smaller *vecindad* (neighborhoods). This chunk of Mexico City offers herds of homeless, various street markets, small art communities and seemingly endless crime (drugs, piracy, kidnapping, murder).

Organization: The brood doesn't appear well organized on the surface. Casual examiners would see a broken network of coteries doing their own thing with little direct connection to one another — and, on some level, this is probably true.

Colon makes sure that the gang is connected in ways both subtle and overt, however. First, in every coterie he appoints a *teniente*, or lieutenant, to be an emissary and go-to figure. Usually, Colon deals with the lieutenants indirectly, sending along his ghouls or childer to parlay messages or give orders. From time to time, however, Colon holds meetings of all lieutenants, and attends those meetings personally.

Every lieutenant is responsible for making his coterie tithe resources to Colon. This usually means money, but Colon takes other things as payment: the service of thralls or childer, kidnapping victims, a transfer of herd, havens, whatever. (While few recognize this directly, this means Colon is sitting on a rather substantial pile of these resources, all of which he claims go toward the fight against the ruling vampires.)

La Santa Muerte, Saint Death

While none of the vampires within this brood are members of the Lancea Sanctum, many do attend Midnight Mass (some as a simple remnant of their old faith, others as a way to help salve their souls without giving in fully to the covenant's dogma).

Oddly, many have taken a patron saint popular in Tepito, a saint wholly unrecognized by the Catholic Church or the Sanctified. This saint — Santa Muerte, or Saint

Death — is represented as a female corpse in a wedding dress. This icon is kept in a glass box in the middle of the Tepito district, literally out on the street for all to see and worship.

Some in the brood don't believe her to be a passive, metaphorical figure — they accept her as an actual creature, a living force of blessed death. Many claim to have seen her stalking the empty streets at night. Some even believe she has come to them near morning, and taught them secret Disciplines and Devotions.

Society and Culture

Approximately three-quarters of the brood are now, or have been, gang members. They are criminals: the crimes they commit not only help contribute to the brood's resources but also contribute to a coterie's reputation on the streets and in the brood. Most of the gangbanger Kindred belong — at least in name — to the Carthian Movement. Several are Acolytes, however, as well. Few belong to the Invictus: only those of the Mentiloso coterie (see below for information on Federico Mentiloso) claim membership with the First Estate.

Those who were at one time gang members belonged predominantly to the gangs local to Tepito: Los Cholos, M-18 (Diezy Ochos), and the Mexican Mafia (La EME). (The Chicos Víriles brood rules over them all, though largely with an unseen hand.) Some members of the brood, however, have come out of the corrupt police force in and around the district. This means dirty "Judiciales" (non-uniformed judicial police) or members of the PFP (Federal Preventative Police).

Because gang culture is tied closely to the brood's own culture, the members tend to practice many customs known to the mortal gangs of Mexico. Some of these customs include the following:

• Tattoos: While few among the Boys get inked *after* death, many were marked beforehand. Gang tats are elaborate. Some indicate favored apocryphal saints, some detail the Lady of Guadalupe in various poses. Many have personal or gang-related axioms inked on arms, chests or backs. (For example: "*Cuándo cogidos de muerte arriba conmigo, estará bienvenido*" means "When death catches me, it will be welcome.") Tats can also indicate the nature and accomplishments of an individual member. Three dots can mean "thief," four might mean "robber." Three slash marks over a star indicates a kidnapper, while three ascending slashes over two horizontal marks reveals a drug dealer.

• Graffiti: Unlike Mexican gang tattoos, gang graffiti is often rather simplistic. This brood signifies territory with its initials in black spray-paint, sometimes with "100%" or a five-pointed star after it. Unlike many vampires, several of the Damned within this brood actually mark their own havens with the gang initials and the star: this signifies to all in the district that they are nearing a forbidden zone. While few mortals or police in the area know that *Chicos Víriles* is a gang comprising vampires, the neighborhood inhabitants do know that its members are at least *human* monsters.

• Clothing: The brood does not wear a consistent "gang outfit," though many Kindred do have armbands or bandanas that feature the Mexican flag, or the colors thereof (green, red, white).

• Initiation: Initiation into the brood goes for any mortal allies, ghouls or vampires who wish to be connected in *any way* to the group. Rites of initiation are always brutal, and often require an individual to bring some kind of harm or chaos to those who live in the wealthy colonial districts of the city. Initiation may involve kidnapping and drinking dry the daughter of a prominent political figure, or maybe climbing up to a cathedral bell tower and opening fire on the plaza below with an automatic weapon. If this can hurt the local vampire regime as well, then that's considered a bonus. After the initiation, a new member is dosed with drugs (if vampire, through a draught of doped blood) and allowed to celebrate in whatever manner befits the drug-addled novitiate.

• Celebration: The night following the Day of the Dead is certainly popular among this brood (largely due to their interest in Saint Death), but even more popular is Cinco de Mayo. That holiday celebrates the Mexican Army's battle against the oppressive French invaders, a feeling that resonates (however hollow) with many of the members of Chicos Víriles.

Characters

Here are several characters of this Mexico City brood.

Amato Colon (Ventrue)

Colon, a true businessman of the street, claims no coterie of his own, instead suggesting that "all of the brood" is his coterie. A seemingly affable man with bright eyes and a powerful presence, his mood can turn dark the moment he senses betrayal. He claims to follow the ideals of the Carthian Movement, though few of the city's Carthians care for him. The city's Primogen and other prominent vampires don't like him much, either — and the feeling is mutual. In fact, Colon hates them so much, he is sometimes surprised that his zealous loathing doesn't jumpstart his heart and bring him back to life. Colon does, in the deepest parts of him, believe that he is fighting a very legitimate fight against what he perceives as the "oppressive monsters," but the reality is that he isn't much more than a thorn in their side. Though he is a thorn in close proximity to many of them — unlike the members of his brood who mostly live in the Tepito *barrio* (some even in total squalor), Colon resides in the San Angel district, where a few of Mexico City's vampire lords make their havens. He enjoys the benefits of leadership perhaps more than he should.

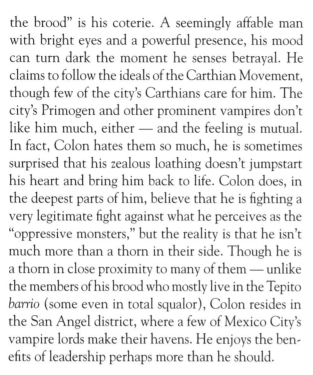

La Ratón (Nosferatu)

She is called "The Mouse," because she dwells in Tepito's various bolt-holes, never settling down in a single haven. She, with her two coterie mates (Guerita and Hugo), are unconventional Acolytes. They do not believe in God, but they do offer a great deal of prayer to La Santa Muerte (see sidebar, above), believing that she is clearly a servant of the Crone. The Mouse and her mates are also accomplished kidnappers, partaking in what has become known as "express kidnapping." They kidnap victims for short periods of time, not protracted episodes. They don't demand a great deal of money — only little things such as credit card numbers, cell phones and ATM PINs. The Mouse, much to the chagrin of her allies, has become increasingly obsessed with Colon, believing him blessed by Saint Death. She stalks him wherever he goes, even setting up her own little "security detail" to protect him. She knows he wouldn't care to look upon her — she is, as her name suggests, ratty and unkempt. But that doesn't stop her from watching him from the shadows.

Federico Mentiloso (Mekhet)

Federico is a man who has risen from the streets — once a gang member, he is now a businessman who wears bolo ties and suits made of fine cotton. He has traded pistol for checkbook, and an old bicycle for a fine Cadillac. He knows that many in the Invictus (to which he belongs) look down upon him, but he also knows that they cannot ignore his prowess and power. Yes, much of his clout is still connected to the streets (crime does pay, after all), but power is power no matter where it comes from. He both loathes and loves Amato Colon. Colon is charismatic, a quality Federico does not possess. But Colon is also a liar, a pretender. If offered entrance to the halls of power, would Amato turn on the brood? Perhaps. If that happens, Federico knows that he will be there to take his place. And if it doesn't happen — well, then, he is fine with being Colon's right-hand man.

Adaptation

Any city has its slums, and in its slums dwell the downtrodden and oppressed. Vampires are not above belonging to these unfortunates, and may find themselves truly exploited by the ruling class of Kindred.

It's therefore pretty easy to take the core ideas of this brood — the down-and-out seemingly working against a powerful minority — and drop it into any big city in the world. Moreover, hidden beneath this is the fact that many of the brood members are duped by a charismatic figure who claims to have their interests at heart — but really, truly, only gives a shit about his own. This brood could easily function in New York, Bangkok, even London.

The Kingdom of the Maze

Welcome to paradise. You'll never leave.

Chiapas is Mexico's southernmost state: below it, beyond the Usumacinta River, lies Guatemala. Deep in the mountains and rainforests of Chiapas await countless old Mayan ruins, tended to by the various indigenous Indian cultures still present. This region has its sacred places: the ruins of Tonina, Palenque and Yaxchilán.

Chiapas also has its cursed places. One of these places, near the small village of Itsanok'uk in the Lacandon jungle, has long been considered a forbidden blight to the Chol and Lacandon Maya who still live in the region. They call the place K'uxu Yatoch K'un, or the Red God's House. It is a series of underground caves that lead to old ruins — ruins that predate the Mayan civilization and do not match any of the architectural styles of ancient Mexico. The underground passages are marked with seemingly inexplicable hieroglyphs painted in red dye and blood. The countless subterranean passages wind back around upon one another or dead-end entirely. There seems no purpose or end of the maze, only a few miles of tangled hallways.

The natives do not go to the Red God's House, because it is already occupied. A brood of vampires dwells in the dark parts of the jungle — some live within the maze, coming out at night to hunt, while others live in small huts and caves around Lake Istanok'uk. The Indians mark the monsters' territory with red-stained swatches of cloth tied around trees. The message is clear: this is not our land, stay away.

That message does not apply to the Kindred. The vampires of this wild region welcome all who wish to come to it and become part of their kingdom. The area does not have a prominent blood supply, or many places to hide during the day. And yet, the vampires here claim that it is a kind of holy place, a fortunate kingdom in which they are allowed to exist as the beasts and monsters that they are. They needn't play at being humans, here. Those who want to be free can leave the trappings of civilization and come to the Red God's House, deep in the jungle.

Nickname: The Indians call them the "Red Gods," or the K'uxu Yatoch.

Covenant: Kindred of all covenants are welcome, though in the end, covenant affiliation matters little in the dark heart of the rainforest. Certainly, members are allowed to keep and even exhibit their beliefs — Isabel, for instance, retains her belief in Longinus regardless of what the others in the Kingdom believe. She in fact preaches to those who will listen, helping some of the brood divulge themselves of sin and exalt the holy predator within. That said, many find it no longer necessary to maintain the false alliances that covenant membership creates.

Appearance: By necessity, the Kindred of this Kingdom wear meager clothing — loose-fitting rag shirts, no shoes, threadbare pants. Some wear wooden masks. Others paint their faces and bodies in river mud or blood.

Havens: The hieroglyph-marked catacombs make for unorthodox havens, but many among the brood do so anyway. (Vampires existing inside the maze-haven can be assumed to have the both the Haven Size and Haven Security Merits at ••••.) The catacombs do have various rooms, none of which are protected by anything more than a moth-eaten "door" made of burlap or cotton. Some such rooms exist down crumbling hallways and narrow stairways, whereas others are actual pits dug out of the ground and lined with mud-brick.

Not all of the Kindred within this brood make a home inside the subterranean labyrinth. Some of the Gangrel (such as Huemac, one of the Kingdom's founders) sometimes sleep hidden in the slick mud near the lake, whereas other Kindred choose to live in bare-bones huts and longhouses in and around the area. It's worth noting that one of the brood's Kindred, the Nosferatu called Tenoch, dwells hidden among the Lacandon natives of Istanok'uk.

Organization: The only organization mandated by the brood specifically regards hunting. Existing out on the fringes, the blood supply is obviously slim. The rule is, everybody hunts. The blood is not for one, but for the whole collective. *How* a vampire hunts and secures food for the brood is up to individual Kindred or their coteries. Some live off the jungle's animal inhabitants, hunting whole swaths of forest clean of life. Others prey on the natives (or, after thralling them, have the natives bring others as food). Some Kindred draw food from afar by taking advantage of unique circumstances and opportunities (such as the relationship offered by the European mage known as Manfred, found below).

The vampires of the Kingdom hold and attend *comidas de sangre* (blood meals), sometimes simply referred to as "feeding time." The nature of the meal — which happens semi-regularly at midnight — is different every time, depending on the food source. Animals might be drained of blood, with the *sangre* emptied into various ritual cups (*alimentar copas*) for the Damned to drink. If live humans are the food, the group likely passes them around during the gathering — such a gathering may also double as a time for stories, celebrations or mourning. The mortals, when possible, are kept alive. Sometimes, however, the Kindred cannot resist finishing off a delectable meal; they know they are beasts, and their mercy extends only so far.

The Maze

Just what are the catacombs beneath the jungle floor? A stone archway leads to them, with a set of 52 steps leading down

into the maze. The labyrinth itself comprises about 80,000 square feet, which is close to two and a half *miles* of maze. Whoever created the catacombs decorated every inch of every wall with seemingly inexplicable hieroglyphs: for every glyph that looks like a bird or animal, there are three that seem an intricate and meaningless tangle of paint and blood. The maze itself features no human-made traps (though crumbling walls and inadvertent pits make for dangerous walking) other than the ones put there by the brood vampires. The walls offer no sconces or holders for torches — those, too, have been put there by the Kindred.

Nobody knows who put this place here. History and investigation indicate that the maze were there before the Mayans. The nearby Indians offer no real help, saying only that the catacombs were built by the "children of the gods" who were cursed for their arrogance.

Society and Culture

The Kingdom of the Maze is a kind of Kindred commune: a so-called society of teachers, predators and bloodthirsty "free spirits." The brood, at this stage, numbers nearly two dozen Kindred, all of whom have come to the jungle not at the behest of existing members, but predicated instead on rumors and whispers of a vampiric "Shangri-la" (or El Dorado) out in the middle of the Chiapas rainforest.

Brood members are, more or less, allowed to do as they wish. Provided that they hunt and bring blood for the brood, they may dwell and spend their Requiems as they wish, unfettered to any kind of harsh Princely rule or so-called Masquerade. Coteries take advantage of this in different ways. Some exalt their predatory nature, hunting both local Indians and the beasts of the forest. Others instead turn inward, becoming contemplative on the nature of being something that is both human and beast. Some pursue Golconda. Others teach or practice their religions. On the surface, it appears oddly liberated, and amazingly without conflict.

Looks are deceiving. Something troublesome bubbles beneath the surface. The three original Unbound founders of the brood — Huemac, Gilberto and Kahuatli — have recently suggested that the Kingdom could be in danger from outside forces. Other Kindred must be jealous, the three say, and will eventually come to destroy their paradise (and as Gilberto points out, *no* paradise goes unpunished). The proclamation that those who are part of the brood may never leave the brood is recent, within the last year or so. Some of the brood take the decree in stride — they either don't want to leave or believe that if the time comes they are capable of escaping without harm. Others grow concerned. Huemac in particular is powerful. He grows more paranoid every night. And slowly, vampires trickle to his side, ready to support him in whatever endeavor he embarks.

Aside from the tension simmering just out of sight, the brood does function despite consisting of several disparate coteries. Isabel, the group's lone Sanctified, proselytizes and tells story from the canonical and apocryphal books of her covenant. Garcia Garza, once an Invictus Harpy, now spends time with his coterie crusted with blood and dirt, relishing the supposed freedom he has to hunt and feed. Vargas and Guzman, both members of the Dragons, believe that the Kingdom sits at the crux of at least *three* ley lines, and are often lost in their studies of the catacombs and local Lacandon legend.

All exist to do their own thing. Interlopers from outside are given the choice to join the brood or go back home — in an ashen urn. Disputes go largely unmediated: violence is encouraged to solve matters that cannot be answered through discussion. By the far end of the lake sits a circle enclosed with logs and stones. There, combatants "solve" disagreements.

Sometimes the coteries intermingle (usually around feeding time); other times they may go nights or even weeks without dealing with one another. Huemac, above all, has been gone more and more. (Whispers suggest that he has stopped sleeping in the lake bed and now hides somewhere in the catacombs. Others say they have seen him stockpiling weapons — anything from rusty machetes to rifles spattered with blood.)

The brood shares one ritual among all its coteries. Some call it *La Rana de Veneno*, others the "Spear of Kisin's Eye," named after the Lacandon god of death and judgment. The ritual is simple, and one meant to engender trust. Several vampires fashion a stake by sharpening wood from a local tree. One of the Damned then crushes a dart frog — whose skin is highly toxic — and slathers the skin and blood over the stake. Then, they stake the target of the ritual.

The staked vampire suffers the normal effects of staking, but also undergoes a secondary effect: incredibly vivid, lucid dreams. In these dreams, the vampire often finds himself walking about in the sunlight without harm. He may be visited by various creatures of the jungle: Goliath tarantulas, a whirlwind of vampire bats, a boar, a jaguar or even a chattering spider monkey. This creature often acts and speaks as a human would, and details the vampire's sins while they walk together beneath the sunlit jungle canopy. Upon having the stake removed, the vampire awakens. (At the Storyteller's behest, the player may then raise the character's Humanity score with experience points, but at a lower cost: New dots x 2, instead of x 3. This can only be done within *one hour* of waking from the dream. After that, the chance is gone.)

Characters

Here are some of this brood's notable personalities.

Huemac (Gangrel)

The jungle has been talking to Huemac. He's told no one of this, and he doesn't intend to, because the jungle has explained — quite succinctly, thank you — that when they need to know, the jungle will tell them. The whispers have explained that the brood is in danger. Forces from outside will soon come. "Dead men and beast men," the jungle says. So, Huemac has been getting ready. He's been hiding weapons in the maze. Other things, too. The rest of the brood don't know about the tombs in the far back — hidden rooms with painted skeletons tied to racks made of thorny Cuachalala wood. That's where he's been keeping all this stuff. Huemac knows that he's strong. He is a towering monument of bronze skin, like the Mayan kings before him, and he knows that his blood grows more potent as the nights go on. Soon he hopes the jungle will include the others and whisper to them what is coming. Because he suspects that it swiftly approaches.

Isabel (Mekhet)

Isabel finds her own faith is in flux. Living wild out here in the jungle has given her a wider perspective. The local Indians believe in a variety of old gods, and yet they also give faith to Jesus Christ, calling him Hesuklistos. (One appealing rumor suggests that when the Catholics came cutting through the jungle, they found that these natives had — quite independently — already known of Jesus and his connection to God.) Isabel has begun to accept that the divinity of Christ as transferred to Longinus remains true, but perhaps does not comprise the entire spiritual picture. A small, powerful woman, Isabel sees what goes on with her fellow broodmates, but she refuses to worry. God — or the gods — will show them the way.

Guzman (Nosferatu)

Bad things are going down, and nobody wants to admit to it. Huemac, when he's around, seems distant, irritable. The other two founders are tight-lipped, too. Guzman sees it all, and his partner Vargas gets the same bad feeling. He is the only one who saw Huemac dragging a small *generator* down into the catacombs, disappearing into the depths. What for? Why didn't he tell anyone? Worse is the fact that the two members of the Ordo Dracul believe they have found a genuinely powerful nexus. They want to go back to their covenant mates in San Cristobál and show them what they learned — but Huemac made it very clear that "for now" the two are not to leave the jungle. Vargas tried to sneak away, and found himself hunted by a pair of red-eyed jaguars. They haven't told anybody what they've seen, yet, but soon they might have to. What will happen then is anybody's guess. Guzman isn't strong or fast — his squat toad body gives him little physical power. But he's smart. Hopefully smart *enough* to get out of here with his fingers and toes.

Manfred (Mysterium)

Manfred, a Thyrsus mage of the Mysterium, believes that the catacombs represent a ruin of Atlantis, and that the hieroglyphics are an esoteric language yet undiscovered. The walls offer a secret, and he will do whatever he must to be allowed access to them. He knows the place is crawling with a nest of vampires, and so he cut a deal with their leaders: if he brings them food, they will let him into the "Red God's House" to transcribe the glyphs. That deal is currently in place. Manfred can often be found working day and night at those glyphs, and periodically he leaves, returning days later with humans to feed to the vampires. Mostly, he brings cast-offs (addicts, the homeless) or criminals (common thieves, kidnappers), but from time to time he brings those humans who stand in the way of knowledge — *his* knowledge. Manfred has a mage partner, an old *t'o'ohil* (spiritual guardian) from the Mansabok village. His partner, who belongs to no order but believes he can translate the hieroglyph language if given time, would be devastated to learn of Manfred's "deal" with the Kindred.

Adaptation

The world features many wild places where vampires do not belong. And yet, together, they could make it work. It takes more than a single coterie of Kindred to make existence on the fringes work to any acceptable degree, and this brood is representative of that.

A group like this could easily be found in any of the world's remote places: the Tibetan Himalayas, the scrubland of old Route 66 in the United States, Germany's Black Forest or the jungles of Southeast Asia.

The Fortunate Eight

So sorry, I know you come here with word from the Prince. Send him back a message: tell him that tonight, I'm not listening.

Mexico City has a shitload of people, and therefore, it has a shitload of vampires. The city's Kindred population represents a muddled brew of everything imaginable, from every clan and covenant, and peppered with bloodlines so unique that even the Damned from neighboring blocks haven't even heard of them. The domain is choked with blood-hungry leeches, each sucking at one of countless teats. The city is hundreds of little fiefdoms shouldering each other out for mere inches.

Amazing, then, that out of the hundreds of vampires, such power should be unofficially placed in the hands of eight. Some know them as the city's self-made, most vicious Harpies. Others call them the "Shadow Primogen," for the power they wield with stinging rhetoric and cosmopolitan influence. Just as the city's own population, the members of this brood belong to all the covenants and represent all the clans. Their authority, while intangible and unauthorized, is so pervasive that they can change the power structure of the city overnight, should they desire.

Except, they don't desire. The power they have isn't used to rule, at least not directly. Ruling the city in such a way requires too much… *responsibility*. Even the cruelest ruler has to be a little bit selfless, to give so much of himself to the world. The Fortunate Eight, as they call themselves (or El Ocho Afortunado), are only in it for themselves. Together they form a self-serving bastion of influence caught in a chaotic city. What they want, they get. Even the Prince dares not deny them — and when he does, they can make his unlife very difficult, indeed.

Nickname: The Wolfpack, or Wolves

Covenant: Every covenant has representation within the Fortunate Eight. (The eldest Harpy, the Daeva Mariposa, belongs to both the Invictus and the Ordo Dracul.) One thing worth noting is that membership within this brood is not technically restricted to those eight Harpies. The Harpies' childer and vampire thralls all count — in a slightly "unofficial" capacity — as belonging to the brood, as well.

Appearance: Most of this brood dress to the nines. They wear expensive fashions, predominantly by American or European designers. Stark blacks, whites and grays are favored. Some, such as Mariposa, wear extravagant furs and broad-brimmed hats. Others, for example, the Ventrue Buho, wear black suits with white shirts and black ties.

The only real exceptions to this rule are the Nosferatu Araña and Perro, the Daeva. Araña wears diaphanous nightgowns wherever she goes, often made of colorful lace and silk. Perro, on the other hand, is a fashion disaster (a fact in which he takes great pride). It is not unusual to see Perro in a powder blue tuxedo (lapel dotted with blood), brown leather shoes, black belt and a dozen colorful bead necklaces.

Havens: The eight vampires who form the basis for this brood all make their havens in the posh Polanco neighborhood of Mexico City. Polanco offers trendy clubs and fashion boutiques, as well as a veritable fiesta of museums and galleries. Each of the eight dwells within a few miles of another — they essentially possess lockdown of this neighborhood's primary resources, exerting some level of influence over all strata (police, club owners, hoteliers, restaurateurs).

Buho, for instance, has a chief suite at the minimalist-designed hotel, Hotel Habita. Mariposa, on the other hand, resides in a swanky apartment above the chic club, Lime Lite (where all the city's beautiful people seem to coalesce night after night).

The ancillary members of this brood — i.e., childer and thralls — are not allowed to make their homes in Polanco. And yet, they're expected to exhibit the wealth and influence emblematic of the brood, and so many make their homes in adjacent neighborhoods: Condesa, San Miguel or even Tacubaya.

Organization: As the brood's nickname suggests, the Fortunate Eight travel in packs. Rarely is one seen without at least two others (though, it is equally rare to see the eight all together at any given time). To those outside the brood, the vampires of the Fortunate Eight seem to share power equally, acting as almost a vicious social hive mind. The reality is that, behind closed doors, age forms the brood's hierarchy. The older one is, the more respect one garners. Mariposa, being the eldest Damned in the brood, is therefore its de facto leader, and is the one who ushers her fellow "Wolves" to be the cosmopolitan powerhouses that they are, making or breaking a vampire with a single comment.

The vampires of this brood — including childer and thralls — assume new names at the time of joining (or the Embrace). These names are always after some kind of animal. Mariposa means "butterfly." Buho means "owl." Some others are Araña (spider), Perro (dog) and Colibri (hummingbird).

Devotion: The Wolf's Maw

(Majesty •, Nightmare •)

Those who deal with the Fortunate Eight often feel as if they are held in the mouth of a wolf — at any point the beast could lick them, crush them or spit them out. This simple Devotion helps the user enforce this feeling, stirring in a victim's blood feelings of both excitement and unease. The one-two punch of fear and wonder can unbalance even the most unwavering Kindred.

Cost: 1 Vitae per scene

Dice Pool: Presence + Intimidation + Majesty versus Composure + Blood Potency

Action: Contested; resistance is reflexive

If the Devotion's caster is successful, the victim of this power feels socially unsettled. For the rest of the scene, the victim suffers a penalty equal to the caster's Majesty dots on all Socialize, Persuasion and Empathy dice pools.

This power costs six experience points to learn.

Society and Culture

It seems effortless. To vampires outside the brood, the Fortunate Eight maintain and wield their power without a thought. They flit from hot spot to hot spot. They feed. They create legacies with a kind word, destroy them with a cruel stare (or worse, dismissal sharp as a nail). To observers, the Wolfpack operates with a level of social intuition on par with the way a shark can smell blood in the water from miles away. They hone in on the scent. They strike. In the wake of the frenzy, Requiems are ruined.

What appears intuitive, however, takes a great deal of work. The brood members put in a great many hours designing the architecture of shame and empowerment. Some, such as Buho, keep reams of little notes taken throughout the course of each night — who snubbed whom, how that vampire owes a favor to this Santeria sorcerer or which covenant seems suddenly at odds with its allies. The brood meets, usually once a week, and helps keep Kindred society orbiting around the Fortunate Eight. Araña is known as the "spider" because she seems to know which strand of the web to pluck when disrupting the business of other spiders. Mariposa herself orchestrates the majority of the brood's decisions.

After such "war room" briefings, the brood's work is far from done. Every night is a subtle flurry of activity — the eight cannot appear as if they are desperately spinning plates upon broomsticks; it must seem as natural as feeding. They broker deals. They garner favors. They slice up the city's prominent neighborhoods like cuts of meat, dangling it before the hungry Damned. Every night requires a level of upkeep and on-the-fly thinking that, by morning, leaves the members of the brood exhausted. But in the end, they keep their power tight and close.

The brood also finds difficult the nature of split allegiances. Most of the members belong to one covenant or another, and each works diligently to convince their covenant mates that they are, indeed, working for the group's ideals above those of the brood. Some, such as Mariposa, don't care. She belongs to both the First Estate and the Dragons, yes, but she's quite clear with her covenant allies: she is a beautiful butterfly not given over to the whims of either covenant. She will attend to their needs after her own. Should they push her — then she will use her considerable talents and become a wolf, instead, who will promptly chew out their throats and leave them bleeding.

Characters

Here are a handful of the characters belonging to this brood.

Mariposa (Daeva)

Mariposa is nearly three centuries old. For the last 100 years, she has been one of Mexico City's dominant Harpies, holding enough power to turn the society's tides 10 times over. Prior to that, however, she was

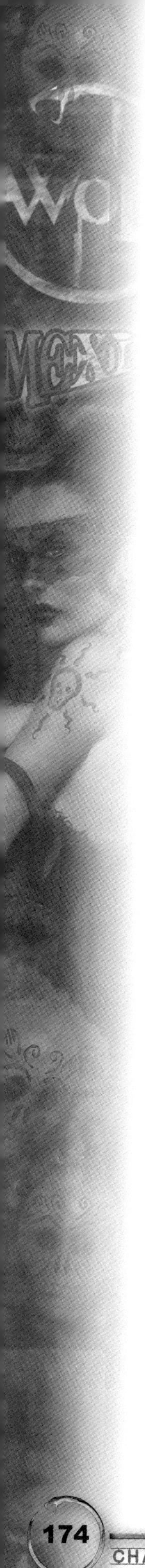

bedraggled, abused, given over to maudlin ideas about morality and salvation. As a member of the Ordo Dracul, she strove to find some way to transcend her condition — or, at the least, to make a kind of peace with it. All of that changed when a vicious coup within the covenant left most of its members missing or destroyed. To survive required a bloodthirsty mindset that Mariposa was not certain she possessed — until the time came, at which point she fought tooth and nail and made some very questionable allies to remain standing. Since that time, something within her has opened its eyes and bared its teeth. The years have allowed her to sharpen her senses — she stands now as a ruthless predator, given over to nearly none of the sentimentality that once plagued her.

Buho (Ventrue)

Buho is a traitor to the brood. They don't know it, not yet. He, just as Mariposa, works with the Invictus. But they don't trust her, and for good reason — she works against their wishes as often as she works for them. Just as Buho takes obsessive notes about the Kindred of the city, he takes similar notes about his fellow broodmates. The time will come when he will bring it all crashing down, slitting their throats. It's regrettable. Some of the brood, such as Araña, he may try to spare. But when the Wolfpack's secrets hit the street, everything will change. His first priority is trying to save himself, but he knows he cannot escape unscathed. It will be like a car crash; his only hope is to steer the wreck in such a way that the damage to himself is as minimal as it can be.

Colibri (Daeva)

Poor Colibri, as delicate as a hummingbird and probably more beautiful. Her sire, Mariposa, treats her like flakes of dried blood under a ragged fingernail — at least, most of the time. Mariposa is unpredictable, which makes it all the worse. In front of others, she humiliates her childe endlessly, subjecting her to all manner of social inequity (and laughing all the while). In private, though, Colibri's sire is surprisingly kind, complimenting her, salving her wounds, feeding her blood from an ornamental cruet. Colibri can't always handle it. She suffers from a terrible case of kick-the-dog syndrome — when outside the company of her sire, Colibri finds herself acting cruel to those around her, even when it isn't called for. It sickens her, that her blood belongs to the brood in this way. She strives to avoid it, to stop acting like her merciless sire — and yet, inevitably, she becomes what she loathes.

Araña (Nosferatu)

She is both beautiful and horrid. Her body, swathed in her see-through robes, is frail like brocade, delicate like bird bones. She was pretty as a human, and still is — at least, empirically. And yet the blue-black veins that show through her skin and her bright eyes are more unnerving than attractive. As an Acolyte, Araña is not given over to any kind of goddess. She believes in the Crone, yes, but only because she believes *herself* to be the embodiment of such a figure. She is, in a way, the Crone. As such, she has developed quite a following of local Acolytes, many of which exist outside the wealthy and influential strata of the city's Kindred (she, in fact, is the only one who seems to hold significant authority over the dregs of local vampire society). Moreover, her cult by no means comprises only vampires. She is the center of various small circles of supplication — mortals worship her as a living heathen saint, and some of the city's sorcerers believe her to hold a shard of magic in the desiccated chambers of her shriveled heart. She is a whore for the attention, so much so that it often distracts her from the brood's overarching purposes.

Adaptation

This brood is easy to drop into any given domain. They are a power clique. They are the "popular kids" — not the student body government, but those bullies who govern with humiliation and invective. Their approval is gold. Their dismissal is damnation. And yet, they have big targets on their backs, and aren't above cannibalizing one another (metaphorically and literally) to avoid losing power.

Allies & Antagonists

Non-Combatants

Outraged Vampire Priest

Quote: *"Stop laughing! This is not a joke! Look at these poor people, at the world you have trapped them in!*

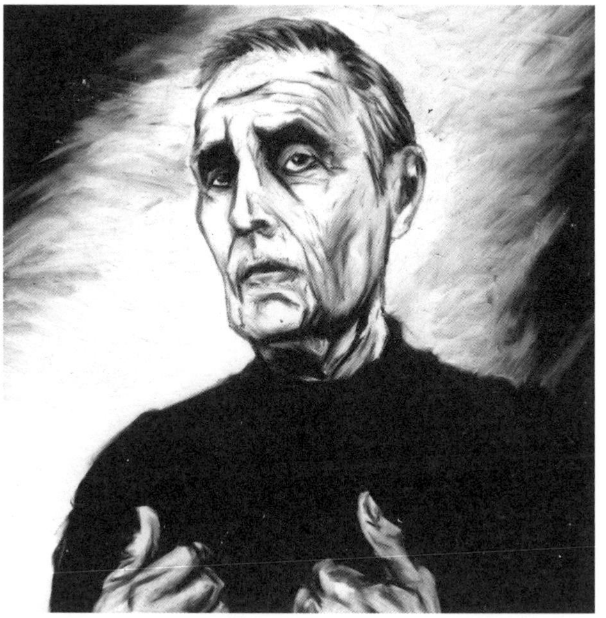

The sin is yours, but the suffering is left to them! How can you go on like this?"

Background: In life, the Outraged Priest always entertained the notion that the lawless border town he dwelt in was edging into Hell more than any earthly country. It just seemed that virtue was always diminished by the brutal ugliness all around it, and there was little that could improve the situation. His faith faltered the night he saw the true face of evil in his town: a band of vampires who took pleasure in terrorizing the living.

These Kindred treated the trembling priest as an entertainment, enjoying his desperate pleas for mercy upon the town. On a perverse whim, one of them Embraced him. Now he is trapped among them, trying helplessly to appeal to their better natures and turn them away from the path of unbridled evil.

Description: The Outraged Priest is a thin, nervous-looking fellow who seems to be in his late 50s. He no longer dresses in his professional garb, preferring shirtsleeves and slacks. His eyes are sunken and dark, his brow wrinkled and high. He is missing two fingers on his left hand from the violent attack that ended in his Embrace.

Storytelling Hints: This is a vampire who believes that he is the last sane man in a world of degraded maniacs and tortured innocents. He is too weak to effect change, but too hopeful to give up — despite the ridicule that he constantly endures. He has been reduced to the status of a clown in his attempts at reforming the evil around him, and he doesn't really know how better to go about it. If characters attempt to deal respectfully with him, he will suspect trickery. He's been fooled before, and now believes that trust can only be followed by further humiliation. Eventually, though, he can't help latching on to anyone who seems determined to rid the town of evil influence. If he feels his faith is poorly placed, for any reason, he will quickly collapse back into dejected, solitary cries against the disgraceful circumstances that surround him.

Abilities

Empathy (dice pool 5) – The Outrage Priest's greatest talent is also his most painful curse. He has a knack for understanding the motives of those around him, and sympathizing with them — whether he likes it or not.

Academics (dice pool 7) – This unfortunate vampire is well educated, and his only retreat from the madness is in quiet study. If a sympathetic character asks him the right questions, the breadth of his knowledge might surprise her.

Occult (dice pool 4) – This is one vampire who knows his saints and truly believes that they watch over all the living (and unliving) beings of the world. His encyclopedic knowledge of their symbols and means of tribute lends itself to the peculiar saint worship among modern Kindred, and may prove to be a hidden asset.

Black Market Conspirator

Quote: *"This piece is absolutely unique. One hundred percent authentic Olmec sculpture, a full figure taken from the tomb of a great warrior. See the markings along the spine? It is a complete, undamaged blessing in the ancient script. This is museum quality. You're lucky I happened to know the people working on the dig."*

Background: Years ago, when she was still a struggling art dealer, the Black Market Conspirator was approached by a charming old man with an irresistible offer: if she would be willing to push certain artifacts on select customers, as directed, she would be richly compensated for her efforts. It didn't take her long to figure out that the pieces she was selling were illegally obtained, but she had to admit that she didn't care. Money was pouring in, and she rapidly gained influence in the exclusive international art trade.

As her power increased, so did her usefulness to the organization that the old man represented. His failing health and growing appreciation for her talents prompted him to introduce her to them as his intended replacement. The Black Market Conspirator soon found herself enmeshed in the workings of a mystic

cult, perfectly happy to sacrifice her soul in exchange for their generous earthly rewards.

Description: A dark-eyed, black-haired *mestizo* beauty, the Black Market Conspirator is demure, stylish and expensively attired. It's important for her to impress the rich and powerful jet set, and she puts a lot of effort into looking right. She flashes an easy, knowing grin at social functions, which most people chalk up to her years of experience and long-term familiarity with the big money crowd.

Storytelling Hints: The Black Market Conspirator is a mortal in service to powers she doesn't quite understand. Ultimately, she is taking part in a grand plan to extend the influence of a dark cult by placing powerful artifacts in the homes of the rich and famous. While she maintains an air of easy, cheerful camaraderie, she is always on the lookout for a new victim. She doesn't like most of the people she deals with (seeing her own greed and unscrupulous drive reflected in them), and is perfectly comfortable subjecting them to an unearthly curse.

If anyone threatens her trade, the Black Market Conspirator will not hesitate to contact her organization and arrange a violent response. She's already had one or two people killed — art dealers or archaeologists who stumbled across one of her secret auctions — and covered it up with the help of her co-conspirators.

Abilities

Persuasion (dice pool 7) – A lot of people don't know what they're looking for until they talk to the Black Market Conspirator — and a lot of them don't know quite why they were looking for it until long after they've made the purchase. Of course, by then it's far too late.

Appraisal (dice pool 5) – This woman is extremely knowledgeable in the minutiae of Mexican antiques and their worth. Forgeries don't do much to further her long-term plan, so she carefully weeds them out of the trade.

Occult (dice pool 5) – The Black Market Conspirator is a practicing occultist, working together with her fellow believers to spread the influence of the slumbering gods of the Maya. She's picked up a thing or two in her dealings with the occult community, and has studied more than one unknown mystic codex.

Hidden Kindred Elder

Quote: *"Time. Time is all I require. Diminished as I am, I cannot possibly make myself known to the others here yet. But soon… soon my strength will restore itself. Soon I will be feared again."*

Background: Six hundred years ago, the Hidden Elder was a god among his people. Thousands feared him, and none dared speak his name without dropping to their knees. His home was the apex of a great stepped pyramid, from which he would emerge to accept immense sacrifices and proclaim his favor. Thunder roared at his behest. The earth would tremble at his step. He destroyed all Kindred who dared to venture into his feeding grounds, tolerating no competition and permitting no threat. The domain was his to mold as he wished. He felt sure his power would never stop growing.

Then one night, he discovered that he could no longer sate his hunger upon the blood of mortals. No matter how many sacrifices were brought to him, no matter how he glutted himself, his undying heart demanded more. The blood he drank began to taste thin and weak, just as that of the birds and beasts. Without fellow Kindred to feed upon, he raged alone, deteriorating rapidly. Within a matter of weeks, he fell helplessly into torpor.

One month ago, he awoke to a thoroughly changed world. He knows that his power has waned seriously, and he understands that most of what he once knew is either forgotten or irrelevant now. Unlike many of his elder compatriots, his mind is undamaged, even if much of his memory is gone. His lesson learned, he makes no claims to special status now, allowing the vampires of the area to believe he is a relatively harmless (if somewhat bizarre) neonate.

Description: The Hidden Elder is distinctly native in appearance. He takes pains to look as modern as possible though, building his concept of proper attire from store catalogs and magazines. He wears off-the-rack suits and simple shoes, but avoids electronics and other modern accessories because he's worried about betraying his anachronistic unfamiliarity with them. There is something obviously constructed about his look, but most vampires would probably chalk that up to an overenthusiastic attempt to fit in.

Storytelling Hints: Play it close to the chest at all times. The Hidden Elder's default position is to feign ignorance. In most cases, he isn't being entirely dishonest — he really doesn't know how things work these nights — but when people talk about history, he has to be careful to avoid revealing himself. Cagey as ever, he is content to seem inconsequential (and even a little stupid) until he has the power to make a play for a position of importance.

Characters who discover the Hidden Elder's true identity might be able to encourage him to speak of the nights of old, assuming they can convince him that they won't betray him to other elders. His knowledge of the ancient peoples and rituals of the region is unparalleled, and can prove incredibly useful.

Abilities

Stealth (dice pool 9) – If there's one power the Hidden Elder has retained, it is the will to remain unseen. He glides through the night, unhindered and unknown. He never seems to be the same person twice, unless it serves him. In a crowd, he's impossible to follow.

Academics (dice pool 7) – He may be absolutely ignorant about details pertaining to the last 600 years, but there probably isn't anyone in the world who knows as much about ancient Mexico as the Hidden Elder does. Languages, myths, social and political practices — he can remember it all when he tries hard enough.

Intimidation (dice pool 5) – It's a little hard not to feel frightened in the presence of the Hidden Elder, assuming he allows you to notice him. There is an undeniable taint of old power about him, something that may be forgotten but not erased. It takes only a momentary effort to show this power to an interloper.

Bottom Feeder

Quote: *"I am never going back — never! Drunks and beggars make better company than you scum. Leave me alone."*

Background: The Bottom Feeder was once a vampire of ambition. Embraced into the world of intrigue and doublespeak, she took pleasure in the complex games of emotional manipulation and maneuvering — until she found herself on the losing side of a furious battle for status and territory. Shamed by her failure and ejected from the familiar streets of her former neighborhood, she abandoned the halls of Elysium in favor of a quiet, relatively unchallenging existence in the back-alleys of the *barrio*.

Several attempts to win her back to the world of politics have failed. On occasion, her kin have paid visits to the seedy neighborhood she haunts, hoping to cure her trauma and benefit from her natural talents. Her determined squalor and reticence have frustrated every attempt. Over the years, she has grown accustomed to a Requiem alone, in poverty, discovering a hidden strength in solitude.

Description: All attempts to maintain a clean, presentable appearance have fallen by the wayside for this vampire. She is filthy, clothing herself in mildewed, layered rags and letting her dry, ratty hair hang loose in knotted mess. It would be easy to mistake her for a madwoman, wandering aimlessly in the streets with her downcast eyes and shuffling gait. There are small clues that she is not entirely what she seems, though: perfect teeth, for instance, and a sense of predatory alertness.

Storytelling Hints: The Bottom Feeder is making a concerted effort to discard the elaborate confections and petty disputes of her past. She knows now that she once devoted too much of herself to conflict that was entirely unnecessary, and that her losses affected her so deeply only because she never applied herself to anything of value. Haunting the worst neighborhoods

of the city is not so much a penance as an attempt to distance herself from the shallow distractions of her previous existence.

Characters who approach her as a victim of tragedy will be playing the wrong card. She believes that she is much improved by her circumstance, no matter how degraded she seems. She feels a genuine sense of calm in these nights, and will only regard vampires who are still caught up in the battles of Elysium with pity.

Those who approach her respectfully will find her cautiously friendly (but not eager to share her new territory with fellow Kindred) and alarmingly open about her feelings. She is willing to advise others on survival in the worst parts of the city, but will offer up no wisdom about Elysium strategy.

Abilities

Survival (dice pool 6) – The Bottom Feeder has a talent for finding blood anywhere in a city. It doesn't matter how blasted the landscape, how inhospitable or dangerous the local structures — she knows where the squatters are. In a pinch, she can locate the favorite hiding spots of local strays, birds and other animals. Things get tight, but she never starves.

Larceny (dice pool 6) – There is nowhere the Bottom Feeder won't go, and, when she applies herself, nowhere she can't go. She can always find her way into sewers, abandoned hovels and all the crude, filthy access points of the city. It's almost impossible to follow her along her complicated, memorized routes, especially when she senses a threat, because she's always got a bolt-hole set up in advance.

Streetwise (dice pool 5) – When you've been on the streets for 20 or 30 years, it's pretty hard not to have a handle on how things really happen. The bottom feeder has a passing familiarity with all of the goings-on in the *barrio*, legal and otherwise. She rarely puts her knowledge to use, preferring to watch rather than participate, but is not above making a connection or interfering with a deal in order to protect her territory.

Combatants

Lucia Herrera Villareal, Nomad Crusader

Quote: *"There… those glyphs on the wall there. See them? Unbelievable! From Guerrero to Campeche, we have searched for this rotten bastard, and he has the gall to sign his own tomb and mark it with the sign of a god. Tonight I shall have his blood."*

Background: Embraced and trained for war, Lucia is a weapon of the Lancea Sanctum in its ongoing effort to erase the influence of pre-Conquest vampires from Mexico. It didn't take much to get her on board: once the local Bishop showed her how much her hometown suffered under the unholy power of the native elders, she willingly dedicated herself to the cause. When the Sanctified brought a torpid ancient in their city low, she was at the forefront of the final assault.

For years, she and her fellow crusaders combed the city, searching for others. In time, she was convinced that none remained. Against the advice of her Bishop, she decided to take the hunt on the road. Lucia recruited two strong mortals, gifting them with the power of her blood and piling into the camper trailer that would serve as her mobile base of operations for years to come. She now has almost two decades of hunting under her belt, and the experience has only toughened her resolve. Six vampires of the old country have fallen to her, and with each, she has descended further into single-minded intent. Two years ago, she committed the ultimate sin, diablerizing one of her enemies in the ecstatic throes of battle. The next time around, the temptation proved too strong to resist, and she did it again. Now she hunts with more dogged hunger than ever before. An addiction to the power of old has arisen in her, matching the fervor of her faith.

Description: Lucia is an unremarkable, dust-swept brunette who appears to be in her mid-20s. Astute observers might notice the knife holsters in her jacket, and those with the sight will see the fierce black lines in her aura — if they bother to look. Her unobtrusive presence has a lot to do with her training, and she does whatever is necessary to back it up whenever she's out in public, often playing the meek wanderer. No matter what she does, though, she can never dull the intense zeal reflected in her dark eyes.

Storytelling Hints: As an antagonist or an ally, Lucia is equally dangerous. She is single-minded, violent, thirsty for elder blood, and will stop at nothing to destroy her prey. Her diablerie brands her as an outlaw no matter where she goes, and she is likely to find many enemies among her own covenant. Slowly, with each step she takes, she moves further into insane addiction and away from her original purpose. She never stops moving, always hunting, always closing in on her next target — and the next diminishing of her soul.

Lucia makes a great threat for physical characters on the low-to-mid power scale. She can easily dispatch a single neonate, but will likely leave any vampire alive if she feels that he is sympathetic to her cause.

Clan: Nosferatu
Covenant: Lancea Sanctum
Embrace: 1968
Apparent Age: 22
Mental Attributes: Intelligence 3, Wits 2, Resolve 4
Physical Attributes: Strength 4, Dexterity 3, Stamina 3
Social Attributes: Presence 2, Manipulation 2, Composure 4
Skills: Academics (Mayan Glyphs) 2, Investigation 2, Brawl 2, Drive (Off-Road) 3, Weaponry (Knife) 3, Survival 4, Stealth 4, Streetwise 3, Intimidation 2

Merits: Ambidextrous, Disarm, Fighting Style: Two Weapons 3 (Whirling Blades, Deflect and Thrust, Focused Attack), Quick Draw, Retainers 4
Willpower: 8
Humanity: 4 (Fixation at 5)
Virtue: Fortitude. Lucia's hunt springs from a genuine core of belief and dedication. Nothing will sway her from that core, even if it is sometimes obscured. When forces are arrayed against her, her resolve only grows.
Vice: Pride. She has taken it upon herself to crusade endlessly, and is beginning to believe that any crime or sin will be justified by her actions. The notion that she is somehow separate from all others, somehow immune to the same judgment that they must face, is where her vice takes root.
Health: 8
Initiative: +7
Defense: 2
Speed: 12
Blood Potency: 3 (12/1 Vitae/per turn)
Disciplines: Vigor 3, Obfuscate 2

Cipactli, the Risen Xipe

Quote: *Translated from Nahuatl: "This is not my land. This is not my home. You — tell me what has become of my people. I am Cipactli of the Xipe, and I have need of sacrifice."*

Background: At the apex of Aztec civilization, the god-nobles of Tenochtitlán moved among the people, directing their prayers and demanding their sacrifices on behalf of the vast and terrible powers above. One such creature, Cipactli, was among the ranks of the Xipe, servants of a powerful Gangrel who identified himself as Xipe Totec, the flayed god of plenty. Cipactli was lowly in vampire terms, but he lorded his power over the trembling mortals of his time, enjoying the fear and devotion they showed him.

For a time, Xipe Cipactli was tolerated by his superiors because of his fervor. He was allowed to direct elaborate rites and deliver the heavenly messages of his Lord to the people in his assigned district, at first under the direction of a fellow god-noble, and then on his own. Unfortunately, Xipe Cipactli quickly lost sight of his position in the hierarchy of Kindred society and began to aggravate the elders with his pretensions to power. Increasingly unable to take direction, he clashed with messengers of Xipe Totec's will and was eventually put down by a warrior of the Daeva. Ceremonially buried and set aside for sacrifice, Cipactli slept through the arrival of the conquistadors and the centuries that followed. He awoke to the nights of the 21st century, finding that his mortal followers and Kindred prosecutors are long dead and long forgotten.

Description: Cipactli is a dark-skinned, well-muscled Toltec man who appears to be in his early 20s. He has short hair and hard, scarred features that suggest a lifetime of violence and tribulation. There are long scars running down his chest and back, where strips of skin have been removed many times over in demonstration of his divine power. Even when dressing in modern clothes, Cipactli will take pains to expose these scars — either by going shirtless or by wearing his top open all the way down the front. He will never wear modern shoes, finding them impossibly restrictive.

Cipactli speaks only Nahuatl.

Storytelling Hints: Cipactli's bearing is haughty and cruel, his voice rough and deep. He has a habit of expounding even when in conversation with a single person — he just can't help acting like he's always up on a platform, directing the faithful to do his bidding. He will brook no challenge, and constantly interrupts speakers, expecting that everyone will stop to listen to him. He only has a vague notion of his own history and overestimates the importance of his knowledge and the influence he once exerted. The hidden truth lurks within his subconscious, manifesting as a deep-set melancholy mood whenever he makes an effort to recall the details of his nights in Tenochtitlán.

He cannot tolerate a dispute. If a vampire overpowers him, he will curse the interloper for daring to touch a true servant of the gods and promise bloody retribution. Cipactli is not likely to integrate well into modern nights, and may find himself subject to a blood hunt if nobody can find a way to rein him in. If he can find a group that worship the old gods and speak his language, he will integrate easily — assuming they are willing to make him feel like the most important vampire in the temple.

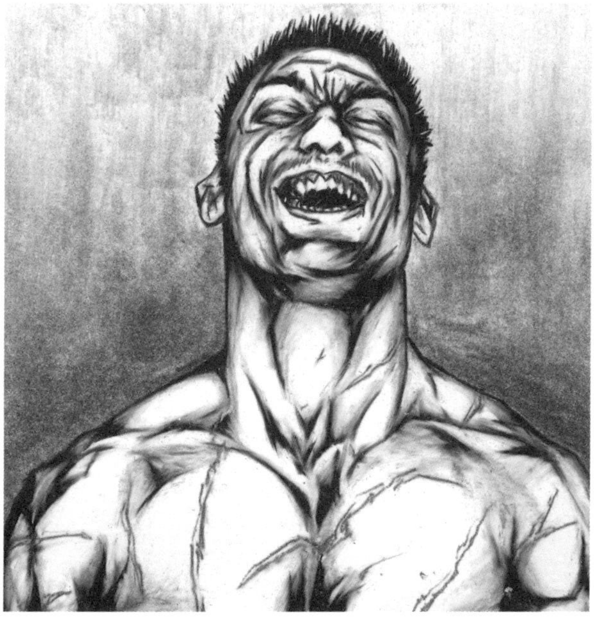

Clan: Gangrel
Covenant: Circle of the Crone
Embrace: 1449
Apparent Age: 22
Mental Attributes: Intelligence 3, Wits 3, Resolve 2
Physical Attributes: Strength 4, Dexterity 2, Stamina 4
Social Attributes: Presence 5, Manipulation 3, Composure 3
Skills: Occult (Aztec Sacrificial Magic) 3, Athletics 2, Brawl 4, Stealth (Jungle) 3, Survival 2, Weaponry 1, Expression 2, Intimidation (In Borrowed Flesh) 4, Persuasion 2
Merits: Brawling Dodge, Fighting Style: Boxing (Body Blow) 1
Willpower: 5
Humanity: 2 (Melancholia at 4, Narcissism at 5)
Virtue: Faith. Cipactli truly believes in the gods of old and their influence. To him, the chaos and unpredictability of modern night make perfect sense in ancient terms, and that knowledge lends him a sense of purpose.
Vice: Pride. In his night, Cipactli was a servant of the gods, gifted with divine power. To him, the mortals were little more than chattel and most of the Kindred were not much better. His Pride gave rise to the narcissistic urges that feed his ambition.
Health: 9
Initiative: +5
Defense: 2
Speed: 11
Blood Potency: 4 (13/2 Vitae/per turn)
Disciplines: Protean 4 (Jungle's Sting at ••• instead of Claws of the Wild. Animal form: Jaguar), Resilience 3, Vigor 2

Paolo Obregon Lopez, Xibalba Cultist

Quote: *"Your world is done. Soon the great city of Xibalba will open its gates again, transforming the whole of this nation into an arena of pain and tribulation. When that happens, I will be there to take my place as a minister of the true church of the dead."*

Background: For the first few years of his unlife, from 1968 to 1985, Paolo was a thoroughly average

member of the Ordo Dracul in Mexico City. Embraced for his scientific acumen, he served as an analyst of archaeological and geological data, noting and cataloging features that supported previous investigations into the spiritual energies of the central and southern Mexico. His personal studies didn't progress very quickly, but he was satisfied with his work (and much preferred it to his living days).

On September 19, 1985, Paolo's world fell apart. The Great Mexican Earthquake struck, and his mortal family, whom he had nearly forgotten in favor of his studies, was utterly wiped out. Worse yet, the change in local geography was enough to render the sum total of his Kindred researches obsolete. His sire was destroyed in an attack led by an opportunistic Carthian enemy in the night that followed, and Paolo was left to wander the devastated city in a daze, observing the carnage.

His absolute inadequacy in aiding the injured, combined with the sudden irrelevance of his existence, broke his mind, and he gave in to his Beast. He moved without purpose, feeding on corpses and burying himself in their ruined homes to hide from the sun. Months later, he was found by a Kindred priest of a vicious Xibalba Church and indoctrinated as a full member.

Description: Wild-eyed, gaunt and unkempt. Paolo was once a man of understated elegance, but he has long forgotten himself and now pays no attention to his appearance. His clothes are stained with old blood, and his face is smeared with dirt. He carries a high-caliber pistol and a hunting knife at all times, often relying on his Disciplines to hide them.

Storytelling Hints: A vampire without hope or mercy, Paolo is desperately in need of help. He roams the streets, convinced he can see and hear coded signals that indicate the coming of Xibalba, often interpreting them as instructions to unleash his cruelty on an unsuspecting mortal in the vicinity. Anything can set him off — a flickering neon sign, a torn garbage bag spilling its contents to the street, a broken taillight on a passing car — anything at all. When he strikes, he always seeks to maximize the pain and confusion of his target, toying with her in an attempt to prove to the Xibalban gods that he deserves to join their ranks. His Schizophrenia encodes every happenstance with hidden layers of meaning, layers that he is convinced only he and his Xibalban compatriots can understand because they are "chosen." His depravity is encouraged (and rationalized) by his madness.

The truth is, Paolo can be saved. He's most interesting if presented as a challenge to characters who might want to reform him, not just a straight villain. Once, he was a rational, intelligent neonate. If he felt he had a purpose in a stable world of Kindred, he could be set on the path to recovering his Humanity and his sanity. To get him there would be difficult for all but the most charitable and patient of vampires, though. The Ordo Dracul might send new members after him in an effort to demonstrate the necessity for individual redemption (and to attempt to win back a valuable scientific mind).

Paolo avoids any confrontation with an equal or greater foe. He attempts to vanish whenever the odds seem stacked against him, hiding so that he can escape and continue his work unchallenged. If a superior foe captures him, he will attempt to win that foe over to his cause. Failing that, he will consider any rough treatment a test from the Xibalban gods, rapidly deciding that he is advancing in their esteem, and must now face a tribulation calculated to shake his faith. Without gentle encouragement, he will fail to redeem himself and will never overcome his madness.

Clan: Mekhet
Covenant: Unaligned (formerly Ordo Dracul)
Embrace: 1968
Apparent Age: 40
Mental Attributes: Intelligence 4, Wits 3, Resolve 3
Physical Attributes: Strength 2, Dexterity 3, Stamina 2
Social Attributes: Presence 3, Manipulation 1, Composure 3

Skills: Academics 4, Investigation 3, Occult 2, Science (Archaeology, Geology) 4, Brawl 2, Firearms 3, Stealth 3, Weaponry 3, Expression (Impassioned Speeches) 3, Intimidation 2, Persuasion 2, Subterfuge 1
Merits: Language (Nahuatl, English), Resources 2, Allies (Cult Members) 3, Contacts (Archaeological Community) 2, Haven Size 1, Haven Security 3
Willpower: 6
Humanity: 3 (Schizophrenia at 4, Depression at 6)
Virtue: Faith. The collapse of Paolo's sanity came about because of the failure to reconcile his faith with the devastating trauma he experienced in the great earthquake of 1985. It remains, but is now clouded by his belief in the supremacy of Xibalba and its place in the grand plan.
Vice: Lust. Paolo indulges his darkest urges by cloaking them in the rhetoric of his cult. He inflicts pain, but only for "ritual purposes." He torments his mortal victims, but only to "prepare" them for their inevitable admittance to the City of the Dead and prove his own readiness for godhood.
Health: 7
Initiative: +6 (+8)
Defense: 3
Speed: 10 (30)
Blood Potency: 1 (10/1 Vitae/per turn)
Disciplines: Celerity 2, Obfuscate 4, Coil of Banes 1

Thirsty Spirit

Quote: *"Señor, señor... what you have, I need...."*

Background: This spirit is one of the many that wander the desert stretch along the border between the United States and Mexico, brought forth by the deaths of desperate men and women on the verge of escape to a better life. In truth, it is not a spirit at all, but a ghost. It was once a man who died for lack of water and rose again, unaware of his passing, still searching, always searching, for the water he believes will give him the strength to complete his journey.

For 30 years, the Thirsty Spirit has wandered aimlessly in the desert, anchored to its bones in the sand and assaulting anyone unlucky enough to wander across its path. All of the stolen water in the world could not release the poor spirit, and it wanders still, maddened by thirst and growing more and more ruthless.

Description: The ghost seems to be a man in his early 40s, weathered and lined with sorrow. He is emaciated and half-blind. Anyone who can see into

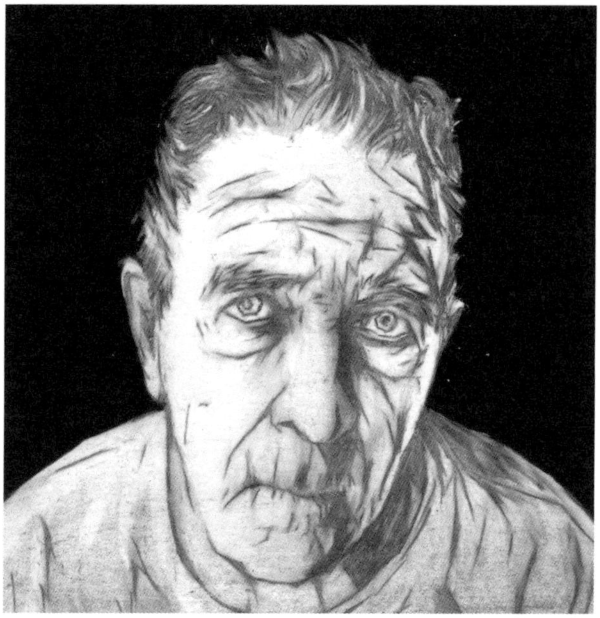

the spirit realm, though, will see a nimbus of hungry energy pulsing within him, shining through the strips of his ragged clothing.

Storytelling Hints: The Thirsty Spirit is not likely to manifest directly to most people. Instead, it will try to compel them to abandon their water containers so that it can try to take a drink. If mortals prove resistant to the compulsion, the spirit will attempt to isolate them by disrupting their communications equipment (if they have any) and navigation aids. Attempts at communication are normally restricted to Ghost Sign manifestations — a plaintive voice on the radio asking for water or a quick image of a dying man on film, his hands outstretched in a sign of need.

Attributes: Power 4, Finesse 2, Resistance 3
Willpower: 7
Morality: 4 (Fugue at 5)
Virtue: Hope
Vice: Envy
Corpus: 8
Initiative: +5
Defense: 4
Speed: 16
Essence: 8
Numina: Compulsion (6 dice), Ghost Sign (6 dice), Magnetic Disruption (4 yards), Manifestation Site (Chihuahuan Desert +2)

Ghostly Thirst (6 dice): This desperate ghost can draw the moisture out of any living mortal it can "touch" while manifested. To do so, the ghost pits its Power + Finesse against the subject's Strength + Stamina in a contested action. If the ghost succeeds, it draws water out of the subject's body in the form of sweat, tears or even a clear, vomited spray (in the event of an exceptional success). This causes the victim one point of bashing damage per success. Once an individual subject has suffered an amount of damage equal to his Health, he is dehydrated and the ghost gives up on him and resumes his search for water. This leaves the subject deprived of water as if he had gone days or weeks without drinking (see "Deprivation," p. 175-176 of the World of Darkness Rulebook).

The ghost tries to lick the sweat from a subject's skin. He tries to suck it from the dirt at his feet. He kisses subjects and dries away their spit. But none of it helps him — it's too late.

New Numina: Manifestation Site

Most ghosts are only able to manifest where the influence of mortals and the atmosphere of the world are conducive to a belief — or even just a temporary fear — in the restless dead. Some ghosts find it easier to manifest in some locations rather than others. Typically, these are ghosts whose mortal lives were ended as a result of a such a location, such as the crushed specter that haunts the intersection where his car was smashed by a drunk driver or the airport where a fatal flight took off.

A ghost with this Numen gains a bonus to its Power + Finesse roll to manifest within a select environment. This bonus is usually about half the ghost's Power, to a maximum of +3. The location described by this Numen — e.g., the Sonoran Desert, Chichen Itza or "the mouth of the old silver mine" — must be very specific (not just any desert, for example) for all but the most powerful ghosts, such as La Llorona.

CHICHEN ITZA

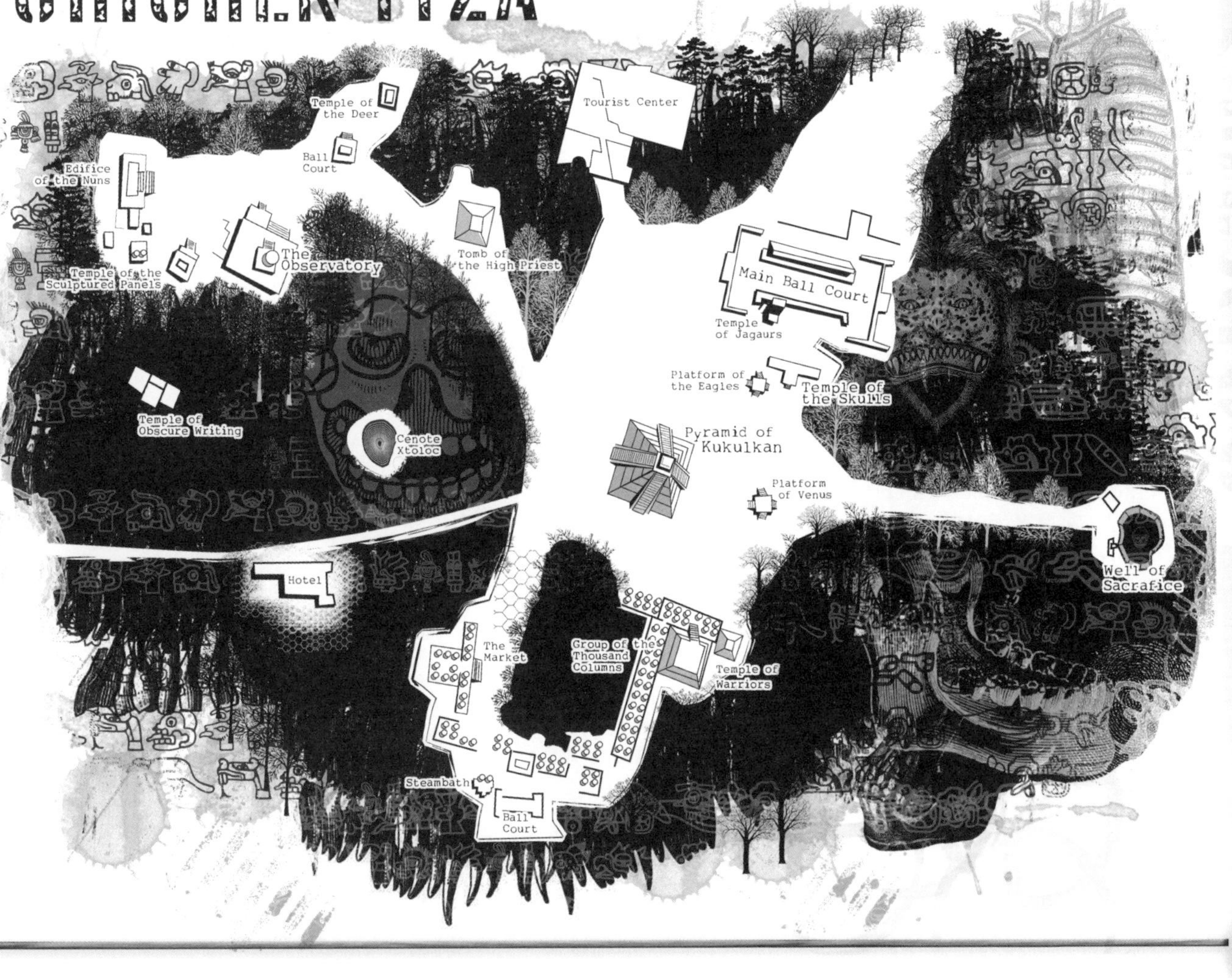

El Chupacabra

The goats were getting restless again. Probably a fox or a coyote, Miguel thought. Sure, he'd heard the stories, everyone had — they made T-shirts with pictures of it for the touristas in town — but Miguel had gone to school until he was 13, he knew enough to know that the goat-sucker was just an urban legend. He took the shotgun, just in case — goat-sucker or no, coyotes could be ornery when they were hungry.

The light from the back door barely reached the goat pen, so Miguel approached cautiously, not wanting to trip over a stone and give the animal time to get away. The goats were milling around frantically, bleating their panic into the night. Miguel circled the enclosure, shotgun ready to deal with the critter that had been harassing his herd. He saw the body first — one of the older male goats was lying on its side, one eye wide and staring. Then he saw the thing perched over it. Miguel only had an instant's glimpse of red, beady eyes and long, sharp spines, then it was leaping at him, hissing like an angry cat and rattling like a diamondback.

The report of the shotgun blast was still echoing on the hills when Miguel started to scream.

Background: In the United States, El Chupacabra has become a joke — a pop culture phenomenon more amusing than terrifying. T-shirts, key chains and every imaginable kind of merchandise have been plastered with the creature's image. It has been the star of cartoons and comic books, featured in popular television series and music and even had toys made in its likeness. But in Mexico, and in many other rural areas throughout Latin America, the creature is still very much a figure of fear. Farmers and herders whose entire livelihood is tied up in their livestock find little about a creature that devours herd animals kitschy or chic. Belief in El Chupacabra is very much alive in many rural communities across Mexico, despite assurances from zoologists and other experts that such a thing does not exist.

Theories as to El Chupacabra's nature abound. Among mortal cryptozoologists, the creature is sometimes thought to be a previously unknown species of canid, or more radically a creature of extraterrestrial origin, a subspecies of vampire or even a demonic being. Scientific-minded individuals contend that "Chupacabra" sightings are the result of mass hysteria and natural animal attacks, and that most sightings can be attributed to malnourished, diseased or deformed animals, usually dogs. Those with more insight into the supernatural usually write sightings off as particularly repulsive Nosferatu or blood-spirits that have Claimed animals.

In fact, it's very possible that El Chupacabra does not exist — reliable reports are sketchy, and not every supernatural creature that appears in human mythology truly lurks in the shadows of the World of Darkness. Perhaps paradoxically, many of the actual supernatural denizens of the World of Darkness consider El Chupacabra to be nothing more than a myth, or at best a misunderstanding of another supernatural creature such as a ghouled animal or a large Rat Host. Others are more open-minded: if vampires, werewolves and zombies can exist, why not the goat-sucker? Still others, mostly werewolves and mages (simply by dint of the fact that they are the most likely to venture into the rural areas where Chupacabras are often said to hunt), claim to have seen or even fought the creature.

Description: Different sightings have described El Chupacabra in different ways: most common is that of a scaly or leathery creature, roughly three to four feet tall, with grayish-green skin and bright red eyes. A line of spines or quills like a porcupine's run down the back. The creature has a face like a panther's, and a mouth full of needle-like fangs with a forked tongue like a snake. El Chupacabra is said to stand on two legs and hop like a kangaroo — in some cases, it has been said to clear 20 feet in a single hop. In some accounts, the creature leaves a sulfurous stench behind, possibly the source of its purported demonic origin.

A second variation ascribes the creature a body structure similar to the previous example, but instead of a reptilian appearance, this version of El Chupa-

cabra has short, coarse fur and a dog-like head with a mouth full of distended fangs. Whether these are two separate, similar creatures, subspecies of the same beast or even different life-cycle stages of the same animal is unknown.

Storytelling Hints: El Chupacabra is a creature best used sparingly. As mentioned previously, el Chupacabra has become a pop-culture cliché, the butt of late-night talk show jokes and sketch comedies. If you try to place el Chupacabra as the ultimate source of a rash of mysterious animal mutilations, your players are probably going to lose any sense of gravitas or fear they might have had (assuming they didn't break out the goat-sucker jokes as soon as they found the first animal carcass).

Instead, try playing up the human angle of the story. Sure, to a bunch of sophisticated, big-city players, el Chupacabra is a big joke, but when they see a village of farmers and herders terrified that their livelihood is being destroyed by some unknown, alien force, it might not be so funny. All of humanity's monsters can be traced back to our most basic fears: fear of death, fear of betrayal, of the unknown. El Chupacabra is a product of the fear that we aren't as self-sufficient as we think, and that we aren't the masters of the animal kingdom we think we are. Play up that angle, and the very fact that el Chupacabra is a figure of comedy for the players will work for you: the different perspective will make the creature seem all the more horrific.

Story Seeds

- A rash of animal exsanguinations has the mortal tabloids talking Chupacabra and the Prince of the city thinking "Masquerade breach." The players' coterie is charged with investigating the livestock mutilations to determine whether the perpetrator is Kindred or something else.
- Spirits of herd animals in the pack's territory are growing restless. It seems that they are being stalked by a strange, spiritual predator that drains Essence from them like a vampire drawing blood. The local spirits have little information to impart, but they seem to be of the opinion that the creature is *not* a spirit, but a physical being that can enter the *Hisil* and stalk spiritual prey.

Mental Attributes: Intelligence 1, Wits 4, Resolve 2
Physical Attributes: Strength 3, Dexterity 4, Stamina 2
Social Attributes: Presence 3, Manipulation 1, Composure 2
Physical Skills: Athletics 4, Brawl (Grapple) 3, Stealth 4
Social Skills: Intimidate 3
Merits: Brawling Dodge, Fast Reflexes 2, Fleet of Foot 3, Iron Stomach
Willpower: 4
Morality: —. El Chupacabra is an animal, with no notions of right and wrong. All it does is hunt and eat and make little Chupacabras.
Health: 6
Initiative: +8
Defense: 4
Speed: 22 (species factor 12)
Size: 4

Weapon	Damage	Dice Pool
Claws	1L	7
Bite	3L	9

Bounding: El Chupacabra is capable of making astonishing leaps for a creature of its size. The creature automatically gains a +6 bonus to all Athletics dice pools when jumping.

Hypnotic Gaze: El Chupacabra's gaze is capable of mesmerizing any creature that looks into its baleful red eyes. To use this power, the creature must make eye contact with its target and roll Presence + Intimidate versus the target's Resolve + Composure. If the creature's total successes exceed the subject's, the subject may take no action beyond standing and staring at the creature in rapt horror. This effect is broken one turn later if el Chupacabra breaks eye contact or immediately if it attacks the subject. The subject may also spend a Willpower point to make a second Resolve + Composure roll at any time. If the subject rolls more successes than el Chupacabra achieved on its initial roll to activate this power, the spell is broken and the subject may act normally.

Drain Blood: Similar to a vampire, el Chupacabra must drink blood to survive. El Chupacabra must drink approximately 10 Vitae worth of blood each week, or the creature begins to starve. Chupacabras normally attack animals, but a starving one may attack a human if desperate enough. Note that the blood el Chupacabra consumes does not technically become Vitae, and el Chupacabra does not use blood to fuel healing or supernatural powers. El Chupacabra drains blood in much the same way as a vampire, however: by making a successful bite attack. Since el Chupacabra's bite does not confer the effects of the Kiss, the creature must usually grapple its target if it wishes to draw more than one "blood point" at a time. As long as the creature can maintain its bite, el Chupacabra can drain enough blood to cause one point of lethal damage to its victim each turn.

Bloody Birth: El Chupacabra reproduces by infecting an animal's blood with its own DNA, either through its spines or its bite. An animal that suffers lethal damage from the creature's bite or spines must attempt a Strength + Stamina roll after 24 hours. This roll is penalized by el Chupacabra's Stamina. If the animal succeeds on this roll, it fights off the creature's infection. If not, the animals suffers five points of lethal damage when it next sleeps as its blood seeps out through eyes, mouth or wounds in just a few minutes. Contained in this bloody leakage is the tiny body of a new Chupacabra, which grows from Size 1 to Size 4 within a few nights' time. Only cows, goats, horses and similar animals seem to be subject to the Chupacabra's infectious reproduction.

Natural Attacks: El Chupacabra's claws inflict lethal damage, and have a +1 Damage bonus. The creature's massive, distended fangs give it a +3 lethal Damage bonus when biting. In addition, any creature grappling with el Chupacabra suffers one lethal wound per turn from the sharp quills. Creatures grappled by el Chupacabra do not suffer this damage, as the spines run down the creature's back and el Chupacabra grapples with its limbs and mouth.

Alternative Chupacabras

Depending on what sort of chronicle you're playing in, el Chupacabra might end up being a weird variation on any sort of monster that's more in theme with your game. For example:

• In a Vampire chronicle, it might be some kind of Vitae-hungry vampire-hound created by Aztec blood-sorcerers during the Conquest. Thus el Chupacabra might be controllable with the proper Crúac ritual — if the ritual can be rediscovered.

• In a Werewolf chronicle, el Chupacabra might be a manifested hunger-spirit or a spirit-ridden goat of some kind. Thus it's just another monster for the Uratha to put in its place. Or it might be some kind of deranged, deformed werewolf!

• In a Mage chronicle, the goat-sucker might be a beast from the Abyss let loose in the Fallen World to undermine the power of some long-dead Mayan mage who gave goats as gifts to distant nobles for the sake of forging sympathetic connections with them. Or it might be the agent of some living archmage who's looking for a particular portentous goat — the Red Goat — whose death will foretell a new age of Awakened power in Mexico.

• In a Promethean chronicle, el Chuacabra could be a Pandoran created from goat parts by a Promethean hoping to test out some alchemical theory before proceeding on to the creation of a more humane being.

Any one of these beasts could terrorize and challenge a mortal hunting party or band of psychic investigators armed with powers from World of Darkness: Second Sight or guns from World of Darkness: Armory.

La Llorona, the Crying Woman

Quote: "*¡O hijos mios!*"

Background: La Llorona, "the crying woman," is a widespread and long-lived folktale from Mexico and Central America. Over the decades, through storytellers from Texas to Panama, the tale has been twisted and changed into countless variations. She's an infamous horror-tale figure, like Resurrection Mary or Bloody Mary. La Llorona is even sometimes said to have been named María.

Just who the crying woman is, and whether she is a murderer or a victim, can probably never be known for sure. Here are two versions of the tale:

Some say La Llorona was a Mexica peasant girl who had fallen in love with a wealthy young man. Though they'd secretly married and had several children, their love was not to be. His father demanded that he go through with an arranged marriage that had been planned for him, and the wealthy young man gave in. All at once, La Llorona lost her lover to a Spanish nobleman's daughter and her children were left fatherless. With no way to feed her children, and her heart still broken, she went mad with grief. She drowned her children in the river (some say the Rio Grande) and then wept for their sad ends. Their bodies were carried away by the water.

Another version of the story supposes that La Llorona's children were swept away in a disastrous flood foretold by a fortune-teller. Her house, with her children inside, was washed away when the river overflowed. Others say the children were drowned by her husband, in an attempt to escape their burden. They say she died trying to save them.

Whatever version of the tale you hear, whichever version you choose to believe, it is well known in Mexico that La Llorona scours the riverbank, weeping and searching for her lost children. She may want to recover their bodies and say goodbye. She may be cursed by God to find salvation only when she finds the corpses she has made. She may be wandering as a ghost, terrified that her lost children could be swept away to Hell. Whether she searches with a murderer's guilt or a mother's grief, she cannot give up her quest.

To the living, La Llorona is a harbinger of death. If you should hear her weeping, you will suffer, especially if you are a child. If you should catch sight of her, you may be doomed to die.

Description: Her features change, shifting like smoke. Some say that her endless, spectral tears are always washing away the face of one tortured woman to reveal another grieving woman underneath. She is Aztec, Mayan, Spanish, Mexican. She is a child, a sister, a wife, a mother. All that is ever the same is her sorrow, which falls from her eyes like tears from Heaven.

Storytelling Hints: Is La Llorona a ghost or a spirit? She is both. Or, rather, there are several ephemeral beings treaded the Mexican night that can be described as La Llorona.

As a spirit, the Crying Woman hungers for the potent Essence of grieving mothers and the terror of drowning children. She is, in fact, several spirits operating independently of one another, inspired by the resonant fear of a horror story spread through whole generations of mortal imaginations. The goal of these spirits is to compel mothers to drown their children, then surrender them to their grief so they may feed on the mothers' sorrow. If necessary, a Crying Woman spirit will simply drive children to drown themselves, then visit their mothers and sup.

But the ghost of La Llorona also walks the land, insane with grief. If you decide that she is the grim shade of a wicked soul, then her motive is to drown children so that no mother shall enjoy what she has lost. If you decide that La Llorona was wronged, or that she is at least genuinely mournful and desperate to save the souls of her children, her motive is less wicked, but her actions are no less deadly. She drowns children so that she can follow their corpses downstream in the hopes that they will lead her to the corpses of her own poor babies.

Even the ghost of La Llorona may not be unique anymore, however. The Crying Woman spirits have created many aggrieved mothers in the past hundred years, and more than one of them has left the same crazed, spectral echo in Twilight — the ghost of La Llorona.

The Spirit
Rank: 3
Attributes: Power 7, Finesse 7, Resistance 7
Willpower: 14
Essence: 10-15 (20 max)
Initiative: +14
Defense: 7
Speed: 21
Size: 5
Corpus: 9
Influences: Sorrow ••• or Grief ••• or Mourning •••
Numina: Chorus (14 dice), Claim (14 dice; grieving or sorrowful mothers), Discorporation (14 dice), Living Fetter (14 dice; grieving and sorrowful mothers), Materialize (14 dice), Material Vision (14 dice)
Ban: A La Llorona spirit cannot cross the Gauntlet unless it is within 3.5 miles of a river, shoreline or coast. Its Numina only affect sad or grieving mothers and their children.

La Llorona and La Malinche

Some Mexican legends relate La Llorona with La Malinche. La Malinche, by this reckoning, is a harbinger of doom who participated in the destruction of her children — the native peoples of Mexico — by marrying a man who did not truly love her (Hernán Cortés or, simply, Spain). Now she wanders Mexico as a mourning ghost, crying over the damage she caused and the world that she lost.

The Ghost

Attributes: Power 5, Finesse 5, Resistance 4
Willpower: 9
Morality: 3
Essence: 10
Virtue: Faith
Vice: Envy
Initiative: +9
Defense: 5
Speed: 20
Size: 5
Corpus: 9
Numina: Compulsion (10 dice), Ghost Speech (10 dice), Terrify (10 dice), Manifestation Site (Riverbanks +3)

La Llorona, The White Woman

Quote: *"Where are my children? Bring me the children."*

Background: The Kindred are not immune to the frightening influence of local legends. For vampires, who must now take every horror tale they hear at least seriously, the threat of other restless dead is quite real. In time, some vampires becomes the local folklore, whether they inspire new tales with their monstrous Requiems or whether they become the legends they were raised on in life.

The White Woman is another incarnation of the La Llorona legend, this time made of Kindred flesh and stolen blood. The White Woman is a deranged nomadic vampire that feeds especially on children. Kindred from Los Angeles to Honduras have claimed to witness her stalking riverfronts, canals, flood channels and beaches. Some vampires claim that she Embraces children only to leave them trapped, chained or pinned to the bottom of a river so that she may feed from them later. Even if she is so old that only the blood of her fellow Kindred will sustain her, the White Woman continues to hunt and drown children wherever she goes.

Some vampires who dwell along the U.S./Mexico border equate the White Woman with the dreaded vampire known as the Unholy (see p. 109 of the Vampire supplement Nomads). Though the motives of these two vampires seem very different, their legends have some commonalities. Both have monstrous hands they cannot hide. Both are cold and deadly nomadic women. The White Woman is starkly white, the Unholy is starkly black. Perhaps they are sisters in Damnation, sired by the same potent (and possibly sleeping?) vampire elder? Or perhaps the White Woman is the Unholy's mother, and the Unholy is the best-known clue as to the fate that befell the White Woman's children? If this is true, it gives the Unholy a legendry pedigree throughout Mexico: the Daughter of La Llorona.

Description: When you see her, it's easy to understand why a hundred years of vampires have mistaken her for an evil spirit. Her appearance is unearthly, though her body is flesh and her teeth and claws are as hard as iron. She is as pale as death, dressed all in white, with eyes the color of eggshells and lips like chalk. Only the black pinpricks of her irises and the wet black tangle of her hair defy her name. She dresses all in white — robes, jackets and gowns have all been seen on her over the years — except when she has been found striding nude from the ocean or the dark trenches of a desert river. Some say she has eagle talons for hands and the feet of a coyote. Her pristine white teeth are punctuated by serpentine fangs.

Storytelling Hints: The White Woman's motives are long since lost to her. She has drifted in and out of torpor — a decade here, a decade there — for more than 200 years. She sleeps in the black waters of ruined rivers and concrete canals, fused with their flows through the power of her mystic blood. Her Final Death has been reported more than once, yet still she wanders the land.

The White Woman is a sad, ferocious shark. Her existence has become little more than an endless ongoing parade of cold-blooded sin. She feeds, she drowns, she moves on.

The self-awareness afforded her by the last shred of her Humanity enables her to negotiate with local Princes, however. She may barter with local Kindred to determine just what child she should drown in this town

or that — provide her with a child and she may help you maintain the Masquerade. Help her find her own children (perhaps actually her childer?) and you may free her from a degree of her madness, thereby saving the lives of countless children over the next century.

The White Woman is a cautionary example for Kindred. She is the future for those vampires who let their Humanity slip away from them. She holds onto hers as if by the end of a rope. She is not so unlike any vampire.

Clan: Mekhet
Covenant: Unaligned
Embrace: ?
Apparent Age: Early thirties
Mental Attributes: Intelligence 2, Wits 4, Resolve 4
Physical Attributes: Strength 4, Dexterity 4, Stamina 4
Social Attributes: Presence 4, Manipulation 3, Composure 3
Mental Skills: Academics (History) 1, Crafts (Weaving) 2, Occult 4
Physical Skills: Athletics (Swimming) 4, Brawl (Claws) 5, Larceny 1, Stealth (Hide) 4, Survival (Desert) 5, Weaponry 1
Social Skills: Animal Ken 3, Empathy 5, Intimidation 5, Persuasion 2, Subterfuge 4
Merits: Language: Spanish, Language: Cree, Status: Legend 5, Status: Kindred Legend 4, Striking Looks 2
Willpower: 7
Humanity: 1 (Delusional Obsession ("Must drown one child a month or perish") at 5, Power Fetish Obsession ("The Water is the source of my powers") at 3, Depression at 2)
Virtue: Fortitude. The White Woman endures. Whatever else the legends may say about her, all tales agree that she has survived sorrow and hardship and pain. She will probably continue to do so for centuries.
Vice: Gluttony. The vampire they call the White Woman feeds beyond necessity. She has an inhuman thirst to take in anguish, to soak herself in tears and drown herself in blood. The Requiem allows her to drink and drown and rise to do it again for eternity.
Health: 9
Initiative: +7
Defense: 4
Speed: 14
Blood Potency: 7 (Vitae/per turn: 20/5)
Disciplines: Animalism 3, Celerity 4, Obfuscate 4, Protean 5, Resilience 5, Vigor 4

Weapon	Damage	Dice Pool
Feral Claws	1A	12

The Dead Desperado

Quote: *"I heard what you did. He told me through the dirt. You should'a buried him deeper."*

Background: The Dead Desperado is an enigma to the undead and the living alike. Many Kindred who have heard of him assume the folktales were invented to provide prestige to a violent undead assassin. They are wrong. Mortals who hear tales of the Dead Desperado assume he's some kind of cowboy joke. They're wrong, too.

The Dead Desperado is a unique being, not a ghost or a zombie or a revenant. He is a vengeful corpse, long-since dead. That much is clear to any who lay eyes on his slashed and ruined flesh, his bullet-ridden body and his jutting bones. Just how he came to be is unknown.

Some say he used to be a vampire, others say he was once a mage. Surely he was a living man, but not even the human heart should be able to conjure the hot vengeance necessary to push on for centuries after death. Mortal folktales say he crawled back to earth from Hell and dug himself out of his own grave. Kindred legends claim he came back for revenge against a vampire who's been asleep for 200 years, and the Desperado's waiting him out.

The truth is in there somewhere. The Desperado was shot dead in the middle of the 1800s by a vampire who had turned his robber partner into a ghoul. That partner's name is long forgotten by the Desperado and by Mexico. But the Desperado wouldn't stay dead

— his wrath crawled back into his skin and came looking for that old vampire.

For 150 years he's been looking and waiting and practicing. The Desperado's motives are so decayed, so rotten in death that he now seeks revenge of any kind, whether it's his or someone else's. He hears about a murder from this ghost or that and then sets out to do unto others.

Description: Even those who consider themselves to be familiar with the undead gasp at the sight of the Dead Desperado. His flesh is rotten and ruined by 150 years' worth of gunfire. His teeth leer out through collapsed cheeks. His nose, slashed and broken, still juts out from beneath his black hat. His remaining eye, lidless now, is always on guard, watching gun hands and shaking wills. His jaw, broken off a hundred years ago, is stitched on now with barbed wire.

Storytelling Hints: The Desperado is a big, bad monster to throw at players who like such things. How exactly the Desperado comes after them is up to you to decide, but you've got plenty of options. The Desperado might be pointed at a coterie of vampires by an enemy who claims they are the grand-childer of his arch-enemy. Uratha may come to find the Desperado by following the trail of death-eating spirits in his wake. Mages might provide the Desperado with a new target, using him against their enemies. Mortals may find him coming in search of vengeance for some poor soul they accidentally killed in a past story.

The Dead Desperado has been trapped in a kind of bizarre loop of damnation. His powers and his passions have lead to the creation of a guiltless undead killing machine. If that's all you need in your story, then you're all set.

If you want more than that, have Storyteller characters share legends and tales from the Desperado's past. His fate was sealed in life when he gave up on living like a human being and withered down to nothing by hate and a gun. The Desperado is not sexy or glorious or awesome. He is tragic, even pathetic. He gave up everything good in life for the sake of the gun and has passed almost into oblivion because of it. The man he once was is gone, dead and forgotten. When his work is finally finished, the Desperado will be dust and his entire prolonged existence will amount to nothing more than bones and bullets.

Mental Attributes: Intelligence 2, Wits 4, Resolve 5
Physical Attributes: Strength 3, Dexterity 5, Stamina 4
Social Attributes: Presence 3, Manipulation 2, Composure 5
Mental Skills: Crafts (Blacksmithing, Carpentry) 3, Investigation 1, Medicine 1, Occult 3
Physical Skills: Athletics 3, Brawl 4, Firearms (Revolvers) 5, Larceny 2, Stealth (Stalk) 4, Survival (Desert) 5, Weaponry (Guns as clubs) 3
Social Skills: Animal Ken (Horses) 3, Intimidation (Stare down) 5, Streetwise 1, Subterfuge (Spot Lies) 4
Merits: Ambidextrous, Danger Sense, Fast Reflexes 2, Gunslinger, Iron Stamina 3, Language: English, Quick Draw, Status: Kindred Legend 4, Status: Uratha Legend 3
Willpower: 10
Essence: 15 (max)
Morality: 1
Virtue: Fortitude. This heartless spirit is an incarnation of patience and devotion. His dedication to its mission has completely subsumed whatever man he once was. He has all the time in the world and he knows it.
Vice: Wrath. Wrongs cannot go unpunished. No one hurts him and gets away with it. Not until everyone understands that he must be taken seriously. Not until everyone fears him enough to leave him be.
Health: 19
Initiative: +12
Defense: 4
Speed: 13
Supernatural Advantage: 5 (Substitute this trait for Blood Potency, Primal Urge or Gnosis when determining the Desperado's resistance to supernatural powers)

Weapon	Damage	Size	Special	Dice Pool
Spectral revolver (x2)	3L	1	No ammo	14
Spectral rifle	5L	2	No ammo	15

Armor: *Entropic Shield* (••)

Supernatural Powers

The Dead Desperado is a unique being whose powers cannot be easily categorized. To facilitate his use in play, his supernatural powers are described in terms drawn from various World of Darkness books. If your chronicle isn't using one of these books, simply ignore the power or adjudicate its use from the information below.

Dead Skin: By spending one Willpower point and one Essence, the Desperado can defy the material limits of his corpse and become incorporeal for a number of turns equal to his Composure. He is still visible, but ghostly and semi-translucent; light passes through his flesh and clothes as if he was a single screen of fabric. In this form, the Desperado cannot be affected by material weapons and cannot affect material objects or persons except with his *Decay* spell from the Death Arcanum. At the Storyteller's discretion, the Desperado may still be susceptible to magical or spiritual weapons in this state.

Death Arcanum (7 dice): Though the Dead Desperado is not and never was a mage, some of his abilities seem to draw on the same magical properties as the Arcana of the Awakened. The Desperado has the equivalent of Death ••, plus Supernatural Advantage 5, but can only cast the equivalent of the spells *Speak with the Dead* (•), *Decay* (••) and *Entropic Shield* (••) (see p. 135-137 of **Mage: The Awakening**). Using these powers, the Desperado can communicate with ghosts, lower an object's Durability by one point per success with a touch of his hand or supply himself with two points worth of Armor. Each of these abilities requires the expenditure of a single point of Essence and lasts for one scene. The Desperado's very touch seems to rot wood and rust metal. Bullets soften and even crumble before they strike him. Ghosts follow in his wake.

Essence: The Desperado requires supernatural fuel to continue his existence — each night the Desperado must spend one Essence to animate his corpse. The Desperado gains Essence like a revenant (see p. 37-38 of World of Darkness: Antagonists), drawing it from other creatures or from the resonance of its actions. To siphon power from a mortal, the Desperado must touch his target and roll Intelligence + Presence (5 dice) versus the target's Resolve + Composure. If the Desperado wins, every success of his converts one of the target's Willpower points into two Essence for the Desperado. The Desperado also has a chance to gain Essence by fulfilling his Virtue and Vice. Whenever the Desperado gains one or more Willpower points by fulfilling his Virtue or Vice, he also rolls five dice. Each success on this roll grants the Desperado another point of Essence. Finally, at the Storyteller's discretion, the Desperado may gain Essence via instances of *momento mori*, like a ghost (see p. 208 of the **World of Darkness Rulebook**).

Magnetic Disruption: This power works like the Numen (see p. 211 of the World of Darkness Rulebook) out to a range of three yards, based on the Desperado's Presence.

Obfuscate ••••: The Desperado is shrouded in ghostly shadows. His presence tricks peoples' minds into dressing him in their own fears. The Desperado has the equivalent of Obfuscate •••• (see p. 135-138 of Vampire: The Requiem). In his unique case, however, the Mask of Tranquility power disguises his aura as little more than a cold and pale glow, like a weak candle's light straining through thick glass. When using the •••• power, The Familiar Stranger, the Desperado appears as someone the subject expects might come to kill him. If no such person exists, the power cannot be used.

Regeneration: The Desperado can restore functionality to his undead body by spending Essence. Each point of Essence he spends heals one point of bashing damage. Two Essence may be spent to heal one point of lethal damage and five Essence may be spent to heal one point of aggravated damage. The Desperado cannot heal without Essence. Even through this mystic power, his body is gradually falling apart from centuries of abuse.

Spectral Guns: The Desperado's guns are solid, rusted remnants of guns he has collected in his decades haunting the desert. In his hands, however, they require no ammunition; the bullets they fire are utterly real for the time they spend flying through the air and punching into flesh, but after that they are just harmless smoke and ash. Still, the Desperado must reload his guns every six shots — not because they need ammunition but because that is what his body did in life.

Tough 5: The Desperado has the equivalent of five ranks of the Tough Aspect, normally used to describe the formidable resilience of zombies (see p. 28 of World of Darkness: Antagonists). Each purchase of the Touch Aspect grants an additional two Health points.

I pray that everybody may also forgive me,
and my blood which is about to be shed will bring pe
I am the gods' mouth. I am their teet
IN A BLUE PLASTIC TARP IN THE DESERT
A SNAKES SHED SKIN